Aspen Handbook on The Media
1977–79 Edition

William L. Rivers Stanford University

Wallace Thompson Aspen Institute for Humanistic Studies

Michael J. Nyhan Aspen Institute for Humanistic Studies

Published with the
Aspen Institute for
Humanistic Studies

The Praeger Special Studies program—utilizing the most modern and efficient book production techniques and a selective worldwide distribution network—makes available to the academic, government, and business communities significant, timely research in U.S. and international economic, social, and political development.

641

Aspen Handbook on The Media

1977-79 Edition

A Selective Guide to Research, Organizations and Publications in Communications

PRAEGER SPECIAL STUDIES IN U.S. ECONOMIC, SOCIAL, AND POLITICAL ISSUES

Modern Media Institute
556 Central Avenue
St. Petersburg, FL. 33701

Praeger Publishers New York London

Library of Congress Cataloging in Publication Data

Rivers, William L.
  Aspen handbook on the media.

  (Praeger special studies in U.S. economic, social,
and political issues)
  "Published with the Aspen Institute Program on
Communications and Society."
  1. Mass media—Directories. I. Thompson, Wallace,
joint author. II. Nyhan, Michael J., joint author.
III. Aspen Institute Program on Communications and
Society. IV. Title.
P88.8.R44   1977   301.16'1'025   77-14556
ISBN 0-915436-67-1 Paper
ISBN 0-03-023141-8 Cloth

ASPEN INSTITUTE FOR HUMANISTIC STUDIES
717 Fifth Avenue, New York, N.Y., 10022, U.S.A.

Published in the United States of America in 1977
by the Aspen Institute for Humanistic Studies

All rights reserved

© 1977 by the Aspen Institute for Humanistic Studies

Printed in the United States of America

FOREWORD

The *Aspen Handbook on the Media* was first published in 1973 as a project of the Aspen Institute Program on Communications and Society. Since that first edition, the scope and the size of the *Handbook* has grown enormously, and the task of indexing the broad range of media interests in the United States and abroad has expanded beyond the immediate purview of the Aspen Communications Program. Nevertheless, this new edition continues to reflect the interests of the Program.

Established in 1971, the Aspen Institute Program on Communications and Society is, in the words of Lloyd N. Morrisett, president of the Markle Foundation, "a major attempt to bring together men, ideas, and institutions to pioneer in the communications field, to identify the main communications issues confronting society, and to develop effective programs to implement policies." In its initial years in Palo Alto, California, under the leadership of Douglass Cater, the Program concentrated on four areas: public broadcasting, government and the media, television and social behavior, and cable television and new technologies. Its major activities consisted of organizing workshops, meetings and seminars; commissioning research and writing; participating in discussions of communications issues organized by other groups and individuals; and publishing papers, studies, reports and books useful to professionals, policy-makers and students in the field of communications.

In 1976, under new leadership, the Program moved its operations to Washington, D.C. While past interests and activities continued to be pursued, the change in location signaled a more intense focus on federal telecommunications policy-making. A task force of leading independent experts was convened to conduct a year-long study of the policy options raised by recent developments in telecommunications technologies and the challenges posed by these developments and options to the processes by which government policy is formulated. Their report should be available in 1978.

Collateral activities have involved work in rural telecommunications, public interest law, television and politics, and international activities. In addition, the Program conducts a continuing series of seminars on telecommunications issues for government decision-makers. For all of these activities, the Aspen Communications Program has been supported entirely by the generosity of numerous private and government foundations—a support that gives the Program a welcome independence that enables it to confront the issues and to propose alternative remedies and policies.

In the future, the former varied interests of the Program will doubtless remain strong. But in addition the Program will always be ready to turn its energies to the exploration of new areas and new issues on the frontier of communications in contemporary society.

Forrest P. Chisman
Associate Director
Aspen Institute Program on
   Communications and Society

PREFACE

Each edition of the *Aspen Handbook on the Media* has been significantly larger than its predecessor. The first edition (1973-74) contained only 97 pages; the second (1975-76) was doubled to 193 pages. The size of the third edition has again more than doubled. This expansion of the *Handbook* is the result not merely of an increase in the number of new listings within each subject category but also of the addition of several entirely new subject and conceptual categories as the field of communications has grown and broadened.

From the first edition, a principal objective of the *Handbook* has been to stimulate greater exchange and cooperation between policy-makers and researchers and among the diverse and widely dispersed membership of the research community in communications. Thus, in the 1977-79 *Handbook*, as in past editions, we have given primary emphasis to the organizations, publications, research efforts and government agencies particularly concerned with national policy issues in mass communications. In addition, we have incorporated new information which will be of particular interest to students, scholars, researchers and policy-makers involved in

(a) the growing number of interdisciplinary communications programs shared among university departments and colleges (economics, business, and law, for example);
(b) the expanding concerns of science and engineering departments with the new media technologies;
(c) the dynamic fields of point-to-point and common-carrier communications;
(d) the frequently overlooked fields of photography and film;
(e) the emerging industries of information technology and information storage and distribution;
(f) the many humanistic questions raised by this new, dynamic, and elusive field.

The active involvement of Canadian institutions and

agencies in the communications field is recognized in this volume by a significant expansion of Canadian entries.

Clearly, communications is on the threshhold of a major breakthrough. As Professor Ithiel de Sola Pool pointed out at a recent Aspen Institute seminar, "In the coming decades, the most dynamic sector of our economy is likely to be communications services." Rather than talking of the mass media only in the traditionally distinct categories of broadcasting, print, film, etc., researchers and policy-makers must now increasingly refer to communications—mass and point-to-point—in the broader context of information resources and services in an emerging Information Age.

The beginnings of this breakthrough are already evident in the complexion of the listings and subject categories for this edition of the *Handbook*. At the academic level, for example, there is an increasing focus on interdisciplinary studies and research on communication/information issues and problems. What was previously the exclusive domain of a mass communication department has come more and more to involve engineering, computer science, business and law departments as well. The interest is apparent even among undergraduates: enrollments in journalism and communications departments have increased markedly, while other courses of study have found drastic cutbacks necessary.

At the policy-making level, several major efforts are underway to rethink our communications structures and the processes by which communications policy is made. The House Communications Subcommittee is currently reviewing the Communications Act of 1934, while a task force of the Aspen Institute Program on Communications and Society has been at work for two years reviewing the dominant policy issues and policy-making options for the future. (The result of the Institute study and the task force's recommendations will be published in 1978 as *Communications for Tomorrow: Policy Perspectives for the Future*.) Also, as this edition goes to press, the Carnegie Commission on the Future of Public Broadcasting is beginning an 18-month study of the American noncommercial communications system.

The technologies of communications are themselves expanding in an almost exponential rate. Making clear distinctions among the subject categories in this *Handbook* has become increasingly difficult as the new technologies overlap and bridge traditional boundaries. The dynamics of the technology, the experts tell us, are now resulting in a convergence of modes. For example, with the increased usage of satellite communications and electronic editing, the previously distinct separation of telecommunications and print media is now beginning to blur. Other examples of such growth and convergence abound.

The information that is contained in this edition of the *Handbook* required well over a thousand letters and phone calls. Most of our requests for information were answered, but some were not—which accounts for any gaps that may be found in the listings. Among the organizations and publications that *did* reply, some provided much more information than others, despite the fact that all requests for information in each category were the same. For this reason, some of the listings are much more detailed than others.

As with the two previous editions, we consider the 1977-79 edition of the *Aspen Handbook on the Media* a work in progress, and we therefore ask for continuing input, not only from the many experts who have helped us compile the *Handbook* but also from our readers. To make such input convenient, we have included a questionnaire inside the back cover which can be filled out and mailed to us postpaid. We hope that most of our readers will take advantage of the questionnaire, and we will welcome and utilize your suggestions. In many instances, the new perspectives and expanded coverage of this present volume reflect the needs expressed by readers of previous editions of the *Handbook*.

In his Introduction to the first edition of the *Aspen Handbook*, Douglass Cater, founder of the Aspen Institute Program on Communications and Society, suggested three initiatives which will be needed to raise research activities in communications to a level of effectiveness for policy purposes:

1. To define a wider horizon for communications research, which until now has been mostly devoted to what John Gardner calls "sub-policy" problems.

2. To build bridges of genuinely interdisciplinary study.

3. To integrate research meaningfully into the formation of policy options for a media system experiencing ever more entangling relationships with government.

This third edition of the *Handbook* gives ample evidence of the burgeoning efforts in the communications field toward meeting these important goals. It is the desire of the editors of the *Aspen Handbook on the Media* to continue to support these efforts by anticipating the rapidly evolving needs of the research and policy-making communities in information and communications.

Palo Alto, California
October 1977

William L. Rivers
Wallace Thompson
Michael J. Nyhan

Postscript: Publishing and researching the *Handbook* over the past five years has given the Aspen Institute a unique perspective on the special needs of the communications research community. One need which became evident several years ago was for a single, up-to-date compilation of statistical information on the rapidly expanding communications industry. This information gap has seriously handicapped researchers in their efforts to locate and collect relevant data. It has also stymied the communications policy-makers who have searched with great difficulty to find evidence of trends and statistical indicators.

Thus, the Institute decided that it would publish, in addition to the *Handbook*, a companion sourcebook which would provide a comprehensive statistical overview of American communications industries, both domestic and international, from 1900 to the present. After two years of research and writing, this highly recommended companion volume, *The Mass Media: Aspen Guide to Communication Industry Trends*, edited by Christopher H. Sterling and Timothy R. Haight, is now available from Praeger Publishers and the Aspen Institute. Order information and further details on this new sourcebook are included at the back of this volume.

M.J.N.

ACKNOWLEDGMENTS

It would have been impossible to compile and edit the *Handbook* without the help of many people. We are especially grateful for the help of Professor Christopher Sterling of the School of Communications and Theater, Temple University, who compiled Section XI, A Selection of Books on Communications, and Section XII, A Selection of Communications Bibliographies, as well as the listing of research materials on government organizations and publications in Section VI. Professor Sterling also provided invaluable guidance in helping us compile Section X, Communications Periodicals, and in critiquing other parts of the book.

Special thanks also go to Professor Herbert Terry of the Department of Telecommunication, Indiana University, and Chairman Robert O. Blanchard of the Department of Communication, American University, for assistance in compiling the listing of U. S. governmental agencies in Section VI; to Monica Schouten of the Centre for Canadian Communication Studies, University of Windsor, for the materials on the Canadian government in Section VI; to Professor Norman Felsenthal of the School of Communications and Theater, Temple University, for most of the information gathered in Section XIII, A Selection of Films on Communications; to Catherine Heinz, Vice President-Secretary of the Broadcast Pioneers Library, for assistance in compiling Section IX, Communications Libraries and Archives; and to Professor Theodore Mark Hagelin of the University of Cincinnati College of Law for information found in Section VII, Communications Law Courses.

We owe a special vote of thanks to our Clearinghouse Correspondents and to other professionals in the field who commented on the last edition and who suggested many new listings which have been incorporated into this edition.

We are also appreciative of the additional information and assistance provided by Sister Sharon Dei of the Communication Arts Program, College of Notre Dame of Maryland; Professor John DeMott of the Department of Journalism, Temple University; Professor Richard D. MacCann of the Broadcasting and Film Division, University of Iowa; Kjell Nowak, Research Fellow in Social Communication at the Stockholm School of Economics Research Institute; Professor Leslie D. Polk of the Department of Journalism, University of Wisconsin-Eau Claire; and Dr. Benno Signitzer of the Department of Mass Communication, University of Salzburg.

In addition to the above contributors, a number of other people provided important editorial guidance and research assistance. They are Richard P. Adler of the Aspen Institute for Humanistic Studies, Palo Alto; Forrest P. Chisman, Associate Director of the Aspen Institute Program on Communications and Society, Washington, D.C.; Timothy Haight, Institute for Communications Research, Stanford University; and Richard E. Kuhn, Publishing Coordinator, Aspen Institute for Humanistic Studies Publishing Program, Palo Alto.

Finally, we gratefully acknowledge the assistance of all the staff of the Aspen Institute Publishing Program, especially that of Linda Brandt, Gertrud Browatzki, Ann Diefenbaugh, Carol Westberg and Diane Willis.

Palo Alto, California

William L. Rivers
Wallace Thompson
Michael J. Nyhan

CONTENTS

Foreword v

Preface vii

Acknowledgements xi

SECTION 1 Universities with Research
Programs in Communications 2

SECTION 2 Non-academic Institutions
Conducting Communications Research 66

SECTION 3 Organizations Supporting
Communications Research 90

SECTION 4 Communications Organizations............ 106

    Advertising and Public Relations....... 107
    Broadcasting 111
    Educational/Instructional Media....... 118
    Film and Photography............... 123
    Journalism........................ 129
    New Communications Technologies 136
    Print Media 143
    Related and General 148

SECTION 5 Media Action Groups 156

SECTION 6 A Guide to Government Policymaking
Bodies in Communications in the
United States and Canada 174

SECTION 7 Communications Law Courses............ 210

SECTION 8 International and Overseas
Communications Organizations............ 230

SECTION 9 A Guide to Special Libraries and
Resources on Communications 264

SECTION 10	Communications Periodicals	282
	Annuals, Directories and Indexes	283
	Research	289
	General	295
	Advertising and Public Relations.	305
	Broadcasting	309
	Cable and Pay Television.	316
	Educational/Instructional Media.	320
	Film and Photography.	324
	Journalism.	335
	Journalism Criticism Reviews	342
	Print Media	344
	Technology and Telecommunications Policy	347
SECTION 11	A Selection of Books on Communications . . .	356
SECTION 12	A Selection of Communications Bibliographies	372
SECTION 13	A Selection of Films on Communications. . . .	398
	Index.	419

1

UNIVERSITIES WITH RESEARCH PROGRAMS IN COMMUNICATIONS

In previous editions of the *Handbook*, this section focused exclusively on current communications research projects in colleges and universities. In this edition the section has been expanded to include information on the degrees offered and the financial assistance available for programs in communications at the listed institutions. The emphasis is on studies at the graduate level, but some information on undergraduate programs is included. It should also be noted that at many universities and colleges, several different departments, schools, institutes or centers may offer communications programs. We have tried to identify and list as many of these programs as possible.

Prospective students of communications should be aware that there are a number of other valuable guides that can be consulted. A list of these general reference works, as well as a number of more specialized guides to communications studies, appears at the end of this section. (See also Section VII, Communications Law Courses.)

The American University
Washington, DC 20016
School of Communication
(202) 686-2055
Robert O. Blanchard, Dean

Degrees offered: B.A., Communication; B.A., Interdisciplinary Studies (Communication, Law, Economics and Government); B.A., Foreign Language and Communication Media; M.A., Public Affairs Journalism; M.A., Media Studies; M.A., Public Communication. Students in the undergraduate communication program focus on one of four professional programs: print journalism, broadcast journalism, public communication, or visual communication. Graduate students in public affairs journalism may also select from broadcast or print foci.

Financial assistance: Society of American Travel Writers Scholarship: $500; Sigma Delta Chi Foundation scholarship in print or broadcast journalism: $1,500; John Merriman Award of the Writers Guild of America, East: $500; Jack Jurey Award in broadcast journalism: $500. The School of Communication also awards assistantships for direct teaching, administrative, research and development purposes.

Research and other projects: The Newspaper Survival Study, a research project funded by the John and Mary R. Markle Foundation, is designed to identify factors that cause failure among newspapers. Data base for the study are the 164 dailies that ceased publication, merged or reverted to less-than-daily status during the years 1961-1970. Undertaken by media critic Ben Bagdikian, one part of the study has been produced so far: *Report of an Exaggerated Death: Daily Newspapers That Failed, 1961-1970.* Other parts will follow as stages of the project are completed. Base for the study is Box 2948, Rockridge Station, Oakland, CA 94618.

A survey entitled "Public Esteem for the U.S. House of Representatives" was undertaken by the School of Communication's Congress and the News Media course. A total of 166 representatives responded to the opinion survey in September/October 1976, which concluded that the representatives believe the media does an inadequate job of informing the public about Congress.

The American NewsService, one of the School's outlets for publication of student reportorial efforts, added the regional bureau of the Associated Press and the *Wash-*

ington Post-zoned weekly edition to its growing list of client news organizations. In its third year, the News Service currently serves more than a dozen news organizations in the Washington metropolitan area.

Arizona State University
Tempe, AZ 85281
Department of Mass Communications
(602) 965-5011
Joe W. Milner, Chairman

The Mass Communications program is designed to develop individuals who can perform professionally in their chosen field of study in broadcasting or journalism. In addition to the necessary technical expertise, the program includes background in journalism and/or broadcasting and the liberal arts essential for a student to cope with the responsibilities of a profession. Areas of specialization: broadcast journalism, broadcast production, journalism, photojournalism, and public relations.

Degrees offered: B.S. and B.A. in both broadcasting and journalism. M.S. in journalism and education.

Financial assistance: The Department has numerous scholarships ranging in value from $100 to $1000 for the academic year. Students are eligible to apply after one semester of successful academic performance in the Department.

Research: "A Descriptive Analysis of Utilization of Cable Television Distribution by Institutions of Higher Education in Selected Locations" assesses the contractual and programming agreements which exist between selected cable television systems and institutions of higher learning. "Determining Optimum Newspaper Column Width and Leading" is a study conducted among several hundred university students to determine optimum newspaper column width and leading for readability and retention. "Children's Television Programming" is a study to develop a class outline and content for a new university class for both broadcasting majors and other areas, such as elementary education. "A Case Study in International and Intercultural Communication: The Arabs and the West," financed in part by a grant from the Ford Foundation, was launched with the Beirut Seminar on East-West Communication in 1972 and includes content analyses of the mass media, follow-up surveys, statements by communications experts, and specific examples.

Boston University
640 Commonwealth Avenue
Boston, MA 02215
(617) 353-3450
School of Public Communication
John Wicklein, Dean

Department Chairpersons: Broadcasting & Film: Robert R. Smith; Communications: C. Bruce MacKenzie; Journalism: James W. Brann; Director, Communication Research Center: Richard D. Ferguson.

The School of Communication is professionally oriented to train students in the following undergraduate fields: broadcasting and film, broadcast journalism, communications, journalism, public relations, advertising and photojournalism.

Degrees offered: Master's degrees are offered in broadcasting, broadcast journalism, broadcast administration, communications, journalism, Afro-American journalism, science communication and public relations.

Financial assistance: A number of assistantships, fellowships, scholarships and loans are available and may be applied for through Boston University Office of Financial Aid.

Research: Faculty and students are active in media research, production projects, and publications. Some of the activity is funneled through the new Institute for Democratic Communication, Bernard Rubin, Director, which sponsors research, conferences and publications. Among the topics included in recent grant and research projects at the School are Afro-American journalism, children's television, science news, media ethics, and science communication on public television.

Brigham Young University
Provo, UT 84602
Department of Communications
E-509 Harris Fine Arts Center
(801) 374-1211, Ext. 2077
M. Dallas Burnett, Chairman

Degrees offered: A.A. in Photo Technology; B.A. in Advertising, Broadcasting, Journalism, Film, Photography, Public Relations/Organizational Communications, Speech Communication, and Speech Education; M.A. in

Communications.

Financial assistance: 20-25 graduate assistantships are available fall and winter semesters, with 2-3 available spring and summer terms.

Research: Current research studies in the Department include the role of divergent value systems in intercultural communication, factors accounting for the displacement of normal news values in the world press, research into curriculum relevance to mass communication careers, research on the communication problems of mass media organizations, factors that influence the acceptance or rejection of advertising philosophies, and the utility of biofeedback training in helping audiences handle the arousal potential of certain media fare. Two autonomous units of Brigham Young University, listed below, also support media research.

Communication Research Institute
Gordon Whiting, Director

The Institute is in the design stage and the precise focus of the research it will embark upon has not been determined. Both applied and basic research aimed at improving the media's communication of significant content will probably be included in the focus, and the Institute will be structured to foster interdisciplinary efforts where the research problem requires them. Funding for the development of the Institute is being provided in part by Bonneville International Corporation.

Language Research Center
Ernest J. Wilkins, Director

The Center has developed an Intercultural Data Bank. Similarities, differences, and unique concerns between and among cultures and societies are noted and projected for analysis and multi-purposed retrieval.

Brooklyn College of the City University of New York
Brooklyn, NY 11210
(212) 780-5555

Department of Television and Radio

Offers B.A. and M.A. degrees. The M.A. degree tends to emphasize production because of the extensive facilities present. Most of the research deals with content analysis and production variables. Twelve graduate assistantships for approximately $2,500 are available each year.

Television Research Institute

Robert C. Williams, Chairperson
   The Institute is composed of faculty and graduate students who conduct research in such areas as societal effects of the media, production variables, content analysis, demographics, and industry personnel.

University of California, Berkeley
Berkeley, CA 94720
Mass Communications Project
(415) 642-3410
Charles Y. Glock & Karl D. Jackson, Co-directors
   A proposed undergraduate, interdisciplinary major in mass communications is currently being developed. The projected opening date for the major is fall, 1978. The focus of the proposed major will be on the effects of mass communications, mass media institutions, and mass communications and public policy.
   In addition to basic courses in mass communications and a two-quarter sequence in research methods, majors will be required to take elective courses organized under two subfields: communications effects, emphasizing topics such as attitude measurement and change, language, perception, public opinion and the analysis of micro-level communications; and communications and public policy, emphasizing analysis of mass media institutions and their relationship to the political system. Majors will be encouraged to take courses in both fields, but it is assumed that students will concentrate in the area of their predominant interest.

University of California, San Francisco
401 Parnassus Avenue
San Francisco, CA 94143
Department of Psychiatry
Human Interaction Laboratory
(415) 681-8080, Ext. 207
Paul Ekman, Director
   Laboratory research is centered on nonverbal communication. Research focuses on quantitative measurements of body movement and facial expression in relation to emotion, personality and psychopathology. This includes cross-cultural studies, studies of psychiatric interviews, and studies of normal conversation. There are opportunities for postdoctoral research fellowships and visiting appointments.

California State University, Chico
Chico, CA 95929
(916) 895-5751
Center for Information and Communication Studies
George Arnovick, Director

Degrees offered: The Center offers B.A. and M.A. degrees in public communication, instructional technology, and a combined option incorporating information science.

Research: The department does not have a separate research division, but most members of the faculty conduct individual research. Current projects include an examination of instructional media preference compared to actual choice; the effect of public opinion polls on media coverage of political campaigns; evaluation methods for instructional media; automated non-print educational resources inventory, indexing, and distribution; systems concept for network connecting of government on-line information data systems; the status of libel insurance, a study of the Alioto libel trials; and the investigation of public opinion polls on agenda setting. In addition, the Center assists in media research and evaluation for the NASA Educational Services Division project.

Carleton University
Colonel By Drive
Ottawa, Ontario K1S 5B6
School of Journalism
(613) 231-5530
G. Stuart Adam, Director

Degrees offered: The School of Journalism offers three programs: a four-year course for undergraduates leading to a Bachelor of Journalism (Honours) degree; an intensive one-year course leading to the same degree for students who hold a degree in another discipline; and a one-year program leading to the degree of Master of Journalism for students holding a Bachelor of Journalism degree (or its equivalent) and for experienced journalists.

Financial assistance: The School has a number of entrance and in-course scholarships for the various programs offered. All students accepted into graduate programs are considered for Carleton fellowships ranging from $2,800 to $3,200 for the academic year. In addition, all students are considered for teaching assistantships, with a remuneration of up to $1,800 for the academic year.

Research: Among the research projects currently

under way in the school are the following: telecommunication policy formation, communication in crisis situations, teleconferencing, the literary tradition in journalism, agenda setting, and research on the parliamentary press gallery.

Central Missouri State University
Warrensburg, MO 64093
Department of Mass Communication
(816) 429-4841
David Eshelman, Head

Degrees offered: The Department of Mass Communication offers a B.A. degree in mass communication, B.S. degrees in broadcasting and film, and in journalism, and a functional major in public relations.

Financial assistance: Three graduate assistantships providing $2,100 for a nine-month assignment in the area of radio-TV; graduate assistantships in several areas of the University in noninstructional capacities; and award scholarships for students in public relations and journalism.

Research: The Department maintains a continuing program of research by both faculty and students in the various areas of public relations, broadcast, and print media. Current and recent research projects include violence to women on TV, small market radio promotion techniques, the current status of electronic news gathering, the effect on editors of financial disclosure laws in Missouri, animation as an art form, and legal issues in mass communication. Research leading to an M.A. in the form of thesis studies is designed for individual students to provide the basis for effective media utilization and an understanding of the role of the media in society.

University of Cincinnati
Cincinnati, OH 45221
Department of Communication,
Speech and Theater
637 A Pharmacy
(513) 475-4335
Roger B. Fransecky, Chairman

Degrees offered: The Department offers academic programs on the B.A., M.A., and Ph.D. levels, leading to professional preparation in theater, communication arts, and speech pathology/audiology.

Financial assistance: Scholarships and assistantships are available for graduate students interested in applying for the program.

Research: The Communication Arts Program offers academic concentration in group and interpersonal communication, film and media studies, and telecommunications policy research. Through its relationship with the Faculty Resource Center, an all-University instructional design, development and research group, the Department engages in ongoing research in academic program development. In addition to operating programs, three major local and regional telecommunications studies were completed during 1972-1975.

Division of Broadcasting
130 Emery Hall
(513) 475-4335
William Randle, Head

Research: Research programs are: 1) multi-channel perception—training in expansion of professional broadcasters in attending to and coordinating multiple-channel messages within professional work situations: directors (TV), sportscasters and newscasters in the field, camera operators, audio-visual controllers, airplane controllers; 2) popular music and the media: programming, computer analysis, impact of popular music on various aspects of society (age, ethnic, class), residual strength, ephemeral aspects; 3) exploitation of media systems by demographic forces within the structure of American society: historical studies of personalities such as Father Charles Coughlin, Huey Long, Joseph McCarthy; and 4) broadcast simulators and research methodologies: the use of simulated broadcasts as training techniques and analysis sources for performance, intensity, and focus of radio and TV performers at various levels of expertise and audience acceptance.

Colorado State University
Fort Collins, CO 80523
Department of Speech and Theatre Arts
(303) 491-6858
G. Jack Gravlee, Chairperson

The Department offers undergraduate and graduate programs with coursework in the theory, production, and criticism of rhetoric and communication; and in the criticism of public discourse. In addition to curricular offerings, the Department sponsors annual broadcasting conferences, institutes, and international debates.

Financial assistance: Scholarships and teaching assistantships are available for graduate applicants. Intern programs in television-radio are also available.

Research: Opportunities for historical, contemporary and applied research are offered in all areas. Current research projects include "Impact of Religious Radio on the Lay Community," "Diagnosing Organizational Communication Problems," "Pamphlets and the American Revolution: Rhetoric, Politics, Literature, and the Popular Press," "Aristotle's Concept of Practical Wisdom and the Basis of Effective Communication for Public Policy Deliberation," "The Negative Image of Campaign Speaking in Fiction Films," "Refocusing on Ethics," and "George Saintsbury's View of Rhetoric."

Department of Technical Journalism
(303) 491-6310
David G. Clark, Chairman

Degree offered: B.A. Areas of undergraduate specialization: broadcast news/documentary film; news/editorial; public relations; technical/business.

Research: The Department is engaged in a broad range of theoretical and applied research dealing with communication patterns and behavior; professionalism studies; the use of media in community resource development; and production of films and videotapes for governmental, educational, and private institutions. Research projects include interpersonal and mass communication patterns of the aging; application of videotape of community problem-solving under a Title IV grant; a film production unit which includes research and evaluation of audience and effectiveness; and designing, administering and evaluating a program aimed at reducing communication barriers within large organizations.

Columbia University
New York, NY 10027
Graduate School of Journalism
(212) 280-4150
Elie Abel, Dean
Frederick T.C. Yu, Associate Dean

Degrees offered: Master of Science in Journalism (M.S.J.). The School offers graduate programs only. All candidates for the Master's degree participate in intensive programs in reporting and writing, editing, and other fundamentals during the fall term. In the spring, each student specializes in print, broadcast, or magazine journalism and also chooses one or more substantive areas of journalism—*e.g.*, international reporting, science writing—on which to concentrate.

Financial assistance: The acute rise in educational costs has forced the School to consider *need* as the single most important criterion in awarding financial aid to degree candidates. An applicant's financial requirements are *not* considered in the admissions process. In recent years, approximately half of each class has received scholarship assistance. The Walter Bagehot Program in Economics and Business Journalism provides fellowships of approximately $13,500 for the academic year, plus full tuition, to ten highly qualified journalists with at least four years' working experience. Special programs are arranged for other mid-career journalists who are sponsored by foundations or other programs.

The Center for Advanced Study of Communication and Public Affairs, W. Phillips Davison, Director, is a division of the School that assists faculty members and visiting journalists with their research. It also provides a meeting place for journalists and scholars from other fields who are concerned with the study of communication, arranges conferences on subjects affecting the mass media, and conducts research in the fields of communication and public opinion. Activities of the Center during 1976-1977 included a study of the role played by mass media in the lives of aged persons, a conference on press coverage of national elections, and an analysis of attitudes held by "attentive publics" toward various foreign policy options facing the United States. Visiting journalists from other countries studied such matters as techniques of investigative reporting, science writing in magazine journalism, and the role of house organs in industrial organizations.

Publications: Columbia Journalism Review, bimonthly (see listing on page 342); *Public Opinion Quarterly* (see listing on page 294); *Columbia Journalism Monographs*, irregular, price varies according to length.

Cornell University
Ithaca, NY 14853
Program on Science, Technology and Society
628 Clark Hall
(607) 256-3810
Raymond Bowers, Director

The Program on Science, Technology, and Society (STS) was established in 1969 to stimulate and initiate teaching, research, and dissemination of information on the interactions of science and technology with society. The Program is interdisciplinary and campus-wide, drawing its students, faculty, and researchers from a wide range of academic fields. Topics of special concern to the Program are studied through courses, graduate and faculty seminars, workshops, conferences, and research projects. Research activities vary widely in both scale and approach, ranging from one-month projects undertaken by individuals to highly structured, long-term efforts involving several participants.

One longstanding component within the STS research program is the multidisciplinary Technology Assessment Project, working in the area of communications. While the Project group is concerned in some measure with social impact and policy analysis of technology already in use, the principal interest is in the long-range policy implications of technology currently emerging from research organizations and likely to be deployed within the next one to two decades. Basic goals are to appraise new communications and related computer technologies; to survey those that seem ripe for major proliferation; to analyze the social implications of these technologies; to investigate future impacts on administrative law and public policy; to assess technological innovation in communications; and to identify, create, and improve methodologies in technology assessment. Technologies chosen for detailed assessment in the past have included microwave diodes and the video telephone. Project members are currently completing a book-length assessment of emerging mobile communications technologies with a broad range of new uses for the private citizen and the commercial user.

University of Denver
Denver, CO 80210
Communication Arts Center

(303) 753-2166
Harold Mendelsohn, Chairperson

Research: The Center conducts both basic and policy-oriented research on mass communications processes and audience behavior. Projects involving both faculty and students have included production and evaluation of public service communications dealing with traffic safety, health-related issues, and reaching "unreachable" disadvantaged populations. Recent faculty research also includes studies of the influences of mass media on voter behavior, and of communication and other sociopsychological factors as related to voter turnout.

Denver Research Institute
P.O. Box 10127
(303) 753-3502

The Denver Research Institute is an integral part of the University of Denver. It is engaged in sponsored research in science, engineering and applied economics for government and industry at the international, national and local levels.

Communications Research is part of the Industrial Economics Division of DRI. Its activities fall into two broad categories: (1) policy and evaluation projects focused on communications media and activities (*e.g.*, cable television, computerized information systems, microform technology, library networks), and (2) projects or tasks that essentially support research in other substantive areas of divisional concern (*e.g.*, energy and resource economics, science and technology policy, business planning).

Telecommunications policy studies have been performed for local, state and federal government and for industry. Projects in this area have encompassed technological, regulatory, market and financial factors affecting the telecommunications industry, including television (*e.g.*, cable, broadcast, satellite, microwave), telephone, and land mobile radio communications.

1977 projects include two studies funded by the National Science Foundation, a study of the social effects of citizen-band radio, and preparation of guidelines for rural telecommunications demonstration projects.

Duke University
Durham, NC 27706
Institute of Policy Sciences and Public Affairs
4875 Duke Station
(919) 684-6612
Joel L. Fleishman, Director

The Institute's Center for the Study of Communications Policy conducts research and develops undergraduate and graduate courses dealing with government regulation of, and relations with, electronic and print media. Current research in progress focuses on media decision making about, and impact upon, politics. Other research involves exploration of public policy toward print journalism.

University of Florida
Gainesville, FL 32611
College of Journalism and Communications
(904) 392-0466
Ralph Lowenstein, Dean

Degrees offered: The College offers degrees for undergraduates in the areas of advertising (B.S. Adv.), broadcasting (B.S. Br.), and journalism and public relations (B.S.J.). The M.A. degree is offered for graduate students in advertising, broadcasting, public relations, international communications, communications research, media management, and journalism.

Financial assistance: Approximately 15 graduate assistantships are offered each academic year. For one-fourth time, these pay about $2,000 for the academic year. Some assistants are placed on one-third time at approximately $2,500 for the academic year and waiver of out-of-state tuition fees. Students interested in assistantships should contact Dr. Kurt E.M. Kent, Director of Graduate Studies, College of Journalism and Communications, 400-B Stadium Building. Telephone: (904) 392-6558.

The University of Florida is one of three major universities to share in the estate of Karl and Madera Bickel, an estate that provides assistantship and work/scholarship funds for approximately 25 graduate and undergraduate students each year. For information prospective students should write Prof. Edward Yates, Chairman, Scholarship Committee, College of Journalism and Communications. Telephone: (904) 392-0448.

Communication Research Center
Kurt E.M. Kent, Director
John Paul Jones, Associate Director
   The Center coordinates communication research in the Departments of Advertising, Broadcasting, Journalism and Public Relations, as well as the Graduate Division within the College. Current research projects include studies on communications problems of older Americans, technology transfer, legislative news play, video systems for news, communication and national development, President McKinley and the press, Third World news agencies, medià images of minority groups, shoppers and free newspapers, and subpoenas of reporters and editors.

University of Georgia
Athens, GA 30602
**Henry W. Grady School of Journalism and
   Mass Communications**
(404) 542-1704
Scott M. Cutlip, Dean
   Degrees offered: A.B.J. and M.A. with majors in advertising, public relations, newspapers, magazines, broadcast news, publication management, and telecommunication arts (including radio, television, and film).
   Financial assistance: Professor Margaret Johnston, Undergraduate Student Services Office, School of Journalism provides information on undergraduate aid. Graduate students should contact Dr. A. Edward Foote, Graduate Coordinator, School of Journalism.
   Research: Research activities in the School of Journalism and Mass Communications cover a wide spectrum of topics in the areas of communications. Major grants include one from ABC for a project entitled "Television Viewing and Techniques of Coping with Problems Among Young Children," and a grant from the National Endowment for the Arts to make a film about the Rev. Pearly Brown. Contemporary Broadcast Programming Policy Research is a continuing program undertaken by the faculty and students of the radio-TV-film sequence. The focus of the research is the development of research-centered routines by which a greater diversity of broadcast programming responsive to citizen needs can be made available within the present organizational framework of commercial and noncommercial broadcasting in the United States. Research includes study of var-

iables in program production, trends in broadcast content, and interaction of management and financial organization with program outputs.

Publications: The School houses the editorial offices for both the *Journal of Broadcasting* (see listing on page 292), and the *Journal of Advertising* (see listing on page 291).

University of Hartford
West Hartford, CT 06117
New England Instructional Television Research Center (NETREC)
(203) 243-4552 (Director)
(203) 243-4551 (staff)
Bernard Z. Friedlander, Director

The objectives of the Center are to:

1. Provide impartial, independent evaluation of the effectiveness of instructional/informational television programs in communicating to their intended audiences, and to conduct evaluations independent of any commitment to a particular production or broadcasting function, publishing interest, or educational point of view.

2. Devise general models for systematic assessment of comprehensibility and comprehension of instructional/informational television programs by specific target audiences as a routine part of the television production process.

3. Disseminate technical expertise for conducting comprehension and comprehensibility assessments among agencies and personnel concerned with television production in education and mass communications.

4. Contribute to the advancement of television as a major learning resource in contemporary education.

Areas of specialization include assessment of comprehension and comprehensibility of instructional television programs; effects of educational and broadcast television on child socialization and development; general mass communications research; and the effects of television advertising on children.

Financial assistance: A limited number of undergraduate and graduate teaching and research assistantships are available in the Departments of Psychology and Communication Arts, the two academic departments of the University with which NETREC is associated.

Research: Ongoing research projects include evaluations of bilingual (English/Spanish) television programs directed toward children and adults; consumer education and television advertising; and children's identification with television characters and personalities.

Harvard University
Cambridge, MA 02138
Center for Research in Children's Television
Larsen Hall, Fourth Floor
Harvard Graduate School of Education
Appian Way
(617) 495-3541
Gerald S. Lessor and Aimée D. Leifer, Co-directors

The Center for Research in Children's Television is a joint activity of the Harvard Graduate School of Education and CTW (Children's Television Workshop). Its purpose is to discover how children learn from the visual media and to utilize its findings in the design of television for children. Both doctoral and master's-level programs are available on research in children's television.

Program on Information Resources Policy
200 Aiken Computation Laboratory
(617) 495-3986
Anthony G. Oettinger and John C. LeGates, Directors

The Program aims to develop an understanding of information systems and information technologies and to use that understanding to illuminate public discussion of information policy and the information industries. High priority areas are the Postal Service, the communications industries, the media, and electronic funds transfer systems.

University of Hawaii at Manoa
Honolulu, HI 96822
Department of Education Communications and Technology
Wist Hall 105
1776 University Avenue
(808) 948-7671
Geoffrey Z. Kucera, Chairperson

Degrees offered: The Department offers a Master's degree program for both media specialists and media generalists. Approximately 50 majors are enrolled in this program.

Research: The Department faculty is engaged in informal research pertaining to the efficacy and efficiency

of the use of different kinds of media in informal and formal teaching situations. All graduate students in the Department undertake research, either experimental or action, under the direction of one of the faculty members. Among the research projects already completed are a study of communication for the promotion of agricultural development in the Fiji Islands, quality development of creative thinking through process-based experiences, and a study about attitudes towards a videotaped one-act play. Also included is a bibliographic project on educational films for Korean studies.
East-West Center
See listing on page 231

University of Illinois
Urbana-Champaign, IL 61820
College of Communications
119 Gregory Hall
Urbana, IL 61801
(217) 333-2350
Theodore Peterson, Dean

Degrees offered: B.S. and M.S. in advertising and journalism; Ph.D. in communications. Admissions to the B.S. and M.S. programs in radio-TV have been temporarily suspended.

Financial assistance: Approximately 10 quarter-time graduate assistantships in advertising (through James Webb Young Fund), and 10 quarter-time graduate assistantships in journalism. The Institute of Communications Research has a varying number of part-time assistantships for doctoral candidates. Payment for full-time assistant is $7,600 plus remission of tuition.

Research: Although the Institute of Communications Research is the formal research wing (see below), members of other departments conduct their own research in such areas as international communication, consumer behavior, and press history and philosophy.
Institute of Communications Research
222B Armory Building
Champaign, IL 61820
(217) 333-1549
Howard Maclay, Director

The Institute conducts research projects in three major areas: language and meaning, attitudes and opinion, and cultural studies. Within these areas researchers are currently working on: (1) Language and meaning: history of language and linguistic notions; human memory; reading and cognition; intercultural communication. (2) Attitude and opinion: history of public opinion in the United States; opinion and attitude formation and change relative to drugs and drug abuse; population, the law, immigration, and integrational relations. (3) Cultural studies: the significant cultural forms of news stories, melodies, ritual, popular rhetoric, and propaganda; history of the press; structure of the film and music industries; history of popular culture.

Indiana University
Bloomington, IN 47401
School of Journalism
Ernie Pyle Hall
(812) 337-9247
Richard G. Gray, Director

Degrees offered: The School offers bachelor's and master's degrees in journalism and a Ph.D. in mass communications (journalism track). On the undergraduate level, all journalism majors are required to take seven core courses (21 semester hours) in journalism history, writing, editing, nonverbal communication, communication law, and journalism ethics. Beyond these core courses, journalism majors must take at least two, and not more than four, additional courses in a variety of areas, including magazine writing and editing, photojournalism and graphics, broadcast and television news and editing, mass media economics, newspaper management, public opinion, advertising, public relations, and international newsgathering systems.

On the master's level, all students without professional or academic journalism backgrounds must take up to four deficiency courses (news writing, communication law, news editing, and journalism ethics). Graduate credit is offered only for the journalism ethics course (J410). Beyond the no-credit deficiency courses, each student must take a total of 30 hours, of which 21 hours must be in journalism. Three core courses are required of all journalism master's students: research methods, public affairs reporting, and either a thesis or a creative or professional reporting project. Students may take up to nine hours in a minor field such as economics or history.

On the doctoral level, all students must take a history

and philosophy core of three courses, and a methodology core of three journalism courses and one statistics course. In addition to these core requirements, each student specializes in two concentration areas (international communication, history of communication, communication law, communication and culture, the media and public policy, communication theory, economics and media management, or educational applications of mass communication).

Financial assistance: The School of Journalism offers more than 20 different scholarships, totaling more than $20,000 each year, to undergraduate journalism students. In addition, the School offers seven graduate fellowships and numerous associate instructor and research assistant positions to both master's and doctoral students. These A.I. and R.A. positions presently pay $3,400 for a full position, plus a fee remission, and require about 20 hours of work each week. Some half-time assistantships are also available.

Research and other projects: The School of Journalism undertakes a large number of research and other projects. Among them are: (1) A survey of Associated Press managing editors for their opinions of reactions to teletext (text on demand on a home television screen) by readers, writers and editors, advertisers and consumers, and regulators.

(2) A year-long study of the 1976 election campaign, in conjunction with Syracuse University and the University of Illinois Chicago Circle campus, which looks at the influence of newspapers and television on voters' practical knowledge, concern over issues, and voting behavior.

(3) A study funded by the American Newspaper Publishers Association (ANPA) which relates the content and appearance of 100 morning-evening daily newspapers in the U.S. to their audience penetration.

(4) A survey of newspaper editors to check on what qualities they look for in potential employees and what things they think should be stressed in journalism education.

(5) A study of the structure and methods of gathering science news.

(6) An annual Foreign Journalists' Project which brings 20 to 25 journalists from all over the world to study at Indiana University and to work on U.S. media.

Publications: The Center for New Communication of

the School of Journalism is planning to issue both research and conference reports. One conference report on problems of declining newspaper circulation among young adults has been published. Contact Professor John Schweitzer, (812) 337-0550.

The Poynter Center on American Institutions
410 North Park Avenue
(812) 337-0261
William Lee Miller, Director

The purpose of the Poynter Center is to provide citizen education, in whatever setting and at whatever level it is effective: in the high school; in the college classroom; in the graduate or professional school; in seminars of moral inquiry for professionals; in adult or continuing education. It is an undertaking in normative teaching, writing, original thinking, and public education dealing with the nonspecialist's understanding of contemporary American institutions, including the mass media.

The Center provides a resource library of reprinted articles, videotapes, and films, and originally commissioned essays, films, and videotaped conversations with Poynter Fellows (prominent representatives or critics of the institutions). The Citizen and the News Project, which has a grant from the Ford Foundation, seeks to promote discriminating news reading and watching. The project offers courses, conducts workshops, and creates materials for courses in the humanities and the social sciences that use print and electronic news as a subject of study. A recently published bibliography and syllabi of undergraduate and continuing education courses that have been offered are available by writing the Poynter Center.

Department of Telecommunications
Radio-TV Center
(812) 337-3818
Charles E. Sherman, Chairman

On the undergraduate level, the curriculum is designed for those who desire knowledge of electronic media, their effects, economics, ethics and relationship to other aspects of contemporary society; those intending to enter the electronic media industries or associated careers requiring an understanding of telecommunications processes such as advertising, communications planning or regulations; and those who aspire to graduate study in mass communications. Instruction is organized in four general areas: management and policy; production; research and effects; and broadcast journalism.

On the graduate level, the curriculum prepares students for teaching and research in mass communications, careers which demand advance training within professional media organizations, and careers in government agencies which relate to mass media. Specialized areas include policy and law; management and economics; effects and theory; instruction and education; and international communication. Production is not offered as an area of specialization in the graduate program.

Degrees offered: The Department offers a B.A., M.A., and M.S. in Telecommunications and a Ph.D. in Mass Communications.

Financial assistance: The Department awards at least two fellowships a year valued at $2,000 each. In addition, there are twelve full-time associate instructorships valued at over $5,000, including salary and full fee remissions. Recipients of these awards have to pay incidental fees of approximately $70 per semester. The Department also has at least two research assistantships a year, which have the same remuneration as the associate instructorships. Special scholarships are also available for minority students, ranging from $800 to $2,000.

Research: The Department carries out a large number of research projects. Among recent ones are a study on the effects of television on human behavior, including subjects relating to violence, humor, erotica and sports; a study on parenting education; an evaluation of television series; a study on the development of pay television, especially those aspects related to cable; a study on the legal and political aspects of how Section 315 (equal time provisions) were re-interpreted to make the 1976 presidential debates possible; a study on international organizations affecting broadcasting; and a study of production techniques utilized in the 1976 debates and what influence they might have had.

The University of Iowa
Iowa City, IA 52242
School of Journalism
(319) 353-5414
Kenneth Starck, Director

Degrees offered: The School of Journalism, founded in 1924, offers degree work from the undergraduate through the doctoral levels. The doctorate in mass communication is an interdisciplinary degree with the objective of developing scholars who will make significant contributions to teaching and research in communication. Two Master's degree tracks are available: a Master's degree with thesis and a Master's degree emphasizing professional performance in the media. The undergraduate program offers three sequences: news-editorial, mass communication laboratory, and communication. Focal point of the graduate program is the **Iowa Center for Communication Study**, which encourages and facilitates inquiry into communication problems by faculty, students and alumni. The Center draws upon diverse approaches—philosophical, critical, theoretical, systems design, historical, legal, behavioral, conceptual, empirical and literary.

Financial assistance: More than $15,000 is available annually in scholarships. More than a dozen teaching and research assistantships and fellowships are available to graduate students.

Research: The Communication Research Program, John W. Bowers, Director, is designed for individual students, providing a background for experience in research on interpersonal communication, group communication, and the mass media. Related work in speech, linguistics, psychology, education, social science or philosophy can be taken, as well as work in advanced statistics or computer science. Opportunities for varied research in addition to that required for thesis or dissertation projects are available in the department's Communication Research Laboratory.

Research activities range from the applied to the theoretical. Projects include the social and cultural context of news; the functional role of editors in the journalistic system; the development of methodological approaches to multivariate communication and mass communication research; family photography; the idea of the press as an instrument of social action in 19th century German sociology and its influence on American sociology; the social effects of the electronic telegraph; news and public affairs programming of television stations and the decision-making process in the broadcast, cable and satellite industries; the study of dialectical and rhetorical elements in television network news; and the idea of control as manifested in American communication theory.

Publications: The Center publishes a Working Paper Series, a Working Bibliography Series, a Simulations and

Games Series, a Modular Learning Unit Series, a Worked Example Series, an Occasional Paper Series, and a Monograph Series. A complete listing of publications and prices is available on request. The Center also publishes *The Journal of Communication Inquiry* (see listing on page 293), which is devoted to exploring philosophic issues as they pertain to communication and the media.

Department of Speech and Dramatic Art
(319) 353-4717
Samuel L. Becker, Chairman
 Division of Broadcasting and Film
 (319) 353-4403
 Robert Pepper, Associate Head (Broadcasting)
 Dudley Andrew, Associate Head (Film)

  Degrees offered: The Division of Broadcasting and Film offers the B.A., M.A. and Ph.D. degrees. At the undergraduate level students can concentrate on a wide variety of areas in both broadcasting and film, including history, theory and criticism, production, research, and public policy and control systems. At the graduate level students are expected to develop coherent and substantial programs and may specialize in film production (M.A. only), theory and criticism of film, history of film or broadcasting, broadcast criticism, the process and effects of mass communication, or in public policy and control systems. The sole emphasis of the Ph.D. program is the development of original scholars in the field, whatever the specialization. Accordingly, doctoral students are encouraged to undertake independent and collaborative research projects.

  Financial assistance: On the average, between 20-25 broadcasting and film graduate students have fellowships or teaching or research assistantships. The 1976-1977 stipend for a one-half teaching assistant was $4,760, plus remission of nonresident tuition.

  Research: Current ongoing research includes several extensive projects on political communication and the 1976 campaign; the uses and gratifications of network news; the uses and impact of mass communication; cross-cultural communication; broadcast program decision-making; the history of public television; sex-role stereotyping and television; film esthetics and criticism; the visual variables of political news on television; the interface of film and video; intermedia relationships; European documentary film; American film of the 1930s and 1940s; the life and work of André Bazin; and the social construction of reality through television.

University of Kansas
Lawrence, KA 66045
William Allen White School of Journalism
105 Flint Hall
(913) 864-4755
Del Brinkman, Dean
  Degrees offered: B.S. and M.S. in Journalism. Sequences available in news-editorial, advertising, photojournalism and radio-television-film.
  Financial assistance: Eight graduate assistantships are available each year. Journalism students are eligible for general university scholarship and loan assistance and for financial aid from nearly $25,000 in special scholarships and loans administered by the School of Journalism.
  Research: Individual faculty members conduct research in areas such as advertising, broadcasting and film history, communications law, international communications, mass communications theory, and minority journalism.

University of Kentucky
Lexington, KY 40506
College of Communications
(606) 258-4838
Robert D. Murphy, Acting Dean
  The College includes the Department of Human Communication and the School of Journalism.
  Degrees offered: B.A. and M.A. degrees are offered.
  Financial assistance: Teaching assistantships paying $3,000 and up are available for half-time service. A limited number of all-University fellowships for especially qualified students carry stipends of $3,000.
  Research: Faculty members conduct a wide range of research projects which currently include mechanisms of information selection; family communication patterns; law of libel, privacy, and obscenity; communication and voting behavior; public and interpersonal communication

as conditions of social change; mass-mediated political learning; telecommunication transportation trade-off; television and conflict resolution.

University of Maryland
College Park, MD 20742
College of Journalism
(301) 454-2228
Ray Hiebert, Dean

Degrees offered: The College offers B.S. and M.A. degrees and is preparing a Ph.D. program. At undergraduate level, courses in news editing, public relations, news broadcasting, news photography and advertising are offered, and at graduate level, courses in commmunications research and specialized reporting, with special emphasis on government and politics. 1977 topic of the Department's Distinguished Lecture Series: "Women and the Mass Media."

Financial assistance: Scholarships, fellowships and teaching assistantships are available.

Research: Research projects have been completed on political communication, government-press relations, internal communications, international communications.

Publications: International Communications Bulletin (see listing on page 301); *Public Relations Review* (see listing on page 295); and *RTNDA Communicator* (see listing on page 340).

Massachusetts Institute of Technology
Cambridge, MA 02139
Center for International Studies
(617) 253-3141
Eugene Skolnikoff, Director

Although MIT offers no program in journalism, it is actively concerned with communications research through the Research Program on Communications Policy, which operates under the auspices of the Center for International Studies, the Center for Policy Alternatives, the Center for Advanced Engineering Study, and the Electronic Systems Laboratory. Current MIT studies include political reactions to direct satellite television broadcasting, the economic and technological feasibility of pay television for the performing arts, international data and text transmission networks, and experiments in the use of video and film in classroom seminars. Ithiel de

Sola Pool is working under an NSF grant on Telecommunications Policy Planning and Research.

MIT also has an active team of faculty members and students organized as the News Study Group. Among its initial projects the group videotaped and analyzed coverage of the 1972 presidential campaign, the Watergate hearings, events preceding the resignation of former President Richard Nixon, and the 1976 presidential primaries and election campaign. Current work includes studies of the impact of mass communications on public attitudes.

University of Michigan
Ann Arbor, MI 48104
(313) 764-1817
Interdepartmental Program in Mass Communication
F. Gerald Kline, Chairperson

The Departments of Journalism, Political Science, Psychology, and Sociology supervise the Interdepartmental Doctoral Program in Mass Communication. Research done by faculty and students affiliated with the Program is conducted in a variety of settings, among them the Institute for Social Research, the Institute of Public Policy Studies, and the individual departments. Current major research areas: human information-seeking and processing; the social context of mass media use and adolescent information-seeking; media effects on electoral behavior; the functions of new communication technologies.

Michigan State University
East Lansing, MI 48824
College of Communication Arts and Sciences
(517) 355-3410
Erwin P. Bettinghaus, Dean

Department chairpersons: Gordon E. Miracle, Department of Advertising; Leo V. Deal, Department of Audiology and Speech Sciences; Gerald R. Miller (acting), Department of Communication; George A. Hough III, School of Journalism; and Robert W. Schlater, Department of Telecommunication.

Degrees offered: The College offers B.A. and M.A. degrees in the Departments of Advertising, Audiology and Speech Sciences, Communication, Telecommunication, and the School of Journalism. The Ph.D. is offered by the

Departments of Audiology and Speech Sciences and Communication, with an interdepartmental Ph.D. among the other three units in Mass Media.

Financial assistance: Financial aid for undergraduate students at the college or department level consists of a limited number of undergraduate assistantships, student labor money and, in the School of Journalism, a few scholarships. At the graduate level there are graduate traineeships available in Audiology and Speech Sciences and research assistantships in both Audiology and Speech Sciences and in Communication. Graduate training assistantships are available in all five units.

Research: Among the many research projects currently conducted by the College are the impact of media in the political process; analysis of communication effects in large and complex organizations; family communication; uses of interactive two-way cable TV systems; media management; effects of television; and effects of the use of videotape on courtroom communication.

Graduate School of Business Administration
   Institute of Public Utilities
   (517) 355-1876
   Harry M. Trebing, Director

   The Institute of Public Utilities, which was established in 1966, conducts programs in three areas: it awards doctoral fellowships and faculty grants to applicants on a nationwide basis; it sponsors a series of annual conferences, with participants drawn from the academic community, government and industry; and it maintains an active publications program.

   The annual conferences and publications focus on topics in the fields of public utility economics, commission regulation, and industry studies on the subjects of electricity, natural gas transmission and distribution, and all phases of common carrier regulation. The Institute has published a number of pioneering studies dealing with telephone separations and settlements; innovations in communications pricing; market structure, competition and entry in telecommunications; and cable television in Canada. Announcements of conferences and a catalog of publications are available upon request.

University of Mid-America (UMA)
P.O. Box 82006
Lincoln, NB 68501
Public Affairs and Information Sciences
(402) 467-3671
Milan Wall, Director

The University of Mid-America (UMA) is a regional educational experiment in "teaching at a distance" or "open learning." The UMA, funded primarily by the National Institute of Education, is governed and administered by a consortium of midwestern state universities committed to providing educational opportunities for adults seeking learning alternatives at the post-secondary level.

As an experimental educational model, UMA has three objectives: to develop multimedia college-level courses for home study; to conduct research on adult learning, including an evaluation of learner response to open-learning courses: and to provide assistance to consortium members in developing open-learning systems.

UMA courses utilize both traditional and nontraditional components, including video lessons for broadcast by local educational stations, popularized material for newspaper publication, and audiocassette tapes, study guides and textbooks for independent study at home.

Additional assistance to learners often is provided through regional learning resource centers and toll-free WATS telephone lines that can put a learner in touch with an instructor on a moment's notice.

University of Minnesota
Minneapolis, MN 55455
School of Journalism and Mass Communications
111 Murphy Hall
206 Church St., S.E.
(612) 373-3565
Robert L. Jones, Director

Degrees offered: Bachelor of Arts degrees may be taken in one of four sequences: news-editorial, advertising, broadcast journalism and photocommunication. All of these sequences are accredited by the American Council on Education for Journalism. M.A. degrees are offered under two plans: Plan A requires a thesis and foreign language capability; Plan B requires more credits but shorter papers in lieu of the thesis and usually does not require foreign language competence. M.A. degrees with a professional emphasis in advertising, broadcast journalism, urban journalism, photocommunication, science communication and general news-editorial are usually taken under Plan B. Ph.D. degrees are earned by work in two of four concentration areas: theory and methodology, history of communication, international communication, and communication agencies as social institutions. Students concentrate on one field and offer a second as a supplementary field. An outside minor or supporting program is required, as is, of course, a dissertation.

Financial assistance: Approximately 30 scholarships restricted to journalism majors are available for undergraduates. In addition, journalism undergraduate majors may compete for many hundreds of all-University scholarships and awards. Each year approximately 10 teaching, research or administrative assistantships are available for graduate students. These typically require some service and afford opportunity to gain laboratory supervising and teaching experience. Doctoral candidates usually hold from two to five duty-free Graduate School fellowships. Mass communication graduate students may compete for several hundred assistantships available in various all-University offices and programs.

Research: The School supports a communications research division which provides research space, equipment and offices for research assistants. Mass communication graduate students and faculty have access to University computing centers and data processing facilities. Typical division projects currently under way include research on children learning to be consumers, advertising for children, and developmental psychology models applied to childrens' consumer information processing. Other research includes profiling social, attitudinal and demographic data for metropolitan daily newspaper and TV news reporters, analysis of the media coverage of children, studies of American graphic humor, studies of mass communication in developing nations, earth satellite communication, studies of mass media and community leadership, analysis of press council organizations and procedures, studies of the specialized press in metropolitan centers and studies of international news agencies.

Department of Speech-Communication
317 Folwell Hall
9 Pleasant St., S.E.

(612) 373-2617
Robert L. Scott, Chairman

Degrees offered: B.A., M.A. and Ph.D. All degrees granted are in speech-communication. Students stress special interests in broadcasting, interpersonal and small group communication, organizational communication, international and cross-cultural communication, and rhetorical studies.

Financial assistance: The Department recommends persons for various scholarships and fellowships in the Graduate School. These are few in number, but important. Recommendations are made by a departmental committee based on application for financial aid. The committee also considers persons for teaching associates. The Department currently has about twenty half-time teaching associates who earn $5,252 and pay tuition at the resident's rate.

Research: Current research includes projects on small group communication in natural settings and contemporary political persuasion; cross-cultural communication workshops as teaching tools and research sources; British public access and the use of the mass media in political causes; international broadcasting systems; communication between sexes and age groups; the philosophy of communication systems; and satellite communication and media management.

University of Missouri
Columbia, MO 65201
School of Journalism
(314) 882-4821
Roy M. Fisher, Dean

Degrees offered: The School of Journalism offers a Bachelor of Journalism, a Master of Arts and a Ph.D. degree.

Financial assistance: A number of scholarships, fellowships, internships, prizes and awards, lectureships and loans from special funds are available. In addition, the Department of Journalism names more than 500 Curator Freshmen Scholars each year, for whom the full amount of the incidental fee is waived. Missourians who are sophomores, juniors or seniors, including transfers from other institutions, are designated University Scholars and receive a $100 waiver-of-fees if they achieve a cumulative grade point average in the upper five percent of their classes.

Research: Although the advanced degree program is research-oriented, there is not a separate facility or group at the school. Several faculty members conduct individual research in the following areas: communication theory development, international journalism, journalism ethics and philosophy, journalism history, communications law and media usage. Among the facilities available to students and scholars is the Frank Lee Martin Library, one of the largest journalism libraries in the world (see listing on page 271).

Freedom of Information Center. (see listing on page 269).

University of Montreal
Outremont, P.Q. H2V 2J2
Department of Communication
1420 Mt. Royale Blvd.
(514) 343-6043, 343-6039
Annie Mear, Director

The Department integrates American and European schools of thought in communications. Among its recent projects: the effects of information overload on individuals and groups; the impact of TV on Eskimos; the role of TV and new technologies in community social development; the role of communication in an intercultural setting; and semiotic analysis of the media.

New York University
New York, NY 10012
School of the Arts
    Alternate Media Center
    144 Bleecker Street
    (212) 598-3338/9
    Ms. Red Burns, Director

The Center was formed in 1971 to create models for access to cable television. Projects have since grown to include research and consultation in educational access, library access, local organization, and telemedicine-electronic community information systems.

Current projects include sponsoring short stand-alone courses on the applications of interactive telecommunication systems for both technical and nontechnical professionals in the field. Examples of course topics are "Two-Way Television: A

Case Study," which covers such areas as technical and organizational design, training of users, securing institutional cooperation, and adapting technology; and "Recent Research and Current Developments in Great Britain," covering areas such as audio and video teleconferencing, communications planning in government and industry, and the educational application of interactive telecommunications.

The University of North Carolina at Chapel Hill
Chapel Hill, NC 27514
Department of Radio, Television and Motion Pictures
Communication Center
(919) 933-2311
A. Richard Elam, Chairman

Degrees offered: B.A. in radio, television and motion pictures, including an emphasis on broadcast journalism done in conjunction with the School of Journalism; M.A. in communications.

Financial assistance: Several undergraduate scholarships are available, including the Jefferson Pilot Broadcasting Scholarship for $1,000 per year ($1,250 if out-of-state). Eight graduate assistantships of about $1,000 per year are presently awarded.

Research: All faculty members of the Department conduct individual research. Research areas include feasibility studies on radio reading services for the blind; sources of meaning in film; federal regulation of broadcasting; and television effects on black children.

School of Journalism
Howell Hall 021 A
(919) 933-1204
John B. Adams, Dean

Degrees offered: B.A. in journalism, with sequences in news-editorial, advertising, and broadcast journalism; M.A. in journalism, with two paths—news-editorial and general curriculum—plus an interdisciplinary Ph.D. in mass communication research.

Financial assistance: In addition to undergraduate financial aid available from the University generally, the School of Journalism awards many undergraduate scholarships to its majors, including the $1,500 per year L.C.

Gifford Distinguished Journalism Scholarship. Research assistantships of $2,600 are awarded to qualified graduate students. University fellowships, each with a stipend of $2,000 or more, are available upon nomination by the School of Journalism to a limited number of graduate students.

Research: Major areas of research include political communications, international communications, economics of the mass media, historical and cultural influences on the press, impact of technology on the mass media, press-bar relations, and studies of newspaper circulation patterns. Representative projects: Charlotte (North Carolina) voter study of the agenda-setting function of the mass media; productivity of communications scholars; completeness of press coverage in the 1972 presidential campaign; communications, technology and culture and the decline of American regional thought.

Northern Illinois University
DeKalb, IL 60015
Department of Journalism
(815) 753-1925
Donald F. Brod, Chairperson

Degrees offered: B.A., B.S., and M.A. degrees are offered. There are undergraduate sequences in advertising, broadcast news, journalism education, news-editorial, photojournalism, and public relations.

Financial assistance: The Department offers about 8 to 10 graduate assistantships per year.

Industrial Press Research Project
Albert Walker, Director

The Project conducts research into the effectiveness of editorial content and treatment and of graphic design; investigates employee-stockholder-public communication methods and theory; and conducts occasional specially funded projects.

Suburban Press Research Center
Anthony Scantlen, Director

The Center receives and collects newspapers from members of Suburban Newspapers of America and uses them for research and critical reviews.

Northwestern University
Evanston, IL 60201
College of Arts and Sciences
   Transportation Center
   (312) 492-7286
   Leon Moses, Director
   The Center's work is focused on five main categories: to what extent present and potential telecommunications can substitute or supplement personal travel; telecommunications used for the transfer of information, such as postal or library services; telecommunications as a factor in land use and regional development; the impact of telecommunications on transportation in such cases as the radio-dispatching of trucks and the use of CB radios; and the interrelationship of telecommunications and transportation in the area of policy and regulatory matters such as rate-making, intermodal competition, barriers to entry, and innovation.
Medill School of Journalism
1845 Sheridan Road
(312) 492-3741
I.W. Cole, Dean
   Degrees offered: B.S. in journalism, with broadcast, newspaper and magazine sequences. M.S. in journalism, in editorial (broadcast, newspaper, or magazine), and advertising.
   Financial assistance: Undergraduate financial aid is handled by the Financial Aid Office, Northwestern University. If a student is admitted to the University and there is financial need, Northwestern will meet that need through grant assistance, loans, and/or jobs on campus. Graduate financial assistance is awarded by the Medill School of Journalism and includes scholarships, work-study, and loans.
   Research: The School's **Frank E. Gannett Urban Journalism Center** has conducted research relating to the adaptability of social science surveys and techniques to augment analytical reporting. Parts of this research effort have been introduced to both graduate and undergraduate Medill curriculums, resulting in published survey material in two metropolitan newspapers *(Chicago Tribune* and *Wilmington News-Journal).*
School of Speech
(312) 492-3741

Roy V. Wood, Dean
Degrees offered: The School includes the Department of Radio, Television and Film (Martin J. Maloney, Chairman) and the Department of Communication Studies (David Zarefsky, Chairman). Degrees offered include the B.S. in speech, the M.A. (M.F.A. in radio, TV and film), and the Ph.D.

Financial assistance: The Departments of Radio, TV and Film and Communication Studies annually award 6 to 8 fellowships and employ 17 teaching assistants.

Research: The Department of Radio, Television and Film concerns itself with research studies and projects related to those media. Historical, critical and empirical studies have been conducted. In recent years, attention has been given to broadcasting in foreign countries. The Department of Communication Studies conducts research in survey and experimental studies in small group and interpersonal communication, problems in freedom of speech, and critical analyses of the communication strategies of political and social movements.

Ohio State University
Columbus, OH 43210
School of Journalism
(614) 422-6291
William Hall, Director

Degrees offered: The School offers both B.A. and M.A. degrees. At the undergraduate level the School has been accredited in news-editorial, broadcasting, and public relations sequences. At the graduate level the degree is research-oriented, and, while a student may take a number of courses in any of the three above areas, he/she does not specialize. The degree is a broad one, with emphasis on theory and research methodology as well as on an understanding of the social and legal roles played by the mass media in our society, both historically and today.

Research: Recent research projects include the policies and practices of television stations in hiring news staff; a survey of radio and television news executives' judgments of broadcast problems that can best be studied by academic researchers; a study of the professional, academic and media experience of professors who teach basic skills courses in schools of journalism; and a study of the comparative efficacy of question-and-answer and traditional news story forms in communicating complex issues.

Department of Communication
205 Derby Hall
(614) 422-3400
James L. Golden, Chairman
   Degrees offered: B.A., M.A., and Ph.D. Master's and doctor's degrees available in mass communication, communication theory, rhetoric and public address, and cross-disciplinary combinations of these.
   Financial assistance: Undergraduate financial assistance is available through the University. Persons entering the graduate program with only a B.A. degree, and selected as teaching assistants, receive $3,015 for nine months, plus a waiver of all University fees. Those entering with an M.A. degree receive $3,600, plus the fee waiver.
   Research: Research projects have been carried out by the Communication Department on the effect of camera angle on source credibility and interpersonal attraction; the effect of humanistic psychology on broadcasting; the influence of "Mister Rogers' Neighborhood" on the learning capabilities of handicapped children; the effect of TV violence and subsequent aggression level on kindergarten children; how people become visually literate correlated with cognitive styles; the effects of television advertising on grade school children; and how children form impressions of television characters.

Ohio University
Athens, OH 45701
(614) 594-5511
College of Communication
John Wilhelm, Dean
   The College has approximately 1,700 undergraduate majors and 171 graduate students in communication.
   Degrees offered: Degrees are offered through the doctoral level. They include a B.S. in Communication, an M.S. in journalism, a B.S. in Communication, an M.S. in Communication, and a Ph.D. in Mass Communication.
Broadcast Research Center
(614) 594-6338
   The Center is a nonprofit research institute which undertakes contract research aimed at assisting both public and commercial broadcasters in making specific managerial decisions. Toward this end the Center maintains a continuing analysis of the specific nature of the

economy and its effect on the media industry. A list of publications is available on request.
School of Journalism
The School conducts a number of research projects related to the mass media. They include how readers respond to veiled attribution; census of foreign correspondents; reader reaction to newspaper front page formats; and a comparison of the quality of copyreading on videoterminals and on paper.
School of Radio-Television
Among research projects carried out by the School of Radio-Television are information dissemination patterns in the broadcast media; the regional broadcast audience; and audiences for locally originated cable programming.

University of Oregon
Eugene, OR 94703
Division of Broadcast Services and Televised Instruction
(503) 686-4242
John Shepherd, Director

In addition to the operation of radio station KWAX-FM, the Division assists both students and faculty in research projects focusing on public radio and television, as well as research projects dealing with instructional media.
Communication Research Center
(503) 686-4198
William Elliott, Director

The Communication Research Center serves to develop and assist in the implementation of research dealing with both interpersonal and mass communication. Current research activities include mass media influences on the political process, communicative patterns of the elderly, and the normative aspects of the interaction process.
School of Journalism
(503) 686-3738
Galen R. Rarick, Dean

Degrees offered: B.A., B.S., M.A., and M.S. degrees are offered. Accredited sequences include news-editorial, radio-television news, public relations, and advertising.

Financial assistance: Graduate teaching fellowships are available, as are undergraduate scholarships.

Research: The Division of Communication Research is

headed by James B. Lemert. Current research includes study of how community leaders process information about public opinion and what they do with it; examination of the comparative importance of demographics and content in subscribing to a daily newspaper; and investigation of media accessibility as a function of group identity.

Department of Speech
(503) 686-4171
Carl Carmichael, Chairperson

The Department consists of four areas: theater, telecommunications, film studies, and rhetoric and communication theory.

Degrees offered: Graduate degrees (Master's and doctorate) are offered in all four areas.

Research: Current departmental research includes several projects dealing with nonverbal communication, as well as individual research activity by faculty members within their own areas of specialization.

University of Pennsylvania
Philadelphia, PA 19104
The Annenberg School of Communications
3260 Walnut Street, C5
(215) 243-7041
George Gerbner, Dean

Degrees offered: The School offers a graduate program of studies leading to the M.A. and Ph.D. in Communications.

Financial assistance: Scholarships and assistantships are available to qualified candidates on a competitive basis. Areas of specialization include codes and modes (study of symbolic processes), communications behavior, and communications systems and institutions.

Research: Every faculty member is an active researcher, and every degree candidate is qualified in making contributions applicable to the conduct of communications inquiry, practice, and policy. Current research projects include a long-range study of television content and effects, called Cultural Indicators; the annual release of the TV Violence Profile and Index; the analysis of pictorial and other nonverbal communications; political communication studies; social cybernetics; research on broadcast news and commercials; historical analysis of crime coverage; economic aspects of programming; and international studies in the global flow of communications. A major international symposium and policy conference on "World Communications Flow—A Reassessment" is planned for the fall of 1978.

Publications: The Annenberg School is the publisher of the *Journal of Communication* (see listing on page 292).

The Institute for Applied Communications Studies, under the direction of Associate Dean Harold H. Frank, extends the work of the school to problems of business and government by holding short courses and conducting applied projects.

Rice University
Houston, TX 77001
Department of Economics
(713) 527-4878
Gaston Rimingler, Chairman

The Department's communications research program has focused on the economics and regulation of the television industry. Its principal emphasis has been on the impact of government policies on the extent of competitiveness within the industry. Specific research projects have included the economics of the network-affiliate relationship; viewer behavior during the Watergate hearings; the impact of the frequency allocation plan on entry into television broadcasting; the determinants of television station time rates; FCC policy for cable television; copyright liability and cable television; and evaluation of the effect of cable on broadcasting. Work on the determinants of entry and on industry behavior are continuing.

Simon Fraser University
Burnaby, British Columbia V5A 1S6
Department of Communication Studies
(604) 291-4341
William H. Melody, Chairman

The Department has organized its courses at both the undergraduate and graduate levels into three major areas: communications institutions—the structure and functioning of organizations related to technically mediated communication systems; communications processes—the nature and effects of the interactions that occur within and between individual persons and human systems; communication systems—the theoretical and pragmatic consequences of a communication approach to societal and environmental analysis.

The Department is in the process of acquiring a ground station for satellite communication as part of the PEACESAT project and video record and playback equipment for the establishment of a video research library. A colloquium series of invited lecturers is offered throughout the year, and distinguished outside scholars frequently appear as visiting professors.

Degrees offered: The Department offers a Major and Honors in Communication at the undergraduate level and a Graduate Program leading to an M.A. Students working for the Ph.D. must be admitted under special arrangements. A formal Ph.D. program is planned for introduction in the near future.

Financial assistance: Attempts are made to provide financial aid through teaching and research assistantships for students in their second through fourth semesters. The University, in addition, provides a one-semester thesis research stipend to students who have completed their second semester in the program.

Research: The following research projects are part of the Department: The *Telecommunications Research Group*, Professor Patricia Hindley, Director, (604) 291-4694. The TRG carries out policy analyses and field studies in broadcasting, telecommunication and development of intermediate communication technology systems in Canada and developing countries. The *World Soundscape Project*, Professor Barry Truax, Research Director, (604) 291-4261. The WSP conducts research into individual and community relationships to the acoustic environment. Their major facility is the Sonic Research Studio, which is completely equipped for tape production/analysis. There are extensive archives of environmental sounds from many countries. The *Social Communication Research Group*, Professor Tom Mallinson, Director, (604) 291-4381. The Group conducts research into interpersonal and organizational communication. A research facility available is the Social Communication Laboratory, which utilizes video and sound systems for the observation of small group dynamics.

University of Southern California
Los Angeles, CA 90007
Annenberg School of Communications
(213) 746-6273

Frederick Williams, Dean

The Annenberg School of Communications is a new and nontraditional graduate training and research institution that specializes in management of, and research into, contemporary and future communications problems. A particular focus is the study of the impact of modern technologies, such as television and computer communication systems, upon organizations and the public.

Degrees offered: Academic programs are designed for advanced training of managers of communication activities (Master of Arts degree in Communications Management) and for training of behavioral scientists with expertise in communications problem-solving (doctoral program in Communication Theory and Research).

Financial assistance: To facilitate full-time attention to their first year of doctoral study, all students accepted into the doctoral program in Communication Theory and Research are awarded an Annenberg fellowship stipend, in addition to a tuition fellowship. As long as a student maintains adequate progress and level of performance in the doctoral program, the tuition fellowship will continue for up to four years. Additionally, there are a variety of research and administrative positions that are a part of contract and grant projects. There are tuition support options for students in the Management Program, although at this time there are no regular fellowship stipends.

Research: Research activities in the communications policy area are administered through the School's *Center for Communication Policy Research*, Gerhard Hanneman, Director. Major projects of the Center have been studies of communication-transportation trade-offs, urban uses of interactive television, evaluation of communication technologies in medical settings, and evaluation of drug abuse communication. The Annenberg School also undertakes research specializing in human interaction with computers. Research projects in this area include investigation of network information systems and automated office communications. The school is the recipient, through 1980, of the formative evaluation component of a $3.7 million television project to develop a career awareness series for nine-through-eleven-year-olds. The new $3.5 million Annenberg Building houses a variety of research facilties and equipment, including a physiographic lab and a 100-seat electronic audience response system.

Publication: The School's newsletter, *The Record*, may be obtained free by writing or calling the Dean's office.

Graduate Program in Communication
(213) 741-2490
James H. McBath, Chairperson

The Communication Program is concerned with human and mass communication phenomena from a behavioral perspective and leads to graduate degrees in several areas of specialization.

Degrees offered: Ph.D. in Communication (major emphasis on cinema, drama, journalism, and speech-communication).

Financial assistance: Full tuition awards as teaching assistant; also partial tuition awards.

Research: Current research problems under investigation include the impact of television advertising on children; interpersonal communication networks among urban groups; the effect of nonverbal communication on task-oriented group interaction; reducing school violence through communication; the effects of television viewing on family communication patterns; research into barriers to cross-cultural communication; interpersonal communication in legal negotiation settings. The *Office of Communication Research and Service*, E.M. Bodaken, Director, provides support for research and public service activities.

Southern Illinois University
Carbondale, IL 62901
School of Journalism
(618) 536-3361
George C. Brown, Director

Degrees offered: B.A., M.A., and Ph.D. degrees are offered. Undergraduate areas of specialization are news-editorial, advertising, and photojournalism. Graduate areas of specialization are communication theory and methodology, communication law, and media history.

Financial assistance: Doctoral and master's fellowships and doctoral dissertation grants are offered by the Graduate School. Both teaching and research assistantships are offered within the School. The majority of graduate students in journalism receive financial aid.

Research: The Mass Communication Research Center of the School of Journalism focuses on the legal questions and the social effects of the mass media in the areas of advertising regulation, college and high school press law, political campaign communication, editorial persuasion, economics, and health communication. Current projects include dissemination of health/drug information; mental health institutional use of the mass media; political campaign communication; college and high school press law; the use of persuasion theory in editorial writing; historical perspectives on newspapers' economics; and history of new journalism.

Publications: Graduate Communication Studies, and occasional technical reports.

Stanford University
Stanford, CA 94305
Department of Communication
(415) 497-2753
Lyle Nelson, Chairman

Degrees offered: The Department offers curricula leading to the B.A., M.A., and Ph.D. degree. The Master of Arts degree prepares students for careers in journalism or documentary film, or in evaluation research for mass media projects in developing countries. The Ph.D. degree leads to careers in teaching and research or other related specialties. Specifically, the Ph.D. program is offered in communication theory and communication behavior through the life cycle, communication media and social change, communication health, information sciences, and public affairs communication.

Financial assistance: A few research assistantships are available to qualified graduate students. The Department sponsors the Professional Journalism Fellowship Program, with the assistance of the National Endowment for the Humanities, which brings promising young journalists to study at the University in a nondegree course of study.

The *Institute for Communication Research* is directed by Professor Nathan Maccoby and is funded in part by grants from foundations, communication media and other agencies, and by government grants and contracts. Serving as the research division of the Department of Communication, the Institute's principal programs are within the fields of international communication, health communication, information science, communication technology and public policy, and communication and the media. Ongoing research at the Institute includes investigation in how media and the processes of communication provide the most effective and economical service, preliminary analysis and proposed expansion of a community-wide communication education program to reduce cardiovascular risk, and working with Third World nations to seek solutions to development problems through improved use of low-cost media.

Department of Economics
(415) 497-3701
Bert Hickman, Chairman

Periodically, the Department's Studies in Industry Economics program sponsors Seminars in Industry, and Workshops in Regulation and Communication at Stanford. A number of publications and discussion papers are produced in association with the seminars and workshops on topics such as "Economic Patterns of Information Seeking," "Economic Issues in the Joint Ownership of Newspaper and Television Media," and "Interdisciplinary Study of the Mass Media: A Syllabus." A complete list of titles can be obtained from the Studies in Industry Economics program.

Syracuse University
Syracuse, NY 13210
School of Education
ERIC Clearinghouse on Information Resources
(315) 423-3640
Donald P. Ely, Director

ERIC is an information system which makes available unpublished, hard-to-find documents on all phases, levels, and subject areas of education. Sixteen Clearinghouses, each focusing on different facets of professional education, locate, acquire, and organize these materials for use by educators, researchers, students, and others interested in the field. ERIC includes citations to more than 200,000 technical reports, articles, speeches and other documents related to education. More than 16 million ERIC microforms are purchased each year, most of them by the 600 institutions and organizations which maintain complete collections of the ERIC file. It is sponsored by the National Institute of Education of the Department of Health, Education and Welfare.

The Information Resources Clearinghouse is concerned with the handling and delivery of information. Specific topics include the management, operation, and use of libraries, together with the technology to improve their operation; the education, training, and professional activities of librarians and information specialists; educational techniques stemming from use of technology, e.g., systems analysis, programmed instruction utilizing audiovisual teaching materials, television, radio, computers, and films; and any medium which may be adaptable to education, such as cable television, microforms, and public television. ERIC specializes in noncopyrighted, unpublished educational materials, such as project reports, speech texts, research findings, how-to-do-it items, locally-produced materials, and conference proceedings. Teachers, administrators, supervisors, librarians, researchers, media specialists, and others are invited to share such materials through ERIC.

Bibliographic citations and abstracts of materials acquired by ERIC are published in a monthly catalog, *RIE* (Resources in Education). Most of these materials are available in microfiche and may be used at many of the 584 institutions in this country with ERIC collections; or personal copies may be ordered in microfiche or photocopy. As an additional service to educators, ERIC also supplies information for *CIJE* (Current Index to Journals in Education), a monthly listing of journal articles with bibliographic citation and annotation. The text of the articles is not supplied.

In-house publications usually take the form of overviews, guides to the literature, bibliographies, or state-of-the-art papers. An occasional newsletter reports on latest developments in ERIC's area of interest, as well as Clearinghouse activities. ERIC answers questions for individuals ranging from queries about the ERIC system to locating specialized information in the ERIC files. It also presents workshops, participates in conventions, cooperates with professional organizations, schools and universities, and furnishes information to professional journals on current additions to the data base.

S.I. Newhouse School of Public Communications
(315) 423-2301
Henry F. Schulte, Dean
　　Degrees offered: B.A., M.A., and Ph.D.
　　Financial assistance: Fellowships, teaching assistant-

ships, and research assistantships are available.
ANPA News Research Center
Maxwell E. McCombs, Director

The Center is the planning and coordinating body for an ongoing program of theoretical and empirical research on newspaper readership. The Center also publishes the *ANPA News Research Bulletin,* which features reviews of the literature and special data analyses developed by the Center's staff on newspaper readership and other topics; reports of projects funded by the Center; and independent articles submitted by outside scholars.

Canadian Communications Program
(315) 423-3215
Vernone Sparkes, Director

The Program has conducted research on news flow between Canada and the United States and on comparative analysis of American and Canadian policy for the electronic media. As part of the Program, the Newhouse School of Public Communications conducted a conference in September, 1976 on problems in news flow between Canada and the United States. The conference was conducted primarily for professional journalists and government workers involved in the information exchange process. Another dimension of the Canadian communications program has involved research into cross-cultural effects from television signal spillover along the Canadian-U.S. border.

Communications Research Center
(315) 423-3363
Maxwell E. McCombs, Director

The Center is involved in a broad range of communications research, with special attention to three ongoing areas: political communications, press performance, and Canadian communications. Included in the political communications program are a series of studies delimiting the press's influence in the agenda-setting area, and other studies analyzing how voters use the media for political information. Work in the area of press performance includes a long-range study of foreign news flow in the Canadian and American press, and in-depth analyses of press operations in several eastern states. The Center has coordinated the preparation

of a new book on precision journalism, *The Handbook of Reporting Methods.*
Department of Television and Radio
Lawrence Myers, Chairman
Recent studies carried out by the Department include an experimental study of the influence of the experienced teacher on television; the impact of an educational television program on its audience; and the Syracuse FM study.

Temple University
1601 N. Broad Street
Philadelphia, PA 19122
Institute for Survey Research
(215) 787-8355
Leonard LoSciuto, Director
The Institute occasionally conducts communications research projects, within a broad range of other projects. Examples: a national sample survey of television viewing, and a survey of public attitudes toward and exposure to erotic materials, including the media of erotica.
School of Communications and Theater
(215) 787-8422
Kenneth Harwood, Dean
The School consists of three Departments: Journalism, Radio-Television-Film, and Theater. The former two cooperate to offer graduate degrees (M.A. and Ph.D.) in Communications. Members of both Departments cooperate in issuing *Communications Research Reports* with research studies, bibliographies, and other analyses—about four to six a year.
Department of Journalism
(215) 787-7433
Jacqueline Steck, Chairperson
Degrees offered: The Department offers B.A. and M.J. degrees, as well as communication graduate degrees. Areas of specialization include advertising, magazine, news-editorial, and public relations.
Research: Ongoing research includes work on media and minorities and photojournalism; media in Latin America; and media in Asia.
Publications: The Department helps support *Mass Comm Review* (see listing on page 301), and *BERITA Newsletter of Malaysia-Singapore Studies.*

Department of Radio-Television-Film
(215) 787-8424
Timothy J. Lyons, Chairperson
   Major research includes work in documentary film history; on broadcasting in America, Africa, foreign and comparative media; on media effects and research methodology; on broadcast journalism; on media regulation and communication policy; on cable; on educational communication; on foreign film education; on television drama; and on media bibliography and communications history and ownership. The Department helps support *Mass Media Booknotes* (see listing on page 302), and *Journal of the University Film Association* (see listing on page 331). There is also a great deal of production activity by faculty and students in both undergraduate and M.F.A. programs. The Department also conducts a London-based program in communications. Summer seminars are conducted yearly in theater, journalism, broadcasting, film, and the media in general all over the world.

University of Tennessee
Knoxville, TN 37916
College of Communications
(615) 974-3031
Donald Hileman, Dean
   The College of Communications was founded in 1969, building on the base established by the School of Journalism since 1947. The College consists of the School of Journalism, the Department of Advertising, the Department of Broadcasting, Graduate Studies, and the Communications Research Center.
   Degrees offered: B.A., M.A., and Ph.D. degrees are offered in all Departments.
   Financial assistance: Graduate assistantships are available to qualified students on a quarter-time basis. Minimum pay is $1,960 per year, with waiver of tuition and fees. A limited number of scholarships and fellowships are also available. In addition, students may apply for loans.
   ### Communications Research Center
   Jack B. Haskins, Director
      The Center was established in 1973 to conduct research on and for the mass media and other com-

munications organizations. The present emphasis is on mass and public communications in order to capitalize on faculty strengths and interests. The Center publishes a quarterly research newsletter, distributed to the mass media and other communications organizations in Tennessee. Current emphasis is on mass media research relating to public service communications, especially energy and associated environmental problems. Other projects deal with advertising, broadcasting, and journalism.

Among other supporting facilities for research at the University are a "laboratory" library, which includes trade journals and research publications in the professional and academic fields of communications, the Learning Research Center, a University Computing Center, and the Institute for Public Service.

The University of Texas at Austin
Austin, TX 78712
School of Communication
(512) 471-5775
Wayne Danielson, Dean

The main themes followed in instruction are communication technology (the School emphasizes computer applications in communication fields); creativity (theory is combined with practice in the School's labs); responsibility (the faculty is strong in law and ethics in the media and society); service (students and faculty do public service work for governmental and community non-profit agencies); and professionalism (the bond combining all fields is that students work or plan to work as professionals in communication fields).

Degrees offered: Some 2,700 undergraduates and 300 graduate students annually enroll in the School of Communication, considered to be the nation's largest. Undergraduate degrees are offered in journalism, advertising, radio-television-film, and speech communication. Of the graduate students, 200 seek M.A. degrees in communication in the various departments. Approximately 100 students enroll each year for the Ph.D. in Communication, which is interdepartmental and interdisciplinary in nature.

Research: Research interests of the 87 faculty members are broad, ranging from audiological measurement to the esthetics of film. Representative projects under way include speech synthesis from newspaper text; automatic indexing of news stories; a descriptive study of Spanish-language broadcasting in the United States; a history of the first years of photography in the United States; a nationwide survey of the writing skills of beginning journalism students; developments in the law of privacy; a series of studies on television violence and its effects; organizational communication patterns in a state agency; and attitudes toward press freedom and responsibility among state legislators.

University of Utah
Salt Lake City, UT 84112
Department of Communication
Building 013
(801) 581-6302
Richard D. Rieke, Chairman

Degrees offered: The Division of Journalism and Mass Communication of the Department of Communication offers courses of study leading to the B.S., B.A., M.S., M.A., M.Phil. and Ph.D. degrees. Undergraduate sequences of study include advertising-public relations, broadcast journalism, news-editorial and radio-television-film. A description of the undergraduate program and scholarship information is available upon request from Professor Robert Tiemens. Major areas of study available to graduate students include advertising-public relations, mass communication effects, international communication, mass communication history and law, noncommercial telecommunication, broadcast economics, visual communication and mass communication research methods. Graduate programs are designed to meet each candidate's professional needs. Additional information concerning the graduate program is available from Professor Robert Avery.

Financial assistance: Research scholarships and teaching assistantships are available to graduate applicants who show demonstrated evidence of scholarly potential and productivity.

Research: Current research projects by faculty and graduate students are reflected in each of the areas of graduate study.

Washington University
St. Louis, MO 63130
Center for Development Technology
(314) 863-0100, Ext. 4506
Lester F. Eastwood, Jr., Associate Director
  for Communications
  Communications activity of the Center is concerned with applying science and technology to needs in education, communication, and information. It is also concerned with public policy issues and the economic, environmental, and societal impact of information systems and new communication devices, systems, and methods. Although the Center is in the School of Engineering and Applied Science, its work is interdisciplinary.
  Courses offered: Programs of academic study are available in traditional departments as well as in the Department of Technology and Human Affairs (THA) in the School of Engineering. For further information about THA graduate degree programs write to Robert P. Morgan, Chairman, Box 1106.
  Financial assistance: The Center occasionally has research assistantships available.
  Research: Center research projects have included analysis of educational needs, telecommunications requirements, and opportunities for use of fixed broadcast satellite services in American education; development of a low-cost broadband receiver for satellite community broadcasting; synthesis of alternative educational satellite systems for U.S. education in which both technical and nontechnical factors have been analyzed; analysis of opportunities, economics, and development of models for delivery of nontraditional, postsecondary education using telecommunications; assessment of cable and fiber-optic communication systems for educational network; identification of government options in educational communications policy; and earth observation data management systems for state agencies.

University of Washington
Seattle, WA 98105
School of Communications
(206) 543-2660
Alex Edelstein, Director
  Degrees offered: B.A. in Communications (concentra-

tion in one of five sequences—editorial journalism, broadcast journalism, advertising, radio-television, and communication), Master of Arts, Master of Communications (Option A or B), and Ph.D. The M.A. is the research degree and leads to work toward the Ph.D. The M.C. (Option A) is a terminal degree for teachers at community college and secondary levels and has possible vocational application for government, industry, and other public sectors. The M.C. (Option B) is a special studies program in a substantive field for media professionals or those who wish to prepare more intensively for media.

Financial assistance: The School awards graduate student assistantships at the pre- and post-Master's levels. Pre-Master's are laboratory assistants in the editorial laboratory, radio and television production, and undergraduate counseling. Some pre-Master's assist in courses in the communication process and the mass media. Post-Master's assist and teach a variety of small sectioned classes. Research assistants work on contract projects. Approximately 20 awards are made each year.

Communications Research Center
Keith Stamm, Director
Brenda Dervin, Associate Director

The Center engages in both theoretical and applied research in the United States and overseas. Recent studies have included cross-cultural studies of mass media use and decision-making; public television; credibility studies of the media; theoretical approaches to uses of cable television; use of mass media and environmental policies; minority portrayals and use of the mass media; and experiments in applied communication. Other studies have addressed themselves to methodology and societal issues in public opinion and mass communication; transactional interpersonal communication; and journalistic policies, personnel, and reporting procedures.

The Milo Ryan Phonoarchives (see listing on page 274).

Center for Quantitative Studies in Social Science
117 Savery Hall/Mailstop DK-45
(206) 543-8110
Gael Welch, Director

The Center is an interdisciplinary resource center for computer applications, both instructional and research, in the social science area. It provides noncredit programming instruction, consulting on program debugging and study design, an archive of data sets for secondary statistical analyses, computer equipment and facilities, and related administrative services. A *Newsletter* is published monthly containing information about the computer system, class offerings, programming hints, and notes about statistical packages available on campus.

Washington State University
Pullman, WA 99163
Social Research Center
(509) 335-1511
James F. Short, Jr., Director

The Center coordinates and administers research in the full range of the social and behavioral sciences. It consists of an administrative staff, a Public Opinion Laboratory, a Social Data Processing Center, and units devoted to activities in criminal justice, human values, aging, and alcohol and drug abuse. In addition, principal investigators utilizing research grants outside of these units constitute an important part of Center activities. Current research activities related to communications are centered in the Human Values Unit, directed by Milton Rokeach. Social Research Center Associate Director Sandra Ball-Rokeach is collaborating with him in a large-scale experimental field study of the impact of television communications on human values.

The Social Research Center is not a degree-granting unit, though much of its research is carried out with faculty and graduate students in cognate disciplines. Other professional personnel associated with the Center include Philip Kuhn, Coordinator of the Public Opinion Laboratory and Bernard Babbitt, Director of the Data Processing Center. Research assistants work with professional personnel in a variety of research and administrative functions associated with operation of the Center and its constituent units.

University of Western Ontario
London, Ontario N6A 5B7
School of Journalism
Room 218, Middlesex College
(519) 679-2441
Andrew MacFarlane, Dean

Degrees offered: With a full-time faculty of seven professors and a complement of over thirty visiting adjuncts, the School offers a varied program that strives to balance the practical with the academic. Within recent years the program has evolved from a combination Honours Bachelor of Arts degree and/or Diploma course to a Master of Arts degree.

Students enter the program from a variety of academic backgrounds that prepare them to concentrate on learning the tools of broadcast and print media. The first two terms provide in-depth exposure to every facet of newspaper, radio, television and magazine production. A three-week internship, a bimonthly school newspaper, a twice-weekly radio newscast, and the availability of campus and local publications all enable the student to combine classroom teaching with practical experience.

Financial assistance: The Ontario Graduate Scholarship and research assistantships are available for eligible students (usually A-average). At graduation, the School recognizes distinction with the following prizes: J.B. McGeachy Award, Dean's Medals, Journalism Faculty Medal, Bob Gage Award, and The Western News Award. Further information about the exact nature of the prizes and scholarships is in the Journalism School's calendar.

Research: In keeping with its professional orientation, the School conducts a program of research through its *Research Centre,* Christie McQuarrie, Director. It is concerned with applying scientific principles of what will help the journalist's understanding and practice of his/her calling, with measuring and interpreting the effect of the public media, with seeking out and recording the contributions of individual practitioners and their media to the development of Canadian society. Thus far a foundation study on "Priority Problems in the News Area of Canadian Dailies" has been completed. Professor C.E. Wilson heads the research area of the Journalism School and, along with Alistair M. Hunter, Editor-in-Residence, oversees publications in the *Western Journalism Library* Series.

An annual media conference in the fall brings together well-known personalities in the print and broadcasting arena and related fields to sound each other out on specific topics. In the area of continuing education, priority has been directed towards developing projects with and for the professional community. These include a Quebec-Ontario Journalist Exchange, the Canadian Centre for International and Development Journalism,

African Student Programme, and a Programme in Communications for Native Peoples.

University of Windsor
Windsor, Ontario N9B 3P4
Department of Communication Studies
Garth S. Jowett, Head
   Centre for Canadian Communication Studies
   (519) 253-4232 Ext. 726
   Garth S. Jowett, Chairman
   Degrees offered: B.A., B.A. (Hons.) M.A. The Department specializes in the examination and analysis of the problems of Canadian mass media and telecommunications within an international context, and in Canadian-American media relationships. While the undergraduate program is broad-based, the graduate program has three areas of concentration: communications policy and research; communications and national development; and media and education.
   Financial assistance: Some teaching assistantships are available. Canadian graduate students and those with landed immigrant status are eligible for the Canada Council graduate fellowships. Occasional research assistantships are also available.
   Research: Some current research projects: Canadian broadcasting policy; the history of communications; an analysis of documentary film; the nature of communications overflow between the U.S. and Canada; a study of the Parliamentary opposition leadership; and policy development toward media use and media study in the schools.

University of Wisconsin—Madison
Madison, WI 53706
Department of Agricultural Journalism
   The Department undertakes studies concerned with media behavior of audiences; attitudes toward controversial issues and sources of information; communications patterns among rural audiences; and comprehension, style-readability, and media presentation techniques with regard to agricultural home economics, international economic development, and natural resources communications.

Department of Communication Arts
Vilas Communication Hall
821 University Avenue
(608) 262-2544
Ordean G. Ness, Chairman

Degrees offered: B.A. in Communication Arts with three concentrations: communication and public address, radio-television-film, and commuication arts education, through the School of Education. M.A. degrees may be earned in either communication and public address or radio-television-film. There are both thesis and nonthesis options. The Ph.D. program is tailored to the student's interests and career needs.

Financial assistance: Undergraduate financial assistance is handled through the University. Graduate students may qualify for teaching assistantships, research assistantships, fellowships and part-time positions as project assistants. Stipends and awards vary from $5,382 per year to $296 per month. Many awards result in reductionof fees for tuition.

Research: Experimental facilities of the Center for Communication Research assist ongoing faculty and graduate research. Current projects include the analysis of interaction sequences, the study of physiological responses to mediated messages, and the study of the processes of visual perception. Other recent departmental research includes research on structures of visual communication; study of film theory, esthetics and criticism; experimental research on emotional responses to entertaining communications; development of a system for ascertaining and teaching the esthetic elements of television; analyses of national and international telecommunication regulatory policies, especially as they relate to evolving communications technology; research on the television coverage of the Indo-China War 1965–1970; the development of television programming; history of broadcasting, film and television documentary; and work on a history of American film and teaching courses in film history.

School of Journalism and Mass Communication
5115 Vilas Communication Hall
(608) 262-3691
William A. Hachten, Director

Degrees offered: J.B.A., J.B.S., M.A. in Journalism and Ph.D. in Mass Communication. Undergraduate sequences include news-editorial, public relations, broadcast journalism, and advertising. Other areas of undergraduate emphasis include community newspapers, magazine writing and editing, international communication, communication theory, and mass communication history and law.

Financial assistance: A number of awards and scholarhsips are granted each year to undergraduate journalism students. About 40 or so graduate students are supported each year by teaching assistantships, fellowships, research and project assistantships. Most graduate assistantships carry waiver of out-of-state tuition. Special financial aid is available for disadvantaged and minority students at both undergraduate and graduate levels.

Research: In addition to the research done in the Mass Communication Research Center (below), an integral part of the School, additional research studies in communication history and law, international communication and other areas are carried out by faculty and graduate students. Some of this research is done at the Mass Communications History Center at the Wisconsin State Historical Society (see listing on page 277).

Mass Communications Research Center
Vilas Communication Hall
(608) 262-3691
Jack McLeod, Chairperson

The Center emphasizes basic research on communication processes and provides assistance on professional and service-oriented studies by faculty and graduate students. Recent projects include adolescent TV use in the family context, influences on reporters, social determinants of information-seeking, assessments of political advertising, dynamism and familiarity in TV content, political participation of young voters, economic simulation model of cable TV systems, and immunization of children against media violence.

University of Wisconsin—Milwaukee
P.O. Box 413
Milwaukee, WI 53201
Department of Mass Communication
(414) 963-4436
Earl S. Grow, Chairperson

Courses offered: The Department offers three undergraduate sequences: news-editorial, radio-television, and mass communication. A Master's degree is offered in conjunction with the Department of Communication.

Financial assistance: Teaching assistantships are available, and a scholarship program is available through the Department.

Research: Faculty research interests include TV news coverage of the Vietnam war, new media technology, economics and history of the film industry, the new journalism, minority media, and semantics and urban telecommunications systems.

SOURCES OF INFORMATION ON HIGHER EDUCATION IN COMMUNICATIONS

The following general works offer a wealth of information on communications programs in colleges and universities. They are all regularly revised, some of them annually.

American Universities and Colleges (Washington: American Council on Education, revised every four years). Provides detailed application and program information on 1,400 institutions.

Barron's Profiles of American Colleges (Woodbury, NY: Barron's Educational Series, frequently revised). Contains less general information than the source above, but provides state-by-state data on 1,350 colleges and universities.

Education Directory: Part 3, Higher Education (Washington: Government Printing Office, annual). A standard guide that lists more schools but provides less data than the sources above.

Lovejoy's College Guide (New York: Simon and Schuster, roughly biennial). Comparable to the second item in this listing.

To find out more about educational programs in the varous branches of communications, any of the following works may be consulted. They are nearly all regularly (often annually) revised, and many of them are free on request. Guides to graduate programs often reflect a sense of the undergraduate program at the same institution. While most of these guides deal with college and university courses or degrees, a few (specifically noted) include other kinds of education, such as trade school courses. This list is by no means an exhaustive census of all such publications, but it provides a sense of what is available.

The American Film Institute Guide to College Courses in Film and Television (Washington: Acropolis Books, 1975). This guide contains the most detailed analysis of departments, faculty, and courses on film and television. A new edition is due in late 1977 or early 1978. It provides information on specific course titles (the only media education guide which does so), facilities and equipment, number of students, and areas of departmental emphasis.

The Annual Guides to Graduate Study, Book V: Communications (Princeton, NJ: Peterson's Guides, Inc., annual). A page each is devoted to schools which pay to be listed, resulting in a very selective and noncomprehensive book. Emphasis is on journalism and speech communications programs, with some broadcasting and film programs included.

Broadcast Education 1975 (Washington: National Association of Broadcasters, 1975). This volume, normally issued every two years (this is the 14th edition, with another due in early 1978), provides a state-by-state listing of colleges and universities offering degrees and courses in broadcasting, as well as two-year colleges having broadcasting programs. For each school listed information is provided on the number of courses, credits, facilities, scholarships offered, and faculty.

The Bowker Annual of Library and Book Trade Information (New York: R.R. Bowker). Among many other sections in this nearly 700-page hardback is a section on library education, which includes material on placement, salaries, a guide to library placement sources, continuing education for library personnel, trainee and library technician programs, and a listing of accredited library schools by state. More complete information on the latter can also be found in the annual *American Library Director*. See also the regularly revised *Guide to Library Education* (Chicago: American Library Association).

Colleges and Universities Offering Courses and Degree Programs Involving Educational Broadcasting (Washington: National Association of Education Broadcasters, 1974). A second edition, this guide is compiled from answers to a 10-point mail survey sent to each of the colleges and universities listed.

Directory of Graduate Programs in the Speech Communication Arts and Sciences: 1977-78 (Falls Chruch, VA: Speech Communication Association, 1977). This 292-page volume, issued every two years, provides a state-by-state listing of some 270 departments across the U.S., providing a full page for each with information on application, program emphasis, degrees, number of faculty and students, costs, deadlines for application, financial support, etc. It includes broadcasting and film education in most cases. For briefer listings, see the annual *Speech Communication Directory* (same publisher).

"Doctoral Programs in Instructional Technology," by Paul W.F. Witt, in James W. Brown, ed. *Educational Media Yearbook 1977* (New York: Bowker, 1977), pp. 351-354. An annual listing of nearly 40 universities, with a lengthy paragraph on each providing data on addresses, personnel, financial aid, and program content.

"Doctoral Programs in Library and Information Science," by Margaret Myers, in James W. Brown, ed. *Educational Media Yearbook 1977* (New York: Bowker, 1977), pp. 355-364. Another annual listing using the same approach as the article above. It includes a guide to further sources of information.

A Guide to Film and Television Courses in Canada, 1973-74 (Ottawa: Canadian Film Institute, 1973). This parallels the American Film Institute guide listed above. It is shorter partly because of the relative newness of these fields in Canadian colleges and universities.

Journalism Education Directory (found in annual January issues of *Journalism Educator*). This is a directory of schools and departments of journalism that lists addresses, faculty, sequences of courses offered, and facilities. It also lists education organizations and other associations and contains a brief statistical review. See also the regularly revised series of leaflets such as "Education for Journalism Careers," "Graduate Study in Journalism and Mass Communications," "What Foreign Students Should Know about Journalism Education," and "Journalism Education in the United States: Its Organized Structure"

(Minneapolis: Association for Education in Journalism, provided free on request).

Public Relations Sequences and Courses in United States Colleges and Universities (New York: Public Relations Society of America, annual, free on request). This booklet lists institutions with one or more courses in public relations, as well as majors in public relations, along with a brief description of each program.

A Survey of Motion Picture, Still Photography, and Graphic Arts Instruction (Rochester, NY: Eastman Kodak, 1975). This brief booklet, the fifth edition of a standard guide, provides a highly abbreviated guide to education in the areas named. It covers technical institutes and schools of photography as well as colleges and universities.

Where Shall I Go to College to Study Advertising? (Washington: American Advertising Federation, annual). This 30-page booklet discusses advertising education in general, and lists advertising programs (courses and majors) on a state-by-state basis.

World Film and TV Study Resources (See listing on page 395).

For a general overview of media education in the United States, Canada, and the rest of the world, see May Katzen's *Mass Communication: Teaching and Studies at Universities* (Paris: Unesco (New York: unipub), 1975) which provides a brief history and analysis of trends in media education (mainly journalism, but including broadcasting and film) on both the graduate and undergraduate levels. The list of references provides a key to specialized publications on media education both in the U.S. and Canada and abroad.

2

NON-ACADEMIC INSTITUTIONS CONDUCTING
COMMUNICATIONS RESEARCH

Many of the institutions in this section are involved in policy-oriented communications research. Some of the organizations listed here (such as A. C. Nielsen and Arbitron) carry out research primarily for the media themselves, but their data is often of broader interest. Support for this research comes from a variety of sources: business, government grants and contracts, and private foundations.

The non-academic research described here can be characterized, in general, as more *technical* and *applied* than that conducted at universities and colleges. Much of this non-academic research falls into four broad categories:

1) economic analyses of communications systems

2) market surveys of the demand for communications services

3) development of new communications technologies

4) studies of the social effects of the media.

It is impossible, however, to draw hard-and-fast lines between academic and non-academic research. Examples of significant academic research can be found in all four of these categories.

Selected lists of published reports are included in many of the entries. Private industry research is not always available for public access. Federally-funded non-classified research is usually accessible through the National Technical Information Service or from the contracting agency.

ABC Television Network, Research Services Department
1330 Avenue of the Americas
New York, NY 10019
(212) 581-7777
Marvin S. Mord, Vice President

The Department plans and initiates all television research efforts, with primary emphasis on providing information, guidance and recommendations on all television-related activities to ABC management. The Department's research figures heavily in decision making, particularly in the formation of television programming, scheduling, pricing and broadcast standards policy. Original social research includes two seprate five-year studies on the effects of television on children by Dr. Melvin Heller, Samuel Polsky and Dr. Seymour Lieberman, as well as five pilot studies on television's effect upon viewer attitudes and perceptions.

Abt Associates
55 Wheeler Street
Cambridge, MA 02138
(617) 492-7100

Abt Associates is a social and economic research firm that conducts studies and experimental social programs. Its current work in telecommunications is in designing a demonstration project on the use of telecommunications technologies in public service delivery. Various integrated service delivery systems, employing technology ranging from videotape to two-way television and teleprocessing, have been designed and analyzed in terms of efficiency, cost, institutional relationships and constraints, and suitability of the technology.

Academy for Educational Development
680 Fifth Avenue
New York, NY 10019
(212) 265-3350
Alvin C. Eurich, President

The Academy is a nonprofit, tax-exempt planning organization that assists universities, colleges, schools, government agencies, and other organizations in developing future plans and improving operations and programs. Beginning with long-range planning in higher education, the Academy now includes programs in mass communications, higher education management, instructional technology, international education, and recruitment of executive personnel for educational institutions.

The Academy has established several divisions and institutes to deal with specific areas of activity.

    1. *Communications Institute*, Edward W. Barrett, Director. The Communications Institute was established in 1969 because of the close relationship between mass communications and the problems and potentials of education. A panel of advisors assists the staff in executing projects which cover such issues as journalism manpower, new trends in communications, the government and media, and general publishing planning.

    2. *Division of International Operations*, Stephen F. Moseley, Director. The Division has been involved in project planning for communications programs in developing countries since 1974, when a series of planning studies was initiated in the areas of educational technology and nonformal education, with emphasis on improved systems of education for health, nutrition, family planning and agriculture, especially in rural areas. The program was reviewed and expanded for 1977 to include special emphasis on the planning of telecommunications projects. Four primary activities are included:

    a. Country planning studies to plan for national communications-based development programs.
    b. Studies to address specific problems requiring communications for existing or planned projects.
    c. Studies and planning services to support the new AID/SAT (space age technology program).
    d. Hosting conferences and seminars of international experts to address major policy and technical issues in the field of communications application to development.

For these studies the Academy assembles teams of specialists from its own staff and other national and international institutions. Studies and consultations under this project have been carried out in Honduras, Nicaragua, Panama, Indonesia, Bangladesh, Afghanistan, South Korea, Bolivia, Lesotho, Ivory Coast, Upper Volta, Central African Republic, Costa Rica and India. Specific projects include a basic village education project in Guatemala, a rural radio education program in Paraguay, a rural information service in Bangladesh, provision of technical assistance to a state-wide educational television network in Brazil, design of a low-cost mass media-based alternative for extension of better health to rural populations in Costa Rica, conducting a cost-benefit analysis of an educational television program for junior high school students in El Salvador, developing a software system related to a planned educational radio project utilizing satellite transmission in Indonesia, a case study of the use of the ATS-6 satellite for village information and education programs in India, and an evaluation of the educational television system in the Ivory Coast.

The Division has also developed a plan for the establishment of international educational technology networks composed of directors and managers of instructional radio and television systems. It has also developed methodology for applying communications media to health and nutrition problems in developing countries.

The Clearinghouse on Development Communication (formerly the Information Center on Instructional Technology) serves as an international center for materials and information on important developments in the application of communication technology to development problems. The Clearinghouse provides services through publications, including *CDC Report*, a series of project profiles, and a series of information bulletins; through referral services; and through information collection/library services. Members of the professional staff of the Clearinghouse have backgrounds in various media applications and experience in development programs in many areas of the world.

 3. *Presidential Search Division*, Ruth G. Weintraub, Director.

 4. *Management Division*, John D. Millett, Director.

 5. *Enrollment Planning Division*, Rexford G. Moon, Director.

 6. *Division of Philanthropic Management*, W. Homer Turner, Director.

The ANPA Research Institute
(American Newspaper Publishers Association)
Post Office Box 593
1350 Sullivan Trail
Easton, PA 18042
(215) 253-6155

William D. Rinehart, Vice President/Technical

Principal department heads of the ANPA Research Institute include the Director of the Production Department and the Director of the Research Center. The American Society of Newspaper Editors (ASNE) has its office at the same location (see listing on page 000).

The Research Center is a major activity for newspaper research, development, testing and training. ANPA invests more than $1 million of its $3 million-plus annual budget in this facility and its related functions. Services include:

1. Basic research and development on newspaper production problems, including mail-room equipment, occupational safety and health administration-related problems, computer programming, newsprint and ink testing service, standardization of color inks, shallow-relief plate development, etc. The Research Center works with many manufacturers to stimulate development of new equipment needed by newspapers.

2. Liaison for advanced research with the Massachusetts Institute of Technology on advanced computer program technology, and with other research organizations and equipment suppliers in the development of pagination devices, advanced communications systems, lasers and plateless printing.

3. A variety of technical training seminars held throughout the year on a less-than-cost basis. Most are "hands-on" working sessions emphasizing practical application. These include Basic Offset Press and Plate; Camera Techniques; Direct Plate Quality Control; Electronic Editing for the Newsroom; Photocomposition and Paste-Up; Management Orientation to New Technology; and Environmental Control.

4. Objective and professional in-plant technical advisory services (TAS), which are available to member newspapers on request. ANPA production engineers spend whatever time is needed (usually two days) at nominal charge at a newspaper plant as consultants on specific production problems.

5. Research bulletins and the annual Production Management Conference.

The Arbitron Company
1350 Avenue of the Americas
New York, NY 10019

(212) 262-5133
Theodore F. Shaker, President

The Arbitron Company, founded in 1949, is the nation's largest broadcast audience measurement company. Each year Arbitron contacts almost 1½ million families in every county in the United States in order to study and report on their television viewing and radio listening habits, resulting in the Arbitron television and radio rating reports. These reports, along with special broadcasting research services, are used by broadcasters, advertisers, and advertising agencies. Arbitron Marketing Research maintains consumer panels and measures and reports purchase behavior, advertising awareness, and commercial recall; re-interviews diary keepers; and samples public opinion on a variety of topics. It conducts surveys via telephone interviews, personal interviews, direct mail questionnaires, and consumer panels. In addition to its headquarters in New York, the Arbitron Company maintains offices in Atlanta, Chicago, Dallas, Los Angeles, San Francisco, and Beltsville, Maryland.

Aspen Institute Program on Communications and Society
1785 Massachusetts Avenue, N.W.
Washington, DC 20036
(202) 462-2011
Glen O. Robinson, Special Adviser to the Aspen Institute
Roland S. Homet, Program Fellow
Henry Geller, Program Fellow
Marc Uri Porat, Program Fellow
Forrest P. Chisman, Associate Director

The Aspen Communications Program has operated since 1971 as one of several inter-related thought-leading-to-action programs of the Aspen Institute for Humanistic Studies. Its purpose is to identify major issues relating to the use and governance of the mass media and point-to-point communications systems, and to develop policies and actions dealing with those issues. In an era of accelerating technological change, the Program has judged it especially important to concentrate on the communications policy-making process as the mediator between new service opportunities and basic value structures in society. Workshops, seminars, and conferences are conducted on selected subjects within the Program's field of interest, and the results of these meetings and of research conducted and commissioned by the Program are published as the Aspen Series on Communications and Society. Publications: *The Mass Media: Aspen Guide to Communications Industry Trends*, edited by Christopher Sterling and Timothy Haight; *The Future of Public Broadcasting*, edited by Douglass Cater and Michael J. Nyhan; *Television As a Cultural Force*, edited by Richard Adler and Douglass Cater; *Television As a Social Force: New Approaches to TV Criticism*, edited by Douglass Cater and Richard Adler; *Freedom of the Press vs. Public Access*, by Benno C. Schmidt, Jr. The Program also publishes a Policy Paper Series, which includes "Refocusing Government Communications Policy," "Issues and Images/Confessions of a Conference Organizer," and "The Public-Interest Media Reform Movement: A Look at the Mandate and a New Agenda."

Battelle Memorial Institute
505 King Avenue
Columbus, OH 43201
(614) 424-6424

Battelle is a nonprofit multidisciplinary research institute. Its Communication Research Laboratory has conducted research and planning for the federal government and other public agencies, including major research on educational telecommunications; has developed concepts for highway safety communications; and has designed external evaluation techniques for the educational satellite. The Institute has also developed and designed cable television franchising procedures and conducted analyses of the potentialities of cable. In addition, the Institute makes technical films.

Bell Telephone Laboratories
600 Mountain Avenue
Murray Hill, NJ 07974
(201) 582-5646
James B. Fisk, President

In addition to the laboratories at Murray Hill, there are three other Bell Telephone Laboratories:
- Everett Road, Holmdel, NJ 07733. (201) 949-3000
- Whippany Road, Whippany, NJ 07981. (201) 386-3000.
- Naperville, IL 60540. (312) 690-2000.

Bell Laboratories, the research and development unit

of the Bell System, is jointly owned by The American Telephone and Telegraph Company (the parent company of the Bell System) and Western Electric Company (the System's manufacturing and supply unit). Incoporated in 1925, Bell Labs performs the basic research, development, design, and systems engineering necessary to provide the Bell System with new and improved equipment and services for telecommunications. Bell Labs also assists the national defense in fields where the company has special competence. The engineering and design of components, devices and systems for Bell System use is the major part of Bell Labs work. In its research activities, Bell Labs scientists seek new knowledge in fields relevant to telecommunications. Bell Labs, with the guidance of AT&T, helps analyze the Bell System's requirements for new services, plans development programs to assure compatibility of new equipment with existing systems, and assists in the introduction of new equipment into the nationwide telecommunications network. Bell Labs also develops systems for use by operating telephone companies to handle increasing business information needs.

Over the years, Bell Labs has made many contributions to the field of telecommunications and to the creation of new industries. Some of these contributions include: discovery of the wave nature of matter; creation of information theory; origination of radio astronomy; invention of the laser, negative feedback amplifier, transistor, solar battery, magnetic bubble devices, and the electrical digital computer; and development of TELSTAR communications satellites and electronic switching systems. The current work of Bell Labs falls into four categories: materials science; electronics technology; communications and information processing; and systems engineering. Publications: *Bell Laboratories Record* (see listing on page 348); *Bell System Technical Journal* (see listing on page 348).

The Brookings Institution
1775 Massachusetts Avenue, N.W.
Washington, DC 20036
(202) 797-6000
Bruce K. MacLaury, President

Brookings occasionally supports and conducts communications research, but nearly always in the context of its major interests—economics and governmental studies. Stephen Hess, a member of the Institution's resident staff, currently is studying the allocation of news-gathering resources in Washington, D.C.

The Bureau of Social Science Research (BSSR)
1990 M Street, N.W.
Washington, DC   20036
(202) 223-4300
Robert T. Bower, Director

BSSR is an independent nonprofit organization devoted to the development of social science knowledge and its application to contemporary social problems. Established in 1950 as a university-affiliated research center, it was separately incorporated in the District of Columbia in 1956. Research is supported equally by contracts and grants from government agencies and public and private institutions. Major program areas in 1977 are manpower, education, health and welfare, crime and justice, mass and intraorganizational communication, social indicators, social sciences as institutions, urban problems and consumer protection. Communications research has been an area of interest since the 1950s. A *Bibliography of Reports and Staff Member Publications* and a quarterly *BSSR Newsletter* are available upon request. Since 1973, BSSR has had a continuing program for improving the use of graphics in social data analyses and communication. Some of BSSR's more recent publications are: *Television and the Public* by Robert T. Bower (Holt, Rinehart, 1973); *Southern Newcomers to Northern Cities* by Gene Petersen, Laure M. Sharp and Thomas Drury (Praeger Publishers, 1977); *Social Graphics Bibliography*, edited by Barry Feinberg and Carolyn Franklyn (BSSR, 1976); and *Social Patterns and Attitudes in the Greater Washington, D.C. Area: A Social Indicators Handbook 1973/1975* by Albert E. Gollin and Mary Eileen Dixon (BSSR, 1976).

Canadian Communications Research Information Centre (CCRIC)
255 Albert Street
Post Office Box 1047
Ottawa, Ontario K1P 5V8
(613) 237-3400 ext. 411 or 493
Ash K. Prakash, Executive Director

Founded in 1974, CCRIC is a UNESCO-initiated organization co-sponsored and funded by the Canada Council through the Canadian Commission for UNESCO and the research services of the Canadian Broadcasting Corporation, the Canadian Radio-Television and Telecommunications Commission, the Federal Department of Communications and the Agency for Tele-Education in Canada.

The Centre was established to create a national clearinghouse for the collection, exchange, and dissemination of information on communications policy, research, resources, activities, and innovations. The general goal of the Centre is to cover the social aspects of electronic mass media and communications, with major emphasis on research and policy. The Centre functions as a referral and consulting service rather than as a research library or documentation source.

Its activities include information services and a data collection encompassing four main files: 1) specialists on human resources, 2) institutions and organizations, 3) research, and 4) documentation and publication.

Publications: *Newsletter*, bimonthly (see listing on page 289); *Communications: Research in Canada*, annual (see listing on page 290).

CBS Broadcast Group, Research Department
51 West 52nd Street
New York, NY 10019
(212) 765-4321
Jay Eliasberg, Vice President

The Research Department of the CBS Broadcast Group functions in the areas of television network research, television station research, and radio research. Basically the Department serves the programming and sales needs of the various divisions of the CBS Broadcast Group, by regularly analyzing audience data provided by such rating services as Nielsen and Arbitron; by analyzing the appeal of programs and personalities through its Program Analyzer facilities; and by conducting special projects on such subjects as concept tests, advertising effectiveness, and audience behavior.

CBS also maintains an Office of Social Research (Joseph Klapper, Director), which conducts studies on subjects relating to the social effects of broadcasting, such as the effect of television on children, and the effects of broadcasting on voter behavior.

Citizens' Research Foundation (CRF)
245 Nassau Street
Princeton, NJ 08540
(609) 924-0246
Herbert E. Alexander, Director

Established in 1958 to provide a center for impartial, comprehensive information on the financing of American politics and to disseminate facts about the role of money in politics. Besides collecting data on campaign financing, fund raising, expenditures, and the groups involved, CRF also sponsors research papers by political scientists for publication in the *Studies in Money in Politics* series. CRF also services the media with current information on political finance. CRF's study and publication program includes continuing work on political broadcasting as it relates to political campaigning.

Committee for Economic Development (CED)
477 Madison Avenue
New York, NY 10022
(212) 688-2063
William H. Franklin, Chairman

The Committee is an independent research and educational organization composed of 200 leading business men and women and educators. CED trustees conduct research and formulate recommendations in four major policy areas: the national economy; the international economy; education and urban development; and the management of federal, state and local government. Although CED's project on broadcasting was completed with the publishing of *Broadcasting and Cable Television: Policies for Diversity and Change* in 1975, the Committee still maintains an interest in broadcasting and cable and continues to monitor new developments in the various telecommunications fields.

Goldmark Communications Corporation
98 Commerce Road
Stamford, CT 06904
(203) 327-7270
Dr. Peter C. Goldmark, President

Goldmark is involved in the design and development of CATV and CCTV systems and services, telecommunications, satellite communications, medical electronics and electronic publishing. The Corporation is engaged in marketing its Rapid Transmission and Storage system (RTS), which was designed and developed to provide lifelong learning opportunities for adults primarily in learning centers, under the auspices of community colleges. The Corporation recently completed a study for the Department of Transportation on the substitutability of communications for transportation as part of NRS activities. In addition, it is actively engaged in additional research and development efforts for an advanced version of the RTS system. Its Transcan operation supplies transfers of motion pictures to tape to various hotel, motel, airplane, and other distributors for use over cable TV systems.

Horizon House International (HHI)
610 Washington Street
Dedham, MA 02026
(617) 326-8220
Paul Polishuk, President

HHI is a subsidiary of Horizon House, publisher of *Telecommunications, Microwave Journal*, and Artech House Books. Its objectives are to supply information, especially to small and medium-sized companies, on markets, industry and government activities; to provide mechanisms for bringing telecommunications buyers and sellers together to trade on a free and competitive worldwide basis; to provide information on worldwide telecommunications activities; and to provide telecommunications consultation services. HHI sponsored INTELCOM 77, an international telecommunications exposition held in Atlanta in October, 1977. Publication: *Communications Satellite Systems Worldwide 1975/1985*, two volumes. Also provides update information service.

Information Futures
2217 College Station
Pullman, WA 99163
(509) 332-5726
Gerald R. Brong, President

Information Futures originated in 1975 with the drawing together of 30 associates from a variety of backgrounds—educational technology, library science, education, information science, heuristics, mathematics, religion, law, plant pathology, communications, public administration—and with a common interest in the ability to maximize the utilization of information to facilitate human performance.

The association develops conferences, seminars, and publications addressing issues of critical importance. These offerings are made available in an attempt to have a positive impact on the future of library/information services. Research projects, program evaluations, information analysis, or other activities may be contracted for with Information Futures. The association also becomes involved with facility design, telecommunications systems development, bibliographic control, budget forecasting, and network development projects.

In 1976-1977 Information Futures developed the following critical issues conferences: Media in Higher Education, Copyright and the Teaching/Learning Process, and Educational Technology—the Alternative Futures. Other critical issues conferences under development deal with: Alternative Futures for Public Libraries, Informational Resources Production for Libraries, and Electronic News Reporting—New Technologies for Information.

Publications: *Media in Higher Education—The Critical Issues: A Resources Prediction and Allocation Model for Audiovisual Programs in Higher Education*. A series of "INSTANTERS" (short essays on library/information-service topics) is planned, as is a series of issues papers on the future of educational technology.

Institute for the Future
2740 Sand Hill Road
Menlo Park, CA   94025
(415) 854-6322
Roy Amara, President

The Institute for the Future is an independent, nonprofit, research organization founded in 1968—the first organization in the United States dedicated exclusively to systematic and comprehensive studies of the long-range future. Its work is supported by business and industrial organizations, government agencies, and private foundations. It conducts research in the field of communications, as well as in other fields.

A publications program has been developed to encourage wide distribution and discussion of the Institute's substantive and methodological research. Among the reports, papers and working papers published by the Institute are: *The Camelia Report: A Study of Technical*

Alternatives and Social Choices in Teleconferencing, by Robert Johansen, Jacques Vallee and Kathleen Spangler; *Group Communication Through Computers, Volume 1: Design and Use of the Forum System,* by Jacques Vallee, Hubert M. Lipinski, and Richard H. Miller; *Potential Market Demand for Two-Way Information Services to the Home, 1970-1990,* by Paul Baran; *The Future of the Telephone Industry, 1970-1985,* by Paul Baran and Andrew J. Lipinski; *The Future of Newsprint, 1970-2000,* by Paul Baran; *Toward a Framework for Communications Policy Planning,* by Andrew J. Lipinski; *Modeling as a Communication Process: Computer Conferencing Offers New Perspectives,* by Jacques Valee; *Computer Conferencing: Measurable Effects on Working Patterns,* by Robert Johansen, Jacques Vallee, and Michael Palmer; *The Forum Project: Network Conferencing and Its Future Applications,* by Jacques Vallee; *The Computer Conference: An Altered State of Communication?,* by Jacques Vallee, Robert Johansen, and Kathleen Spangler; *Network Conferencing,* by Jacques Vallee; *Group Communication Through Electronic Media: Fundamental Choices and Social Effects,* by Robert Johansen, Richard Miller, and Jacques Vallee; *Computer-Communications for the Community Information Utility,* by Paul Baran; *Computer-Based Communication in Support of Scientific and Technical Work,* by Jacques Vallee and Thaddeus Wilson; *Teleconference on Integrated Data Bases in Postsecondary Education, A Transcript and Summary,* by John Ferguson and Robert Johansen.

A complete list of publications and prices can be obtained from the Institute.

Kalba Bowen Associates, Inc.
12 Arrow Street
Cambridge, MA 02138
(617) 661-2624
Konrad K. Kalba, President

Kalba Bowen Associates, a research and consulting firm, was established in 1973 to engage in grant and contract research, private consulting, and related educational projects in the communications field. Projects generally fall into one of the following areas: (1) public policy and regulation, (2) corporate and market strategy, (3) information management, (4) technology assessment, (5) telecommunications planning, and (6) media use and evaluation. Some of the specific research areas in which the firm is active include: legislative options and economic impact of state CATV regulation; vertical "separations" policies in communications industries; the pay TV, video player, and mobile radio markets; measurement of the cognitive and behavioral effects of technological change; information retrieval and analysis systems for decision making; and use of the mass media for scientific, technical, and medical communication. Publications: Research reports, some of which are available for purchase.

Arthur D. Little, Inc.
Acorn Park
Cambridge, MA 02140
(617) 864-5770

The Telecommunications Section of Arthur D. Little, Inc., an international consulting firm, has worked for virtually every common carrier in the United States and in many other countries, for telecommunications equipment manufacturers, for major users of telecommunications, and for the U.S. and other governments. Recent work for public agencies has included the preparation of scenarios of plausible developments in several areas of telecommunications over the next fifteen years. The areas studied included citizen-band radio, broadband services to the home, a possible government domestic satellite operation, international satellite competition, and U.S. Post Office development.

Marketing Science Institute (MSI)
14 Story Street
Cambridge, MA   02138
(617) 491-2060
Thomas B. McCabe, Jr., President
Prof. Stephen A. Greyser, Executive Director

Associated with the Harvard Business School, MSI does research on many aspects of the marketing system: practices and effects of the system, methods of studying and analyzing marketing practices and behavior, and social and economic issues related to marketing. MSI has pioneered research on such subjects as the effects of television advertising on children, consumer information processing, and the impacts of consumerism on marketing. The Institute publishes a series of research reports and a program of priority subjects on which it will fund research. Recent monographs include: *Children Learning to Buy* (Ward, Wackman, and Wartella); *The Evolution of Retail Institutions in the U. S.* (McNair and May); *Consumer Information Processing: Perspectives and Implications for Advertising* (Wilkie and Farris); and *Advertising and Promotion in Brand Strategy* (Strang, et al.).

METREK Division, The MITRE Corporation
Westgate Research Park
McLean, VA 22101
(703) 790-6000

The METREK Division is a nonprofit systems-engineering organization that conducts research, system engineering, planning, and project design for the federal government and other agencies. Much of its communications research is designed to improve military communications and communications between government offices and agencies, but some is media-related. METREK is studying the use of cable communications and computers to provide a variety of consumer and government services into homes and remote communities.

For information on military applications, consult Dr. Walter A. Yondorf, (703) 790-6304. Mr. William F. Mason, (703) 790-6204, manages the civil and media communications work.

National Broadcasting Company, Social Research Department
30 Rockefeller Plaza
New York, NY 10020
(212) 247-8300
J. Ronald Milavsky, Vice President

The Social Reseach Department, a division of NBC's Research and Corporate Planning Department, William S. Rubens, Vice President, studies television's effects on society. Its initial assignment was to conduct a study of the effects of violence in television on aggressive behavior in children, using the method of a large-scale longitudinal panel study. The division's responsibilities have subsequently been expanded to include other social and psychological effects of the medium. In addition to conducting original research, the Department is responsible for analyzing the research of other social scientists in order to keep the company's management continuously informed of relevant developments.

National Research Council (NRC)
2101 Constitution Avenue
Washington, DC 20418
(202) 393-8100

The National Research Council (NRC), established in 1916, is the operating arm of the National Academy of Sciences and the National Academy of Engineering. The NRC provides support for the federal government, upon request, in all areas of science and engineering.

The Committee on Telecommunications. R. V. Mrozinski, Executive Director. (202) 389-6414/6538. The Committee, which was formed in 1968 to provide support for a Presidential Task Force on Telecommunication Policy, focuses on research on the development and application of evolving civil telecommunications-information systems, their social and economic implications, and their impact on federal policies and regulations. Authorized under a core contract which is renewed yearly, the Committee's current activities include: providing support to its sponsors in the area of telecommunications-information research, development and application; publicizing those findings considered beneficial to society; and performing agreed-upon studies in the field of telecommunications-information.

The consortium of government agencies sponsoring the committee includes the Department of Commerce, the Department of Health, Education and Welfare, the Department of Transportation, the Department of Housing and Urban Development, the Federal Communications Commission, the National Science Foundation, and the U. S. Postal Service.

Publications: *Communications Technology for Urban Improvement, Application of Social and Economic Values to Spectrum Management, Telecommunications for Enhanced Metropolitan Function and Form, Telecommunications Research in the United States and Selected Foreign Countries: A Preliminary Survey Summary (Volume I)* and *Individual Contributions (Volume II), Local Government Information Systems—A Study of USAC and the Future Application of Computer Technology, An Information Systems Resource Center for Local Governments* (supplementary report to *Local Government Information Systems*), and *Electronic Message Systems for the U. S. Postal Service.* Microfiche copies may be ordered from the National Technical Information Service,

U. S. Department of Commerce, Springfield, VA 22161, at a cost of $2.25 each. Telephone orders: (703) 557-4650.

A.C. Nielsen Company
Nielsen Plaza
Northbrook, IL 60062
(312) 498-6300
James D. Lyons, Manager, Media Research Division

The Nielsen Company supplies reports on national and local television audiences to advertisers, advertising agencies, broadcasters and others. The Nielsen Television Index (NTI) provides weekly estimates of the size and demographic composition of audiences for national network programs. The Nielsen Station Index (NSI) measures audiences of local television stations in over 200 markets up to eight times each year. Nielsen also provides similar television audience measurements in Canada and Japan. In addition to its headquarters in Northbrook, Illinois, the A.C. Nielsen Company maintains offices in New York, Chicago, Hollywood, Dallas, Atlanta, and Menlo Park, California.

Rand Corporation
1700 Main Street
Santa Monica, CA 90406
(213) 393-0411
Leland L. Johnson, Director,
  Communications Policy Program

The Rand multidisciplinary program in communication was established in 1970 after a history of Rand research on communications satellites, computer technology, radio spectrum management, and telephone and television industries. Recent research has been involved with cable franchise decisionmaking, assessment of public policy relating to media ownership and control, effects of television on human behavior, and regulation of the telephone industry.

Among recent communications policy publications: *Cable Television: A Handbook for Decisionmaking* by Walter S. Baer; *New Television Networks* by Rolla Edward Park; *The Fairness Doctrine in Broadcasting: Problems and Suggested Courses of Action* by Henry Geller; *Two-Way TV Teleconferencing for Government: The MRC-TV System* by Rudy Bretz and L. A. Dougharty; *Evaluation of Intergovernmental Communication: Statistical*

Baseline Analysis by Harold Sackman; *The Mandatory Origination Requirement for Cable Systems* by Henry Geller; *Neighborhood Communications Centers: Planning Information and Referral Services in the Urban Library* by Robert Yin, Brigette Kenney, and Karen Possner; *Concentration of Mass Media Ownership: Assessing the State of Current Knowledge* by Walter Baer, Henry Geller, Joseph Grundfest, and Karen Possner; *Newspaper-Television Station Cross-Ownership: Options for Federal Action* by Walter Baer, Henry Geller, and Joseph Grundfest; *Expanding the Use of Commercial and Noncommercial Broadcast Programming on Cable Television Systems by Leland L. Johnson;   Watergate and Television: An Economic Analysis* by Stanley Besen and Bridger Mitchell; *jtkelevision and Human Behavior: A Guide to the Pertinent Scientific Literature* by George Comstock and Marilyn Fisher; *Television and Human Behavior: The Key Studies* by George Comstock, F. Christen, Marilyn Fisher, R. C. Quarles, and W. D. Richards; *Television and Human Behavior: The Research Horizon, Future and Present* by George Comstock, G. Lindsey, and Marilyn Fisher; *Television News and Local Awareness: A Retrospective Look* by William Lucas and Karen Possner; *Projecting the Growth of Television Broadcasting: Implications for Spectrum Use* by Rolla Edward Park, Leland L. Johnson, and Barry Fishman; *Citizen Participation in Broadcast Licensing Before the FCC* by Joseph Grundfest; and *Optimal Pricing of Local Telephone Service* by Bridger Mitchell.

The Roper Organization, Inc.
One Park Avenue
New York, NY 10016
(212) 679-3523
Burns W. Roper, Chairman

The Roper Organization, which was cofounded with Elmo Roper in 1933, is a national marketing and opinion research firm. Its major activities include custom studies for individual clients, a unique subscription research service which monitors public opinion on a range of social and economic issues, and continuing studies and consultation for specific clients. Roper has also conducted studies on consumer behavior, marketing opportunities and strategies, advertising effectiveness, corporate image, and political, social and economic attitudes. Studies have been conducted for the Television Information Office—a 1959-76 series of studies on changing public attitudes toward television and other mass media; for the Corporation for Public Broadcasting—a continuing study to determine the subject matter interests and programming preferences of public broadcasting viewers; for the American Broadcasting Company—a study to determine the effects of various methods of promoting programs in advance of their appearance; and for *Time* magazine—a series of studies to determine subscribers' readership of various items and departments. Studies have also been conducted for various newspapers on the demographics of readers and their areas of interest, both in terms of editorial content and advertising.

Social Science Research Council (SSRC)
605 Third Avenue
New York, NY 10016
(212) 557-9504
Eleanor B. Sheldon, President

The SSRC's purpose is the advancement of research in the social sciences. It does not fund research, but does award pre- and postdoctoral fellowships.

The Council currently has two committees concerned with mass communications. The first is the Committee on Television and Social Behavior, chaired by Stephen B. Withey of the University of Michigan. The committee was appointed to assess the current state of research on the influence of television viewing on social behavior and to suggest needed and promising directions for future research. Funds for the committee have been made available to the council by the National Institute of Mental Health. The committee is currently preparing its final report, which will be completed in the fall of 1977.

The second is the Committee on Mass Communications and Political Behavior, chaired by Eleanor B. Sheldon. The committee was organized in order to prepare a coordinated set of research projects on the role of the mass media in the 1976 Presidential election. It is preparing reports on those projects and considering new projects for the coming years. The committee has been supported by a grant to the council from the John and Mary R. Markle Foundation.

Ronald P. Abeles serves as SSRC staff for both committees.

SRI International
333 Ravenswood Avenue
Menlo Park, CA 94025
(415) 326-6200

Formerly Stanford Research Institute, SRI International conducts hundreds of research projects, some related to the media. Most SRI media research is in telecommunications and includes studies of the economic aspects, spectrum utilization, and earth-station siting of domestic communications satellites. SRI has done extensive development work on devices used by the media. These include office copiers, facsimile systems, electrostatic and ink jet printers, color television cameras, document handling systems and video disc systems.

For several years the SRI Augmentation Research Center has been offering service on its interactive office automation system, NLS, to a growing number of subscriber organizations. NLS is unique in that it provides word processing, text editing, document production, electronic mail, teleconferencing support, file management, and library archiving capabilities within a single integrated easy-to-use system. It is being used effectively by managers and researchers as well as secretaries and computer programmers.

SRI has also completed an extensive survey of the market for home information centers that will be developed with cable television as a base.

Systems Applications, Inc. (SAI)
950 Northgate Drive
San Rafael, CA 94903
(415) 472-4011
George P. Mandanis, President

Systems Applications was established in 1968 to provide analytic, technical, and other consultative services in telecommunications, environmental control, and information processing to clients in government and industry, both in the United States and abroad. Activities of its Telecommunications Studies Group embrace a broad spectrum of technical, economic, and systems analyses in long-haul transmission, switching, local distribution, and land mobile communications. Studies performed include analyses of technical feasibility, costs, and prices; demand forecasting; investment analyses; and analyses of the effects on telecommunications markets of governmental policies and of the regulatory environment of the industry. The following examples of SAI's orientation and approach to consultative assignments in the telecommunications field summarize its services, which focus on analyses of common carrier facilities and on evaluations of telecommunications equipment and services:

Common carrier facilities analysis. The distinguishing feature of SAI's approach is its explicit consideration of demand-supply interactions over time. Specific services include demand forecasting for all principal services; least-cost supply analysis; network implementation planning; financial analysis (including the setting of rates for common carrier services); and technical and cost studies for equipment source selection.

Market research for telecommunications products or services. SAI's approach to market research encompasses demand forecasting and market share analysis. Forecasting is based on contingency analysis as well as on analysis of statistical trends. Market share analysis is used to assess, over time, the cost/price competitive position of the client vis-à-vis other suppliers.

In addition, SAI's services in the area of public policy include economic and technical analyses of alternative industry structures and related regulatory controls and incentive mechanisms; assessment of the adequacy of current telecommunications-service offerings for meeting current and anticipated service requirements of public and private users; and contingency analysis of the costs and economic/social benefits of technological and service innovations, as well as evaluation of the alternatives.

Yankelovich, Skelly and White, Inc.
575 Madison Avenue
New York, NY 10022
(212) 752-7500
Daniel Yankelovich, President

Yankelovich, Skelly and White is a national marketing and social research firm that was founded in 1958. Its clients include business corporations, media organizations, government agencies, universities, and associations. It offers three custom research services to its clients: consumer marketing studies; studies of industrial marketing, financial services and corporate communications; and public opinion and behavioral science studies.

The firm also offers three standardized research services: The Laboratory Test Market, The Yankelovich Monitor, and Corporate Priorities.

Custom studies include newspaper readership and marketing studies, audience evaluation studies for cable television, and an investigation of public participation in public broadcasting. Corporate Priorities investigates the credibility of the electronic and print media with both the general public and elite groups, as well as the perception of the media by media professionals themselves. In addition, corporate clients are advised on how to use the various media forms both to participate in the public policymaking process and to reach the general public. The Yankelovich Monitor tracks extant and newly emerging social trends which have an impact on communications.

3

ORGANIZATIONS SUPPORTING
COMMUNICATIONS RESEARCH

Included in this section are private foundations, government agencies, trade associations and other industry groups that support communications research. Some of these organizations have established on-going programs in communication; others provide support for communications-related projects only on an occasional basis.

Traditionally, communications *per se* has not been a high-priority area for foundation support. The Markle Foundation is unique in that it confines its support exclusively to the field of communications. However, many other foundations will fund communications projects if they are related in some way to the institution's major interests.

In addition to the national foundations listed here there are many local and regional foundations which may fund communications projects relevant to local concerns. For a comprehensive listing of both national and local foundations, see *The Foundation Directory*, published annually by the Columbia University Press for The Foundation Center.

Among government agencies, the National Science Foundation is currently the principal source of support for communications research. Other government agencies, such as NIMH and NIE, will occasionally fund communications projects that fall within their mandated areas of interest. In addition, government regulatory agencies, such as the FCC and FTC, sometimes fund outside research that is related to current policy-making areas. (For further information on these agencies, see Section VI.)

As might be expected, the funding provided by trade associations and other industry groups is almost exclusively restricted to research on topics of immediate relevance to their particular industries. As a result, grants from these groups are usually (but not always) for applied rather than basic research projects.

Most of the organizations listed in this section issue annual reports, statements of their areas of interest, and/or guidelines for proposals. Interested researchers should write for such materials before submitting a full-scale proposal.

The A.A.A.A. Educational Foundation
American Association of
Advertising Agencies
200 Park Avenue
New York, NY 10017
(212) 682-2500

The A.A.A.A. Educational Foundation, Inc., is a private nonprofit Foundation established in 1967 by the American Association of Advertising Agencies. Designed originally as a bridge between advertising and university research, the Foundation has served over the years as a vehicle for stimulating basic research to enlarge the body of knowledge about advertising, marketing, communications, and consumer behavior. The goals of the Foundation have evolved since its inception, reflecting the changing environment of the marketing and advertising business, and are currently stated as follows:

(1) To stimulate and fund basic strategic research on issues in the marketing and advertising process that may be subject to public policy decisions and legislative and regulatory programs, so that credible facts may be substituted for opinion in such discussions.

(2) To stimulate and fund tactical research on common industry problems which would have direct and practical value to agencies and their clients.

(3) To improve communications between the academic research community and the marketing and advertising industry to help translate basic conceptual research into practical applications.

(4) To continue to enlarge the body of knowledge about advertising and marketing, advance the professionalism of the industry by research into the nature of the advertising process, and attract outstanding academic talent to the study of advertising and marketing.

Background: Phase I. From 1967 through 1972, the Foundation awarded substantial monetary grants to 22 universities to support basic research into a wide variety of topics related to marketing and advertising. This work was conducted by 28 research professors, and 64 doctoral candidates. A summary of the 22 research grants, including the purpose, results and application of each grant project, was prepared and published by the Foundation in 1973 and is available from Foundation headquarters.

Phase II. In 1973, a decision was made to suspend fund raising for the Foundation and to channel available funds through joint sponsorship projects with two distinguished organizations, the National Bureau of Economic Research and the Marketing Science Institute. These efforts have produced a series of scholarly reports on various aspects of marketing and advertising. A bibliography of this material is available through the Foundation.

Phase III. The statement of goals above was adopted in late 1976, and represents the beginning of *Phase III* for the Foundation.

Research Projects: As outlined in the statement of goals, the Foundation concentrates its attention on research in areas of public policy related to advertising, and in areas of industry-wide practical concern. Subject areas are delineated by the Foundation's Academic Committee, and appropriate proposals will be sought from the academic research community. The Foundation's Board of Trustees will make the final determination on the allocation of funds among specific projects.

Interested parties may communicate directly with the Academic Committee at the Foundation's headquarters in New York City.

Other Activities: In its brief history, the A.A.A.A. Educational Foundation has twice sponsored national conferences for university professors of advertising. The Foundation has also joined with the Association of National Advertisers in sponsoring a continuing successful program of "Case Histories for College Students," and in a pilot seminar program designed to introduce government officials to the marketing and advertising function. This seminar program was developed by the School of Government and Business Administration of George Washington University.

The William Benton Foundation
39 E. 51st Street
New York, N.Y. 10022
(212) 759-5660
Jack Howard, Secretary-Treasurer

The Foundation's objective is to encourage experimental and innovative uses of the communications media in order to inform and improve the effectiveness of the political process. Because the Foundation operates on a limited basis it makes very few grants and stays strictly within its declared mandate. In recent years the Foundation has approved grants to: 1) The League of Women

Voters' Education Fund for sponsorship of the Presidential Forums, which paved the way for the 1976 presidential debates; 2) Northwestern University for a conference on new uses of communications media in education; 3) The National Citizens Committee for Broadcasting for a conference held at Airlie House in Spring 1977 on "Communications Policy—The Public Agenda."

Canada Council. See listing on page 200.

Carnegie Corporation of New York
437 Madison Avenue
New York, NY 10022
(212) 371-3200
Alan Pifer, President

In mid-1977 the Carnegie Corporation announced the formation of a private commission to study the future course of public broadcasting in the United States. Among the areas to be studied are the growth of public broadcasting in light of emerging new technologies and the fiscal and structural problems of the present public television system. A decade earlier, the Corporation sponsored the Carnegie Commission on Educational Television, whose recommendations served as the blueprint for the Public Broadcasting Act of 1967.

Traditionally the Carnegie Corporation supports little communications research per se, though some of its grants designed for other purposes contain a research component. Among them: A grant to George Washington University for evaluation and promotion of a radio series on education, "Options in Education," through the Institute for Educational Leadership, Washington, DC; and support for the development of the "Nova" series by WGBH in Boston.

The Ford Foundation
320 East 43rd Street
New York, NY 10017
(212) 573-5263
Fred W. Friendly, Advisor on Communications
David M. Davis, Program Officer in Charge, Office of
    Communications

The Ford Foundation's activities in communications have centered mainly on the establishment of an alternative public broadcasting system in the United States and on general communications research.

Research or research-related grants made in 1976 include a supplement of $300,000 to the Urban Institute for two years of continued support of the Cable Television Information Center, $735,000 over three years in support of the Aspen Institute's Program on Communications and Society, $500,000 over three years in support of the International Institute of Communications, $90,000 over two years to Duke University for support of a study of media-campaign interaction, and $109,300 over three years to the University of Chicago for fellowships in communications for faculty members from developing country universities. The Ford Foundation has also supported mid-career fellowships for journalists in specific fields such as law, international security and arms control, education and manpower/unemployment.

Future grants and projects of the Office of Communications will be allocated among modest support of public television programs, news and the law/journalism activities, communications policy research and international communications. Total actions over the next two or three years will be on the order of $3 million annually.

The Fund for Investigative Journalism
Room 1021
1346 Connecticut Avenue, N.W.
Washington, DC 20036
(202) 462-1844
Howard Bray, Executive Director

The Fund was established in 1969 to make grants for journalistic investigations of abuses of the public interest. Grant applications are reviewed periodically. More than 300 grants have been made since 1969 for newspaper and magazine probes, books and broadcast reports.

Lilly Endowment, Inc.
2801 North Meridian Street
Indianapolis, IN 46208
(317) 924-5471
Landrum R. Bolling, President

Traditionally, the principal emphasis of the Endowment has been on projects that depend on private support, though grants have also been given to governmental institutions and tax-supported programs, in three major areas: education, religion, and community development.

The Endowment has occasionally supported media-related projects in these areas. The full scope of the Endowment's interests is covered in its annual report.

The Markle Foundation
50 Rockefeller Plaza
Suite 940
New York, NY 10020
(212) 489-6655
Lloyd N. Morrisett, President

Since the middle of 1970, all grants made by the Markle Foundation have been devoted to communications. Selected recent grants of the Foundation include:

University of Minnesota, Communication Research Division, Daniel B. Wachman, Director: A study of the ways in which children are influenced by pro-social television content.

Harvard University, Anthony G. Oettinger: Program on Information Resources Policy.

University of North Carolina, William T. Gormley (now of S.U.N.Y., Buffalo): A study of the effects of cross-media ownership on state and local news content.

The Urban Institute, Sheila Mahoney: Cable Television Information Center.

Aspen Institute for Humanistic Studies, Glen Robinson and Robin Homet: Program on Communications and Society.

Media Access Project, Harvey J. Shulman: Litigation on test cases concerning freedom of access by the public to the mass media and others to have access to nonclassified government information; support of participation in an FCC license renewal case; and a project to promote equal employment opportunities for women and minorities in broadcasting.

University of California, Berkeley, Percy H. Tannenbaum: Studies of uses of communications technologies in the delivery of services to the elderly.

New York University, School of the Arts, Ms. Red Burns: Alternate Media Center.

The National News Council, William B. Arthur: General support.

Massachusetts Institute of Technology, Ithiel de Sola Pool: Research Program on Communication Policy.

University of Pennsylvania, Ronald Frank: Study on the identification of special interest audiences for public television.

University of Michigan, Layman E. Allen: Experiment to create community involvement and interaction in an educational game using cable television and local telephone service.

The Rand Corporation, Leland C. Johnson: Communications Policy Program.

University of California, Berkeley, Leroy F. Aarons and Robert C. Maynard: Summer Program for Minority Journalists.

Syracuse University, Thomas Patterson: Study of how national media information is filtered through local media and how local political primaries are covered.

Duke University, James David Barber: Study of how politicians set media strategies for campaigns and how media organizations interact with campaigns to produce a national media agenda of attention.

The National Council on the Aging, Media Resource Center, Louis Hausman, Director: Support of a West Coast Representative.

Harvard University, Project Zero, Howard Gardner, Co-Director: Two studies to examine how children come to understand the television medium and the steps whereby they learn to distinguish between fantasy and reality.

The American University, Ben H. Bagdikian: Investigation of the cause of U. S. newspaper failures in recent years.

Center for Action Research, Eliot A. Daley, President: Study to ascertain feasibility of national endowment for children's television programming and the development of a model for such an endowment.

The Early Learning Center, Brooks Jones and Margaret Skutch, Director: Support of the creation and evaluation of children's television material that teaches with viewer participation.

Middlebury College, Committee on Foreign Languages, Kimberly Sparks, Chairman: Support of the adaption of German and Spanish language versions of "Sesame Street" television program for use in beginning language courses.

National Citizens Committee for Broadcasting, Ted Carpenter, Executive Director, and Nicholas Johnson, Chairperson: General support.

Population Education, Inc., Project on Human Sexual Development, Elizabeth J. Roberts, Executive Director:

Support of workshop for members of the industry and the public to clarify and seek answers to questions related to televised sexuality.

Broadside Video, Lynn Bennett, Executive Director: Support of public affairs programming in local communities of Virginia and Tennessee.

Princeton University, Fritz Machlup: Economic study of communications industries.

London Graduate School of Business Studies, A. S. C. Ehrenberg: Studies of characteristics of U. S. television audiences.

National Opinion Research Center, Center for the Study of American Pluralism, Andrew M. Greeley, Director: Exploratory research on the relationship between the mass media and the ways in which young Americans think about themselves and their society.

University Of Michigan, F. Gerald Kline: Study of adolescents' acquisition from radio of information about such issues as family planning, drug and alcohol use, and occupations.

Lincoln Center for the Performing Arts, Media Development Department, John Goberman, Director: Support for the development of a plan to determine if the televising of live and recorded performances can become a significant source of revenue for Lincoln Center.

National Association of Broadcasters (NAB)
1771 N Street, N.W.
Washington, DC   20036
(202) 293-3500
John Dimling, Vice President, Research

The NAB annual program of grants for research in broadcasting was established in 1966. The program is directed toward the academic community and seeks both to stimulate interest in broadcast research and to aid the professional development of researchers already in the field. Applications are judged by a committee of broadcasters, academicians and broadcast researchers. Grantees are awarded up to $1,200 to cover out-of-pocket expenses incurred in carrying out their proposed research. Topics of projects funded in 1976 include: effect of parental justified and unjustified interpretations of TV programming on children's perceptions of that programming; PSA information and format needs of radio station personnel; the role of the commercial radio station in the local community; market structure, conduct, and performance of station brokerage firms; the uses and gratifications of TV news; a pilot effort at "informed" production of TV material for a young audience; a cognitive developmental study of black children's perceptions of TV advertising; blind people's use of commercial radio; gratification of self-esteem via TV viewing; and historical parallels in the role of mass media in the U. S. over the past fifty years.

National Endowment for the Arts
Washington, DC 20506
(202) 634-6369

The Endowment funds projects in several areas of communications, including television, radio, videotape, the visual arts, the graphic arts, and motion pictures. Recent grants have included a matching fund program to develop curricula for film-related courses and to organize and administer workshops and seminars for teachers of film; a matching grant program to encourage regional film centers to provide regional screenings and to encourage research and study in film education; a matching grant program to support production, research and development to improve arts programming on film, television and radio; and a program employing films, videotapes and other new media to build public awareness of the man-made environment.

National Endowment for the Humanities
Washington, DC   20506
(202) 382-5721

The National Endowment for the Humanities is an agency of the federal government established in 1965 to help teachers, scholars and writers to develop the humanities as sources of insight into human problems and priorities. Although the Endowment has no office that deals with communications research per se, it has a fully established Media Program (Stephen Rabin, Director) to fund humanities programs in the media. The Office of Planning and Analysis (Armen Tashdinian, Director) has also granted support for media-related projects. Among grants made by the Endowment are: a grant to the Aspen Institute for Humanistic Studies for a workshop on humanistic uses of cable television; grants to support research for and production of films in American history, literature, and culture; a grant to the University of Wisconsin to study the use of television for exploration of the humanities; a grant to the University of California at San Diego, to develop a pilot program to print college courses for credit in daily and weekly newspapers; a grant to the American Film Institute for a project of film preservation and film documentation; and a grant to the Center for Policy Research for a study of the social role of the national news media.

National Institute of Mental Health (NIMH)
Division of Extramural Research Programs
National Institute of Mental Health
Room 10-105
5600 Fishers Lane
Rockville, MD 20857
(301) 443-3563

NIMH supports communications research only if it is related to problems of mental health. For example, it commissioned 23 large research projects for the Surgeon General's Advisory Committee on Television and Social Behavior to try to determine the impact of televised violence on the behavior, attitudes and development of children. While that program of research has ended, NIMH is currently supporting research and reviewing research proposals on such topics as pro-social and aggressive behaviors and the influence of television programming on the development of sex-role expectations, perceptions of other persons and groups, and personal and social goals.

National Science Foundation (NSF)
Washington, DC 20550
(202) 655-4000

Created by the Congress in 1950, the National Science Foundation's original purposes were to initiate and support basic scientific research, to foster and support computer and other scientific methods and technologies, and to support curricular innovations and the in-service and pre-service training of science education personnel. Originally limited to biological, physical, mathematical and engineering science, the NSF charter has been broadened (in 1968) to include the social sciences as well as certain areas of applied research. Programs related to research are:

Science Information Service: To improve the dissemination of scientific information, this office awards grants and contracts in the areas of (1) development and improvement of information and data systems, (2) development of new and improved methods of publication, (3) research in science information.

Public Understanding of Science: To enhance citizen knowledge and understanding of the potentials and limitations of science and technology in meeting current and emerging problems, this office awards grants and contracts for: (1) information projects on science that facilitate dissemination of information to the public (examples of projects eligible for support are special-purpose films and television programs and projects that increase the scientific knowledge of media personnel); (2) national, regional, and community communications programs designed to serve either broad or specific audiences; (3) research and methodological studies of the communications process as it relates to public understanding of science.

Division of Advanced Productivity Research and Technology: This division supports research, through grants or contracts, in the broad area of telecommunications policy, including both regulatory questions and questions of applications of telecommunications to social service delivery problems. Past awards have supported work in such areas as telephone regulation, allocation of radio spectrum, transportation-telecommunications tradeoffs, the use of cable television for service delivery, cable television franchising procedures, and the use of telecommunications to facilitate health service delivery.

The Newspaper Fund
P.O. Box 300
Princeton, NJ   08540
(609) 452-2000
Thomas E. Engleman, Executive Director
Robert Skinner, Associate Director

The fund is a nonprofit foundation supported by Dow Jones & Co. Its purpose is to encourage young people to consider careers in journalism. All programs are organized through college campuses throughout the country.

Summer Internships: For students who have finished at least three years of college, and will be returning for one full semester after internship: (1) Reporting internship for nonjournalism or liberal arts majors. Working a full summer as a salaried reporter for a major daily in the country. Receives a $500 scholarship from the Newspaper

Fund at summer's end; (2) Copy-editing internship for journalism or communications majors. Working a full summer for a major daily, salaried. Receives a $700 scholarship from the Newspaper Fund at summer's end.

Minority Programs: Urban Journalism Workshop: for minority high school students. Involves attending journalism workshop on a college campus for approximately three weeks as a general eye-opener and introduction for minority students who may not have had exposure to journalism, but who might want a career in that field.

Visitation Program: Brings professional newspaper or wire service people into a predominantly minority high school to work with students and teachers. Provides peer identification and career advice.

Teacher Institutes: Tuition grants for the inexperienced high school journalism teacher, *i.e.*, one, who has a different major, or has volunteered to take over the program.

Editor-in-residence Program: Cosponsored with the American Society of Newspaper Editors. A day or two in college programs in which editors help students keep up-to-date on work in the professional world.

Career Advising Program: Advertising majors, who design their own work, submit ads to the Newspaper Fund. Three ads are chosen from the program and those students are given $100 scholarships. The ads are then distributed professionally by the Newspaper Fund, and various newspapers around the country agree to run them as a public service.

Publications: Newspaper Fund Journalism Scholarship Guide *A Newspaper Career and You* (published annually); *Newspaper Fund Newsletter* (monthly—see listing listing on page 339).

Rockefeller Brothers Fund (RBF)
30 Rockefeller Plaza
New York, NY 10020
(212) 247-8135
William M. Dietel, President

While the RBF as a general rule does not make research grants, it may from time to time contribute to more general programs or activities of which research is a part. General budgetary or special project support has been given to the Program on Communications and Society of the Aspen Institute for Humanistic Studies; Educational

Broadcasting Corporation (New York Channel 13); Harvard University's Program on Information Resources Policy; International Institute of Communications Ltd. (formerly International Broadcast Institute Ltd.), and the Office of Communication of the United Church of Christ.

The Rockefeller Foundation
Arts, Humanities and Contemporary Values
1133 Avenue of the Americas
New York, NY 10036
(212) 869-8500
Howard Klein, Director for the Arts
Joel Colton, Director for the Humanities

The Arts Program has concentrated its communications funds on artistic uses of public television. Through grants to selected organizations, such as the Long Beach Museum, California, and Electronic Arts Intermix, New York, post-production and editing facilities have been made available to large numbers of video and television artists. The Humanities Program is investigating ways of using television and film as media to convey humanistic ideas. The American Humanist Association received support for a television series on Ethics and American Society; WGBH received a grant for research and scripting of a television series of important episodes in American labor history; and another grant helped establish the Yale University Media Design Studio. The Aspen Institute Program on Communications and Society received a grant for its Workshop on Television for the development of a television criticism curriculum.

The Alfred P. Sloan Foundation
630 Fifth Avenue
New York, NY   10020
(212) 582-0450
Nils Y. Wessell, President
Robert N. Kreidler, Executive Vice President
Arthur L. Singer, Stephen White, Vice-Presidents

The Sloan Foundation has occasionally supported research and development projects in communications, particularly in the area of technology assessment. In 1970 the Foundation established the Sloan Commission on Cable Communications which led to the report *On the Cable*. Recent grants in communications have included support for research and development in the use of broadband communications systems in higher education (MIT) and support for the development of methods for televising and distributing live cultural events (Lincoln Center, New York). Such grants, however, represent only a small area of the Foundation's broader interests in science and technology, economics and management, and related problems of society.

The Twentieth Century Fund
41 East 70th Street
New York, NY   10021
(212) 535-5441

The Fund is one of the major institutions supporting a wide range of communications research. It does not make grants but commissions research and arranges for publication of findings and conclusions in book form. Some of its projects are undertaken by independent Twentieth Century Fund task forces. An example is the Task Force on a National News Council, which surveyed local and regional press councils in the United States and Britain, then recommended the establishment of the National News Council that is supported by a consortium of foundations.

Other projects: A study on *The Economics of the Daily Press in the United States*, by James N. Rosse, of Stanford University, who is analyzing the forces moving the press toward monopoly and possible public policies to deal with the situation; the Task Force on Justice, Publicity and the First Amendment, which examined the controversy surrounding judicial attempts to assure defendants their Sixth Amendment rights to a fair trial by restricting the freedom of the press to cover trial proceedings; *Wholesale News: How the Wire Services Select, Shape, and Distribute Information*, by Edward Jay Epstein, who is assessing the impact of the services' organizational structures on news judgment and selection decisions; the Task Force on Broadcasting and the Legislature, which recommended broad access to the Congress and state legislature for the broadcast media; the Task Force on Government Power and Press Freedom, which issued a report, *Press Freedoms Under Pressure*, that was concerned primarily with the impact of government subpoenas on the free flow of news; *Freedom of Information: Problems of Access and Privacy*, by Allen Weinstein, who is evaluating the conflicts between the Privacy and Freedom of Information Acts.

4

COMMUNICATIONS ORGANIZATIONS

The organizations listed in this section are primarily trade associations, professional groups, and labor unions involved in the field of communications. Although these groups vary greatly in terms of size and scope, most of them conduct similar activities, which include:

- Issuing publications that report on developments of interest to their members (some of the professional associations also publish scholarly journals containing new research in their fields).

- Holding regular, usually annual meetings for their members.

- Giving awards that recognize outstanding individuals or achievements.

- Representing the interests of their members before government and other policy-making bodies, as well as to the public at large.

In addition, many of these organizations either carry out research or sponsor outside research projects relevant to their interests. Some of the organizations provide scholarships and/or fellowships for students preparing for careers in communications. The professional groups often provide job-directory services for their members.

The organizations in this section are broken down into the following categories:

1) Advertising and Public Relations 107
2) Broadcasting 111
3) Educational/Instructional Media 118
4) Film and Photography 123
5) Journalism 129
6) New Communications Technologies 136
7) Print Media 143
8) Related and General 148

1. ADVERTISING AND PUBLIC RELATIONS

AAF/ADS
1225 Connecticut Avenue, N.W.
Washington, DC 20036
(202) 659-1800
Cathy Molo, Manager, Education Services

Formerly ADS, National Professional Advertising Society, AAF/ADS is the academic division of the American Advertising Federation (AAF). It has a membership of 25,000 as well as 39 active college chapters. It serves as a job clearinghouse for graduating college students, sponsors a National Student Advertising Competition, and maintains a library of 800 volumes. Publication: *AAF/ADS Communicator*, monthly.

Advertising Council
825 Third Avenue
New York, NY 10022
(212) 758-0400
Robert P. Keim, President

The Council was founded and is supported by American business to conduct public service advertising programs. It encourages advertisers and advertising media to contribute time and space, and advertising agencies to supply creative talent and facilities to further causes of national significance. Specific campaigns include carpooling, nutrition and health, forest fire prevention, rehabilitation of the handicapped, the U.N., child abuse, consumer information, the United Way, and fighting pollution. Publication: *Public Service Advertising Bulletin*, bimonthly.

Advertising Research Foundation (ARF)
3 East 54th Street
New York, NY 10022
(212) 751-5656
Edgar Roll, President

An organization devoted to promoting advertising and marketing effectiveness by means of objective and impartial research; through developing new research methods and techniques; through analyzing and evaluating existing methods and techniques and defining proper applications; and through establishing research standards, criteria and reporting methods. Members include advertisers, advertising agencies and media, as well as commercial research organizations, advertising associations and colleges and universities. Publication: *Journal of Advertising Research* (see listing on page 292).

American Academy of Advertising (AAA)
202 Communications Building
University of Tennessee
Knoxville, TN 37916
(615) 974-3048
Richard Joel, President

The Academy, founded in 1959, is the national association of teachers of advertising and is dedicated to the advancement of advertising education. Membership is open to both teachers and professional advertising practitioners. Its objectives are to provide a forum for the exchange of ideas; to seek ways in which to draw educators and practitioners more closely together; to disseminate research findings and scholarly contributions to the understanding of advertising, its role in society, the ways in which it functions, and to advertising education; and to stimulate research focusing on these and related matters. Publications: *Journal of Advertising*, quarterly (see listing on page 291); *Newsletter*, four times a year.

American Advertising Federation
1225 Connecticut Avenue, N.W.
Washington, DC 20036
(202) 659-1800
Howard H. Bell, President

An organization with over 25,000 members consisting of advertising clubs, advertisers, ad agencies, advertising trade associations, the media, and allied firms. Its purpose is to further a better understanding of advertising through government relations, public relations, and advertising education, and to further an effective program of advertising self-regulation. Publication: *Exchange and Washington Report*, 10 times a year.

American Association of Advertising Agencies (AAAA)
200 Park Avenue
New York, NY 10017
(212) 682-2500
John Crichton, President

The Association is a national organization of the advertising agency business. Founded in 1971, it has 425 member agencies. To obtain membership in the Association agencies must demonstrate that they meet the AAAA Agency Service Standards and Standards of Practice. The functions of the Association are to foster, strengthen and improve the advertising agency business; to advance the cause of advertising as a whole; and to provide services to members, in particular those which they cannot provide for themselves.

American Marketing Association (AMA)
222 South Riverside Plaza
Suite 606
Chicago, IL   60606
(312) 648-0536
Wayne A. Lemburg, Executive Vice President

The Association is a professional society of marketing and marketing research executives, sales and promotion managers, advertising specialists, teachers and others interested in marketing. It sponsors research, seminars, conferences and student marketing clubs and maintains a placement service. Publications: *Marketing News* (see listing on page 307); *Journal of Marketing* (see listing on page 306); *Journal of Marketing Research* (see listing on page 293); and *Proceedings*, annual. It also publishes books, monographs, bibliographies and pamphlets on marketing.

Association of Canadian Advertisers
159 Bay Street
Suite 620
Toronto M5J 137
Ontario
(416) 363-8046
W. David Buller, Secretary

The Association, which is over 60 years old, has a membership of 230 advertisers throughout Canada. It holds seminars and workshops on advertising which are open to anyone interested as well as to its members, and represents its members in legislation involving government at both federal and provincial levels. Publication: *Newsletter*, three times a month, for members only.

Foundation for Public Relations Research and Education
845 Third Avenue
New York, NY 10022
(212) 826-1774
Frederick H. Teahan, Executive Secretary

The Foundation sponsors and conducts basic research in the field of public relations. It offers fellowships to full-time teachers of public relations at university level; offers an annual graduate scholarship to a student of public relations; and sponsors an annual lecture on the historic antecedents of public relations. It has established an audiovisual archive containing motion picture, audiotape and videotape interviews with leading public relations figures. Publications: *Annual Foundation Lecture*; *Public Relations: A Comprehensive Bibliography*; *Public Relations Law*; and *Public Relations Review*.

Public Relations Society of America, Inc. (PRSA)
845 Third Avenue
New York, NY 10022
(212) 826-1750
Rea W. Smith, Executive Vice President

The major professional association for public relations practitioners, PRSA was chartered in 1947 and has more than 8,250 members and 75 chapters throughout the U. S. PRSA has nine sections of specialized professional groups: counselors, government, corporate, utilities, associations, health, investor relations, financial institutions, and educational institutions. Each section is designed to provide a specialized forum for its members. Its functions are to advance the standards of public relations and to provide the means for members' self-improvement through a series of continuing educational activities, information exchange programs, and research projects. Publications: *Public Relations Journal* (see listing on page 308); *National Newsletter*, monthly, for members only; *Public Relations Register* annual, $40 to nonmembers.

2. BROADCASTING

Agency for Instructional Television (AIT)
See listing on page 118

Alpha Epsilon Rho
College of Journalism
University of South Carolina
Columbia, SC 29208
(803) 777-4102
Dr. Richard M. Uray, Executive Secretary
   Alpha Epsilon Rho is the national honorary broadcasting society. It has regional offices throughout the United States. It sponsors awards to outstanding figures in broadcasting and holds a competition for broadcast productions. Publications: *Monitor*, quarterly; *Directory*, annual.

American Federation of Television and Radio Artists (AFTRA)
1350 Avenue of the Americas
New York, NY 10019
(212) 265-7700
Sanford I. Wolff, Executive Secretary
   Founded in 1937 as the American Federation of Radio Artists, AFTRA is a labor union representing 30,000 actors, announcers, singers, dancers, newsmen, sports specialists and others in radio, television, recording, and other areas of the industry. Its purposes are to improve wages and working conditions for all talent employed within its jurisdiction through collective bargaining; to administer contracts to insure conformance by multiple employers; and to study and develop terms covering new areas of employment such as the field of cassettes, audio recordings used with slide films, and other supplemental video materials. Publications: *AFTRA Magazine*, quarterly (see listing on page 309); regional and local newsletters published periodically by some of the 43 locals and chapters of the organization.

American Women in Radio and Television, Inc. (AWRT)
1321 Connecticut Avenue, N.W.
Washington, DC 20036
(202) 296-0009

Francine P. Proulx, Executive Director

AWRT was established in 1951 as a national nonprofit professional association of women working in radio, television and allied fields. Its current membership is over 2,500. Overall goals include job advancement of qualified women and improved quality of radio and television. AWRT gives awards to programs that promote positive images of women, and it maintains local and national professional skills registries of its members. Publication: *News and Views*, bimonthly newsletter for members.

Association of Maximum Service Telecasters, Inc. (MST)

1735 DeSales Street, N.W.
Washington, DC 20036
(202) 347-5412
Lester W. Lindow, President

MST is a private association of television broadcasters which lobbies for the broadcasters' interest before government agencies, primarily the FCC. Its objectives are to prevent interference with television broadcast signals; to foster technical expertise by television broadcast stations and others; to maintain the primacy of the local station as a basic element in the nationwide broadcast system; to preserve free over-the-air television; and to preserve the spectrum already allocated for local television service.

Association of Public Radio Stations (APRS)

See National Public Radio (NPR).

Bilingual Children's Television, Inc. (BC/TV)

2150 Valdez Street
Suite 1550
Oakland, CA 94612
(415) 839-5678
Rene Cardenas, Executive Director

BC/TV produces a daily half-hour television show, "Villa Alegre," which is intended for children from four through eight. The show is conducted in both Spanish and English and uses the various cultures of Latin America in order to highlight the nation's cultural diversity. BC/TV has also done extensive research on programming for Latino audiences.

Broadcast Education Association
1771 N Street, N.W.
Washington, DC 20036
(202) 293-3518

Founded in 1955, the Association was formerly known as the Association for Professional Broadcasting Education. Its 200 institutional members include universities and colleges offering degrees and courses in radio, television and film; and radio and television stations which belong to the National Association of Broadcasters. The Association also has 350 individual members.

Its functions are to encourage the adoption and practice of high standards for teachers in the field of broadcasting; to provide for exchange of teaching materials and information; to foster close relationships between teachers and broadcasters; to improve the capabilities and understanding of students who enter the profession of broadcasting; and to facilitate employment. Publications: *Journal of Broadcasting*, quarterly (see listing on page 292); *Feedback*, bimonthly newsletter for members only; seminar proceedings, composite course outlines, and bibliographies (all published irregularly).

Canadian Association of Broadcasters
P. O. Box 627
Station B
Ottawa, Ontario K1P 5S2
(613) 233-4035
Dr. Pierre Camu, President

A nonprofit trade association incorporated in 1926, CAB represents 284 AM radio stations, 64 FM radio stations, 63 television stations, 82 associate organizations and several television networks.

The CAB's major role is to represent the interests of Canadian private stations before governmental, legislative, regulatory, judicial and consultative bodies. It provides leadership and information in areas of programming, advertising, self-regulation, copyright, technology and public service and encourages the development and exposure of talented Canadians.

A department of the CAB exchanges radio programs among member stations and produces a long-running public service series which permits Members of Parliament to make regular radio reports to their constituents.

CAB publishes "Careers in Broadcasting," a booklet

for aspiring broadcasters. A Broadcast Code of Advertising to Children has been developed by the Association, to which all members subscribe and which is endorsed by the Canadian Radio-television and Telecommunications Commission, a government regulatory body.

Among its wide range of services CAB also coordinates educational and management training programs and distributes ideas and suggestions from the Canadian and world communities.

Canadian Broadcasting Corporation.
See listing on page 201

Corporation for Public Broadcasting (CPB)
See listing on page 177

CTW
1 Lincoln Plaza
New York, NY 10023
(212) 595-3456
Joan Ganz Cooney, President

Formerly Children's Television Workshop. CTW is an independent, nonprofit company whose activities include the creation of educational and informational programs and many associated educational products, including "Sesame Street," "The Electric Company," and "The Best of Families." It also conducts an extensive program of research on the educational effectiveness of its programs. Publication: *CTW Newsletter*, published intermittently. Free.

Joint Council on Educational Telecommunications (JCET)
1126 16th Street, N.W.
Washington, DC 20036
(202) 659-9740
Frank W. Norwood, Executive Director

JCET was founded in 1950 as a consortium of organizations concerned with educational communications and with the need to persuade the FCC that certain television channels should be reserved for noncommercial, educational broadcasting. The Council acts as education's instrument for coordinating policy on telecommunications planning. Publication: *JCET Data Base*, irregular.

National Academy of Television Arts and Sciences (NATAS)
291 South La Cienega Boulevard
Beverly Hills, CA 90211
(213) 659-0990

Founded in 1946, the Academy is devoted to the advancement of the arts and sciences of television and to fostering creative leadership in the television industry for artistic, cultural, educational and technological progress. It recognizes outstanding achievements in the television industry by presenting its annual Emmy Awards. Its 11,100 members consist of persons engaged in television performing, engineering, film editing, music, production and writing. It maintains a television film and tape library at UCLA. Publications: *Television Quarterly*; *Emmy Award Directory*, updated annually; *Awards, Rules and Regulations*, annual.

National Association of Broadcasters (NAB)
1771 N Street, N.W.
Washington, DC 20036
(202) 293-3500
Vincent T. Wasilewski, President

NAB was founded in 1922. Its 5,000 members include radio and television stations, all seven national radio and television networks, and various associate members. Its purpose is to foster and promote the development of the arts of aural and visual broadcasting; to protect its members from injustices and unjust exactions; and to encourage and promote customs and practices which will strengthen and maintain the broadcasting industry. Publications: *NAB Highlights*, weekly newsletter; *Code News*, monthly newsletter; *Radioactive*, monthly newsletter. Available only to members of the Association. Also publishes booklets on broadcasting.

National Association of Educational Broadcasters (NAEB)
1346 Connecticut Avenue, N.W.
Washington, DC 20036
(202) 785-1100
James Fellows, President

The Association's membership of 3,000 work in or are concerned with all areas of telecommunications—the new technologies, including cable, audio and video cassettes, and closed-circuit operations; and communication within industry and the professions. Its purpose is to further the interests of professionals in telecommunications by providing a variety of services, particularly in professional development, research and publications, information and publications, and research and planning; to assist institutions in the techniques of applying communications technology to their specific problems and to the professional growth of their staffs; to act as a catalyst for various joint activities by professionals; and to work with governmental agencies to foster the growth of telecommunications. Publications: *Public Telecommunications Review* (see listing on page 313); *NAEB Letter* (see listing on page 323); *NAEB Directory of Educational Telecommunications*, annual.

National Public Radio (NPR)
2025 M Street, N.W.
Washington, DC 20036
(202) 785-5400
Frank Mankiewicz, President
James P. Barrett, Director of Public Information

NPR, a private, nonprofit corporation, is a membership organization of public radio stations. It is the national programming center for more than 156 members which operate 182 stations in the U. S. and Puerto Rico. It produces, acquires and distributes programming through a two-way interconnection system with its members. In 1977 the Association of Public Radio Stations (APRS), which had represented the interests of the country's public radio stations before Congress, the executive branch, regulatory agencies and the Corporation for Public Broadcasting, became a part of NPR.

National Religious Broadcasters (NRB)
Box 2254 R
Morristown, NJ 07960
(201) 540-8500
Dr. Ben Armstrong, Executive Secretary

NRB is a trade association dealing with religious communicators, in both the religious and secular fields, throughout the world. It gives annual awards of merit for the best religious program, the best religious station, and for distinguished service. It sponsors regional workshops and seminars, compiles statistics, provides a placement service, and holds an annual convention. Publications: *Hotline*, monthly; *Religious Broadcasting*, bimonthly; and *WEF Communications Report*.

Public Broadcasting Service (PBS)
475 L'Enfant Plaza West, S.W.
Washington, DC 20024
(202) 488-5000
Ralph Rogers, Chairman
Lawrence K. Grossman, President

The Public Broadcasting Service is the member organization of the nation's public television stations. Owned and governed by the stations, it serves both as the national distributor of public television programs and as the coordinator of numerous station services. While not a "network" in the familiar sense, PBS manages and services the public television interconnection—the system through which over 260 stations are linked together. Through the interconnection, programs are distributed from PBS across the nation and can be broadcast at a time of the individual station's choosing. As the stations' national representative organization, PBS has many other responsibilities. It administers the station program cooperative and provides stations with many support services, including acting as their spokesman before the Congress, the executive branch and the Federal Communications Commission. PBS is governed by a 52-member board elected by the membership and comprised of both public television lay leaders and station managers. There are 35 lay representatives on the Board, all of whom play an active role in the affairs of their local stations, and 15 professional representatives. In addition, both the PBS Vice Chairman and the President serve on the Board. Publications: Periodic brochures and special reports.

Radio-Television News Directors Association (RTNDA)
1735 De Sales Street, N.W.
Washington, DC 20036
(202) 737-8657
Len Allen, Managing Director

A professional society of heads of news departments for broadcast news, teachers of broadcast journalism, and others involved in industry services, public relations departments of business firms, public relations firms, and networks. Founded in 1946, the 1,400-member society sponsors annual awards for news reporting, editorials and outstanding contributions to broadcast journalism; operates an employment service, speaker's bureau, and workshops; and conducts an annual international conference and regional seminars.

Functions: To improve standards of broadcast journalism; to defend rights of newsmen to access to news; to promote journalism training to meet specific needs of broadcasting. Publication: *RTNDA Communicator* (see listing on page 340).

**Society of Motion Picture
and Television Engineers (SMPTE)**
See listing on page 128

Television Information Office (TIO)
745 Fifth Avenue
New York, NY 10022
(212) 759-6800
Roy Danish, Director

Founded in October, 1959, and supported by the three major television networks, individual commercial stations and groups, educational stations and the National Association of Broadcasters, TIO provides a continuing information service to meet the needs of educators, students, government agencies, the press, the clergy, librarians, allied communications professionals and the general public, as well as broadcasters. Its purpose is to provide "a two-way bridge of understanding between the television industry and its many publics," and to increase knowledge and understanding of the medium among those individuals and groups who have a direct interest in its impact upon our society. Publications: *informaTIOn*, a newsletter; *TIO Index*, a reference guide to information for community education, programming, promotion and sales activities.

3. EDUCATIONAL/INSTRUCTIONAL MEDIA

Agency for Instructional Television (AIT)
Box A
Bloomington, IN 47401
(812) 339-2203

Edwin G. Cohen, Executive Director

AIT's predecessor organization, National Instructional Television, was founded in 1962. AIT is a nonprofit American-Canadian agency created in 1973 to strengthen education through television and other technologies. It believes that television can and must become a prime force in the improvement of education; that considerable resources are necessary to bring this about; and that these resources can be mobilized by expanding and strengthening cooperative production ability. AIT develops joint program projects involving state and provincial agencies, and acquires and distributes a wide variety of television and related printed materials for use as major learning resources. It makes many of the television materials available in audiovisual formats. Publications: *AIT Newsletter*, quarterly, free.

American Science Film Association (ASFA)
3624 Science Center
Philadelphia, PA 19104
(215) 387-2255
Randall M. Whaley, President

ASFA is an organization of scientists, educators and film producers, and film distributors who are interested in the use of motion pictures, television and related media as tools of research, as a means of communicating the results of research, and as instruments for science education and for public understanding of science. It provides information services related to the production, cataloging, evaluation, distribution and utilization of audiovisual media in the field of science. Publication: *Notes*, quarterly newsletter.

Association for Educational Communications and Technology (AECT)
1126 16th Street, N.W.
Washington, DC 20036
(202) 833-4180
Howard B. Hitchens, Jr., Executive Director

The AECT has 9,000 members concerned with learning and instructional technology. It was founded in 1923 as a professional association for individuals involved in the systematic application of communications media and instructional materials to learning. Affiliates are the American Student Media Association, the Armed

Forces/Government National Affiliate, the Association for Multi-Image, the Association for Special Education Technology (ASET), the Community College Association for Instruction and Technology (CCAIT), the Division of Educational Media Management (DEMM), the Division of Instructional Development (DID), the Division of Telecommunications (DOT), the Educational Communication and Technology Foundation, the Industrial Training and Education Division, the Information Film Producers of America, the Information Systems Division (ISD), the International Audio-Tutorial Congress (IATC), the International Division (ID), the International Visual Literacy Association, the Media Design and Production Division, the Regional Media Centers National Affiliate, and the Research and Theory Division. Publications: *Audiovisual Instruction* (see listing on page 320); *AV Communication Review* (see listing on page 320); *Technology and the Management of Instruction; Extending Education through Technology; Educational Facilities with New Media; Visual Literacy: A Way to Learn, a Way to Teach; Standards for Cataloging Nonprint Materials;* newsletters for ASET, CCAIT, DEMM, DID, DOT, ISD, IATC and ID.

Association of Media Producers (AMP)
1707 L Street, N.W., Suite 515
Washington, DC 20036
(202) 296-4710
Daphne Philos, Executive Director

Membership of the Association is comprised of producers and distributors of educational media, materials and related services. Its function is to stimulate greater and more effective use of the media as an integral part of all educational programs and to promote the creation of quality materials for use in such programs. It works with educational organizations to improve educational curricula and methodologies and assists its members in analyzing the needs of, and in providing more effective services to, consumers of educational media and materials. It conducts an annual industry-wide survey of educational media sales by product format, grade level, subject area and type of customer. Publications; *Federal Tie Line,* biweekly; *Reports,* monthly; *State Tie Line,* monthly; *Membership Directory,* semiannual.

Educational Communication Association (ECA)
822 National Press Building
14th and F Streets, N.W.
Washington, DC 20045
(202) 393-6267

The purpose of the Association is to develop and promote multi-media educational programs which are designed to strengthen and enhance those ethical and human values which are basic to the continuity of progress in modern society. It develops, distributes and implements programs which cover diverse educational interests and it encourages other organizations and institutions to seek its assistance in developing similarly oriented programs. It maintains a multi-media library offering material on a rental or purchase basis. It distributes radio and television programs for use during free public service time. Publication: *The Torch*, a quarterly newsletter.

Educational Press Association of America (EDPress)
Glassboro State College
Glassboro, NJ 08028
(609) 445-7349
Jack R. Gillespie, Executive Director

EDPress was established in 1895 by the editors of eight educational journals. A national organization with regional chapters, its membership is comprised of institutions, periodicals and individuals actively engaged in educational communications. Its purpose is to improve the quality of educational communications and to advance the aims of education generally. It sponsors workshops and an Annual Awards Program for excellence in educational journalism. It also offers a publication evaluation service to its members. Publications: *EDPress Newsletter*, members only; *America's Educational Press; The Idea Book*.

EDUCOM
P.O. Box 364
Princeton, NJ 08540
(609) 921-7575
James C. Emery, President

EDUCOM, a nonprofit corporation founded in 1964, is a consortium of over 250 college and university campuses concerned with the more effective use of computing, communications and information technology in higher education. Emphasis has been placed on working toward a national computer network for higher education and related organizations. Specific research projects include development and use of a computer-based simulation of an interuniversity computer network; projects connected with the development of a prototype network, EDUNET; and analysis of statewide efforts toward cooperative computing. EDUCOM's functions are to provide a forum for professional interchange among faculty and staff of member institutions interested in using computer and information technology in higher education through associational activities, including an annual conference, spring seminars, a magazine, and informal memoranda; to provide services to members through obtaining discounts on computers and related equipment and providing consulting assistance through the EDUCOM Consulting Group; and to conduct cooperative research projects with member institutions. Publications: *EDUCOM*, Bulletin of the Interuniversity Communications Council (see listing on page 322); *Planning for Cooperative Computing; Charging for Computing Services; Computer Networking in the University: Success and Potential;* proceedings of EDUCOM conferences.

Joint Council on Educational Telecommunications (JCET)
See listing on page 114

National Association of Educational Broadcasters (NAEB)
See listing on page 115

National Audio-Visual Association (NAVA)
3150 Spring Street
Fairfax, VA 22030
(703) 273-7200
Harry R. McGee, Executive Vice President

Membership in the Association is comprised of more than 750 dealers, manufacturers, producers and suppliers of audio-visual products and equipment such as motion picture projectors, film, and tape recorders. Publications: *NAVA News*, semimonthly; *Audio-Visual Equipment Directory*, annual.

National Center on Educational Media and Materials for the Handicapped (NCEMMH)
The Ohio State University
Columbus, OH 43210
(614) 422-7596
S.C. Ashcroft, Director

The NCEMMH, in cooperation with the National Instruction Materials Information System and with professional associations, various other public and private agencies, and interested individuals, provides a comprehensive program of activities to facilitate the use of new educational technology in instructional programs for handicapped persons. The Center provides coordination services for 13 Area Learning Resource Centers and four specialized offices serving the entire country. Publication: *Apropos*, a newsletter. Quarterly.

National Public Radio (NPR)
See listing on page 116

4. FILM AND PHOTOGRAPHY

American Film Institute (AFI)
John F. Kennedy Center
  for the Performing Arts
Washington, DC 20566
(202) 833-9300
George Stevens, Jr., Director

The Institute is an independent, nonprofit organization established by the National Endowment for the Arts to preserve the heritage and advance the art of film and television in the U. S. With more than 35,000 members nationwide, the AFI serves students, scholars, professionals and members of the public whose interests or careers revolve around the moving image. AFI activities are supported by grants from the National Endowment for the Arts, the National Endowment for the Humanities, and contributions from foundations, corporations and individuals. In addition, individual memberships at $15 per year are available. The AFI film preservation program administers funds for the preservation and cataloging of American films. A major adjunct project to preservation is publication of *The American Film Institute Catalog of Motion Pictures*, a decade-by-decade compilation and cross-indexing of films distributed in the U. S. As an educational organization, the AFI operates the Center for Advanced Film Studies to train young filmmakers; special summer workshops for film educators; and the National Education Services, which helps to determine the extent and needs of secondary, graduate and post-graduate level film education in the U. S. and which answers inquiries about film and film education from the general public. The AFI also administers the Academy Internship Program (funded by the Academy of Motion Picture Arts and Sciences), the Independent Filmmaker Program (funded by NEA), and the Directing Workshop for Women. The AFI Theater, a repertory cinema at the John F. Kennedy Center for the Performing Arts in Washington, D.C., offers classic and foreign film series and organizes tours of specialized film packages throughout the country. Publications: *American Film* (see listing on page 324); *AFI Guide to College Courses in Film and Television* (revised annually); *The American Film Institute Catalog of Motion Pictures* (volumes on the 1920s and 1960s completed); *FilmFacts* (bibliographic and informational sheets compiled by the National Education Services).

American Science Film Association (ASFA)
See listing on page 119

Canadian Film Development Corporation
See listing on page 201

Consortium of University Film Centers (CUFC)
c/o Visual Aids Service
University of Illinois
1325 South Oak Street
Champaign, IL 61820
(217) 333-1362
Thomas H. Boardman, Executive Secretary

Membership of CUFC is comprised of over 200 university and college film rental centers and producers of 16mm film. Its purposes are to assist in making film more accessible, to promote its widespread and most effective use, and to recommend optimal standards of service and distribution; to foster cooperative planning among universities, institutions, agencies, foundations and organizations in solving mutual problems; to gather and disseminate information on improved procedures and new developments and to report useful statistics through common reporting terminology; to reduce waste of resources and unnecessary duplication of effort; to develop and provide programs which have economic benefits and priveleges to its membership; and to inspire, generate and coordinate research and scholarship which may further these purposes. Publications: *CUFC Leader*, biennial newsletter; *Proceedings and Membership list*, biennial; *CUFC Leaders*.

Council on International Nontheatrical Events (CINE)
1201 16th Street, N.W.
Washington, DC 20036
(202) 785-1136
Shreeniwas R. Tamhane, Executive Director

Formerly the Committee on International Non-Theatrical Events, (CINE) is concerned with entering quality non-theatrical, television documentary and short subject motion pictures in 74 international film festivals. Screening juries include Adult, Youth and Student Amateur; Agriculture; Art; Avant-garde; Business and Industry; Education; Environment; Experimental; History; Human Relations; Medical; Religious; Science; Sports; TV and Government Documentary; Travel. The Council presents Golden Eagle and CINE Eagle certificates annually. Publications: *Cinegrams*, three or four times a year; *CINE Yearbook*.

Educational Film Library Association (EFLA)
17 West 60th Street
New York, NY 10023
(212) 246-4533
Nadine Covert, Administrative Director

EFLA publishes evaluations of films, books, pamphlets and bulletins on various aspects of audiovisual education. It sponsors the American Film Festival and presents Blue Ribbon Awards to outstanding films. It maintains a film information library on nontheatrical film. Publications: *Evaluations*, 10 times a year; *Sightlines*, quarterly. Available only to members of the Association.

Film Library Information Council (FLIC)
Box 348
Radio City Station
New York, NY 10019
(212) 790-6418
William Sloan, Editor

FLIC gathers, codifies and disseminates information about characteristics, standards and library performance of films and other non-print materials, equipment and personnel for public libraries, museums and other community service centers in North America. It helps librarians evaluate materials in the non-print media field; increases the exchange of information between film librarians, distributors and film producers; encourages experimentation and innovation by calling attention to new materials, methods and support for film library programs; and takes an active role in effecting the shape of technological media development. It sponsors workshops on film history, selection, utilization, and other subjects relevant to public libraries. Publications: *Film Library Quarterly* (see listing on page 328); *Directory of Film Libraries in North America.*

Motion Picture Association of America, Inc.
522 Fifth Avenue
New York, NY 10022
(212) 867-1200
Also:
1600 I Street, N.W.
Washington, DC 20006
(202) 293-1966
Jack J. Valenti, President

The Association was founded in 1922. Members include producers and directors of motion pictures and motion picture production companies in the United States. Its purpose is to preserve, protect and enlarge the global market for American films and to raise the level of creative excellence and artistry in American film. The Association maintains offices in countries on every continent through the Motion Picture Export Association.

National Board of Review of Motion Pictures (NBRMP)
210 East 68th Street
New York, NY 10021

(212) 988-4916
Charles Reilly, Executive Director
Members of NBRMP are concerned with the social effects of the motion picture and with the technical and artistic phases of movies. The Committee on Exceptional Films annually selects the ten best movies of the year, the best actor and actress, the best supporting actor and actress, and the best director. Publication: *Films in Review* (see listing on page 329).

National Film Board (of Canada).
See listing on page 202

National Free Lance
Photographers Association (NFLPA)
Four East State Street
Doylestown, PA 18901
(215) 348-2990
H. Jeffrey Valentine, President
NFLPA is an organization of amateur and professional photographers throughout the world. It assists and cooperates with news media in obtaining photograp.is when regular coverage is not available. It maintains a members' photographic file for industry use, and sponsors contests and exhibitions. Publications: *Freelance Photo News*, irregular. Also publishes guides, directories and pamphlets.

National Press Photographers Association (NPPA)
Box 1146
Durham, NC 27702
(919) 489-3700
Charles Cooper, Executive Secretary
NPPA is an organization of professional news photographers and others whose occupation has a direct professional relationship with photojournalism, the art of news communication by photographic image through publication, television film, or theater screen. It sponsors a TV newsfilm workshop, competitions and contests, and maintains a library of tapes, recordings and slides on all aspects of photojournalism. Publications: *News Photographer*, monthly; and *Membership Directory*, annual.

Society for Cinema Studies (SCS)
c/o Timothy Lyons, President
Radio-Television-Film Department
Temple University
Philadelphia, PA 19122
(215) 787-8432

(Location is dependent on who is President.) The SCS is a learned society founded in 1959 and composed of college and university film educators, filmmakers, historians, critics, scholars, and others concerned with the study of the moving image. Publications: *Cinema Journal* (see listing on page 326); *Newsletter*.

Society of Motion Picture and Television Engineers (SMPTE)
862 Scarsdale Avenue
Scarsdale, NY 10583
(914) 472-6606
Denis A. Courtney, Executive Director

The Society's aims are to advance engineering technology, to disseminate scientific information, and to sponsor lectures, exhibitions and conferences advancing the theory and practice of engineering. It develops standards for motion pictures, television and optical and magnetic recording and sponsors standards promulgated by the American National Standards Institute in order to promote interchangeability and provide for operating efficiency. It makes available visual and sound test films for use as standardized measuring tools. It sponsors technical courses at universities on subjects such as sound techniques, laboratory processing, and film handling for television station technicians. It also presents eight annual awards for outstanding contributions to motion pictures and television. Publications: *Journal*, monthly; lists of motion picture technical terms in English, Spanish, French, Italian and German; a list of TV studio lighting terms; technical reports; and bibliographies on television and high-speed photography.

University Film Association (UFA)
c/o Peter Dart, President
Department of Radio-Television-Film
The University of Kansas
Lawrence, KS 66045
(913) 864-2700

(Location is dependent on the current President.) Founded in 1946 as the University Film Producers Association, the UFA now comprises over 800 members producing films, and teaching and studying film production, criticism and history. Its purpose is to further and develop the potentialities of the motion picture medium in instruction and communication throughout the world; to encourage the production of motion pictures in educational institutions; to engage in the teaching of the art and science of motion picture production techniques, film history, criticism and related subjects; to serve as a central source of information on film instruction and film production by educational institutions; and to provide a means for sharing ideas on the various activities involved in teaching film courses. UFA also produces and distributes motion pictures and allied materials. Publications: *Journal of the UFA* (see listing on page 331); *UFA Digest* (see listing on page 334); *Directory*, a biographical directory of UFA members.

5. JOURNALISM

American Council on Education for Journalism
School of Journalism
University of Missouri
Columbia, MO 65201
(314) 882-4821
Milton Gross, Secretary-Treasurer

ACEJ is the formally recognized agency for the accreditation of programs for professional education in journalism and mass communications. It consists of a 22-person council representing three educator and fourteen professional associations and has accredited programs in 64 institutions of higher learning throughout the United States. Its functions are to ensure that schools and departments of journalism continue to adhere to suitable educational standards and that their staffs, facilities and curricula meet the educational needs of their students and the demands of the profession. Publication: ACEJ annually publishes a booklet, *Education for a Journalism Career*, which lists membership, standards for accreditation, and schools which have programs accredited.

American Press Institute (API)
11690 Sunrise Valley Drive
Reston, VA 22091
(703) 620-3611
Malcolm F. Mallette, Director

API is a nonprofit educational institution that was founded at Columbia University in 1946. Members are required to have at least five years of newspaper experience and must be nominated by a principal executive of a newspaper. The purpose of the Institute is to contribute toward the continuing education and training of newspaper men and women in the United States and Canada. Towards this end the Institute holds an annual series of approximately 20 seminars, mostly of two weeks' duration, for newspaper executives and staff members of all departments. The seminars are also open to journalism educators and a limited number of newspaper men and women from abroad.

American Society of Journalists and Authors
123 West 43rd Street
New York, NY 10036
(212) 586-5650

The purpose of the Society is to provide contacts, fellowship, and tangible supporting services for freelance writers of nonfiction, and to promote and reward professional excellence in nonfiction writing. The Society's 435 members are primarily free-lance writers of non-fiction magazine articles. It holds monthly meetings in New York City and publishes a confidential monthly newsletter carrying market news, job offers, news of awards and competitions, and news of member activities.

American Society of Magazine Editors (ASME)
575 Lexington Avenue
New York, NY 10022
(212) 752-0055

ASME, the professional society of magazine editors, was founded in 1963. It has 250 members. Its purposes are to serve as a visible presence for magazine editors, giving them a leadership position among magazine executives; to serve as a forum for discussions on professional problems in editing; to serve as a voice to express their concerns and viewpoints; and to serve as a means for developing public relations programs of long-range benefit to magazine journalism.

American Society of Newspaper Editors
1350 Sullivan Trail
P.O. Box 551
Easton, PA 18042
(215) 252-5502
Gene Giancarlo, Executive Secretary

The Society was founded in 1922. Its 800 members are editors of daily newspapers. Its purposes are to promote acquaintance among its members; to develop a stronger professional *esprit de corps;* to maintain the dignity and rights of the profession; to consider and establish ethical standards of professional conduct; and to exchange ideas for the advancement of the profession. Publications: *The Bulletin of the American Society of Newspaper Editors,* nine times a year; *Problems of Journalism; Read All About It!: Fifty Years of ASNE.*

Associated Press Managing Editors Association
50 Rockefeller Plaza
New York, NY 10020
(212) 262-4091
John E. Leard, President
Bruce Nathan, Associated Press liaison with APME

The Association was founded in 1933. Its membership consists of some 500 managing editors, executive editors and editors. Its purpose is to enable its members to meet in some 20 study committees every year in order to improve by criticism, evaluation and suggestion the Associated Press news report, as well as to exchange information on how editors can improve their newspapers and their own performance. Publications: *APME News,* 10 times a year; the *Red Book,* a compilation of proceedings of the annual convention incorporating summaries of study committee reports; numerous study committee reports prepared separately.

Association for Education in Journalism (AEJ)
102 Reavis Hall
Northern Illinois University
DeKalb, IL 60115
(815) 753-1000
Quintus Wilson, Executive Secretary

Founded in 1912, the Association is a professional

organization of college and university teachers of journalism and communications with a membership of 1,150. It has two co-affiliates: the American Association of Schools and Departments of Journalism, an organization of accredited journalism institutions; and the American Society of Journalism School Administrators, which is composed of administrators of accredited and non-accredited institutions. It also has 18 professional affiliates. Its functions are to improve methods and standards of teaching, to stimulate and conduct research, and to promote professional freedom and responsibility. The Association compiles statistics on enrollments and current developments in journalism education and maintains a listing of journalism teaching positions. Publications: *Journalism Quarterly* (see listing on page 294); *Journalism Educator*, a quarterly magazine published in cooperation with the American Society of Journalism School Administrators; *Journalism Abstracts* (see listing on page 286); and *Journalism Monographs* (see listing on page 294).

Journalism Education Association (JEA)
Paula Simons, President
Monchalet Apartments, Apt. 203 C
Leavenworth, KS 66048
(913) 651-5241

JEA is an independent professional organization for those involved in journalism education. It holds two national conventions yearly in conjunction with the National Scholastic Press Association, an organization serving journalism students at the secondary level. JEA officers are elected every two years, and editors are appointed semi-annually. Publications: *Communication: Journalism Education Today (C:JET)* (see listing on page 336); *Newswire*, a newsletter, three times a year; *Me and My TV*, a research report of a project tested at St. Mary's Center for Learning in Chicago and funded by the Ford Foundation; print and cassette materials derived from convention programs.

National Conference of Editorial Writers
1725 N Street NW
Washington, DC 20036
(202)785-1081
Clarke M. Thomas, Pittsburgh Post-Gazette

President for 1977

Editorial writers on daily newspapers of general circulation in the U.S. and Canada are represented in this organization of 400 members. It was founded in 1947. Its purpose is to stimulate the conscience and the quality of the editorial page. Publication: *The Masthead*, quarterly magazine (see listing on page 339).

National Federation of Press Women (NFPW)
312 Cannon Building
Washington, DC 20515

The NFPW was founded in 1937. It now has a membership of 3500 and serves as a federation of 28 state associations of professional women writers for daily and weekly newspapers, company and general magazines, other publications, and radio and television. It conducts an annual writing contest, provides a scholarship in journalism, and gives an annual award to an outstanding newswoman. Publications: *Press Woman*, monthly; *Directory*, annual.

National News Council (NNC)
One Lincoln Plaza
New York, NY 10023
(212) 595-9411
Norman E. Isaacs, Chairman
William B. Arthur, Executive Director

Founded in 1973 following recommendations of a task force commissioned by the Twentieth Century Fund, the Council consists of 18 members, ten of whom are not connected with the news media. Its purpose is to hear complaints regarding fairness or accuracy of news disseminated by national media and to report on attempts to infringe on the media's First Amendment rights. Anyone—individual or organization—may bring a complaint to the Council. Publication: *NNC Newsletter*, eight times a year.

Quill and Scroll Society
School of Journalism
University of Iowa
Iowa City, IA 52242
Richard P. Johns, Executive Secretary

Quill and Scroll, organized in 1926, is an international scholastic organization that has granted charters to over

11,000 high schools in every state of the Union and in 32 foreign countries. The honorary society for high school journalists was proposed in the fall of 1925 by George H. Gallup and organized by him with a group of 26 high school advisors. Any high school—public, parochial or private—publishing a newspaper, a yearbook or a magazine or involved in other journalism activities may apply for a charter. Membership in the Society may be obtained only through a local chapter. Its functions are to encourage and reward individual student achievement in journalism and school publications; to raise standards in the field of scholastic journalism; and to conduct programs of service and activities for member schools leading to the improvement of school publications. Publications: *Quill and Scroll*, bimonthly during the school year (see listing on page 340); numerous other publications designed to provide practical help for advisors and staff members.

Society for Collegiate Journalists (SCJ)
c/o John David Reed, Executive Secretary-Treasurer
Student Publications
Eastern Illinois University
Charleston, IL 61920
(217) 581-2814

SCJ, the national honorary collegiate journalism society, was formed in 1975 with the merger of Pi Delta Epsilon, founded in 1909, and Alpha Phi Gamma, founded in 1919. Its active membership includes an estimated 3,000 student journalists at 109 chapters on campuses throughout the United States. Its functions are to recognize and honor individual ability and achievement in collegiate student publications; to serve, promote, and help to improve collegiate journalism; to establish cordial relations between students and members of the profession; and to fraternally unite congenial students interested in journalism. Publications: *The Collegiate Journalist*, biannual newsletter for members, will be expanded to magazine format and made available to anyone interested; occasional papers on topics of interest.

Society of Professional Journalists, Sigma Delta Chi
35 East Wacker Drive
Chicago, IL 60601
(312) 236-6577
Russell E. Hurst, Executive Officer

A professional organization of 30,000 journalists, including teachers and college students, the Society was founded in 1909. Its functions are to advance the standards of the press; to associate journalists "of talent, truth and energy"; to attract talented young people to the journalistic field; and to raise the prestige of journalism. It is open to all ranks of journalists and to all branches of news-editorial journalism. More than 280 chapters hold monthly meetings and conduct a wide range of professional programs and activities. Principal areas of activity include freedom of information issues; professional and student awards and scholarship programs; career information; the marking of historic sites; professional development studies; and national and regional meetings on topics of professional concern. Publication: *The Quill*, monthly magazine (see listing on page 340).

Washington Journalism Center
2401 Virginia Avenue, N.W.
Washington, DC 20037
(202) 331-7977
Julius Duscha, Director

Founded in 1965, the Center serves as a sponsoring body for professional conferences and educational programs for journalists. Eight to ten conferences are held in Washington each year on topics such as welfare reform and the poor, the environment and energy, the arts in America, reading and American education, and the future of the women's movement. Each conference lasts four days and attendance is limited to 20 journalists. Speakers include leading government officials, members of Congress, former government officials, and representatives of various public affairs and special interest groups.

The Women's Institute for Freedom of the Press.
3306 Ross Place, N.W.
Washington, DC 20008
(202) 966-7783
Donna Allen, Director

A nonprofit organization devoted to research and publishing of practical and theoretical works on the communication of information. It engages in research on all aspects of communication, studies ways in which freedom of the press may be extended worldwide, and provides information to women about new developments in the field. The Institute is engaged in a long-term research project on the structure of the communications system and its relation to women. It will also publish works that study the interaction of women and the mass media. Publications: *Media Report to Women,* (see listing on page 303); *Media Report to Women's Index*/Directory, annual; *Women in Media: A Documentary Source Book,* by Dr. Maurine Beasley and Sheila Silver.

6. NEW COMMUNICATIONS TECHNOLOGIES

**American Federation of Information
 Processing Societies (AFIPS)**
210 Summit Avenue
Montvale, NJ   07645
(201) 391-9810
Robert W. Rector, Executive Director

AFIPS is a federation of the Association of Computing Machinery; the Institute of Electrical and Electronics Engineers Computer Society; the Society for Computer Simulation; the American Society for Information Science; the Association for Computational Linguistics; the Society for Information Display; the Special Libraries Association; the American Institute of Certified Public Accountants; the American Statistical Association; the Society for Industrial and Applied Mathematics; the American Institute of Aeronautics and Astronautics; the Instrument Society of America; the Association for Educational Data Systems; the Data Processing Management Association; and the Institute of Internal Auditors. It serves as a national voice for the computing field and disseminates knowledge of the information processing sciences. It presents an annual award for contributions to information processing and maintains a small library. It is the U. S. member of the International Federation of Information Processing. Publication: *Proceedings,* irregular. Also publishes books.

**American Library Association (ALA),
 Information Science and Automation Division (ISAD)**
50 East Huron Street
Chicago, IL   60611
(312) 944-6780
Donald Hammer, Executive Secretary

ISAD is concerned with information dissemination in library automation, video and cable communications, and in the audiovisual field. Interests include electronic data processing, systems analysis, mechanized information retrieval, standards development, management techniques, television and audiovisual activities, telecommunications information networks, and the development of related hardware and software. It sponsors seminars and institutes and provides consultation services. Publications: *Journal of Library Automation*, quarterly; *Library Automation*.

American Society for Information Science (ASIS)
1155 16th Street, N.W.
Suite 210
Washington, DC 20036
(202) 659-3644
Joshua I. Smith, Executive Director

The Society was founded in 1937 as the American Documentation Institute. Most of its 4,000 members are teachers, consultants, researchers, library or information center managers, administrators, and systems designers. The 100-odd institutional members include research organizations, information or documentation centers, libraries of all kinds, university schools of information science, and industrial organizations specializing in information science and technology. Its function is to promote the improvement of the information transfer process through research, application, development and education. Publications: *Journal of the American Society for Information Science* (see listing on page 350); *Annual Review of Information Science and Technology* (see listing on page 347); *Bulletin of the American Society for Information Science* (see listing on page 349); *Proceedings of the ASIS Annual Meetings; Library and Reference Facilities in the Area of the District of Columbia* (in cooperation with The Joint Venture).

Cable Arts Foundation
171 West 57th Street
New York, NY 10019
(212) 541-4666
Russell Connor, Executive Director

The Foundation is dedicated to promoting quality

arts programming on cable and commercial television. Cable Arts produces and distributes both anthology and original arts series to cable systems around the country and encourages local arts production for cable. A secondary goal is to contribute to higher quality arts programming on public and commercial TV. A third project area is the International Television Workshop (ITW), created by Cable Arts Foundation to extend the flow of cultural and arts programming throughout the world.

Specific projects recently concluded or still in process are: 1) the arts anthology series, *A Time for Art*, which was cablecast by 33 systems across the country, and *A Time for Art II*, focusing on New York art and artists; 2) a series entitled *The Critical Experience*, to be distributed to PBS; 3) a survey for the Exxon Corporation on the national production and distribution of museum exhibition TV promos; 4) a cable series entitled *Independent Filmmakers*; 5) a series on New York artists entitled *Group Portrait I*; 6) a program entitled *Nepal/Where the Gods are Young*; and 7) a program on West Germany's salute to the American Bicentennial.

Some existing and planned projects of the International Television Workshop are: 1) International Video Report (Videotape), to be produced abroad and assembled in the U. S. by ITW for dissemination by public and cable television; 2) International Video Bank and Post-production Facility, an open-access international video library and a post-production facility providing logistical support to videomakers and filmmakers in the field, cassette editing, and subtitling capability; 3) International Video Screenings, continuation and expansion of present exchange for interested professionals; 4) International Video Distribution, with ITW providing representation abroad for videomakers seeking international distribution; 5) International Videomakers Exchange, with ITW providing a coordinating service for an experimental video artists'/producers'/directors' exchange program and assisting in organizing artist-in-residence arrangements in the U. S. and abroad; 6) International Video Newsletter, a monthly publication reporting on international video meetings, activities, exchanges, satellite use, co-productions and technical developments related to innovative uses of television; 7) International Video Conferences, organized and hosted by ITW.

Cable Television Information Center
2100 M Street, N.W.
Washington, DC 20037
(202) 872-8888
Harold Horn, Executive Director
 The Center seeks to help local officials and the public arrive at optimum policies and procedures for the development of cable TV in the public interest. It provides analytic tools, points out options available, and aids governments in organizing their resources and thinking through a procedure for implementing a cable system in an urban environment. Publications: *Notes from the Center*, quarterly (see listing on page 318); 14 reports of both a general and technical nature, plus updates, available either individually or as a complete kit; a report series on cable uses; miscellaneous papers. A publication list is available from the Center.

Cablecommunications Resource Center
2000 K Street, N.W.
Washington, DC 20036
(202) 857-4827
Charles Tate, Executive Director
 Established in 1973 by the Booker T. Washington Foundation. The Center's primary function is to develop and disseminate technical and economic data on the cable industry in order to encourage minority ownership of cable television systems. It makes marketing, policy, economic and financial analyses for communities and client groups, and focuses on the uses of telecommunications for the delivery of health, education and welfare services. Publication: *Cablelines* (see listing on page 317).

Canadian Cable Television Association
85 Albert Street
Suite 405
Ottawa, Ontario K1P 6A4
(613) 232-2631
Michael Hind-Smith, President
 The Association is a trade organization with over 300 members reaching more than 3,000,000 subscribers—over half of the television set owners in Canada. It represents licensee-members before the federal government, prepares reports for industry meetings, conducts long-range planning and keeps in touch with provincial gov-

ernments on behalf of its members. Publications: *Communique*, a newsletter, biweekly; *Communique*, quarterly, free to interested libraries.

EDUCOM
See listing on page 121

National Cable Television Association (NCTA)
918 16th Street, N.W.
Washington, DC   20006
(202) 457-6700
Robert L. Schmidt, President

The Association is a national trade organization which represents many of the operating cable systems before the FCC, Congress and state regulatory bodies and on technical television industry committees, as well as in various programs of the television industry. Publications: *NCTA Bulletin*, biweekly; *Perspective on Cable Television*, quarterly (see listing on page 318); periodic surveys; reports with "how to" information, technical and general data.

National Federation of Local
   Cable Programmers (NFLCP)
763½ Chestnut Street
Dubuque, IA   52001

Founded in 1977, the NFLCP is an organization of approximately 200 access and local origination cable programmers throughout the country. Its goals are to preserve and further insure citizens' access rights and to achieve active citizen participation in the media. It engages in advocacy efforts on local, regional and national levels and provides support to those who seek to make information and media use more accessible to all people, and to this end serves as a center for the collection and dissemination of pertinent telecommunications information. Publication: *NFLCP Newsletter* (see listing on page 318).

Public Service Satellite Consortium (PSSC)
4040 Sorrento Valley Boulevard
San Diego, CA   92121
(714) 452-1140
John P. Witherspoon, President

PSSC has a steadily growing membership of public

service organizations which are seeking low-cost telecommunications services via advanced satellite systems. Members range over the public service spectrum from educational associations and universities to hospitals, medical specialty groups and state telecommunication authorities. The common thread is an interest in seeing low-cost telecommunication services evolve through efficient use of satellite systems. The functions of PSSC are to work with users and potential satellite users in a program of experimentation using NASA and commercial satellites; to conduct continuing studies of public service telecommunications requirements; to provide realistic technical and economic analysis of user requirements; to aggregate member requirements and resources for maximum economy; to help public service users render essential services more economically through more efficient use of communications facilities. PSSC is an approved experimenter on NASA communication satellites. Publication: *PSSC Newsletter*, monthly. A basic handbook on satellite communications will be published in 1978.

Teleglobe Canada
See listing on page 202

Telesat Canada
See listing on page 203

The following pay-cable distributors can provide information on subscription cablecasting:

Gary Adams
Bestvision
5540 West Glendale Avenue
Suite 201
Glendale, AZ   85301
(602) 931-9157

Ken Silverman
Cinemerica
9477 Brighton Way
Beverly Hills, CA   90210
(213) 550-8355

John Berentson
Hollywood Home Theatre
1345 Avenue of the Americas
New York, NY 10019
(212) 246-8400

Nick Nicholas
Home Box Office
Time-Life Building
Avenue of the Americas
 and 50th Street
New York, NY 10020
(212) 556-2433

Alan Greenstadt
Optical Systems
433 Airport Boulevard
Burlingame, CA 94010
(415) 348-8650

Jerry Burge
Pay TV Services
3718 Woodsong Court
Dunwoody, GA 30338
(404) 394-1286

Lou Scheinfeld
Prism TV
1516 Locust Street
Philadelphia, PA 19102
(215) 735-7636

Jeff Reiss
Showtime
1211 Avenue of the Americas
New York, NY 10036
(212) 564-6757

Bob Weisberg
Telemation Program Services
Time-Life Building
Avenue of the Americas
 and 50th Street
New York, NY 10020
(212) 556-2433

7. PRINT MEDIA

Alternative Press Syndicate, Inc. (APS)
Box 777
Cooper Station
New York, NY   10003
(212) 674-6550

APS is a nonprofit association of alternative newspapers which was founded in 1966 as the Underground Press Syndicate. It has a membership of 250. Its functions are to increase awareness of the alternative press by seeking and handling publicity for the alternative press in daily newspapers and national magazines and on television and radio; and to maintain a variety of services for member publications, including provision of free reprint rights, publishing a quarterly list of members, and arranging for the microfilming of alternative publications. Publications: *Alternative Media* (see listing on page 344); *APS Directory*, annual; *APS Member List*, quarterly; *How to Publish Your Very Own Underground Newspaper*.

American Newspaper Publishers Association (ANPA)
P.O. Box 17407
Dulles International Airport
Washington, DC   20041
(703) 620-9500
Jerry W. Friedheim, Executive Vice President

ANPA was founded in 1887 and represents more than 1,200 newspapers in the United States, Canada and the offshore islands. Its functions are to advance the cause of a free press, and to serve its members in all fields affecting newspaper publising, acting on behalf of the newspaper publishing business in matters where collective action is appropriate. Its major departments serve newspapers in the fields of labor and personnel relations, production management and technical research, government relations, economic data, credit management, transportation, public relations and news-editorial research. (Also see listing for the ANPA Research Institute.) Publication: *ANPA Public Affairs Newsletter*, monthly.

Association of American Publishers (AAP)
One Park Avenue
New York, NY   10016
(212) 689-8920

Townsend Hoopes, President

The AAP was founded in 1970 with the merger of the American Educational Publishers Institute and the American Book Publishers Council. It has a membership of 280 publishers of general, educational, trade, reference, religious, scientific, technical and medical books, as well as instructional materials, systems of instruction, classroom periodicals, maps, globes, and tests. It sponsors Publishing Forum, an informal discussion group.

**Canadian Daily Newspaper
  Publishers Association (CDNPA)**
250 Bloor Street East
Suite 206
Toronto, Ontario M4W 1E7
(416) 923-3567

A nonprofit organization established in 1925, the Association represents the majority of daily newspapers in Canada, with circulations ranging from several thousand to several hundred thousand. The main purpose of the Association is to disseminate information about the daily newspaper industry and to provide support services in advertising, circulation, editorial, credit information, labor relations, research, technology and the newspaper in education. Two research projects were undertaken in 1975: a National Newspaper Readership Study, which provided daily newspaper readership and audience characteristics for publishers, advertisers and advertising agencies; and a Survey of Teacher Attitudes Toward Use of Mass Media in Education, which sought to explore the general attitudes of teachers toward the mass media. Publications: *Editorial Newsletter*, in both French and English, 10 times a year, a professional development aid directed at newsrooms and journalism schools; *NIE Newsletter*, three times a year, directed to schol teachers; *Selected Data on Canadian Daily Newspapers*, annual.

**Catholic Press Association
  of the U. S. and Canada**
119 North Park Avenue
Rockville Centre, NY   11570
(516) 766-3400

Founded in 1911, the Association has members, both publications and individuals, in the U. S., Canada, Guam and the West Indies who are involved in newspaper and magazine writing and editing and the production of religious publications and books. Its purpose is to promote the welfare, professionalism and expansion of Catholic periodical publishing. It has undertaken a Catholic audience reading study in cooperation with Gallup Polls, Inc. Publications: *Catholic Journalist* (see listing on page   ); *Catholic Press Directory*, annual; *Catholic Press Annual*.

College Press Service, Inc.(CPS)
1764 Gilpin Street
Denver, CO   80218
(303) 388-1608

The press service's 450 members include newspapers and news magazines edited and managed by university or college students and published regularly during the academic year. Its functions are to provide news and feature stories about domestic and foreign youth, student and education activities; and to aid in court cases involving the student press. The service has also developed a code outlining its policy on freedom and responsibility, and it investigates violations of this policy. Founded in 1962, the nonprofit corporation operates collectively, selling its stories and materials to student newspapers, student governments, radio and television stations, college public relations offices, education associations and commercial newspapers and magazines. The CPS Center for the Rights of Campus Journalists offers censorship and harassment counseling for student journalists of member and nonmember papers. It also publishes a bimonthly newsletter of current censorship cases free to CPS member newspapers, along with CPS news releases and working papers on technical aspects of newspaper production. Publications: *The Student Press* (1973); *The CPS Stylebook*.

Comic Magazine Association of America (CMAA)
41 East 42nd Street
New York, NY   10017
(212) 697-6750/51
Ronald R. Lindblom, Administrative Assistant

Founded in 1954, the Association's 12 members include publishers, distributors, printers and engravers of comics magazines. Its function is to conduct research and operate a self-regulation program for the industry in order to raise standards of decency and good taste and to eliminate objectionable material in comics magazines. Toward this end, the Association operates the Comics Code Authority, which previews all material intended for publication in comics magazines produced by members. Publication: *CMAA Newsletter*, quarterly, containing general information on publishing and distribution relative to the comics industry.

Magazine Publishers Association (MPA)
575 Lexington Avenue
New York, NY   10022
(212) 752-0055
Stephen E. Kelly, President

MPA is an organization of 125 members which publish 450 consumer, agricultural, business, educational and religious magazines. Related organizations are the American Society of Magazine Editors and the Media Credit Association. It administers Publishers Information Bureau, which provides statistical information about magazine advertising. It also maintains a library on magazine publishing. Publications: *Newsletter*, six times a year; *Update*, four to six times a year.

National Newspaper Association (NNA)
c/o William G. Mullen, Executive Vice President
491 National Press Building
Washington, DC   20045
(202) 783-1651

The Association was founded in 1885. Its 7,000 members are newspapers and their executives, through 50 affiliated state, regional and national newspaper trade associations. Its purpose is to serve as a professional clearinghouse and voice for daily and non-daily community newspapers. It lobbies before Congress and federal agencies and departments on matters of concern to newspapers, including business issues as well as free-press issues. The Association stages an annual Government Affairs Conference in Washington, D.C. in March, and an Annual Convention and Trade Show, usually in the fall, in various cities around the country. It sponsors an annual national Better Newspaper Contest for members, conducts foreign study missions, and undertakes many other programs typical of trade associations. Publications: *Publishers' Auxiliary*, semimonthly newspaper (see listing on page 346); *National Directory of Weekly Newspapers*, annually; *NNA Washington Letter*, monthly, for members; *Directory of Congressional Press, Legislative and Administrative Assistants*, annually; *Biennial Survey of Newspaper Printing Equipment*; *Annual Cost Study for Weekly Newspapers*; *Federal Laws Affecting Newspapers*.

The Newspaper Guild, AFL-CIO, CLC
1125 15th Street, N.W.
Suite 835
Washington, DC 20005
(202) 296-2990
Charles A. Perlik, Jr., President

Founded in 1933 as the American Newspaper Guild, the Guild is an international union representing some 40,000 employees in news, advertising, promotion, business, circulation and related departments of newspapers and allied enterprises in the United States, Canada, and Puerto Rico. Its functions are to advance the economic interests and improve the working conditions of its members; to guarantee, as far as it is able, equal employment and advancement opportunity in the industry and constant honesty in news, editorials, advertising, and business practices; to raise the standards of journalism and ethics of the industry; to foster friendly cooperation with all other workers; and to promote industrial unionism in the jurisdiction of the Guild. It is currently engaged in a continuing program to increase and upgrade the employment of minorities and women in the news industry; in studies on the effect of video display terminals on vision and related areas; in establishment of an industrywide portable pension plan; and in continuing efforts on behalf of legislation that would provide protection against forced disclosure of newspersons' information and sources. Publication: *The Guild Reporter*, semimonthly tabloid (see listing on page 337).

Newsprint Information Committee
633 Third Avenue
New York, NY 10017
(212) 697-5600, ext. 446
Edward Starr, Executive Secretary

An organization comprising 13 Canadian newsprint producers which disseminates economic and technical information on newsprint. It sponsors advertising and readership research on behalf of newspapers. Publications: *Newsprint Facts*, five times a year; *Newspaper and Newsprint Facts at a Glance*, annually.

Publishers Information Bureau
575 Lexington Avenue
New York, NY   10022
(212) 754-0022

The Bureau was founded in 1947 and has 60 members. Its purpose is to provide statistical information about general magazine advertising in terms of space and revenue, a monthly service which is also available by subscription to nonmembers.

8. RELATED AND GENERAL

**American Association for
   Public Opinion Research (AAPOR)**
817 Broadway
New York, NY   10003
(212) 677-4740
Joan S. Black, Secretary-Treasurer

Founded in 1947, AAPOR is a professional society of 200 individuals engaged or interested in public opinion research and its allied fields. Members include professors, students, government and foundation employees, and employees and executives of commercial organizations which undertake market and opinion research. Its function is to stimulate creative research and study in the field of public opinion and social behavior; to facilitate the dissemination of research methods, techniques and findings through annual conferences, a quarterly journal and other means; to promote the use of public opinion research in democratic policy formation; to encourage the development of professional standards; and to serve as a representative national organization in international opinion research associations and at international meetings. Publication: *Public Opinion Quarterly* (see listing on page 294).

Center for Understanding Media
66 Fifth Avenue
New York, NY   10011
(212) 741-8903

John Culkin, President

The Center conducts research and undertakes projects in communications, education and the arts, specializing in projects involving young people and the new media. It stresses the need for programs in media study and media making at all levels of education and attempts to integrate teaching about the new media with teaching about literature and the traditional arts. Some projects include Master of Arts in Media Studies, a graduate program in conjunction with the New School for Social Research; Film-Makers-in-the-Schools Program, which coordinates programs in 40 states; Young Filmmakers Festival, which coordinates a national festival of student-made films by public television stations and produces a national program; and Children's Film Theater, which programs screenings of short films for children followed by creative activities based on the film. Publications: *Medialog*, quarterly; *Catalogue*; other educational materials.

Council of Communication Societies
P.O. Box 1074
Silver Spring, MD 20910
(301) 953-7100, ext. 2111
Vernon M. Root, Executive Director

The Council is a group of 19 professional associations that have joined forces to provide a focus for improving public awareness of communication as a vital element in human society, for encouraging interaction among a wide range of communication organizations, and for exerting a unifying force within the communication profession. Most of the Council's activities have been in the areas of seminars and publications. Seminar topics have included the future of communication, communication career trends, and continuing education for communication. The Council has also held White House and federal agency briefings in Washington. Publications: *Communication Notes* (see listing on page 297); *Communication Directory*, an irregular periodical issued every three or four years which contains descriptions of 378 communication organizations and 84 communication research centers, as well as lists of sources of communication research, career, and education information; and *Career Trends Seminar Proceedings*, a monograph designed primarily for guidance counselors and students interested in communication careers.

International Communication Association
Balcones Research Center
10100 Burnet Road
Austin, TX 78758
(512) 836-0440, ext. 225
Robert L. Cox, Executive Secretary

The Association has 2,300 members, most of whom are teachers and researchers in universities, colleges, and secondary and primary schools. It encourages and engages in the systematic and interdisciplinary study of communications theories, processes and skills; disseminates information about such theories, processes and skills through publications, educational projects and professional meetings; and encourages the application of research results in these areas toward the development of human understanding and public welfare. Publications: *Journal of Communication*, quarterly (see listing on page 292); *Human Communication Research*, quarterly (see listing on page 291); *Newsletter*; and *Directory*.

Iowa Freedom of Information Council
c/o School of Journalism
Drake University
Des Moines, IA 50311
(515) 271-2838
Dean Herbert Strentz, Executive Secretary

The Council is a nonprofit organization formed by major media associations in Iowa in March, 1977. It is concerned with protection of First Amendment freedoms—with coordination and organization of media response to infringements on press freedom and with education of the public on press freedom. The Council is funded primarily by sustaining membership fees of $500, as well as by other memberships at $100 each. It is possibly the first organization of its kind in the United States.

Media Credit Association
575 Lexington Avenue
New York, NY 10022
(212) 752-0055

Formerly the Periodical Publishers Association, which was founded in 1903, the Association has 130 members. Its function is to provide credit information on advertising agencies doing business with publishers and other media.

Modern Media Institute, Inc.
556 Central Avenue
St. Petersburg, FL 33701
(813) 821-9494
Donald K. Baldwin, Director

    A privately funded educational institution founded in 1975 by Nelson Poynter, Chairman of the Board of The Times Publishing Co., St. Petersburg, and the Congressional Quarterly, Washington, D.C. Its function is to challenge bright high school and college students and professionals with opportunities to explore imaginative mass media techniques while using The Times Publishing Company as a learning laboratory. Classes and workshops are offered in media management, writing and editing, graphics, photocommunications, new technology, video training tapes and communications research.

National Cartoonists Society
9 Ebony Court
Brooklyn, NY 11229
(212) 743-6510
Marge Devine, Scribe

    The purpose of the Society is to further the interests of cartooning and cartoonists. Its approximately 500 members are cartoonists engaged in producing comic strips, television animation, comic books, political cartoons and magazine cartoons. Rules of the Society require that members must earn the major portion of their income by cartooning. Publication: *The Cartoonist*, annual (for members only).

National League of Cities(NLC)
1620 Eye Street, N.W.
Washington, DC 20006
(202) 293-7310
Alan Beals, Executive Director
Fred Jordan, Director of Communications

    Founded in 1924, NLC is the national action arm of the nation's cities. Included in its membership are State Municipal Leagues and their member cities and, as direct members, cities with a population of over 30,000, the 10 largest cities in each state, and all state capitals—a total of 812 eligible direct members and over 14,000 member cities. NLC focuses its National Municipal Policy activity on improving the quality of life for the people who live in our cities. Through comprehensive analysis of national policies and related programs and through advocacy before the Congress and federal executive agencies, NLC officers and staff address the immediate and long-term concerns of city officials and urban citizens. A major objective of NLC is to aid city policy leaders—mayors and council members—in the improvement of their individual and institutional capacity to shape sound local policies and to strengthen their State Municipal Leagues and NLC as the vehicles which these officials use to influence the shape of state and national policies. NLC is participating with other public interest groups and unions in a study of the feasibility of establishing a major national cable television network as an alternative to ABC, CBS, NBC, and PBS. Noncity organizations and individuals can have access to the League through nonvoting associate memberships and through subscriptions to its monthly magazine, *Nation's Cities*, and fortnightly newsletter, *Washington Report*.

Recording Industry Association of America (RIAA)
1 East 57th Street
New York, NY 10022
(212) 688-3778
Henry Brief, Executive Director

RIAA, an organization of manufacturers of phonograph records and other kinds of recording equipment for home use, establishes manufacturing and recording standards for records and tapes; certifies sales figures for Gold Record and Platinum Record awards; and prepares a monthly report on factory shipments of leading types of records, by unit and dollar value, as well as a quarterly report on factory sales of pre-recorded tapes. It maintains a reference library of books, magazines, and other materials on the phonograph record industry. It operates an anti-piracy bureau which assists law enforcement authorities in prosecuting counterfeiters or "pirates" of sound recordings. Publications: technical standards; list of Gold Record Award winners; brochure.

Society for Technical Communication (STC)
1010 Vermont Avenue, N.W.
Suite 421
Washington, DC 20005

(202) 737-0035

The Society is a professional organization dedicated to the advancement of the theory and practice of technical communication in all media. It has 50 chapters and 3,000 members, most of whom are writers, editors, illustrators and teachers in the U. S., Canada and throughout the world. It is the largest society of its kind in the world and was one of the founding members of the International Council for Technical Communication (INTECOM) (see listing on page 242) and of the Council of Communication Societies (see listing on page 149). Publication: *Technical Communication*, quarterly (see listing on page 304); *Intercom*, bimonthly, for members only.

Speech Communication Association (SCA)
5205 Leesburg Pike
Falls Church, VA 22041
(703) 379-1888
William Work, Executive Secretary

SCA is an international association for communications professionals and scholars, organized in 1914. The purpose of the Association is to promote study, criticism, research, teaching, and application of the artistic, humanistic, and scientific principles of communication, particularly speech communication. The Association is divided into nine divisions to allow members an exchange of ideas within specialized areas: 1) Forensics, 2) Instructional Development, 3) Interpersonal and Small Group Interaction, 4) Interpretation, 5) Mass Communication, 6) Public Address, 7) Rhetorical and Communication Theory, 8) Speech Sciences, and 9) Theatre. The SCA provides individual member services, including a placement service and bulletin, annual conventions, and summer workshops. It also sponsors research and development projects designed to strengthen the profession. Publications: The SCA produces cassettes, books and other publications on several aspects of communications. Among them are *Spectra*, a bimonthly newsletter; *Communication Monographs* (quarterly); *Communication Education* (quarterly); *Quarterly Journal of Speech*; *International and Intercultural Communication Annual* (see listing on page 291); and *Free Speech Yearbook* (see listing on page 285).

Women in Communications, Inc. (WICI)
P.O. Box 9561
Austin, TX   78766
(512) 452-0119

Founded in 1909 as Theta Sigma Phi, Women in Communications has grown to a membership of more than 8,000 women and men who represent all fields of the communications industry. Its purposes are to work for a free and responsible press; to unite women engaged in all fields of communications; to recognize distinguished achievement by women journalists; to maintain high professional standards; and to encourage its members to greater individual effort. The organization sponsors a job information service for its members, offers scholarships to high school and college journalists through its individual chapters, sponsors workshops and conferences, and sponsors an annual Clarion Competition for outstanding reporting in any media on human rights, the environment, and community service. Publications: *The Matrix*, quarterly (see listing on page 302); *WICI Newsletter*, eight times a year.

5

MEDIA ACTION GROUPS

The organizations in this section either perform a "watchdog" function on the media or advocate various reforms from a public interest point of view. Some of these groups are primarily concerned with the media in terms of the interests of a particular subpopulation (e.g., women, children, blacks); others deal with a variety of issues related to a specific medium. Yet another category is the public interest law firm, which provides legal services to other media action groups.

Because broadcasting is a federally regulated industry, it has been the focus of most of the initiatives from the media action groups. The strategies of these groups include challenging the license renewals of individual stations, filing petitions for rulings by the FCC and the FTC, bringing about court actions, and encouraging public pressure on broadcasters and advertisers. Many of these groups also sponsor research and issue reports evaluating media performance. In recent years a number of action groups, such as The Public Interest Satellite Association, have focused their efforts on emerging technologies.

While the organizations listed here are primarily national in scope, similar groups have been formed in many local communities to deal with local issues. The National Citizens Committee for Broadcasting (see listing) has published a comprehensive guide to both national and local media action groups across the country.

Accuracy in Media (AIM)
777 14th Street, N.W.
Suite 427
Washington, DC   20005
(202) 783-4407
Reed J. Irvine, Chairman
John R. Van Evera, Executive Secretary

Accuracy in Media is a non-profit, non-partisan organization founded in 1969 to combat inaccurate, distorted and unfair reporting by the major media. It receives complaints of errors or distortions from the public, investigates them and pursues those cases that involve demonstrated errors or unfairness with the responsible publishers or broadcasters. AIM has filed numerous fairness doctrine complaints with the Federal Communications Commission. It has also been active in attending shareholder meetings of some of the major media companies and in proposing shareholder resolutions. It has pressed the three networks to adopt stronger codes of ethics and to employ ombudsmen. AIM recounts some of the more serious cases which it handles in its monthly newsletter, the AIM Report, available for $15 a year. *Writers and Wrongers*, a report on errors in the media, is issued periodically. AIM also syndicates a weekly column by Reed Irvine which goes to over 80 newspapers and magazines.

Action for Children's Television (ACT)
46 Austin Street
Newtonville, MA   02160
(617) 527-7870
Peggy Charren, President

ACT is a national consumer organization working to improve broadcast practices relating to children through education, research, and legal action. ACT maintains a specialized resource library of materials relating to children and television and has commissioned research on program content and on TV advertising practices. ACT presents annual Achievement in Children's Television Awards and holds yearly symposia on children and television.

Publications include: *Pre-Christmas Advertising to Children*, *Television in the Afterschool Hours*, and *Weekend Commercial Children's Television*, all by F. Earle Barcus; *Programming and Advertising Practices in Television Directed to Children—Another Look* by Ralph and

Carol Jennings; *The Family Guide To Children's Television: What to Watch, What to Miss, What to Change and How to Do It* by Evelyn Kay; *Children's TV: The Economics of Exploitation* by William Melody; *Network Children's Programming: A Content Analysis of Black and Minority Treatment on Children's Television* by Gilbert Mendelson and Morissa Young; *Mothers' Attitudes Toward Children's Television Programs and Commercials* by Daniel Yankelovich; *ACT Materials: A Resource List*; *Children and Television: An ACT Bibliography*; *ACT Resource Library Reference Sheets*: Current bibliographies on specific subjects: "Sex Roles Portrayed on TV," "Social and Cultural Roles Portrayed on Television," "Children and Television Advertising," "Children and Television Violence."

Also issued by ACT: *But First This Message*, a 15-minute 16mm color film with sound for rent or purchase, featuring film clips from children's television programs and commercials and statements from children, physicians, a toy manufacturer, a professor of communications and a professor of child development; *Nutrition Games/Juegos de Nutricion*, a bilingual nutrition poster with games and suggestions for alternative snack foods; *Treat TV with T.L.C.*, ACT guidelines for parents in the form of a poster.

American Council for Better Broadcasts (ACBB)
120 East Wilson
Madison, WI 53703
(608) 257-7712 (mornings)
Leslie Spence, Executive Director

Established in 1953, the Council is an organization of local, state and national organizations and individuals other than professional broadcasters that acts as an unofficial watchdog over media performance. The Council monitors programs and submits rating reports to sponsors, networks, broadcasters, congressional committees and government agencies. Publication: *Better Broadcast NEWS*, five times a year. Free to members, $2.00 per year to others.

The Children's Broadcast Institute
3 Charles Street West
Suite 202
Toronto, Ontario M4Y IR4
(416) 967-4624

The Honorable Pierre Juneau,
  Honorary Chairman
  The Institute is concerned with the content quality of mass media programs and broadcasts for children. It distributes a monthly newsletter which reports on and evaluates specific media programs for children in the U.S. and Canada. The Institute conducts workshops throughout Canada and has recently received a grant from WINTARIO for a project entitled "The Power of Television."

Citizens Communications Center
1914 Sunderland Place, N.W.
Washington, DC 20036
(202) 296-4238
  The Center is a public-interest law firm which provides legal representation to citizens wishing to participate in regulatory and court proceedings involving communications issues. General information on citizen rights and action strategy is also a priority, along with supplying students, attorneys, and media reform groups with copies of model briefs/pleadings, usually prepared by staff attorneys and interns, on current regulation development. Charges are usually for duplication and postage costs only, unless request is made for other material published by another organization. The Center occasionally publishes research studies in connection with particular regulatory proceedings.

Citizens for Better TV, Inc. (CBTV)
Route 2, Box 284 I
Oneida, TN 37841
(615) 569-5023
Dr. Flonnie Strunk, President
Reverend Anthony Carson, Executive Vice-President
  Citizens for Better TV was incorporated in 1975 as a non-profit, non-denominational organization for the purpose of combatting excessive violence and permissiveness on TV and to promote more educational and better TV programs through procedures such as (1) recognizing sponsors of desirable programs by awarding them the organization's seal of approval, (2) recommending to its members that they purchase products of manufacturers that sponsor good programs, (3) insisting that the networks develop acceptable guidelines on violence and permissiveness, and (4) providing the networks with letters

written by concerned citizens.

CBTV, Inc., is structured so that it can give every concerned citizen an opportunity to exercise his influence through individual groups that are united by the national office. National, state, or local groups become autonomous chapters of the national office, and members of each chapter elect a leader to become a representative to CBTV.

Publications: *CBTV, INC.*; *Grapevine*, published at unspecified times.

Committee for Open Media (COM)
c/o Department of Philosophy
San Jose State University
San Jose, CA 95192
(408) 277-2875
Phil Jacklin, Director

Organized in 1970 to promote on-air citizen access to radio and television, COM appears before the FCC and in the courts on access policy issues and also negotiates with local broadcasters. The Committee developed the Free Speech Message, a viewer/listener-initiated spot message on issues. In 1977 it instituted an annual citizen access survey, National Voice Count. Other concerns include access for journalists, access alternatives to the Fairness Doctrine, and non-profit news.

Committee on Children's Television (CCT)
1511 Masonic Avenue
San Francisco, CA 94117
(415) 863-9434
Sally Williams, Executive Director

CCT is a racially and economically diverse group of parents and professionals in the Bay Area who are concerned with the problems and potential of television in the lives of children. CCT works with community groups in evaluating, assessing and attempting to influence the quality and content of children's television through workshops, publications, and a Children's Television Fair. "Countdown" is a project involving hundreds of organizations in meetings with broadcasters, monitoring children's TV programs, evaluating station license renewal applications, and in issuing a "Report Card" on programming. Publications include: "TV Violence and Your Child"; "TV and the Young Consumer"; "Know Your Competition," a discussion of highlights of child development issues and their relationship to the content of TV programs; "The Peaceable Kingdom," a discussion of the Report and Policy Statement on Children's Television Programs issued by the FCC in 1974; "Children and Television: A General Bibliography"; "Seeking Solutions to Violence on Children's Television"; "Guidelines for Selecting the Best of Children's TV"; and "Kicking the Junk Food Habit: How to Counter TV Advertising of Heavily Sugared Foods." Members receive a free subscription to *CCT Newsletter.*

Council for Public Interest Law
1250 Connecticut Avenue, N.W.
Washington, DC 20036
(202) 452-1266
Charles R. Halpern, Executive Director

The Council for Public Interest Law was established in recognition of the need for new resources to support public interest law—the legal representation of groups and individuals whose interests traditionally have not been represented in the legal system. The Council has analyzed public interest law financing, and developed proposals to broaden the financial support for these kinds of activities, and to assure that the important developments in public interest law in recent years, including public interest communications law, are preserved and expanded.

Council on Children,
Media and Merchandising (CCMM)
1346 Connecticut Avenue, N.W.
Room 523
Washington, DC 20036
(202) 466-2584
Robert B. Choate, Chairperson

The Council's commitment is to protecting the child in the marketplace. The reform of print advertising and television commercials seen by children is a major focus. It works with broadcasting and advertising self-regulatory groups, the FDA, the FTC, the FCC, Congress and consumer groups to eliminate deception, distortion and misinformation in advertising seen by children.

Federation of Motion Picture Councils (FMPC)
1957 Curtner Avenue
San Jose, CA 95124
(408) 371-1839
Mrs. Joseph Baker, President

A federation of 33 state and local film councils whose purpose is to review and/or endorse motion pictures presenting the highest possible moral and artistic standards. Presents an annual Best Family Film Award and an annual Clara Edwards Memorial Award to a local council. Sponsors "Dial-a-Movie," a telephone service recommending motion pictures, as well as Monthly Youth Forums and a Summer Youth Film Series. Publications: *Motion Picture Ratings Preview Reports*, monthly; *Newsreel*, monthly.

Film Advisory Board (FAB)
1727 North Sycamore
Hollywood, CA 90028
(213) 874-3644
Elayne Blythe, President

The purpose of the FAB is to preview and evaluate films in all media in order to promote better family entertainment on television and in motion pictures. Publication: *Film List*, monthly.

Freedom of Information Clearinghouse
Post Office Box 19367
2000 P Street, N.W., Suite 700
Washington, DC 20036
(202) 785-3704

The Freedom of Information Clearinghouse was established in 1972 as part of Ralph Nader's Center for the Study of Responsive Law. The Clearinghouse gives legal and technical assistance to public interest groups, citizens, and the press in the effective use of laws granting them access to government-held information. The Freedom of Information Act, which became law in 1967, is the primary basis for the public's right of access to federal records, and the Federal Advisory Committee Act, which became law in 1973, is the primary basis for the public's right of access to advisory committee deliberations.

The Clearinghouse has been active in two principal areas. The first has been to gather information on government access laws, to disseminate this information to individuals and groups, and to assist in the effective use of these laws. For example, the Clearinghouse has collected data on all state public records laws, and is developing information as to how these laws might be improved. It has testified before the United States Congress, published articles in several journals, answered hundreds of individual requests about how to get information from government agencies, and has sent thousands of mailings to individual citizens, public interest groups, and press organizations describing the Freedom of Information and Advisory Committee Acts.

The other thrust of the Freedom of Information Clearinghouse has been to litigate cases under the federal Freedom of Information Act and the Federal Advisory Committee Act in an attempt to challenge illegal withholding of information and to secure judicial interpretations in areas where these Acts are unclear. It also encourages groups at the state level, in appropriate circumstances, to go to court to secure the rights of citizens under state access laws.

Publication: "The Freedom of Information Act: What It Is and How To Use It," free. Send a stamped, self-addressed envelope to the above address.

Media Access Project (MAP)
1910 N Street, N.W.
Washington, DC   20036
(202) 785-2613

MAP is a public-interest communications law firm dedicated primarily to representing groups and individuals who seek access to information and the channels of communication necessary to disseminate information. MAP regularly practices before the FCC, federal district courts, and appellate courts.

National Association for
Better Broadcasting (NABB)
Post Office Box 43640
Los Angeles, CA   90043
(213) 474-3283
Frank Orme, Executive Vice President

Formed in 1949 to promote the advancement of public interest in broadcasting, NABB has as its major goal the development of awareness of the public's rights and responsibilities in broadcasting.

National Black Media Coalition (NBMC)
277 Plymouth Avenue South
Rochester, NY 14608
(716) 325-5116
NBMC is composed of 42 local black organizations, each dedicated to eliminating all forms of racism from radio and television and to bringing to bear the resources of the broadcasting industry upon the problems of black communities.

**National Citizens Committee
on Broadcasting (NCCB)**
1028 Connecticut Avenue, N.W.
Suite 402
Washington, DC 20036
(202) 466-8407
Nicholas Johnson, Chairperson
Ted Carpenter, Executive Director
　One of the broadest-based among TV reform groups, NCCB works to secure citizens' rights in broadcasting and to seek broadcasting reform. NCCB is presently focusing on the monitoring of television violence, reporting on advertisers who support violence, an alternative to the Nielsen rating system, and litigation in the area of concentration of ownership. Publications: *Access*, a monthly magazine (see listing on page 309), and *Media Watch*, bimonthly. A *National Directory of Media Reform Groups* is to be published soon.

**National Council of the Churches
of Christ—Communication Commission**
475 Riverside Drive
New York, NY 10027
(212) 870-2574
The Rev. Dave Pomeroy, Director,
　Broadcast Production
　The Commission is an ecumenical agency for the cooperative work of 19 Protestant and Orthodox denominations and agencies in broadcasting, film, cable, print media. It offers advocacy to government and industry structures on media issues. Services: liaison to network TV and radio programming, film sales and rentals, distribution of information about syndicated religious programming and syndication of some programming. The Commission also provides news and information to print

and broadcast news media concerning the work of the National Council of Churches, related denominations and agencies, and general news of religious import. A list of resources from the cable TV and emerging technologies information service is available. Publications: *Chronicles* (work of the NCCC); *Film Information* (see listing on page 328).

National Federation of Local Cable Programmers.
See listing on page 140.

National Gay Task Force (NGTF)
80 Fifth Avenue
New York, NY 10011
(212) 741-1010
Jean O' Leary and Dr. Bruce Voeller,
    Co-Executive Directors

The largest gay civil rights organization in the world, NGTF is a clearinghouse for the gay movement and a political force promoting passage of gay civil rights legislation and fair and accurate portrayals of lesbians and gay men in the media.

Publications: *It's Time*, a monthly newsletter, single copy 25 cents, subscription by membership in NGTF; and *Action Report*, free, are sent monthly to individual members and to the more than 1,700 lesbian and gay groups in the U. S. and abroad.

National News Council (NNC)
See listing on page 133

National Organization for Women (NOW), Task Force on Broadcast Media and the FCC
National NOW Action Center
425 13th Street, N.W., #1001
Washington, DC 20004
(202) 347-2279
Kathy Bonk, National Task Force Coordinator

The Task Force gives technical assistance and advice to chapters of the parent organization, which work to promote the employment and image of women in the broadcast industry.

The National Sisters Communications Services
1962 South Shenandoah Street
Los Angeles, CA   90034
(213) 559-2944
Sister Elizabeth Thoman, Executive Director

A national resource/research office founded in 1973 to stimulate the awareness and more effective use of mass communications in and by religious congregations of women; to train sisters in communications strategies and skills; to provide communications resources, skills and expertise for groups; to develop a network of sister communicators for ongoing education and increased professionalism and involvement in the field of mass communications; to educate religious leaders to the value and necessity of communications activities; and to research contemporary communications issues and inform those interested of the implications of such issues on the policies and practices of communications in the Society—locally, nationally and internationally. The NCS offers workshops, seminars, resources and research services and also provides an evaluation service for brochures, newsletters, slide/tape presentations, etc. Publications: *Quarterly Review*, and *Sistersharing*, bimonthly newsletter.

The Network Project
102 Earl Hall
Columbia University
New York, NY   10027
(212) 923-3900

The Network Project is a collective research and action group formed in 1971 to investigate U. S. television and to focus public attention on communications effects. Much of its research has been broadcast in a series of five radio documentaries, titled "Feedback," which were produced with the assistance of WBAI-FM in New York. The programs have been broadcast by about 25 radio stations around the country.

Publications: Notebook Series (each notebook contains the transcript of a related *Matrix* program): *No. 2 Directory of the Networks, No. 3 Control of Information, No. 5 Cable Television, No. 7 The Case Against Satellites, No. 8 CATV: End of a Dream, No. 9 Government Television; No. 10 Global Salesman, No. 11 Public Access/Public Interest.*

Radio productions: *Feedback: (1) Television: The*

Medium, (2) Television: The Business, (3) The Fourth Network, (4) Broadcast Journalism, (5) Entertainment Programs, (6) Cable Television, (7) Communications Satellites: The New Web, (8) Spreading the Word, (9) Selling the World, (10) Access at Home.

Public Advertising Council
1516 Westwood Boulevard
Suite 201
Los Angeles, CA 90024
(213) 475-5781
Marvin J. Segelman, Director

A non-profit advertising and educational service organization which produces and distributes public service materials—primarily TV, radio, and print—and helps local and national public interest groups gain access to media space and time. Special emphasis given to helping groups utilize media to obtain financial self-sufficiency in their long-term development.

Public Communication, Inc.
c/o Communications Law Program
UCLA Law School
Los Angeles, CA 90024
(213) 825-6211

A public-interest law firm specializing in First Amendment, access, and fairness-doctrine questions, and other free-speech questions in the broadcast area. The firm also assists citizens in the litigation and produces public service announcements for the print and broadcast media, informing consumers of the merits of various products and informing minority citizens of important legal rights.

Public Interest Satellite Association (PISA)
55 West 44th Street
New York, NY 10036
(212) 730-5172
Bert Cowlan and
  Andrew Horowitz, Co-Directors

The Public Interest Satellite Association (PISA) was formed in the Fall of 1975 to mobilize a broad-based public effort to explore the public interest uses of satellite communications technology and to ensure that its future development serves the communications needs and interests of the American people.

PISA's objective is to assure that the benefits of this powerful, publicly-financed resource are made available to non-profit community and citizen organizations, which today have an increasing need to develop alternative, low-cost means of telecommunications.

PISA's goal is the creation of an independent, non-profit satellite communications system tailored to meet the requirements and pocketbooks of this vital non-profit sector of society. Much of its work (e.g., conducting studies on the communications uses and costs of non-profit groups; developing guidelines for future satellite policy directions; educating people about the technology) is being directed towards this end.

A copy of *Toward the Public Dividend: A Report on Satellite Telecommunications and The Public Interest Satellite Association* is available on request.

Public Media Center, Inc. (PMC)
2751 Hyde Street
San Francisco, CA   94109
(415) 527-5730

PMC is a non-profit advertising agency which helps groups working in the public interest present their views more effectively by providing them with the sort of professional mass communications skills that usually only money can buy.

PMC produces and distributes radio, television and print advertising on issues like monopoly control of energy, the dangers of nuclear power, social justice, growth alternatives and the American economic system, for clients like the United Farm Workers, Amnesty International, the American Friends Service Committee, the Oil, Chemical and Atomic Workers, Friends of the Earth and more than 100 other national and community organizations.

PMC also works to provide maximum exposure for ideas which are normally excluded from the mass media, not only by distributing materials which deal with them but by monitoring stations' public service performance and complaining when it is inadequate, petitioning the FCC for rules more sympathetic to controversial and minority viewpoints, and attempting to counteract the Advertising Council's present dominance of free broadcast time slots.

Publication: *Strategies for Access*, a guide on how to get public interest messages on the air. $3 postpaid. PMC also distributes a free catalog of the materials it has produced.

The Reporters Committee for Freedom of the Press
1750 Pennsylvania Avenue, N.W.
Room 1112
Washington, DC   20006
(202) 872-1620
Jack C. Landau, Executive Director

The Reporters Committee is a legal research and defense fund organization founded in 1970 and devoted to protecting the First Amendment freedom of information interests of the working press. Founded on the premise that the constitutional interests of reporters, editors, and photographers may be different from the legal interests of other First Amendment organizations, it is supported mainly by donations from major publishers and broadcasters, supplemented by donations from reporters and editors. It also files original complaints, friend of the court briefs and, upon request, testifies before congressional or executive agencies. Publication: *Press Censorship Newsletter* (see listing on page 346).

The Support Center
1424 Sixteenth Street, N.W.
Washington, DC   20036
(202) 265-2443
and
27 Maiden Lane
San Francisco, CA   94108
(415) 982-4500

The Support Center is a non-profit tax-exempt organization that seeks to increase the effectiveness of public interest organizations by providing them with a full range of management support services and business information. Services encompass all aspects of management in public interest organizations, including: financial management, management planning, office management, communications, financial development, personnel and management systems.

Publication: *You Don't Know What You Got Until You Lose It* (an introduction to accounting, budgeting, and tax planning for small nonprofit organizations and community groups).

United Church of Christ, Office of Communication
289 Park Avenue South
New York, NY 10010
(212) 475-2121

Founded in 1957 and one of the most active groups of its kind, the Office of Communication helps citizens' groups protect their right of freedom of speech by helping them gain access to radio and television. It also aids citizens' groups seeking to improve the broadcast service in local communities.

Publications: *A Short Course in Cable*; a lawyer's guide to broadcast regulation; annual studies of minority broadcasting employment.

Urban Policy Research Institute
321 South Beverly Drive
Suite W
Beverly Hills, CA 90212
(213) 553-4161

A public-interest organization, focusing primarily on California, the Institute is concerned with protecting individual civil liberties and privacy from abuses inherent in the performance of unaccountable police agencies. The Institute sponsors an Investigative Journalism Program which seeks to promote effective investigative techniques, improve press access to information, and increase the dissemination of information to the public, through a series of workshops and publications.

Publications: *News Leads*, a bimonthly newsletter of investigative journalism (see page 339). *Reporter's Reference Guide*, an annotated and indexed description of nearly 200 basic reference works which are available at libraries, $1.00.

Workshop Transcripts: "Essentials of Investigative Reporting," by Jack Tobin, Marv Olson and William Farr; "Libel Law," by Louis Loeb, William Niese and Lowell Bergman; "Accounting, Business, and Real Estate Records," by Alex Auerbach, Richard Gordon, David Stutz and Jeff Gerth. $2.00 each.

Publications available from the Investigative Journalism Project: "Working Paper No. 2: Exploring Ways and Means of Increasing the Quality and Quantity of Investigative Journalism"; "Transcript of a Discussion on How to Organize an Investigation"; by Robert W. Greene; and "Transcript of a Discussion on Team Investigative Reporting," by Bruce V. Locklin.

A complete list of publications is available from the Institute.

6

A GUIDE TO GOVERNMENT
POLICYMAKING BODIES IN COMMUNICATIONS
IN THE UNITED STATES AND CANADA

The following pages provide an outline of selected national governmental organizations and documents concerned with communications policy in the United States and Canada. The section for the United States is divided into two categories: (1) the major agencies of the federal government involved in communications regulation and policymaking, and (2) the government publications and references which are most valuable in making rapid and selective uses of the massive volume of regulatory materials. The Canadian section combines governmental agencies and publications into a single discussion divided into executive, legislative, judicial and provincial categories.

1. Government Policymaking Bodies in the United States.
   A. U.S. Government Organizations   175
   B. U.S. Government References and
      Publications   187
2. Government Policymaking Bodies in Canada
   (organizations and publications combined) 197

Keeping current in a field that changes as much as this does is not easy. Trade periodicals (see Section X) present the most current reporting of events, though such reports may be biased in favor of the industry served by a particular periodical. (Only the *New York Times* and *Washington Post*, among the consumer media, provide a regular and accurate report on media regulation.) The monthly "Where Things Stand" column of *Broadcasting* (first issue of every month), sums up the current status of from 20 to 25 regulatory and policy matters and provides a capsule of the past 6 to 12 months of activity on each problem area.

In addition, most regulatory activity affecting obscenity, pornography, libel, and privacy in print and film media occurs at the local and state or provincial levels. Even broadcast media are affected locally—see, for example, Robert P. Sadowski's "Broadcasting and State Statutory Laws," *Journal of Broadcasting* 18:433-450 (Fall, 1974). Increasing local activity concerning cable regulation is summarized in Vernone Sparkes' "Local Regulatory Agencies for Cable Television," *Journal of Broadcasting* 19:221-233 (Spring, 1975).

A. U.S. Government Organizations

This listing of U.S. governmental bodies involved in communications policy is categorized as follows:
> Executive Branch Agencies, Offices and Corporations
> Congressional Support Organizations and Joint Committees
> House Committees and Subcommittees
> Senate Committees and Subcommittees
> Independent Agencies and Commissions
> Federal Courts

Because government personnel change rapidly, names of officials are not included. This information, and more, can usually be found in agency annual reports, the *U.S. Government Manual* or the *Congressional Directory* (see the next section publications).

Executive Branch Agencies, Offices and Corporations

Many executive branch agencies are subject to presidential reorganization. The following list was current when this book went to press, but new agencies are created, old agencies die, and the duties of agencies are changed or transferred from time to time. The President also names directors of so-called "private corporations." Two of these, COMSAT and the Corporation for Public Broadcasting, are discussed at the end of this section.

Antitrust Division, Department of Justice. Constitution Avenue at 10th Street, N.W., Washington DC 20530. (202) 739-2421. The Division enforces antitrust law and has an interest in media, particularly broadcasting ownership policy. The Department often represents the FCC in court, although it has opposed the Commission in some cases.

Interdepartment Radio Advisory Committee. Executive Secretary, IRAC, Office of Telecommunications, Department of Commerce, 1325 G Street, N.W., Washington, DC 20005. (202) 724-3346. The IRAC, in conjunction with the Office of Telecommunications Policy (OTP, below) advises the president on governmental spectrum needs and management.

Office of Education, Department of Health, Education and Welfare. 400 Maryland Avenue, S.W., Washington, DC 20202. (202) 245-8795. Government funding for many public radio and television programs is distributed by this office.

Office of International Communication Policy, Department of State. Room 5824, 2201 C Street, N.W., Washington, DC 20520. (202) 632-2592. In conjunction with the FCC and OTP (below), this branch of the State Department is preparing the U.S. position for the 1979 World Administrative Radio Conference.

Office of Management and Budget, Executive Office of the President. Executive Office Building, Washington, DC 20503 (202) 395-3000. OMB is the President's advisor on budgets, including those of most communications agencies. OMB also approves federal forms used by executive branch agencies.

Office of Telecommunications, Department of Commerce. 1325 G Street, N.W., Washington, DC 20005. (202) 377-5578. A research and support agency for OTP (below), the agency does advanced economic and technical research on telecommunications.

Office of Telecommunications Policy, Department of Health, Education and Welfare. Office of the Assistant Secretary for Planning and Evaluation, Room 403E, South Portal Building, Washington, DC 20201. (202) 245-1891. The office develops policy and evaluates programs containing telecommunications elements for the purpose of delivering health, education and welfare services. The office currently administers the Telecommunications Demonstration Program, which supports projects using non-broadcast technology for the delivery of instructional and informational services.

Office of Telecommunications Policy, Executive Office of the President. 1800 G Street, N.W., Washington, DC 20504. (202) 395-5800. OTP advises the President on long-range policy for governmental and nongovernmental telecommunications issues, both domestic and international. It has been active in spectrum management and cable television. (As this edition of the *Handbook* went to press President Carter proposed to abolish the Office of Telecommunications Policy, transferring its functions to the Department of Commerce and the Office of Management and the Budget.)

United States Information Agency. 1776 Pennsylvania Avenue, N.W., Washington, DC 20547. (202) 632-5244. USIA conducts U.S. overseas cultural and information programs, runs the Voice of America, and produces films and television programs for foreign distribution.

Communications Satellite Corporation (COMSAT). 950 L'Enfant Plaza, S.W., Washington, DC 20024. (202) 554-6000. COMSAT provides satellite services to American-based international communications common carriers which serve the public. It provides such services through the satellites of the International Telecommunications Satellite Organization (INTELSAT), of which it owns approximately 30 percent, and through U.S. earth stations, of which it owns 50 percent. The INTELSAT satellites and earth stations operating in conjunction with them throughout the world are known as the "global system." Publications: *COMSAT Technical Review,* quarterly; *Report to the President and the Congress,* annual; *Annual Report to Shareholders.*

Corporation for Public Broadcasting. 1111 16th Street, N.W., Washington, DC 20036. (202) 293-6160. CPB is a nonprofit organization created to promote the growth and development of noncommercial television and radio. Its functions are to aid local public television and radio stations in augmenting their ability to serve the community; to expand the national inventory of programs available for local station use; and to support the total public broadcasting system through various activities, including talent development and encouragement of innovative production and instructional techniques. Publications: *Annual Report; Public TV Survey; CPB Report.*

Congressional Support Organizations and Joint Committees

Copyright Office, Library of Congress. Crystal Mall Annex, Arlington, VA 20559. (202) 557-8700. The Copyright Office administers most of the 1976 copyright law, with substantial impact on print, broadcast and CATV media.

General Accounting Office. 441 G Street, N.W., Washington, DC 20548. (202) 275-5067. GAO is Congress' investigative arm, often issuing reports on the effectiveness of communications programs or agencies. It approves FCC forms.

Office of Technology Assessment. U.S. Congress, Washington, DC 20510. The office was established in 1972 to provide Congress with comprehensive information on the beneficial and adverse consequences associated with technology, to be used by Congress in developing public policy and legislation. The office is governed by a board composed of six senators and six representatives, with both political parties equally represented. A council of representatives from the scientific, engineering and administrative fields advises the office. Assessments are completed in-house, by panels of outside subject matter experts, and through contracts awarded to other organizations. The office has undertaken one project in communications: a preliminary assessment of the feasibility and value of providing commercial and public services through broadband communications in rural America. A report was completed in April, 1976, and reviewed and expanded in a major conference cosponsored by the Aspen Institute and the National Rural Center in November 1976. Findings of the report and the conference were considered in hearings held by the Communications Subcommittee of the U.S. Senate Committee on Commerce in the spring of 1977. The office is studying how best to establish a permanent program to advise Congress on communications and related matters.

Joint Committee on Congressional Operations. Room 1628, Longworth House Office Bldg., Washington, DC 20515. (202) 225-8267. Along with Senate and House leadership and the Rules Committees of both houses, this committee has been concerned with press coverage, particularly broadcast coverage, of Congress and its committees and subcommittees.

House Committees and Subcommittees

House Appropriations Subcommittee on the Departments of Labor and Health, Education and Welfare. Room 2358, Rayburn House Office Bldg., Washington, DC 20515. (202) 225-3508. The subcommittee approves appropriations for the Corporation for Public Broadcasting.

House Appropriations Subcommittee on the Departments of State, Justice, and Commerce, the Judiciary and Related Agencies. Room H309, Capitol Bldg., Washington, DC 20515. (202) 225-3351. The subcommittee's authority includes the Board for International Broadcasting, USIA, FCC and FTC.

House Appropriations Subcommittee on the Treasury, Postal Service, and the General Government. Room H164, Capitol Bldg., Washington, DC 20515. (202) 225-5834. The subcommittee supervises OTP appropriations.

House Government Operations Subcommittee on

Commerce, Consumer, and Monetary Affairs. Room B350b, Rayburn House Office Bldg., Washington, DC 20515. (202) 225-4407. The subcommittee is concerned with consumer issues in reform of regulatory agencies. It has held hearings on FTC's Bureau of Consumer Protection.

House Committee on Interstate and Foreign Commerce. Room 2125, Rayburn House Office Bldg., Washington, DC 20515. (202) 225-2927. Most commercial and noncommercial telecommunications matters involve interstate commerce and come under the primary jurisdiction of this committee. Significant hearings and inquiries, however, are usually conducted by the subcommittees below:

House Interstate and Foreign Commerce Subcommittee on Communications. Room B331, Rayburn House Office Bldg., Washington, DC 20515. (202) 225-9034. This subcommittee has the broadest jurisdiction on communications issues in the House. In recent years the subcommittee has examined domestic common carrier competition, CATV, public broadcasting, equal employment opportunity, broadcast advertising, political broadcasting, and the Fairness Doctrine, and has conducted general FCC oversight. In 1976 the subcommittee started a comprehensive review of the entire Communications Act of 1934.

House Interstate and Foreign Commerce Subcommittee on Oversight and Investigations. Room 2323, Rayburn House Office Bldg., Washington, DC 20515. (202) 225-4441. The subcommittee shares oversight functions with the communications subcommittee and has been concerned with the reform of administrative agencies.

House Judiciary Subcommittee on Courts, Civil Liberties and the Administration of Justice. Room 2137, Rayburn House Office Bldg., Washington, DC 20515. (202) 225-3926. The subcommittee has dealt with such issues as wiretapping, pornography and obscenity, and shield legislation for reporters.

House Judiciary Subcommittee on Monopolies and Commercial Law. Room 2137, Rayburn House Office Bldg., Washington, DC 20515. (202) 225-8088. The subcommittee's authority includes legislation or investigations into communications ownership issues.

House Small Business Committee. Room 2361, Rayburn House Office Bldg., Washington, DC 20515. (202)

225-5821. The committee is concerned in part with communications and small business. Through subcommittees it has examined the inability of minority communications companies to get Small Business Administration loans, and it has studied "all-channel (AM-FM) radio" legislation.

Senate Committees and Subcommittees

Senate Appropriations Subcommittee for Labor, Health, Education and Welfare, and Related Agencies. Room 1108, Dirksen Senate Office Bldg., Washington, DC 20510. (202) 224-7283. The subcommittee's responsibilities include CPB appropriations.

Senate Appropriations Subcommittee for the Departments of State, Justice and Commerce, the Judiciary and Related Agencies. Room S146a, Capitol Bldg., Washington, DC 20510. (202) 224-7244. The subcommittee handles appropriations for the Board for International Broadcasting, FCC, FTC and USIA, among others.

Senate Appropriations Subcommittee for Treasury, the Postal Service, and General Government. Room 1406, Dirksen Senate Office Bldg., Washington, DC 20510. (202) 224-0330. The subcommittee considers all OTP appropriations.

Senate Committee on Commerce, Science and Transportation. Room 5202, Dirksen Senate Office Bldg., Washington, DC 20510. (202) 224-5115. As is also the case in the House, this committee's communications subcommittee holds most important hearings. The full committee, however, conducts confirmation hearings for many presidential appointments to agencies such as the FCC and CPB.

Senate Commerce Subcommittee on Communications. Room 233, Russell Senate Office Bldg., Washington, DC 20510. (202) 224-9321. Like its House counterpart, the subcommittee is charged with review of nearly all communications-related legislation. It plays an active role in confirmation hearings conducted by the parent committee. Recent interests have included common carrier competition and rural telecommunications.

Senate Committee on Governmental Affairs. Room 3300, Dirksen Senate Office Bldg., Washington, DC 20510. (202) 224-4943. Through a special study unit, the committee has been actively involved in study of administrative agencies and laws governing their operation. It has also studied freedom of information and privacy.

Senate Judiciary Committee. Room 2226, Dirksen Senate Office Bldg., Washington, DC 20510. (202) 224-5225. The former jurisdiction of the Patents, Trademarks and Copyrights Subcommittee is now assumed by this committee, which is parent to several significant subcommittees (below).

Senate Judiciary Subcommittee on Administrative Practice and Procedure. Room 162, Russell Senate Office Bldg., Washington, DC 20510. (202) 224-5617. The subcommittee is concerned with amendments to the Administrative Procedure Act and with general regulatory reform.

Senate Judiciary Subcommittee on Antitrust and Monopoly. Room A517, Senate Office Bldg., 1919 D Street, Washington, DC 20510. (202) 224-5573. Like its House counterpart, the subcommittee considers communications monopoly practices. It has studied AT&T and other common carriers and, more recently, CATV.

Senate Judiciary Subcommittee on the Constitution. Room 102b, Russell Senate Office Bldg., Washington, DC 20510. (202) 224-8191. The subcommittee combines the responsibilities of the former subcommittees on constitutional rights and liberties and on amendments. It has broad free speech–free press interests and is concerned with free press, fair trial and shield law legislation.

Independent Agencies and Commissions

Two independent commissions, the FCC and the FTC, are so dominant in communications policy that they are listed first and described in detail. Other agencies follow.

Federal Communications Commission. 1919 M Street, N.W., Washington, DC 20554. (202) 632-7000. The FCC was created by the Communications ACT of 1934 and succeeded the 1927-1934 Federal Radio Commission. Its seven members are appointed by the president, approved by the Senate and serve staggered seven-year terms. It regulates nongovernmental interstate and foreign communications by telegraph, telephone, radio and TV broadcast, cable television, CB radio, satellite and special and safety services. Broadcast station licenses and CATV certificates of compliance are granted and renewed by this agency.

The FCC's Consumer Assistance Office (Room 258) helps outsiders deal with the agency and locate information and staff assistance. Press releases and official FCC documents can be obtained from the Public Information Office, Room 202, (202) 632-7260.

In some cases it may be appropriate to call the Office of the Chairman, Room 814, (202) 632-6336. The FCC is organized into offices and bureaus (see organization chart). Offices usually handle professional activities (legal, engineering, etc.), while bureaus are organized by function. Some important offices and bureaus are described below. Addresses are for the main FCC building unless otherwise indicated.

See FCC chart on opposite page

Office of Administrative Law Judges. Room 632, (202) 632-7680. The office conducts hearings and issues initial decisions in adjudicatory cases, including licensing.

Office of General Counsel. Room 614, (202) 632-7020. The office represents the FCC in courts and offers internal legal advice.

Review Board. Room 602, (202) 632-7180. The board reviews initial decisions of administrative law judges prior to further review, if any, by the full FCC.

Office of Chief Engineer. Room 7002, 2025 M Street, N.W., Washington, DC 20554. (202) 632-7060. The office advises the FCC on engineering matters, including spectrum allocation.

Field Operations Bureau. Room 734, (202) 632-6980. The bureau deals with violations of technical and operational rules. It monitors and inspects stations for this purpose.

Broadcast Bureau. Room 314, (202) 632-6460. The bureau has general responsibility for broadcast services. Its Complaints and Compliance Division, Room 332, (202) 632-6968, handles compliance with policies such as the Fairness Doctrine and equal time. The Renewal and Transfer Division, Room 702, (202) 632-6993, processes station license renewals or changes in ownership.

Cable Television Bureau. Room 6008, 2025 M Street, N.W., Washington, DC 20554. (202) 632-6480. The bureau is responsible for CATV rules and issuing

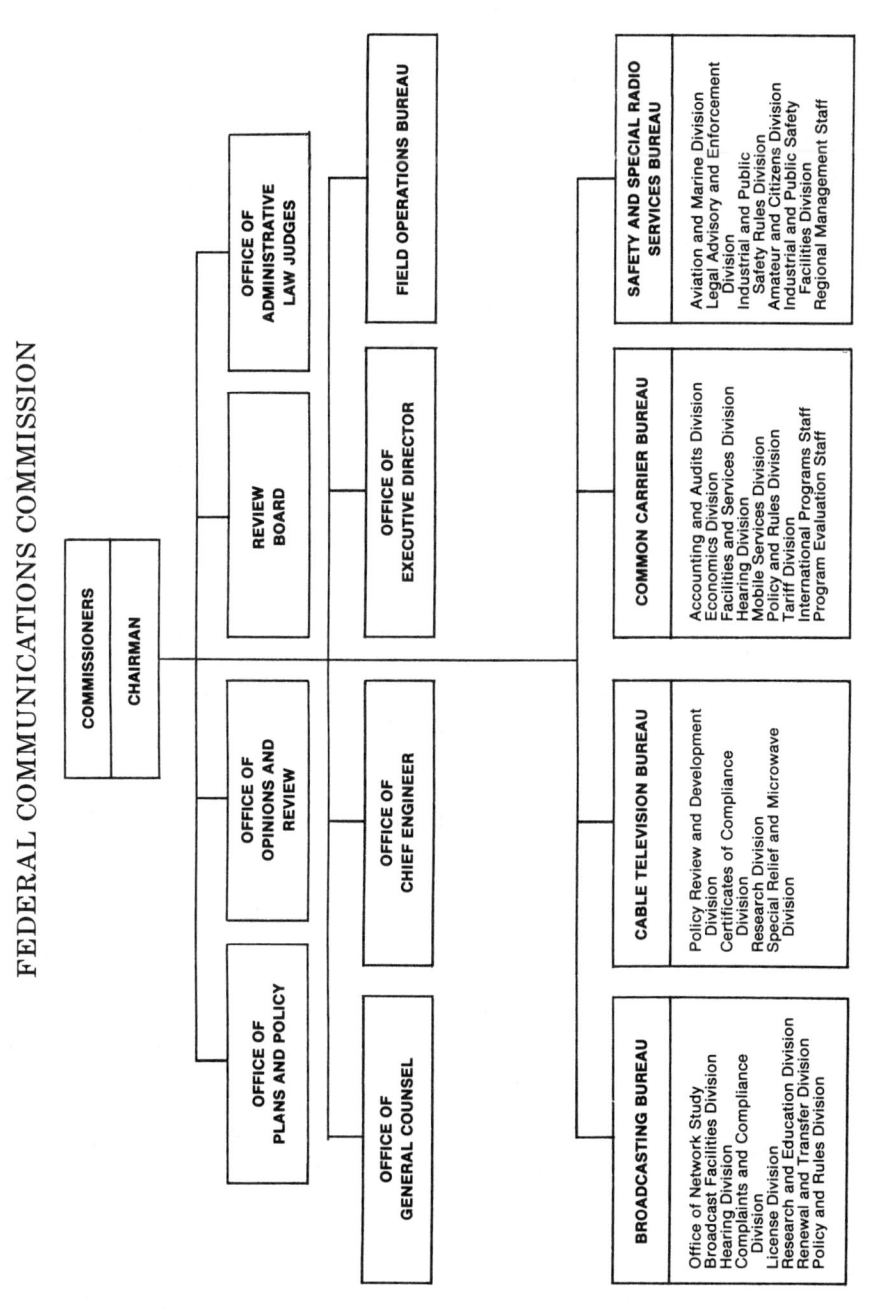

Government Policymaking Bodies: United States 183

Simplified Organization Chart — 1977
FEDERAL COMMUNICATIONS COMMISSION

COMMISSIONERS
CHAIRMAN

- OFFICE OF PLANS AND POLICY
- OFFICE OF OPINIONS AND REVIEW
- REVIEW BOARD
- OFFICE OF ADMINISTRATIVE LAW JUDGES

- OFFICE OF GENERAL COUNSEL
- OFFICE OF CHIEF ENGINEER
- OFFICE OF EXECUTIVE DIRECTOR
- FIELD OPERATIONS BUREAU

BROADCASTING BUREAU
- Office of Network Study
- Broadcast Facilities Division
- Hearing Division
- Complaints and Compliance Division
- License Division
- Research and Education Division
- Renewal and Transfer Division
- Policy and Rules Division

CABLE TELEVISION BUREAU
- Policy Review and Development Division
- Certificates of Compliance Division
- Research Division
- Special Relief and Microwave Division

COMMON CARRIER BUREAU
- Accounting and Audits Division
- Economics Division
- Facilities and Services Division
- Hearing Division
- Mobile Services Division
- Policy and Rules Division
- Tariff Division
- International Programs Staff
- Program Evaluation Staff

SAFETY AND SPECIAL RADIO SERVICES BUREAU
- Aviation and Marine Division
- Legal Advisory and Enforcement Division
- Industrial and Public Safety Rules Division
- Amateur and Citizens Division
- Industrial and Public Safety Facilities Division
- Regional Management Staff

"certificates of compliance," which permit system operation. Its Cable Complaints Service, Room 6330, (202) 632-9703, receives public complaints about CATV system violations of FCC rules and policies.

Common Carrier Bureau. Room 500, (202) 632-6910. The bureau is responsible for all common carriers under the FCC's supervision, including telephone, telegraph, radio and satellites.

Safety and Special Radio Services Bureau. Room 5002, 2025 M Street, N.W., Washington, DC 20554. (202) 632-6940. The bureau licenses and regulates radio for purposes such as aviation, industrial and public safety; and citizens' band.

Federal Trade Commission. 6th Street and Pennsylvania Avenue, N.W., Washington, DC 20580. (202) 523-3625. Created by the Federal Trade Commission Act in 1914 and given significant added powers by Congress in 1938 and 1975, the Federal Trade Commission is charged with protecting the public from anticompetitive behavior and unfair and deceptive business practices. The structure of media industries, including mergers, and advertising practices are supervised by the FTC. Its five members are named by the president, approved by the Senate, and serve rotating seven-year terms. Information about the FTC is available from its Office of Public Information, Room 496, (202) 523-3830.

Like the FCC, the FTC is organized into bureaus and offices, as shown in the organization chart that follows. Major offices and bureaus are described below. Offices are located in the main FTC building unless otherwise noted.

See FTC chart on opposite page

Office of Administrative Law Judges. Room 7118, 1101 Pennsylvania Avenue, N.W., Washington, DC 20580. (202) 724-1511. The judges conduct adjudicative cases and issue initial decisions.

Office of General Counsel. Room 568, (202) 523-3613. The office represents the FTC in court, advises the commission on policy, and issues advisory opinions.

Bureau of Competition. Room 372, (202) 523-3601. In cooperation with the Antitrust Division of the Department of Justice, the bureau enforces antitrust laws against anticompetitive practices and unrea-

Government Policymaking Bodies: United States 185

Simplified Organization Chart — 1977
FEDERAL TRADE COMMISSION

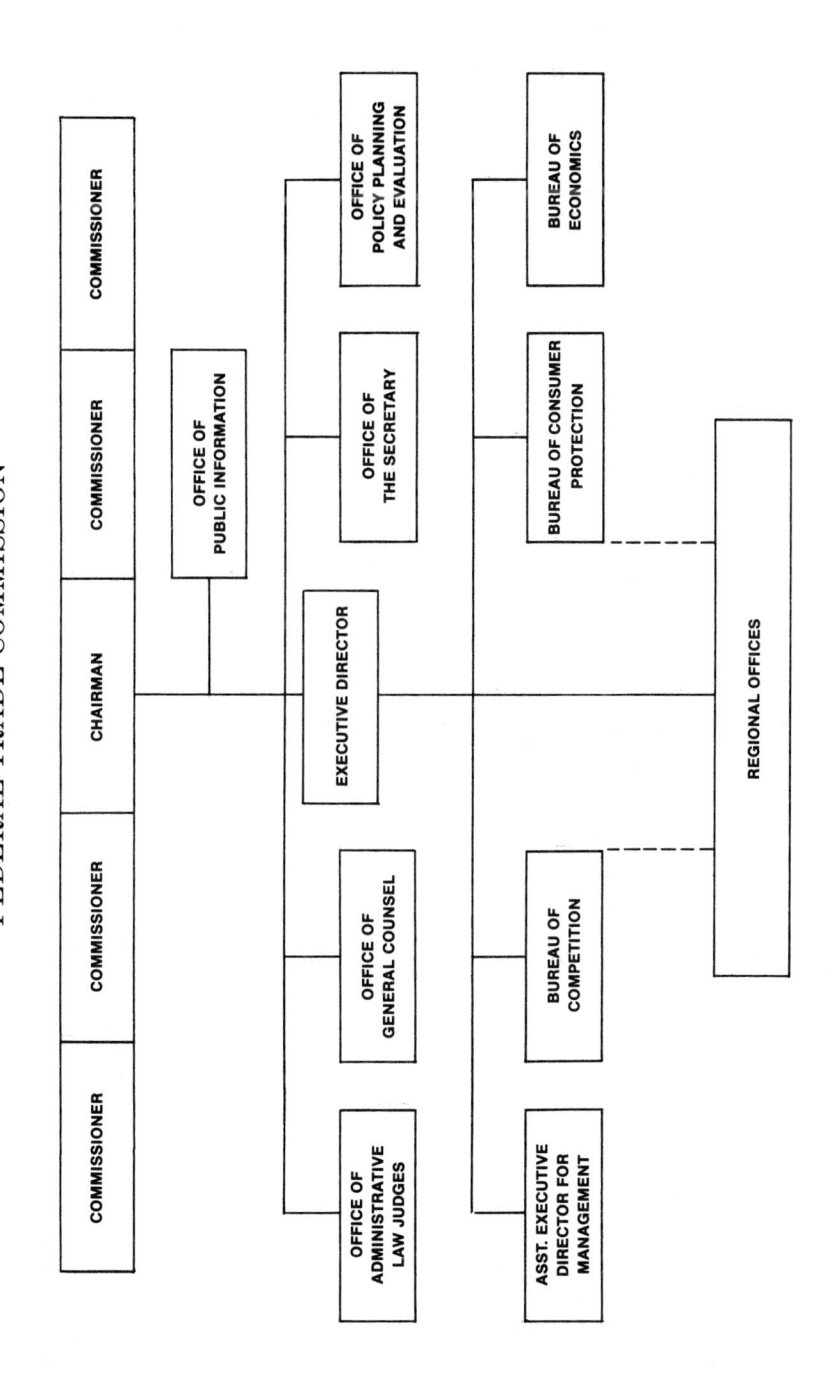

```
COMMISSIONER — COMMISSIONER — COMMISSIONER — CHAIRMAN — COMMISSIONER — COMMISSIONER

                                    |
         ┌──────────────────────────┼──────────────────────────┐
         |                          |                          |
  OFFICE OF                  OFFICE OF                  OFFICE OF
  ADMINISTRATIVE             PUBLIC INFORMATION         POLICY PLANNING
  LAW JUDGES                                            AND EVALUATION

  OFFICE OF                  EXECUTIVE DIRECTOR         OFFICE OF
  GENERAL COUNSEL                                       THE SECRETARY

  ASST. EXECUTIVE            BUREAU OF                  BUREAU OF
  DIRECTOR FOR               CONSUMER                   ECONOMICS
  MANAGEMENT                 PROTECTION

  BUREAU OF
  COMPETITION

                    REGIONAL OFFICES
```

sonable or unfair restraints of trade.

Bureau of Consumer Protection. Room 468, (202) 523-3727. The bureau investigates and litigates cases involving acts or practices thought to be deceptive or unfair to consumers. It is the most active branch of the FCC in advertising regulation, and it prepares appropriate trade regulation rules.

Bureau of Economics. Room 700, 2120 L Street, N.W., Washington, DC 20037. (202) 254-7721. The bureau aids and advises the FTC on the economic aspects of its activities and prepares economic reports and surveys.

Board for International Broadcasting. 1030 15th Street, N.W., Washington, DC 20005. (202) 254-8040. The board has oversight responsibility for Radio Free Europe/Radio Liberty. It is expected to see that broadcasts fit the context of U.S. foreign policy.

Federal Election Commission. 1325 K Street, N.W., Washington, DC 20463. (202) 523-4089. Some commission decisions affect FCC political broadcasting cases.

National Aeronautics and Space Administration. 400 Maryland Avenue, S.W., Washington, DC 20546. (202) 755-8344. NASA plays an active role in satellite policy.

National Foundation on the Arts and the Humanities. 806 15th Street, N.W., Washington, DC 20506. (202) 382-4091. Through its separate endowments on the arts and on humanities, the foundation has participated in funding public television and radio programs.

National Science Foundation. 1800 G Street, N.W., Washington, DC 20550. (202) 632-7970. NSF funds both basic and applied communications research.

U.S. Commission on Civil Rights. 1121 Vermont Avenue, N.W., Washington, DC 20425. (202) 254-6600. The commission has issued several reports critical of equal employment opportunities in broadcasting and of the work of agencies, like the FCC, with equal employment opportunity responsibilities.

Federal Courts

State courts and federal courts make policy contributions through their decisions in litigated cases. The two courts listed below are the ones most frequently involved in important communications cases.

Supreme Court of the United States. 1 1st Street, N.E., Washington, DC 20543. (202) 393-1640. The Supreme Court is the court of last appeal in the United States and is the final arbiter on the meaning of the Constitution. In recent years it has decided significant cases on the Pentagon Papers, CATV, copyright, advertising law, libel, privacy, broadcasting, and press coverage of trials. Information requests should be directed to the Public Information Office.

U.S. Court of Appeals for the District of Columbia Circuit. 3rd Street and Constitution Avenue, N.W., Washington, DC 20001. (202) 426-7182. This court is usually the first to hear appeals of FCC decisions, although some appeals may start in federal district courts or in other appeals courts. As with the Pentagon Papers case, the court is often an important intermediate court of appeal in non-FCC matters involving federal agencies prior to a final decision by the U.S. Supreme Court.

B. *U.S. Government References and Publications*

There are many ways to enter the seemingly confused world of regulatory policy and legal documentation. The first step combines (1) an understanding of the key agencies of government involved, with (2) an understanding of the documents issued by those agencies, what is in them, and how to use them. The second step is to have as clear a conception as possible of either the issue or the specific case or decision being sought. These few pages offer an introduction to this process, by briefly annotating the major sources that regularly present material on communication regulation. For background introductions, see the books noted in Section XI. The most current reports and analyses of government actions are in the trade periodicals and other journals noted in Section X.

To aid in rapid reference, this listing has been divided into the following categories:
- Handbooks for to Legal and Government Documents
- Major Indexes to Regulatory Material
- Specialized Directories and Abstracts on Communications Regulation
- General Guides to Government Organization and Operation
- Executive Branch Documents

FCC and FTC Documents
Congressional Documents
Judicial Branch Documents

Virtually all of this material will be found in federal depository libraries, which are usually located on major university campuses, in large municipal libraries, or in law libraries.

Handbooks for Legal and Government Documents

The following bibliographies and guides are all commercially published materials, since the government publishes little in the way of guides to regulation and policy. The listing progresses from the introductory texts on legal research to useful bibliographies and guides to government documents.

How to Find the Law by Morris L. Cohen (St. Paul, MN: West Publishing Co., 1976, 7th ed.), and *Fundamentals of Legal Research* by J. Myron Jacobstein and Roy M. Mersky (Mineola, NY: Foundation Press, 1977, 5th ed.) are standard, up-to-date, and comprehensive textbook introductions to the paper documentation issued by all branches of government, especially the Congress and Courts. (There are shorter paperback versions of both available from the same publishers.) Details are given on which agency issues what, contents of specific documents, how they are arranged and indexed, and how to use what is available.

"Researching Regulation," *Journal of Broadcasting* 17:131-157 (Spring, 1973) contains "Broadcast Legal Documentation: A Four-Dimensional Guide" by Don R. Le Duc; and "Broadcast Regulation Research: A Primer for Non-Lawyers" by Joseph M. Foley. While these articles focus on broadcasting examples, the general information on sources and citation is invaluable as a brief introduction to a complex subject.

Guide to Reference Books by Eugene P. Sheehy (Chicago: American Library Association, 1976, 9th ed.) is a standard one-volume work found in most libraries. It provides a detailed annotated guide to works on all subjects, including every aspect of government regulation in this country and abroad. An excellent index makes this easy to use.

Research Resources: Annotated Guide to the Social Sciences (Santa Barbara, CA: ABC-Clio, 1971) is a complete annotated guide to publications (and their use)

from all branches of the government. It includes serial publications, annuals, directories, and other material.
Government Publications and Their Use by Lawrence F. Schmeckebier and Roy B. Eastin (Washington: Brookings Institution, 1969, 3rd ed.) remains the classic yet unofficial guide to who publishes what and how best to use each item.

Major Indexes to Regulatory Material

These are the most important general indexes to government and private legal and regulatory publications. Federal depositories and law libraries have many other more specialized indexes, as well as indexes which offer coverage of other countries.

Monthly Catalog of United States Government Publications (Washington: GPO, 1895-date, monthly, with semiannual and annual indexes) lists almost all publications of any branch of the federal government. Since July, 1976, it has been enlarged to provide more information on each document. Arrangement is by listing agency, but the excellent subject index can also be used.

Cumulative Subject Index to the Monthly Catalog of United States Government Publications, 1900-1971 (Washington: Carrollton Press, 1973-1975, 15 volumes) provides a single subject index to 800,000 government publications for a 72-year period, thus lessening search time through the *Catalog* indexes.

The Declassified Documents Reference System Retrospective Collection (Washington: Carrollton Press, 1976, 3 volumes) supplements both the *Monthly Catalog and the Cumulative Subject Index* to it by abstracting and providing a subject index to some 8,000 previously classified titles not listed in the *Catalog*. This publication, which consists of Part 1 (Catalog of Abstracts, two volumes) and Part 2 (Cumulative Subject Index), will have annual updates.

Index to United States Government Periodicals (Chicago: Infordata International Corp., 1972-date) is a privately produced "reader's guide" to some 150 government periodicals. It is computer-generated with quarterly issues and indexes and is bound into an annual volume.

Federal Index (Cleveland: Predicasts Inc., 1976-date, monthly). This service indexes several already indexed publications, but combines them in a single book to help make literature searches easier. Included are the Congressional Record, Federal Register, Commerce Business Daily, presidential documents, and the *Washington Post*, with references to *CFR*, the U.S. Code, and bills and documents in Congress.

Index to Legal Periodicals (New York: H.W. Wilson, 1909-date, monthly) is a "reader's guide" to more than 350 law journals and related periodicals, with monthly, annual, and three-year cumulations. There are earlier and other current services, but this one is the accepted classic for American law periodicals.

Specialized Directories and Abstracts on Communications Regulation

As broadcasting is by far the most regulated of the mass media, the material here primarily refers to radio, television, and CATV. "A Bibliography of Articles on Broadcasting in Law Periodicals," *Journal of Broadcasting* 14:83-156 (Winter, 1969-70) provides annotated subject-divided listings up to 1955, and author-and-subject-indexed nonannotated listings for the period from 1956 through 1968.

Directory of Congressional Press, Legislative and Administrative Assistants (Washington: National Newspaper Association, annual) provides an alphabetical listing of all senators and representatives, followed by a state-by-state listing of congressional delegations. The listing includes rooms and telephone numbers for each senator and representative, followed by the names of their administrative assistants, press assistants and legislative aides. The directory also contains listings of press contacts for the White House, cabinet officers, federal agencies, miscellaneous numbers for Congress, and courts located in the District of Columbia.

Media Law Reporter (Washington: Bureau of National Affairs, 1977-date, weekly) carries selected agency rulings as well as the full text of selected federal and state court decisions affecting newspapers, magazines, television and radio. Each issue contains a topical index, an index-digest, and a table of cases. There are also cumulations and annual bound volumes. The more important earlier material will be published soon in another volume. This appears to be the single most useful source, at least after 1976.

Pike and Fischer Radio Regulation (Washington:

Pike and Fischer, 1948-date, subscription service) reprints nearly all FCC decisions and reports on radio, television and cable communications, plus abstracts and texts of decisions on broadcasting/cable issues made by the Supreme Court, the Court of Appeals for the District of Columbia, and lesser courts. This is a comprehensive but complicated set to use; the "how to use this book" material at the front of the "Current Service" volumes and the indexes in the new "Finding Aids, Master Index, Forms" volume should be consulted first.

Radio Laws of the United States (Washington: GPO, irregularly revised). Not really an index or an abstract, this compilation reprints in chronological order facsimiles of all acts dealing with wireless and radio from 1910 to date, including the 1934 Act and all its amendments. It is issued as an unnumbered document of the House of Representatives.

General Guides to Government Organization and Operation

The following publications provide guides to the organization and operation of agencies of all branches of the federal government and report on their recent activities.

United States Government Manual (Washington: GPO, annual) is an official handbook that details the origin, background, statutory authority and function of agencies of all branches of the federal government, noting how they interrelate and listing their locations, telephone numbers, and principal personnel. There are about 40 charts and a good index. The manual is vital to an understanding of the flow of law and the regulatory process. The title has varied somewhat over the years.

Encyclopedia of Governmental Advisory Organizations (Detroit: Gale Research, 1975, 2nd ed.). In 10 major subject categories (and many subcategories, including telecommunications), this volume lists the various agencies, their background, authority, and publications issued. It is alphabetical, has key word indexes, and is updated by booklet releases about every six months.

National Journal (Washington: Government Research Corporation, 1969-date, weekly) is an authoritative though nonofficial "news magazine" of the previous week's government activities in all branches. Included are decisions of agencies, new laws, presidential announcements, background reports on important topics, and political matters. Each issue is indexed, and there are quarterly and semiannual cumulations. See also *Congressional Quarterly Weekly Report*.

United States Law Week: General Law (Washington: Bureau of National Affairs, 1931-date, weekly) provides texts of selected decisions and orders of executive agencies, decisions of state and federal courts, and information on legislative affairs. It is indexed, by subject, bimonthly and annually.

Executive Branch Documents

Included here are sources of government agency rules and regulations, and publications of the Office of Telecommunications Policy.

Code of Federal Regulations (Washington: GPO, 1949-date, annual in some 70 volumes) provides codification by subject matter of all current administrative rules and regulations. Title 16 provides rules and regulations of the Federal Trade Commission, and Title 47 provides rules of both the Federal Communications Commission and the Office of Telecommunications Policy. Changes in these rules and regulations appear in the *Federal Register* and are then included in the next annual issue of *CFR*. *CFR* has its own general index volume, also revised annually.

Federal Register (Washington: GPO, 1936-date, daily), the best official source for recent agency documents, provides official texts of all presidential executive orders and proclamations, new or modified rules and regulations of all federal agencies (including independent agencies), and decisions of fact-finding bodies. Back issues are usually microcopied in libraries. It publishes monthly, quarterly, and annual indexes.

Specific agency publications (annual reports and sometimes other documents) are available from:
Board for International Broadcasting
Copyright Office (Library of Congress)
General Accounting Office
Office of Education (Department of HEW)
Office of Telecommunication (Department of Commerce)
Office of Telecommunications (Policy Executive Office
  of the President)
United States Information Agency

Agencies can usually provide bibliographies of recent publications, and agency annual reports often contain similar lists.

FCC and FTC Documents

As is the case with most federal agencies, a vast amount of paper comes from the FCC and FTC, and this listing is only selective of the more important material likely to be found in a library.

A useful guide for research on the FCC is Erwin Krasnow and G. Gail Crotts' "Inside the FCC: A Guide for Information Seekers," *Public Tele-communications Review* 3:4:49-56 (July-August, 1975), which details FCC publications, offices and officials, file organization and how to make best use of all these. Major FCC publications are:

Annual Report (1935-date) provides a review of FCC activities for the fiscal year in broadcasting and common carrier communications. Since 1967 it has also included a detailed statistical report on finances and employment in the broadcasting industry.

Federal Communications Commission Reports (1935-date, weekly with bound cumulations). Decisions in cases and docket reports are issued in weekly pamphlets (available from GPO by subscription) and are later bound. While a volume per year was long standard, by the 1970s it took five volumes to cover a year's work. There are separate index volumes for the first (to 1965) and the second series.

Statistics of the Communications Common Carriers (1939-date, annual) contains financial and operating statistics as reported by the telegraph and telephone industries and specialized carriers.

Annual Broadcast Financial Data (annual, processed). Separate reports for AM-FM radio and for television are issued six to eight months after each calendar year, with both national and market data (much of this is found in the *Annual Report*).

Television Broadcast Programming Data (1973-date, annual, processed). Based on licensee reports, this provides market-by-market data on amounts of news and public affairs programming in a typical week.

Rules and Regulations (irregularly revised). The FCC can supply a list of the various volumes and their cost. These are also printed in *CFR* (see Executive Branch Documents).

Major FTC publications are:

Annual Report (1915-date) provides a summary of the previous fiscal year's FTC activities.

Federal Trade Commission Decisions (1915-date, subscription with bound cumulations) is the official reporter of FTC orders and case decisions. It is published in about two volumes per year.

FTC Organization, Procedure and Statutes (revised every several years) is a guide to how the FTC operates, its statutory authority, and the sanctions it can impose.

Congressional Documents

The following are the major publications, directories, and indexes to the two Houses of Congress and their committees:

Congressional Directory (1809-date, one edition per congressional session) lists the organization and membership (including member biographies) of both Houses, including the makeup of committee membership and staffs.

Congressional Staff Directory (Mt. Vernon, VA: Congressional Staff Directory, 1959-date, annual) lists committee assignments of members of Congress and provides details on committee staff personnel and organization for Congress and closely related agencies.

Congressional Quarterly Weekly Report (Washington: Congressional Quarterly Service, 1946-date, weekly) is a news service with a summary of House and Senate developments, both political and legislative, including vote charts. See also *Congressional Quarterly Almanac* (1945-date), which is a fully indexed review of the previous session's legislation, divided by subject. The same publisher's *Congress and the Nation* (volumes for 1945-64, 1965-68, 1969-72, and 1973-76) surveys government and politics, based on material from the annual *Almanacs*.

Federal Laws Affecting Newspapers (Washington: National Newspaper Association) is a six-part pamphlet series on federal laws as they relate to newspapers and newspaper publishing. Subjects covered include laws relating to employment, postal regulations, advertising, the Freedom of Information Act, occupational safety and health, and public notice.

United States Code Congressional and Administrative News (St. Paul, MN: West Publishing Co., 1939-date, semimonthly, while Congress is in session, or monthly, with annual cumulation) contains texts of major public laws and legislative histories, plus executive orders and administrative agency regulations.

Congressional Record (1873-date, daily) is the official journal of both House and Senate, with transcripts of floor debates, presidential messages, and additional material inserted by members. Frequent indexes are published by name, subject, and bills. The annual bound volumes are paginated differently, so it is important to know whether a citation is to the daily record or to a bound copy.

Congressional Index Service (Chicago: Commerce Clearing House, 1937-date, weekly) cumulates to two volumes per Congress (one for the Senate and one for the House), indexing all congressional bills and resolutions of general interest and listing their current status.

Congressional Information Service (Washington: Congressional Information Service, 1970-date, monthly with annual cumulation) provides abstracts (one volume) and index (one volume) to all published House, Senate, and joint committee hearings, committee prints, documents, reports, and miscellaneous documents. It has a detailed index of names and subjects. There is a *Five-Year Cumulative Index, 1970-74*.

Checklist of Congressional Hearings (Lanham, MD: Bernan Associates, Inc., 1958-date, weekly) is an annotated listing, appearing while Congress is in session, of published transcripts of hearings conducted by committees and subcommittees of both Houses. It covers about 1,000 published hearings.

United States Statutes at Large (Washington: GPO, 1875-date, annual) contains chronologically ordered printing of all public laws, reorganization plans, private laws, concurrent resolutions, and proclamations for a given congressional session, one volume per year. Thus the 1934 Communications Act is in the 1934 volume, but the reader would have to search the subject indexes of each later volume for all amendments.

United States Code Annotated (St. Paul, MN: West Publishing Co., 1927-date, irregular revision, 50 volumes). Though unofficial, this is more current (includes quarterly and annual pocket parts) and provides annotations to the official *United States Code* (Washington: GPO, revised every six years: current edition, 1977). USCA provides a subject-organized compilation of laws of a general and permanent nature (*i.e.*, the original law as amended), and it is thus the most useful research source for finding current law.

Judicial Branch Documents

Law libraries contain many official and unofficial court "reporter" series which provide texts of court decisions on all levels of government. Listings begin with the Supreme Court, followed by a very selective list of other sources. Publications issued by West Publishing Co. make use of a common key number system, which makes cross-reference easier.

United State Reports (Washington: GPO, 1922-date, two or three volumes per court session) is the official and complete text of all Supreme Court decisions. Earlier years were reported and published privately. In addition, there are two private reporter systems which also include the official texts, plus additional material: *Supreme Court Reporter* (St. Paul, MN: West Publishing, 1882-date, two volumes per session) includes edited headnotes and other features; and *United States Supreme Court Reports* (Cedarhurst, NY: Lawyers Cooperative Publishing Co., three or more volumes per court session) includes the official texts of decisions, plus case summaries, annotations by the editors, and summaries of briefs of counsel.

United States Law Week: Supreme Court (Washington: Bureau of National Affairs, 1931-date, weekly) carries a complete text of all decisions, a topical index, and a journal and calendar of Supreme Court cases.

Federal Reporter (St. Paul, MN: West Publishing Co., 1880-date, several volumes per year) has covered various courts, but consistently includes the U.S. Court of Appeals (which for the District of Columbia is crucial in appeals of FCC decisions), and the courts of lesser importance (for communications): the Court of Customs and Patent Appeals, and the Court of Claims. This is a commercial reporter; there is no official version for the U.S. Court of Appeals.

American Law Reports (Cedarhurst, NY: Lawyers Cooperative Publishing Co., 1919-date, several volumes per year) contain selected appellate court decisions, supplemented with often extensive comment on the points of law raised. There are three series (1919-1948, 1948-1965,

1965-date), plus a newer service on federal courts (1969-date.)

Shepard's Citations (Colorado Springs, CO: Shepard's Citations, 1873-date, many different series). There are sets of these paralleling most official and commercial law reporters. They do not print cases or decisions but provide a type of historical index telling what happened to cases on appeal, how points of law were used as precedents, and so on. How to use these invaluable tools is detailed in "How to Use Shepard's Citations" (available from the publisher), or can be determined at the desk of most libraries having the Citations.

2. GOVERNMENT POLICYMAKING BODIES IN CANADA (organizations and publications combined)

Executive Branch

Canada Post. Hon. Jean-Jacques Blais, Minister. Sir Alexander Campbell Building, Confederation Heights, Ottawa, Ontario K1A OB1. The Post Office was established in 1867 and now fulfills its function via five directorates: Corporate Affairs, Operational Services, Finance and Administration, Marketing, and Personnel.

Publication:
Annual Report. 1867—.

Communications Canada. Hon. Jeanne Sauvé, Minister. Journal Tower/North Building, 300 Slater Street, Ottawa, Ontario K1A OC8. The Department of Communications, established in 1969, is responsible for ensuring universal Canadian access to a broad range of communications services. In fulfilling its task, the department considers complex social, environmental, human and economic patterns before and after new communications devices are instituted, and also conducts research in technological advances in telecommunications. The minister is responsible for the Radio Act, The Telegraphs Act, the Teleglobe Act, the Telesat Canada Act, and is also the spokesperson to Parliament for the Canadian Radio-television and Telecommunications Commission.

Periodicals:
Annual Report. 1969—.

In Search, the Canadian Communications Quarterly. 1974—. A bilingual magazine of information and opinion offering a selection of articles to generate awareness of all aspects of telecommunications. (See listing on page 300.)

60 Days. 1974—. A newsletter appearing every two months offering brief summaries of departmental research and affairs.

Monographs:
Branching Out. Ottawa, 1972. The report of the Canadian Computer/Communications Task Force, established to develop and recommend specific policies and institutions that will ensure the orderly and efficient growth of combined computer/communications systems in the public interest.

Instant World. Ottawa, 1971. A report of the Telecommission which involved 50 studies, a comprehensive study of the present state and future prospects of telecommunications in Canada.

Privacy and Computers. Ottawa, 1972. A report of the joint task force established by the Department of Communications and the Department of Justice, whose purpose it was to discover and report the practices and laws relating to privacy and computers in Canada.

Publications of the Communications Research Centre, P.O. Box 490, Station A, Ottawa, Ontario K1N 8T5, the principal research facility of the Department of Communications, are:

Index of Research Publications. Ottawa, 1972.

Communications Research Centre Technical Note. No. 1—

Communications Research Centre Report. No. 1—.

Consumer and Corporate Affairs. Hon. Tony Abbott, Minister. 1 Place du Portage, Hull, Quebec. The department is responsible for such areas as consumer affairs, corporations and corporate securities, combines, patents, copyrights, trademarks and industrial designs.

It has been involved in cases of misleading advertising, and multiple and conglomerate media ownership.

Publications:
Annual Report. 1970—.

Bureau of Corporate Affairs Bulletin. Monthly.

Patent Office Record. Weekly.

Trademarks Journal. Weekly.

Restrictive Trade Practices Commission Report. Irregular.

Ministry of State for Science and Technology. Hon. Hugh Faulkner, Minister. Martel Building, 270 Albert Street, Ottawa, Ontario K1A 1A1. Established in 1970, the Ministry is responsible for policy formulation and development regarding the actions of the Government of Canada that affect the growth and application of science and technology. A recent project of the Ministry involved research on the flow of science news to the Canadian public via mass media.

Publications:
Annual Report. 1970—.

Media Impact. Two volumes. Vol. II, "Science, Mass Media and the Public," by Orest Dubas and Lisa Martel. Ottawa, 1975.

Secretary of State. Hon. John Roberts, Minister. 65 Slater Street, Ottawa, Ontario K1A OM5. The Secretary of State is one of the oldest federal government departments. In conjunction with such organizations as the C.B.C., N.F.B., C.F.D.C., and the Canada Council, its Arts and Culture Branch develops policies which encourage artistic and cultural activities in Canada.

Publication:
Annual Report. 1968—.

Statistics Canada. Hon. Jean Chretien, Ministry of Industry, Trade and Commerce, Main Building, Tunney's Pasture, Ottawa, Ontario K1A OT6. Established in 1918 as the Dominion Bureau of Statistics (its name was changed in 1971), Statistics Canada compiles, analyzes, abstracts and publishes statistical information on Canada's economic and social life and conducts censuses of population, housing, merchandising, and agriculture, at five-year intervals.

Publications:
Advertising Agencies, 1974. Ottawa, 1976.

Canada Yearbook, Annual Review of Economic, Social and Political Developments in Canada. 1884—.

Communications: Monthly Survey of Radio Broadcasting Stations.

Communications: Monthly Telephone Statistics.

Market Research Handbook, 1975. Ottawa, 1976.

Motion Picture Production, 1974. Ottawa, 1976.

Motion Picture Theatres and Film Distributors, 1974. Ottawa, 1976.

Phonograph Records and Pre-recorded Tapes.

Telecommunications Statistics, 1974. Ottawa, 1976.

Transport Canada. Hon. Otto Lang, Minister. Transport Canada Building, Place de Ville, Ottawa, Ontario K1A 0N5. Transport Canada is a corporate structure of crown corporations and operating administrations which have varying degrees of autonomy. The department is involved in transport planning, policy formulation and program assessment. The minister is the spokesperson to Parliament for the Canadian Transport Commission.

Publication:
Annual Report. 1974—

Independent Agencies

Canada Council. Mrs. G. Lang, Chairperson, 255 Albert Street, P.O. Box 1047, Ottawa, Ontario, K1P 5V8. The Canada Council was established in 1957 to "foster and promote the study and enjoyment of, and the production of works in the arts, humanities and social sciences." Through its grants, the Council assists organizations and individuals in the fields of music, opera, dance, theatre, visual arts, films, writing, and publishing.

Publication:
Annual Report. 1957—.

Canadian Broadcasting Corporation. A. Johnson, President. 1500 Bronson Avenue, P.O. Box 8478, Ottawa, Ontario K1G 3J5. The C.B.C. was given a mandate in 1936 to offer broadcast services to all Canadians, thereby promoting national unity. Four radio networks have been established (AM and FM in both English and French) and two television networks (English and French). The Corporation is currently involved in its Accelerated Coverage Plan to offer services to all communities of 500 inhabitants or more and is being investigated by the Canadian Radio-television and Telecommunications Commission regarding the corporation's fulfillment of its mandate.

Publications:
Annual Report. 1936—.

Canadian Broadcasting Corporation, A Brief History. Ottawa, 1976.

Canadian Film Development Corporation. Gratien Gelinas, Chairman, 800 Place Victoria, Suite 2220, P.O. Box 71, Montreal, Quebec H4Z 1A8. The C.F.D.C. invests in Canadian productions and offers grants, loans, and other awards to film-makers. It also aids film administration and distribution.

Publication:
Annual Report. 1968/69—.

Canadian Radio-television and Telecommunications Commission. Harry Boyle, Commissioner. Berger Building, 100 Metcalfe Street, Ottawa, Ontario K1A ON2. The C.T.R.C. is a public authority created to license, regulate and supervise radio, television, cable and telecommunications common carriers in Canada. Some of the most notable C.R.T.C. regulations established Canadian content quotas and limited the amount of advertising in broadcasting. Currently, the C.R.T.C. has been empowered to conduct an inquiry into the C.B.C. and the fulfillment of the Corporation's mandate to promote national unity. All decisions of the C.R.T.C. are final, but appeals can be lodged with the Federal Court in matters of law or jurisdiction.

Periodicals:
Annual Report. 1968—.

Decisions and Orders. Irregular.

Cable Systems in Canada, 1975. Ottawa, 1975.

Public Hearings, Transcript of Proceedings. Irregular.

Monographs:
Bibliography: Some Canadian Writings on the Mass Media, Ottawa, 1974.

Canadian Transport Commission. Hon. E.J. Benson, President, Congill Building, 275 Slater Street, Ottawa, Ontario K1A ON9. As a court of record, the commission is required to perform regulatory functions under the *Railway Act,* the *Aeronautics Act* and the *Transport Act* and to generally coordinate transport carrier operations (railways, water, aircraft, extra-provincial motor vehicle undertakings, and commodity pipelines). The commission is also involved in research to achieve the objectives set in the National Transportation Policy. Its former concerns with telecommunications regulation and research have now become part of C.R.T.C. jurisdiction.

Publications:
Annual Report. 1967—.

Decisions and Orders. Irregular.

Canadian Transport Cases. 1969—.

National Film Board. Andre Lamy, Chairman, 150 Kent Street, Ottawa, Ontario K1A OM9. The Board was founded in 1939 and was instructed in 1950 to "initiate and promote the production and distribution of films in the national interest." N.F.B. is the main producer of Canadian documentaries, which are distributed nationally and internationally.

Publication:
Annual Report. 1939—.

Teleglobe Canada. J.C. Delorme, Chairman, 650 Sherbrooke St. W., Montreal, Quebec H3A 2S4. Teleglobe Canada is responsible for Canadian international cable and satellite operations and traffic and is a federal crown corporation. The corporation conducts investigations and research to improve the general quality and efficiency of telecommunication services and makes use of developments in cable and radio transmission. Teleglobe Canada was formerly known as the Canadian Overseas Telecommunication Commission.

Publication:
Annual Report. 1975—.

Telesat Canada. David A. Golden, President. 333 River Road, Ottawa, Ontario K1A 8B9. Telesat Canada was established by Parliament in 1969 to own and operate Canada's domestic satellite system. It is a corporation owned by the federal government, the common carriers and the general public. Canada is the second highest user of microwave communication systems in the world on a per capital/per mile basis.

Publication:
Annual Report. 1969—.

Legislative Branch

The legislature of the Canadian government is the Parliament of Canada. It consists of the elected House of Commons, the appointed Senate, and the sovereign as represented by the Governor-General. Regulation is introduced as bills, all of which must be read three separate times in each House, adopted by both Houses, and receive royal assent in order to become law.

Publications:
Canada Gazette, Part I. 1867—. Weekly. Contains notices of a general character, proclamations, certain orders-in-council and various classes of statutory notices. Indexed.

Canada Gazette, Part II. 1972—. Fortnightly. Contains all instruments and regulations made under statutory authority. Indexed.

Canada Gazette, Part III. 1974—. Monthly. Publishes public acts as soon as reasonably practical after they have received royal assent. Indexed.

House of Commons. Parliament Buildings, Ottawa, Ontario K1A 0A6. The House of Commons is composed of 264 elected members, representing all ten provinces and two territories.

Publications:
Debates of the House of Commons. Official report,

daily edition, later bound and indexed. 1867—.
Order Paper and Notices, daily edition (agenda).

Votes and Proceedings, daily edition.

These publications are revised and printed in bound form at the end of each session as *Journals of the House of Commons*, 1867—.

Minutes of Proceedings and Evidence, Standing Committee on Broadcasting, Films and Assistance to the Arts.

Minutes of Proceedings, Standing Committee on Transportation and Communications.

Senate. Parliament Buildings, Ottawa, Ontario K1A 0A4. The 102-seat Senate consists of appointed members. It can initiate legislation with the exception of appropriation and tax bills.

Publications:
Debates, official report, daily edition.

Minutes of proceedings, daily edition.

At the close of each session, these publications are edited, indexed, and published in bound form as the *Journals of the Senate of Canada*, 1867—.

Special Senate Committee on Mass Media. Report (2nd session, 28 Parliament, 18/19 Elizabeth II, 1969/1970). This three-volume report has been recently reprinted and is still valuable for its discussions of the economics of publishing and broadcasting and for its research studies on Canadian uses and gratifications of the mass media.

Minutes of Proceedings, Standing Committee on Transport and Communications.

Judiciary

Federal Court of Canada. Hon. Mr. Justice W. R. Jackett, Chief Justice, Supreme Court of Canada Building, Wellington Street, Ottawa, Ontario K1A OH9. The Federal Court of Canada is a court of law, equity admiralty, and it is a superior court of record having civil and criminal jurisdiction. The Court is divided into Trial and Appeal divisions. The recent case involving deletion of American commercials on Canadian cable TV was heard in the Federal Court-Appeal Division.

Publication:
Canada Federal Court Reports, 1971—.

Supreme Court of Canada. Rt. Hon. Bora Laskin, P.C., Chief Justice, Supreme Court Building, Wellington Street, Ottawa, Ontario K1A OJ1. The Supreme Court has exclusive jurisdiction over final appeal in civil and criminal cases, as well as matters referred to it by the Governor-in-Council, and jurisdictional matters conferred upon it by statute. The judgment of the Supreme Court is in all cases final and conclusive.

Publications:
Canada Law Reports, 1923—.

Canada Supreme Court Reports, 1970—.

General Publications

The following periodicals are concerned with Canadian communications and are published by nongovernmental agents:

Broadcaster. R.G. Lewis & Co. Ltd., 77 River Street, Toronto, Ontario M5A 3P2. A Canadian periodical covering events in the broadcast industry.

Cable Communications; monthly; *Cable Communications Annual Handbook;* and *Cable Communications Annual Directory and Buyer's Guide.* Pryde Publications Ltd., Suite 301, 30 Bloor St. W., Toronto, Ontario M4W 1A2. These publications treat cable communications from both industrial and technical viewpoints.

Canadian Communications Law Review, 1969—. Faculty of Law, University of Toronto, Toronto, Ontario M5S 1A1. An annual journal of review and opinion on communications law and policy in Canada.

Canadian Communications Reports. Tele-Connect Publications, Suite 405, 150 Metcalfe Street, Ottawa, Ontario K2P 1P1. A bimonthly trade publication in newsletter format.

Canadian Communications Research Information Centre Newsletter and *Annual Register of Communications Research in Canada.* C.C.R.I.C., 22 Queen Street, Ottawa, Ontario K1P 5V9. Publications concerned with the state of communications research in Canada.

Canadian Interconnection. McLean-Hunter Ltd., 481 University Avenue, Toronto, Ontario M5W 1A7. A monthly trade publication in newsletter format.

Provincial Interests in Media Regulation

Regulation of communications in Canada has historically been a matter for federal jurisdiction. Currently the provinces are lobbying for control over communications of a local or educational nature. Of particular provincial interest is the regulation of cable television. Federal-provincial conferences on communications matters have been held in the past few years to resolve the jurisdictional issue, and Federal Communications Minister Jeanne Sauvè, has promised more provincial input into regulation and policy. But the issue is still unresolved. Information on provincial issues in communications can be obtained from the following provincial ministries:

Alberta
    Hon. Dr. A. A. Warrack
    Minister of Utilities & Telephones
    403 Legislative Building
    Edmonton, Alberta T5K 2B6

Manitoba
    Hon. Rene Toupin
    Minister of Consumer, Corporate & Internal Services
    301 Legislative Building
    Winnipeg, Manitoba R3C OV8

British Columbia
    Hon. Jack Davis
    Minister of Energy, Transport & Communication
    Parliament Buildings
    Victoria, British Columbia V8V 1X4

New Brunswick
   Douglas MacIntosh
   Director of Transportation and Communications
   Department of Transportation
   Box 6000
   Fredericton, New Brunswick E3B 5H1

Newfoundland
   Hon. James Morgan
   Minister of Transport and Communications
   Confederation Building
   St. John's, Newfoundland A1C 5T7

Ontario
   Hon. James Snow
   Minister of Transportation and Communications
   Ferguson Block, Queen's Park
   Toronto, Ontario M7A 1Z8

Quebec
   Louis O'Neill
   Minister of Communications
   675 St-Cyrille E.
   Quebec City, Quebec G1R 4Y7

Nova Scotia
   Hon. Harold M. Huskilson
   Department of the Provincial Secretary
   P.O. Box 998, Provincial Building
   Halifax, Nova Scotia B3J 2X3

Prince Edward Island
   Hon. John H. Maloney
   Minister of Industry and Commerce
   180 Kent Street, Box 2000
   Charlottetown, Prince Edward Island C1A 7N9

Saskatchewan
   Hon. Ned Shillington
   Minister of Cooperation and Cooperative Development
   P.O. Box 7121, 2055 Albert Street
   Regina, Saskatchewan S4P 3S1

7

COMMUNICATIONS LAW COURSES

Since the last edition of the *Aspen Handbook on the Media*, the number of law schools offering courses in communications law has continued to grow. At least one university, UCLA, now places special emphasis on communications law. In addition, a number of courses are being jointly taught by law school and journalism/communications professors—e.g., the course entitled "Mass Communications Media and the First Amendment," which is co-taught by Fred W. Friendly of the Columbia Journalism School and Benno C. Schmidt, Jr., of the Columbia Law School. In addition to the courses listed in this section, other courses in communications law and regulation are offered in many of the undergraduate and graduate departments listed in Section I.

A list of lawyers and others interested in communications law may be obtained by writing Alex Greenfeld, c/o Legal Department, *New York Times*, 229 West 43rd Street, New York, NY 10036.

A new journal specializing in communications law, *Comm/ent*, has been established by Hastings Law School in San Francisco (see listing). *Comm/ent* joins the *Federal Communications Bar Association Journal* as a prime resource in this area.

Arizona State University
College of Law
Tempe, AZ 85281
(605) 965-6181
Ernest Gellhorn, Dean

Freedom of Expression, taught by Professor William C. Canby, Jr., (602) 965-6463. A brief introduction to basic historical materials concerning freedom of expression and subsequent concentration on contemporary problems in the free speech-free press area. Included are problems of free press versus national security, freedom of information, reporter's privilege, and executive privilege. Particular emphasis is given to First Amendment problems in broadcasting and other mass media.

Administrative Law, taught by Dean Ernest Gellhorn. Focuses on the FCC and the administrative process concerned with communication.

Boston University
School of Law
765 Commonwealth Avenue
Boston, MA 02215
(617) 353-3115

Seminar in Government Regulation of Broadcasting, taught by Professor Dennis S. Aronowitz. Approximate enrollment: 12. Principal objectives of the course are to provide general familiarity with the subject and to develop research and writing skills.

University of California at Berkeley
School of Law
Boalt Hall
Berkeley, CA 94720
(415) 642-5049
Sanford H. Kadish, Dean

Communications Law Seminar, taught by Professor Stephen R. Barnett. Approximate enrollment: 25—30. Consideration of selected problems of law and policy involving the mass media, particularly television. Study of media access, media control, the relationship between government and the press, and the functioning of today's communications media with respect to the purposes of the First Amendment.

University of California at Los Angeles
School of Law
405 Hilgard Avenue
Los Angeles, CA 90024
(213) 825-6211
William D. Warren, Dean

Communications Law Program, Tracy A. Westen, Director. The Program has seven major components: (1) classes covering principally First Amendment aspects of media regulation, including licensing, fairness and equal-time doctrines, obscenity, censorship, cross-ownership and cable; (2) seminars in broadcast litigation; (3) individual student research into selected topics; (4) work on actual litigation pending before the FCC and federal courts; (5) extensive quarter-away program allowing student interns to practice with public interest and communications organizations; (6) Speaker's Program, bringing to the law school prominent people from government and the entire spectrum of the communications industry; and (7) ongoing liaison with both national and Southern California media organizations.

The Catholic University of America
Columbus School of Law
Washington, DC 20064
(202) 635-5140
Michael O'Keefe, Dean

Seminar in Mass Communications Law, taught by Professor Harvey L. Zuckman (202) 635-5147. Approximate enrollment: 12—16. A research course which considers such areas as First Amendment theory, defamation, invasion of privacy, free press-fair trial, governmental regulation of advertising, copyright as it relates to journalism and federal regulation of broadcasting.

University of Cincinnati
College of Law
Alphonso Taft Hall
Cincinnati, OH 45221
(513) 475-2631
Samuel S. Wilson, Dean

Telecommunications Law, taught by Professor Theodore M. Hagelin. (513) 475-6805. Approximate enrollment: 15—20. Covers broadcasting, cable and satellites. The course is intended to provide students with an introduction to the regulation of communication technologies. Focus is on the operation and structure of the FCC and of the industries implementing these technologies. Special attention is devoted to the interplay between regulatory policy and industry economics, especially as it affects constitutional rights.

Columbia University
School of Law
435 West 116th Street
New York, NY 10027
(212) 280-2640

Seminar in Copyright Law, taught by Professor John M. Kernochan. Approximate enrollment: 18—20. The nature and operation of copyright law, and of related laws affecting the arts, are examined through the medium of selected problems, emphasizing (a) issues raised by recent technological advances affecting exploitation of music, fine arts, literature, and other creative production, and (b) proposals for legislative reform.

Seminar in Intellectual Property, taught by Professor John M. Kernochan. Approximate enrollment: 18—-20 students. Emphasis on student research. Individual and group research pursued under supervision in the general area of "entertainment law," including the law of copyright, misappropriation, ideas, etc., and in the area of trademark, patent, and trade secrets law. The work stresses the collection analysis, negotiation, and drafting of standard instruments in the area concerned. Students are encouraged to make first-hand investigations of current legal and industry practice relevant to their seminar work.

Business Torts, taught by Professor John M. Kernochan. The law of unfair commercial practices, with particular emphasis on the law of trademarks and on such subjects (sometimes referred to as "entertainment law" or "law and the arts") as copyright, misappropriation, and the law of ideas. Trade secrets, commercial disparagement, false advertising, and interference with contractual relations may also be considered, to the extent time permits.

Regulated Industries a: Public Utilities and Public Transportation, taught by Professor William K. Jones. (212) 280-2626. Covers problems pertaining to public utility regulation in general (rate level, rate design, limitations on entry, financial practices, mergers), plus special attention to recent telecommunications problems: customer-owned terminal equipment, specialized common carriers, communications satellites, and the relation between telecommunications and computers.

Regulated Industries b: Electronic Mass Media, taught by Professor William K. Jones. Covers allocation of radio spectrum among diverse uses; issuance and renewal of radio and television broadcast licenses; limitations on multiple ownership and network practices affecting the electronic media; regulation of programming practices of such media; and problems posed by new technological and institutional developments, especially cable television and subscription services.

Mass Communications Media and the First Amendment, taught by Professors Fred W. Friendly and Benno C. Schmidt, Jr. (212) 280-2627. Covers various First Amendment problems pertaining to print and electronic media, including libel, privacy, the Fairness Doctrine, access questions, reporter's privilege, and national security restraints.

Cornell University
School of Law
Ithaca, NY 14850
(607) 256-1000
Roger C. Cramton, Dean

Broadcast Regulation. Current issues in the regulation of broadcast and cable television and of radio: licensing policies, including media control, public service standards, and other issues arising, particularly in the renewal and comparative licensing contexts. Programming questions such as fairness, public affairs, network practices, violence and obscenity. Cable and public television issues. Role and technique of the FCC in developing policy.

Copyright, Trademark, and Patent Law, taught by Professor Harry G. Henn. Problems involving copyrights, trademarks (and unfair competition), and patents, designed both to introduce the student to the basic concepts of those fields and to provide some specialized training for those interested in pursuing careers in the publishing, entertainment and other copyright-related industries, in representing clients with trademark problems, or as patent lawyers.

University of Detroit
School of Law
651 East Jefferson Avenue
Detroit, MI 48226
(313) 927-1541
Richard A. Seid, Dean

Communications Law, taught by Professor William T. Downs. A study of selected problems in modern mass communications, including the impact of the First Amendment, libel and slander, free press and fair trial, free press and the right to privacy. Regulation of the electronic media, structural regulation, the licensing and hearing process, the fairness and emerging concepts of access to media.

Fordham University
School of Law
140 West 62nd Street
New York, NY 10023
(212) 956-5648
Joseph M. McLaughlin, Dean

Law and the Performing Arts, taught by Adjunct Professor Stewart Lavey. Approximate enrollment: 30. A study of basic legal relationships in the performing arts. The course covers the areas of artist-manager relationships; acquisition and disposition of literary properties for motion pictures and stage plays; production, financing and distribution of motion pictures; concert and classical artist agreements; and special taxation problems. The course in Corporations is a prerequisite.

Law and the Visual Arts, taught by Professor Joseph M. Perillo. Approximate enrollment: 25—30. Explores rights of the artist in relation to the dealer and collector, including copyrights, "moral right," and protection by contract; rights of the consumer, including protection from forgery and fraud; governmental intervention, including subsidization and censorship; international looting; and special taxation problems.

Supreme Court Seminar, taught by Professor Charles M. Whelan. Approximate enrollment: 10. Concentrates on Supreme Court practice, the constitutional decisions of the most recent term and leading constitutional issues on the current docket. Enrollment is limited. Constitutional Law course is a prerequisite.

George Washington University
The National Law Center
Washington, DC 20052
(202) 676-6288
Robert Kramer, Dean

Public Policy in the Mass Media, taught by Professor Jerome A. Barron in the fall semester (80-90 students) and Mr. Marcus Cohn, a member of the Washington communications law bar, in an evening class in the spring, is a two-hour course in mass communication law for students who have completed their first year in law school. It covers institutional structure of mass media and their interrelationships; psychological aspects of mass communications; continuing adjustments among public interest goals, the economic system, and technological developments; influence of and controls exercised by government, other institutions, and private groups; conflict between freedom of speech of the media and other major community interests; the media's relationships to the interests of dissident and minority groups and the access of these groups to the media.

Professor Barron gives the student the option of taking an examination or of preparing a research paper. There is considerable student participation in the course. About forty percent of those enrolled write research papers and about one-third of those deal in depth with subjects discussed in the course in survey fashion. Some students who write papers, usually about a dozen, are asked to give short reports on their findings. These reports help to give a large course a seminar feeling.

Mr. Cohn stresses some important law cases, but his main concern is with the sociological and humanistic aspects of mass media. He attempts to show that law is just one of several disciplines that affect public policy toward the media.

Georgetown University Law Center
600 New Jersey Avenue, N.W.
Washington, DC 20001
(202) 624-8320
David J. McCarthy, Jr., Dean

Communications Law Seminar, taught by Adjunct Professor Curtis White. Approximate enrollment: 20. The course examines in detail the regulation of the mass media, with particular emphasis given to the role of the

Federal Communications Commission. Accordingly, it focuses on policy rather than on legal decisions and requires in-depth treatment of regulatory economics.

Communications Law Clinical Seminar, taught by Adjunct Professor Curtis White. Approximate enrollment: 20. The clinic focuses on the representation of consumer interests in broadcasting and cable, with an introduction to new technology. However, the academic knowledge and lawyering skills developed by the student can be used in representing various special interest groups or government in the communications field, as well as in other types of legal practice.

Entertainment Law Seminar, taught by Professor Richard Alan Gordon. Approximate enrollment: 24. The course examines the common and particular legal problems and practices involved in individual artist representation, the motion picture industry, the musical performing and recording industry, and the professional sports industry. Contract forms and individual bargaining options available will be discussed.

Harvard Law School
Cambridge, MA 02138
(617) 495-1234
Albert Sacks, Dean

Copyright, taught by Professor Arthur Miller. Legal problems arising in the production, marketing and distribution of literary, artistic, musical, and related works. The course centers on the law of copyright and the changes brought about by the new statute. It considers also the relation of copyright to other branches of law, including "unfair competition."

Constitutional Law: The Constitution and the Press, taught by Anthony Lewis, (617) 495-1715. The press and other forms of mass communication have acquired a more significant role in the United States than in any other country. Their constitutional protections against official regulation have been greatly enlarged by the courts in recent years. As the press assumes a more significant public role, should its special privileges under the American system be limited or reconsidered? What is the relevance of media concentration? Do new legal responsibilities go with new power?

Regulation of Broadcasting, taught by Professor Douglas Ginsburg. The course examines selected questions that arise in the design of a public policy for broadcasting and cable communications. **Prelude:** Payola. What is it and why is it thought to be undesirable? **Part One:** Industrial Organization. Why and how is entry into broadcasting licensed? What is to be the national policy on economic competition in broadcasting? Its relationship to the policy of competition in the "marketplace of ideas"? By what model of political economy are scarce goods such as classical music (or police dramas, for that matter) to be allocated in a world in which consumers cannot transact with suppliers? In the cable world in which they can transact? **Part Two:** Content Regulation. Are there constitutionally relevant distinctions between print and the electronic media? What are the purpose and effect of the "Fairness Doctrine"? Of the "equal time" provision for political candidates? What are the appropriate limits of consumer protection rules: herein of drug lyrics, controls on sex and violence, and commercial practices on children's programming. **Coda:** Public Broadcasting.

Howard University
School of Law
2935 Upton Street N.W.
Washington, DC 20008
(202) 686-6575
Charles T. Duncan, Dean

Communications Law and Practice, taught by Spencer J. Boyer. Approximate enrollment: 25—30. A review of legal and practical problems in the field of communications law, with emphasis on practice before the Federal Communications Commission and on representation of entertainers and athletes.

Indiana University
School of Law
735 West New York Street
Indianapolis, IN 46202
(317) 264-8523

Seminar in Mass Communications and the Law, taught by Professor James W. Torke, (317) 264-4992. Selected study of the impact of mass media and the propriety and feasibility of legal regulation and protection, with particular emphasis on the First Amendment and the federal Communications Act of 1934.

University of Iowa
College of Law
Iowa City, IA 52242
(319) 353-2121
N. William Hines, Dean

Mass Communication Law, taught by Randall P. Bezanson. Enrollment: 40. Study of selected issues relating to the role of the press in a free society. Issues which may be analyzed include a brief survey of First Amendment theory as it relates to the press and communications media; defamation; privacy; free press and fair trial; reporter privilege; access to and use of governmental information; right of access to the press; and a study of regulation of radio and television broadcasting.

Freedom of Speech, seminar taught by Barry D. Matsumoto. Approximate enrollment: 8. Examines theoretical background for and judicial doctrinal development of the protection of freedom of expression. Special attention to selected areas such as prior restraint, obscenity, libel, loyalty oaths, sedition, symbolic speech, protest in public areas or any other areas of interest to participants in the seminar. In addition to studying selected problem areas, the seminar emphasizes development of overall theoretical understanding of free expression.

University of Kansas
School of Law
Lawrence, KS 66045
(913) 864-4550
Martin B. Dickinson, Jr., Dean

Mass Communications Law, taught by Professor Deanell R. Tacha. Approximate enrollment: 12. The seminar concentrates on general First Amendment issues specifically relating to the communications industry and also deals with legal problems of the press.

Loyola Law School
1440 West Ninth Street
Los Angeles, CA 90015
(213) 642-2902
Frederick J. Lower, Dean

Entertainment Law, taught by Professor Thomas J. Scully. (213) 642-2949. Approximate enrollment: 70. Analysis of the federal copyright statutes, as well as common law and statutory protection for all forms of creative expression. Some emphasis placed on problems peculiar to the motion picture, television, music and book publishing industries.

University of Maryland
School of Law
500 West Baltimore Street
Baltimore, MD 21201
(301) 528-7214

Mass Communications Law, taught by Professor Everett Goldberg, (301) 528-7214. Examines the laws and institutions regulating mass communications, focusing on the press, broadcasting and cable television. Among the problems considered are access to the media, media access to information, regulation of broadcasting and broadband communications by the Federal Communications Commission, state and local regulatory roles and media concentration.

Political and Civil Rights, taught by Professor Peter Quint. (301) 528-7234. Gives a detailed consideration of freedom of expression and association with a somewhat less exhaustive review of certain related topics such as religious freedom and equality in the exercise of the franchise. Although primary attention is devoted to the analysis of legal materials — primarily opinions of the United States Supreme Court — some consideration may also be given to related philosophical and historical problems.

University of Michigan
Law School
Ann Arbor, MI 48104
(313) 764-0514
Theodore J. St. Antoine, Dean

Communications Sciences and the Law, taught by Professor Layman Allen, (313) 764-9339. The course explores implications of recent developments in the communications sciences and technology for legal education and for the organization, storage and retrieval of legal literature.

Freedom of Speech, taught by Professor Vincent Blasi, (313) 763-1372. Freedom of speech, press and the right to petition are covered. Emphasis is placed on classic writings.

Patent Law, taught by Robert A. Choate, Lecturer in Law, (313) 962-4790. An introduction to substantive patent law and the related fields of copyright and trademark registration.

Broadcasting and the First Amendment, taught by Professor Lee C. Bollinger, (313) 763-4575.

University of Missouri
Law School
218 Walter Williams
Columbia, MO 65201
(314) 882-6487

Communications Law Seminar, taught by Professor Dale Spencer. (314) 882-7436. The subject matter of the course varies with current issues and with student interest. Among suggested topics are access to the press; the First Amendment and attorneys; libel and privacy; modernization—labor and the press; copyright; campaign financing; the antitrust—Newspaper Preservation Act; broadcast media—unique public forum or communications media; plea bargaining; computers and the courts; and obscenity.

University of Nebraska—Lincoln
College of Law
Lincoln, NB 68503
(402) 472-2161
John W. Strong, Dean

Mass Communications Law, taught alternately by Professors Josephine Potuto and John Snowden. Law applicable to the various mass communications media. Major topics include the constitutional status of mass communications, the conflict between a free press and a fair trial, and government regulation of electronic media.

New York University
School of Law
Washington Square
New York, NY 10012
(212) 598-2511
Norman Redlich, Dean

Broadcast Regulation, taught by Jerome S. Boros, (212) 247-3040. Course focuses on policy considerations underlying governmental regulation of the broadcast media, the statutory scheme of the Communications Act, and the interaction among the FCC, other government branches, and the public in animating broadcast regulation. Details the FCC's administration of broadcasting and related areas, emphasizing spectrum allocation, licensing and renewals, and content control, including advertising, obscenity, fairness, and political matters. Explores CATV, Pay-TV, and other emerging technology.

Communications Policy and Law, taught by Professor Morton I. Hamburg, (212) 838-0424. The seminar examines the present and future policies and significant legal problems connected with the communications media, particularly broadcasting. Discussion cover development and regulation (including licensing) of American broadcasting; access to the media; the Fairness Doctrine; First Amendment problems as they relate to governmental regulation; and use of new technology, including cable TV and satellites.

Northwestern University
School of Law
357 East Chicago Avenue
Chicago, IL 60611
James A. Rahl, Dean

Regulation of Broadcasting, taught by Professor Robert Bennett, (312) 649-8430. An examination of law covering the broadcasting industry. The regulatory scheme of the Federal Communications Commission provides the major focus for attention, with emphasis on choice among competing applicants, diversification of control of the media, the fairness and related doctrines, and audience involvement in the regulatory process. Attention is given to related matters such as antitrust considerations and regulation of CATV. The course highlights the pervasive tension between concerns of free speech and regulation in the public interest.

The Ohio State University
College of Law
1659 North High Street
Columbus, OH 43210
(614) 422-2631

Mass Media Law, taught by Professor P. John Kozyris. (614) 422-0701. Covers general background on the First Amendment; public law of libel; free press vs. fair trial; privacy; the press and antitrust laws and concentration of ownership; advertising; and regulation of broadcasting media. The last subject includes balanced programming, equal time, diversification, licensing problems, cable TV, and future technology.

University of Oklahoma Law Center
300 Timberdell Road
Normal, OK 73019
(405) 325-3711
James E. Westbrook, Dean

Legal Problems of the Communications Media. Course covers defamation, privacy and other problems encountered in representing clients in the publishing, radio, journalism and motion picture industries.

Patents, Trademarks and Copyright, taught by Professor Elmer M. Million. The nature of the rights, acquisition and enforcement of patents, trademarks and copyrights, and property and contract interests therein.

Practicing Law Institute
810 Seventh Avenue
New York, NY 10019
(212) 765-5700
Thomas T. Heney, Executive Director

The PLI was founded in 1933 and is the nation's oldest and largest continuing legal education organization. It is concerned with helping lawyers to maintain their competence by keeping up with new statutes, current developments in the law courts and government agencies, and changes in the social and economic climate. 283 programs covering 146 topics were offered in 1975, attended by 24,000 registrants. Among its many topics the Institute presents programs in communications law, such as the following, which were scheduled in 1977:

Communications Law. James C. Goodale, Chairman; Lyn R. Oliensis, Program Attorney. November 3—4, 1977, New York City. The seminar covers prior restraints; antitrust; copyright; commercial speech; how to win a Gertz case; what to do about the new privacy cases; how to use the Freedom of Information Act; the effect of cable on the Fairness Doctrine; what to do about subpoenas; and the liability under 10-B-5 for carrying advertising.

Current Developments in Copyright Law. Morton David Goldberg, Chairman; Ruth Druss, Program Attorney. May 18—20, 1977, New York City; June 1—3, 1977, Los Angeles. The seminar covered deposit and registration of copyrighted works; musical works; sound recordings;

preemption; duration; problems relating to magazines, newspapers and other periodicals; terminations of transfers or licenses; pictorial, graphic and sculptural works; motion pictures and other audio-visual works including television; educational and library photocopying; manufacturing requirements; importation restrictions; and infringement and remedies.

This seminar was designed to present a comprehensive coverage of the recent wide-ranging revisions in the U.S. copyright law.

Rutgers University School of Law—Camden
Fifth and Penn Streets
Camden, NJ 08102
(609) 757-6184
Robert F. Lyle, Assistant Dean

Mass Communication Law, taught by Professor Jonathan Mallamud. (609) 757-6188. A study of the laws that govern the mass media and the dissemination of information in our society with the exception of basic constitutional law and libel law insofar as those subjects are covered in Constitutional Law and Torts. The course begins with consideration of the First Amendment theory governing mass communications by means of an examination of the concept of right of access to the mass media and theories concerning the fiduciary responsibility of licensees of broadcasting stations. The next part of the course deals with problems of the relationship of the free press to providing a fair trial and the ability of reporters to get access to information possessed by government agencies. Various problems relating to the impact on mass communications of other areas of law, such as antitrust and labor law, will also be considered. The final portion of the course consists of an examination of the regulation of radio and television by the Federal Communications Commission.

Rutgers University School of Law—Newark
180 University Avenue
Newark, NJ 07102
(201) 648-5551

Federal Regulation and the Electronic Media, taught by Professor Michael Botein. Approximate enrollment: 10–20. The course is oriented largely toward the Federal Communications Commission's jurisdiction and policy.

Copyright and Literary Property, taught by Professor Eugene Aleinikoff. Approximate enrollment: 10–20. The course focuses primarily on the copyright problems of authors and other artists.

First Amendment and the Mass Media, taught by Professors Eugene Aleinikoff and C. N. Paul. Approximate enrollment: 10–20. The course focuses mainly on the constitutional rights of citizens to use the print and electronic media.

University of San Francisco
School of Law
2130 Fulton Street
San Francisco, CA 94117
(415) 666-6307

Broadcasting Law, taught by Professor C. Delos Putz Jr. (415) 666-6385. Approximate enrollment: 15 to 20 students. The course concentrates on the basic policies of the Federal Communications Commission in regulating over-the-air broadcasting by radio and television stations and includes some coverage of the regulation of CATV. Areas covered include the historical development of broadcast media under the First Amendment, the framework of regulation established in the Communications Act of 1934, and the basic programming policies of the Federal Communications Commission. Particular emphasis is placed on the Fairness Doctrine as applied to broadcast journalism, political broadcasting and advertising; problems of public access to the media; FCC policies relating to license renewals and transfers, including citizen participation; rules relating to regulation of competition; and jurisdiction to regulate CATV and copyright problems.

Stanford Law School
Stanford, CA 94305
(415) 497-2465
Charles J. Meyers, Dean

Communication Law 246, taught by Professor Marc Franklin, (415) 497-4934. Considers legal problems involving the mass media. Particular emphasis upon the regulation of broadcast media and asserted legal differences between print and broadcast media. The limits on speech in such areas as defamation, privacy, election campaigns, and fair trial-free press receive extended attention.

Communication Law 149, taught by Professor Marc Franklin. Introduces non-law students to the issues surrounding government regulation of the mass media, issues which emerge in virtually every aspect of the operation of the print and broadcast media —getting permission from the FCC to begin broadcasting; what media may do to obtain desired information; legal controls on what media may publish—or must publish; constraints on dissemination of the final product. Major attention given to decisions of the Supreme Court involving First Amendment issues.

Temple University
School of Law
Philadelphia, PA 19122
(215) 787-8951
Peter J. Liacouras, Dean

Communications Law, taught by Martin J. Gaynes. Enrollment: 80.

Intellectual Property I: Patents; Intellectual Property II: Copyrights, Trademarks, taught by Professor Arthur H. Seidel. Enrollment: 37.

Interviewing, Negotiation and Counseling, taught by Professor Joseph D. Harbaugh. Enrollment: 20.

Entertainment Tax, taught by Professor Joseph W. Marshall. Enrollment: 47.

University of Texas at Austin
School of Law
2500 Red River Street
Austin, TX 78705
(512) 471-1621
T. J. Gibson, Associate Dean

Mass Communications Law, taught by Professors David A. Anderson and Lucas A. Powe, Jr. (512) 471-5151. The course covers First Amendment theory and goals, prior restraint, state-supported media, newsgathering methods, confidential information and sources, access to information, accreditation, fair trial, defamation, privacy, theory of broadcast regulation, broadcast licensing, program content, Fairness Doctrine, equal opportunities, bias and staging, commercial speech, cable television, and concentration of media ownership.

Communications Torts, taught by Professor David A. Anderson. Course covers interference with patronage, defamation, appropriation of trade values, invasion of privacy, trade libel, deceit, misrepresentation, abuse of process.

Copyright, Trademark and Patent Law, taught by Professor David A. Anderson. Course covers rights in ideas, performances, and literary and artistic expressions.

Regulation of Braodcasting, taught by Professor Lucas A. Powe, Jr. Course emphasizes why the public gets the programming that appears on television and radio. Objectives are to teach students First Amendment issues in a special setting, to focus on a single administrative agency, and to learn the importance of economics in comprehending how a regulated industry behaves.

Washburn University
School of Law
1700 College Avenue
Topeka, KS 66604
(913) 295-6660

Communications Law, taught by Professor Carl C. Monk. Course covers regulation of broadcasting, including licensing, control programming, and business aspects such as antitrust; free press-free trial; and rights of reporters, such as confidential sources and newsgathering.

College of William and Mary
Marshall-Wythe School of Law
Williamsburg, VA 23185
(804) 253-4304
William B. Spong, Jr., Dean

Seminar in Mass Communications, taught by Professor Collins. Approximate enrollment: 11. A survey of various legal problems of mass communication, especially the regulation of radio and television; First Amendment theory and mass communications; defamation; pornography; coverage of trials; freedom of information; antitrust and labor law relation to the press.

Yale Law School
New Haven, CT 06520
(203) 436-8895
Harry H. Wellington, Dean

The First Amendment and the Media: Emerging Problems, taught by Floyd Abrams of Cahill, Gordon & Reindel, 80 Pine Street, New York, NY 10005, (212) 944-7400. A seminar dealing in depth with a small number of current problems with respect to the nature of First Amendment protection of newspapers, radio, and television. Includes consideration of recent clashes between the press and the courts with respect to publication of matter with respect to judicial proceedings; the conflict between First Amendment protections and claims of national security; and the Fairness Doctrine. Other current First Amendment issues may be dealt with as the term proceeds. Emphasis is on the critical examination of the legal doctrines involved and evaluation of the performance of the press, the courts, and the FCC and the development of alternative policies in these areas. Guests from the communications industry and the judiciary take part.

Constitutional Law and the Welfare State, taught by Professor Robert M. Cover. Approximate enrollment: 50. Covers various constitutional problems of the welfare state, including regulation of broadcasting.

Communications (News Media) Law, taught by James C. Goodale, Adjunct Professor. Course covers problems faced by counsel for news media organizations, principally publishers. Libel, right of privacy, prior restraint and fair trial-free press cases are covered, as well as cases dealing with the business aspects of publishing.

Regulation of Radio and Television, taught by Professor Telford Taylor of Columbia Law School. Approximate enrollment: 50.

8

INTERNATIONAL AND OVERSEAS COMMUNICATIONS ORGANIZATIONS

By now the fact that we live in an increasingly interdependent world is widely recognized. The growth of international communications—most dramatically symbolized by the communications satellite—has played no small role in stimulating this interdependence. This growth has also produced greatly increased interest in communications issues around the world.

The entries in this section are by no means exhaustive but are meant primarily to suggest the range and diversity of activities in communications beyond the United States and Canada. Two kinds of organizations are listed here: (1) international organizations—groups with members from many countries and with interests in communications which are either regional or world-wide (many such organizations are based in the United States); and (2) overseas organizations—schools, institutes, foundations, etc. whose interests in communications are largely confined to the country in which they are located. In both categories, almost all of the organizations listed issue publications in English.

The listings in this section are divided into the following categories:

1) United States and Canada 231
2) Europe 236
3) Latin America 254
4) Africa and the Middle East 257
5) Asia and Australia 259

A bibliography of directories and surveys of international and overseas communications organizations appears at the end of the section for those interested in information about other organizations in this field.

1. UNITED STATES AND CANADA

Clearinghouse on Development Communication
1414 22nd Street, N.W.,
Washington, DC 20037
(202) 293-5964

Formerly the Information Center on Instructional Technology. The Clearinghouse is concerned with the role that all types of communication activities can play in solving development problems. It is operated by the Academy for Educational Development and supported by the Bureau for Technical Assistance of the U.S. Agency for International Development. It serves as an international clearinghouse for materials and information on the uses of technology to improve education, and it disseminates information on educational applications of communications technology to planners and practitioners from developing countries through publications, consultations and seminars. Publications: *Development Communication Report* (see listing on page 299); a series of Bulletins which include *Tele-Niger: Adapting an Electronic Medium to a Rural African Context*, *A Resourcebook on Radio's Role in Development*, and *A Directory of Sources of Assistance on Educational Technology for Development*. All bulletins are free.

Communications Satellite Corporation (COMSAT)
See listing on page 177

East-West Communication Institute
Jack Lyle, Director
East-West Center
University of Hawaii
1777 East-West Road
Honolulu, HI 96822
(808) 948-8624

One of five problem-oriented institutes within the nonprofit East-West Center, which was founded to promote understanding and better relationships between the United States and nations in Asia and the Pacific, the East-West Communication Institute is concerned principally with education, training, and research in social and economic developmental communication. The Institute's work is organized in several project areas: Social Effects, Process and Context, Communication Policy and Planning, and Flow of News Between Countries. The Communication Institute conducts research and analysis, offers workshops and courses leading to professional development, arranges seminars for discussing key questions, offers grants for graduate study, provides information services, and publishes papers and books. (See also listing for the University of Hawaii on page 18.)

Inter American Press Association (IAPA)
2911 N.W. 39th Street
Miami, FL 33142
(305) 358-1878

IAPA was founded in 1942. It has 1,000 member newspapers whose readers are interested in news of other American countries. It established the Inter American Press Association Scholarship Fund, which distributes annual scholarships among North American and Latin American journalists and journalism students. Its IAPA Technical Center supplies technical information to its members. Publications: *IAPA news*, bimonthly; *IAPA Updater*, irregular; *Noticiero de la SIP*, bimonthly; *Entreboletines*, irregular.

International Advertising Association (IAA)
475 Fifth Avenue
New York, NY 10017
(212) 684-1583
John S. Wasley, Executive Director

The IAA is an organization comprised of individuals in 80 countries who are engaged in advertising and marketing products and services overseas and who are interested in mass communications related to the marketing of goods and services. It conducts research on topics such as restrictions and taxes on advertising; advertising trade practices and related information; and advertising expenditures throughout the world. It has compiled recommendations for international advertising standards and practices. It maintains a library of advertising and marketing periodicals from various countries and reference books on international advertising. It sponsors an annual award for distinguished services in the field of international advertising and marketing. Publications: *IAA Airletter*, bimonthly; *IAA Membership Directory*, annual; *International Advertising Expenditures*, biennial; *Concise Guide to International Markets*, occasional.

International Association of Business Communicators (IABC)
870 Market Street, Suite 469
San Francisco, CA 94102
(415) 433-3400

The IABC was formed in 1970 by the merger of the International Council of Industrial Editors and the American Association of Industrial Editors. Corporate Communicators Canada joined the organization in 1974. The Association has a membership of 3,800, 500 of whom are outside the United States. Members are primarily industrial and organizational personnel engaged in writing, editing, film production, phone information programs, audiovisual programs, closed-circuit television, and speech writing. Its purpose is to encourage effective communication by exchanging ideas, improving training methods and managerial skills, and improving understanding of the economic system of which membership sponsors are a part. Publications: *Journal of Organizational Communication* (see listing on page 293); *IABC News* (see listing on page 300).

International Association of Independent Producers (IAIP)
P.O. Box 2801
Washington, DC 20013
(202) 638- 5593
Edward v. Rothkirch, Executive Director

The Association is an organization of 2,700 members from 102 countries who are involved in all aspects of the audio-visual field. Publications: *Communication Arts International*, quarterly; *Newsletter*, eight times a year, free to members, available on quote to others.

International Communication Association (ICA)
See listing on page 150

International Development Research Centre
P.O. Box 8500
Ottawa, K1G 3H9
(613) 996-2321

The Centre is a training and research agency funded by the Government of Canada. It sponsors various programs throughout the world, especially in Africa, Asia and South America. It focuses on new approaches to development by introducing new technology for information retrieval; by sponsoring conferences and fellowships; by producing films; by publishing books; and by sponsoring research on communication problems between villages, among the urban poor, and in the mainstream of society.

International Labor Press Association (ILPA)
815 16th Street N.W.
Washington, DC 20006
(202) 347-5564

In existence since 1911, the ILPA has a membership of over 500 labor publications in the United States and Canada. About one-third of the membership is made up of national and international union publications; the rest include publications issued by local unions, joint councils, and state and local central bodies chartered by the AFL-CIO. Its purpose is to act as a clearing house for information and ideas in the labor press field; to improve effectiveness of labor press; to provide ways to raise standards; and to exchange information about editorial and typographical problems.

International Radio and Television Society (IRTS)
420 Lexington Avenue
New York, NY 10017
(212) 867-6650
Robert H. Boulware, Executive Director

The IRTS was founded in 1952 by the merger of the Radio Executives Club and the American Television Society. Its 1300 members consist of individuals engaged in management, sales or executive production in the radio and television broadcasting industries and their allied fields. It sponsors an annual Faculty/Industry Seminar, a two-day college conference, and other seminars and workshops. It presents an annual IRTS Gold Medal for outstanding contribution to or achievement in broadcasting or broadcast advertising. Publications: *Newsletter; Roster of Members*, annual.

International Society of Weekly Newspaper Editors (ISWNE)
c/o Department of Journalism
Northern Illinois University
DeKalb, IL 60115
(815) 753-1925

ISWNE was founded in 1954. Its purposes are to promote excellence in editorial comment and content in weekly newspapers; to improve the writing of editorials; to exchange ideas among weekly newspaper editors; and to develop international understanding through weekly newspapers. Publications: *ISWNE Newsletter,* monthly except July; *Grassroots Editor,* quarterly.

International Telecommunications Satellite Organization (INTELSAT)
490 L'Enfant Plaza, E.W.
Washington, DC 20024
(202) 488-2300
Telex: 89-2707

INTELSAT originated as an international joint venture in August 1964 under interim agreements signed by 11 countries to form a single global commercial communications satellite system. The definitive agreements took effect in February 1973. Under the definitive agreements, all states which are members of the International Telecommunication Union (ITU) and all states which were members of INTELSAT under the interim agreements may join the Organization. Membership in INTELSAT is 95. Its objective is to continue to carry forward on a definitive basis the design, development, construction, establishment, operation and maintenance of the space segment of the global commercial telecommunications satellite system. Today INTELSAT is a legal international entity with owners' equity of $378 million. Investment in INTELSAT is based on the investment-use principle; that is, each country invests in INTELSAT in proportion to its use of the system and shares accordingly in revenues which become available for distribution, including a 14 percent return on investment. The INTELSAT system now consists of a combination of six operational INTELSAT IV and INTELSAT IV-A satellites, as well as three in-orbit spare satellites. Each INTELSAT IV has a capacity of 4,000 telephone circuits plus two television channels; while the INTELSAT IV-A has a capacity of 6,000 telephone circuits plus two television channels. A total of six INTELSAT IV-A satellites have been procured by INTELSAT for launch over the next few years. A contract has been awarded for the procurement of seven INTELSAT V spacecraft, each carrying 27 transponders with a capacity for up to 12,000 two-way telephone conversations and capable of transmitting up to two channels of color television. It is currently anticipated that the INTELSAT V series will begin operation in late 1979. The INTELSAT system presently has 163 operational antennas at 131 earth stations in 82 countries around the world.

Society for Technical Communication (STC)
See listing on page 152

United Nations Correspondents Association (UNCA)
Press Trust of India
Room C315, United Nations
New York, NY 10017
(212) 751-0850
R. Chakrapani, President

The Association, which was organized in 1948, has about 200 members. Its purpose is to maintain freedom and prestige of press, radio and television correspondents in their relations with the UN; to secure accreditation and unhindered access to UN headquarters and regional offices for bona fide correspondents; and to facilitate social contact between correspondents and UN delegates and officials.

2. EUROPE

The Konrad Adenauer Foundation (KAF)
Rathausallee 12
5205 Sankt Augustin bei Bonn
West Germany. 02241/1961
Telex: 889727 kas d.

The Foundation has six institutes, one of which, the Institute for International Partnership, works to contribute to the socioeconomic advancement of developing countries, principally in conjunction with partners having similar political values. The Institute and its foreign partners have promoted and supported numerous projects, including projects in the mass media, in different countries at regional and national levels. Another Institute, the Social Sciences Research Institute, is engaged in mass communication research, content analysis and the impact of mass media on political attitudes.

British Broadcasting Corporation (BBC)
Broadcasting House
London W1A 1AA
England
01-580-4468
Telex: 265781
Cable: BROADCASTS LONDON TELEX
Ian Trethowan, Director-General

The BBC is a public corporation established by Royal Charter. It is empowered to operate broadcasting services in the United Kingdom, which include two national television networks, four national radio networks, a number of separate regional services and twenty local radio stations. It also operates an extensive world-wide radio service, with transmitters in the U.K. and at six bases overseas. The home services are financed by the sale of licences, which are required for all television receivers in the U.K. The external services are financed by a grant-in-aid from the Treasury. Neither the home nor the external services accept advertising revenue.

The BBC's Research and Designs Departments embrace such diverse activities as the planning of the UHF transmitter network, the application of digital techniques to the processing and distribution of audio and video signals, studies of quadraphony, and the acoustic design of studios using scale models. BBC engineers have been responsible for such developments as Sound-in-Syncs (conveying the sound signal in digital form in the synchronising intervals of the television waveform), and Ceefax, the data transmission system which uses unemployed lines in the frame fly-back period.

Catholic Media Council
Postfach 1912
D-51 Aachen
West Germany
Dr. Franz-Josef Eilers, Executive Secretary

The Council is an evaluation and advisory office for church funding agencies and for individuals in the field of communications, especially in the Third World. Publications: *Information Bulletin; Service Papers.*

Centre for Public Opinion and Broadcasting Research (OBOPSP)
ul. Woronicza 17
skr Pocztowa 46
00950 Warszawa,
Poland
43 87 92

The Centre is the research department of the Committee of Radio and Television in Poland. It conducts research on the effects of radio and television, both domestic and foreign. Analyses of the activities of foreign radio and television organizations are based on radio and TV periodicals, brochures, and scientific literature, as well as on listening to European broadcasts. Publications: *Messages and Opinions*, quarterly, in Polish but with summaries of articles in English, $13 per year. Available from European Publishers Representatives, Inc., 11-03 46th Avenue, Long Island City, NY 11101. Also publishes *Research Abstracts*.

Commonwealth Broadcasting Association (CBA)
Broadcasting House
London W1A 1AA
England
01-580 4468, ext 5023
Telex: 265781
Alva Clarke, Secretary-General

The CBA embraces 45 national broadcasting organisations in 42 Commonwealth countries in Europe, the Mediterranean, Africa, Asia, the Caribbean, Australasia and the Pacific. Founded in London in February 1945, the Association is pledged to work for the improvement of all aspects of broadcasting in its member organisations through collective study and mutual assistance and to further the concept that public service broadcasting is vital as an instrument to promote social, cultural and economic aspirations. General Conferences of the Association are held every two years. Publication: *Combroad* (see listing on page 311).

Commonwealth Press Union (CPU)
Studio House
184 Fleet Street
London EC4A 2DU
England

01-242-1056

The CPU was founded in 1909 as the Empire Press Union. Its present name was adopted in 1951. Members are publishers or newspaper proprietors in all Commonwealth countries. Its function is to promote the welfare, freedom and efficiency of Commonwealth newspapers and other news media; to watch for measures likely to affect the freedom of the press in any part of the world; to work for improved telecommunication facilities for the reporting and transmission of news; and to promote the education and training of journalists. Publication: *Quarterly Bulletin*, $10 per year; conference reports.

DISTRIPRESS: Association for the Promotion of the International Circulation of the Press
Beethovenstrasse 20
8002 Zurich
Switzerland

The Association was founded in 1955 and has 332 members in 58 countries. Its purpose is to consider matters of international commercial relations, including merchandising; to exchange information on sales and economic questions; to encourage cooperation with publishing houses; and to furnish information and mediate disputes. Publications: *DISTRIPRESS News*, two or three times a year; *News Letters*, monthly; *Who's Who in DISTRIPRESS*, every third year.

The Ditchley Foundation
Ditchley Park, Enstone
Oxfordshire OX7 4ER
England
Enstone 346
Sir Philip Adams, Director
American Ditchley Foundation
39 East 51st Street
New York, NY 10022
(212) 752-6515
Forrest D. Murden. Director

The Foundation, in cooperation with the American Ditchley Foundation, sponsors and supports educational programs at Ditchley Park, Oxfordshire, consisting principally of meetings on issues of common concern to U.K. and U.S. citizens, including communications. Publication: *Ditchley Journal*, semiannual.

European Broadcasting Union (EBU)
1, rue de Varembé
Case postale 193
CH-1211 Geneva 20
Switzerland
Telex: 22 230. 33-24-00
Dr. R. de Kalbermatten, Secretary General

The EBU was founded in 1950, succeeding the International Broadcasting Union. Its Technical Centre is located at 32 Avenue Albert Lancaster, B-1180 Brussels, Belgium. It has 105 members in 75 countries. Its purpose is to promote development of and research in all aspects of broadcasting; to exchange information; to resolve differences; to advise members on contractors and copyright legislation; and to promote the co-production and exchange of news and programs, including programs for Eurovision. Publications: *EBU Review*, monthly, alternating between the Geneva and Brussels editions (see listing on page 312).

Institute of Development Studies
University of Sussex
Fulmer, Brighton BN1 9QN
Sussex
England

The Institute is a research and training center which sponsors research on the problems of developing countries, including communications, and problems between the developed and underdeveloped nations of the world.

Institute of Scientific and Technical Communicators, Ltd. (ISTC)
17 Bluebridge Avenue
Brookmans Park, Hatfield
Herts AL9 7Ry
England
Potters Bar 55392

The ISTC was formed in 1972 by the merger of The Presentation of Technical Information Group, the Institution of Technical Authors and Illustrators, and the Institute of Technical Publicity and Publications. It is the British representative on the International Council for Technical Communciation. Its 1300 members, who work in defense, industry, and in educational institutions, are engaged in technical writing, illustration, publicity, journalism and related fields. Its purposes are to establish professional standards for the communication of technical information; to promote education and training for such standards and to institute examinations and award certificates. Publication: *The Communicator of Scientific and Technical Information*, quarterly, 2 £ per year.

International Association for Mass Communication Research
Centre for Mass Communication Research
University of Leicester
104 Regent Road
Leicester LE1 7LT
England
Prof. James D. Halloran, Director

Founded in 1957 and affiliated with UNESCO, the Association is composed of individual and organizational members, both national and international, in over 46 countries. Its functions are to organize scientific conferences and provide a forum where researchers and others involved in mass communication can meet and exchange information about their work; to encourage the development of research and systematic study; to stimulate interest throughout the whole field of mass communication research; to disseminate information about research and research needs—not only to researchers but also to those working in the various media and to others responsible for media policy—and generally to seek to bring about improvements in communication practice, policy, and research. The Association holds a biennial conference. Publications: monographs.

International Catholic Association for Radio and Television (UNDA)
General Secretariat
12, rue de l'Orme
1040 Brussels
Belgium
734.63.61.
Telex: 21275 CIPINF.B for UNDA

Founded in 1928 as the International Catholic Bureau for Broadcasting, UNDA adopted its present name in 1947. Members consist of autonomous Catholic National Associations approved by competent ecclesiastical authorities in 106 countries, and 11 international associations. Its purposes are to try to ensure that media productions in each country are animated by a human and Christian spirit; to see that the best possible use is made of religious broadcasting; to help in training broadcasters and audiences, especially in the Third World; and to promote media training and media appreciation in schools, colleges and seminaries. Publications: *Unda Documentation*, quarterly, $8 per year; *The Wide World of Unda*, 10 times a year, $5 per year.

International Catholic Union of the Press (ICUP)
10, Avenue de la Gare des Eaux-Vives
Case Postale 313
CH-1211 Geneva 6
Switzerland. (022) 35 09 09

Originally founded in 1927 as the Catholic Journalists' Bureau, the ICUP took its present name in 1936. Its constituent members are the Federation of Catholic Press Agencies, the International Federation of Catholic Dailies and Periodicals, the International Federation of Catholic Journalists, the International Catholic Association of Journalism Teachers, and the International Federation of the Church Press. Its purposes are to link and thereby strengthen Catholics influencing public opinion through the press; to raise professional standards; to exchange information; to research problems of press and religious news; to promote the Catholic press in underdeveloped countries. It is represented in the U.S. and Canada by the Catholic Press Association (see listing on page 144). Publications: *UCIP Information*, quarterly (English, French and two other languages).

International Council for Technical Communications (INTECOM)
A. Tunheim, Secretary-General/Treasurer
Undelstad Terrasse 38B
N.1370, Asker
Norway

Founded in 1971, INTECOM consists of seven technical communication societies: The Institute of Scientific and Technical Communicators, Ltd. (U.K.); The Society for Technical Communication (U.S.A.; see listing on page 152); The Society for Technical Communication, Toronto Chapter (Canada); the Institution of Technical Authors and Illustrators of Australia; Studiekring voor

Technische Informatie (the Netherlands); Foreningen Teknisk Information (Sweden); Norsk Forening for Teknisk Informasjon (Norway). Its purpose is to promote and improve technical communication throughout the world by holding international conferences; establishing international standards and codes of practice; establishing grants and scholarships; and promoting, researching and publishing special reports, proceedings and other publications.

International Federation of Film Archives (FIAF)
74 Galerie Ravenstein
B-1000 Brussels
Belgium
Brigitte Van Der Elst, Executive Secretary

A Federation of national, regional and local film libraries, archives and museums which seeks to preserve the artistic and historic heritage of motion pictures. Promotes cooperation among members through international exchange of films and documents relating to the history and the art of the cinema. Conducts technical and historical research, and publishes books in English, French and German on the preservation of film.

International Federation of Journalists (IFJ)
IPC-Boulevard Charlemagne 1, Bte #5
1041 Brussels
Belgium
02/736.80.15.
Cable: INTERFEDJOUR

The Federation consists of 28 national unions in 24 countries, including the United States. It was founded in 1952. Its purposes are to raise professional standards; to defend press freedom; to contribute to the development of news media in the developing countries; and to issue International Press Cards for journalists. Publications: *IFJ Information* (see listing on page 338); *Direct Line* (see listing on page 337).

International Federation of Newspaper Publishers (FIEJ)
6, Rue du Faubourg Poissoniere
75010 Paris
France
523.38.88.

The Federation, which was founded in 1948, is composed of national newspaper organizations in 30 countries, primarily in Europe but also including the United States and several countries in Asia. Its purposes are to safeguard the ethical and economic interests of newspapers and to study conditions favorable to the development of press activities. Publications: *FIEJ Bulletin,* quarterly; *Newspaper Techniques,* occasional; *FIEJ Notes,* occasional; *FIEJ Documentation.*

International Federation of the Periodical Press
68a Wigmore Street
London W1H 9DL
England

Established in 1925, the Federation includes organizations publishing 22,000 periodicals in 23 countries throughout the world, including the United States. Its purposes are to develop the interests of the periodical press by supporting freedom in the dissemination of news, by protecting its ethical and material interests, by ensuring public and official confidence, by promoting the use and raising the standards of the periodical press, and by encouraging cooperation between members.

International Film and Television Council (IFTC)
Via Santa Susanna 17
00187 Rome
Italy
48 65 09

The Council was founded in 1958. Its membership consists of 42 international organizations, among them the European Broadcasting Union, the International Catholic Association for Radio and Television, the International Catholic Film Office, the International Centre of Films for Children and Young People, and the International Radio and Television Organization. Its purpose is to further the work of its member organizations by arranging meetings and consultation among them and to act as a link for the exchange of information. Publications: *World Screen; Calendar of International Film and TV Events,* annual, 1,200 lira; *IFTC Directory of International Film and Television Organizations and their National Branches.*

International Institute of Communications (IIC)
Tavistock Square East
Tavistock Square
London WC1H 9LG
England
01 388 0671. Telex: 24578
Cable: WIDECAST
Edward W. Ploman, Executive Director

Founded in 1969 as the International Broadcast Institute (IBI), the Institute is a worldwide independent, nonprofit organization with a membership of over 700 individuals, business firms and institutions in 70 countries which represents all interests in communications: policy makers and planners, broadcasters, social scientists, engineers, lawyers, educators, industrialists, researchers and writers. Its purposes are to provide a multi-disciplinary, international forum for the independent analysis of social, cultural, economic, political and legal issues relating to the development, planning, and impact of communications, particularly in the electronic media; to further international and regional cooperation in the field of communications; to initiate and promote research; and to provide information, consultancy and advice. The IIC works through meetings, research studies and publications and has a library of published and non-published material. Research studies include regional studies of communications flow; communications policies and structures; communications and law; and communications technologies. Publications: *InterMedia* (see listing on page 301); *Vision and Hindsight: the Future of Communications; Case Studies on Broadcasting Systems; The Role of New Communications Systems; Communications Policy for National Development; Communications and International Law; IIC Legal Papers.*

International Organization of Journalists (IOJ)
Parizska 9
11001 Prague 1
Czechoslovakia
Jiri Kubka, General Secretary

The IOJ is an organization of 150,000 members, including national organizations, groups, committees and individuals, in 109 countries. It was founded in 1946. It maintains a permanent international institute for the training of journalists in Budapest and international journalists' rest homes in Bulgaria and Hungary. Its purposes are "to defend freedom of the press and journalists and fight for their better material and social position; by free and true information to help to maintain peace and friendship among nations; and to support fully friendly co-operation of all journalists throughout the world and help to achieve their unity." Publications: *The Democratic Journalist,* monthly; *Journalists Affairs,* bimonthly; *Interpressgrafik,* quarterly.

International Press Institute (IPI)
Lindenplatz 6
8048 Zurich
Switzerland
34 54 06
London Secretariat:
City University
280 St. John Street
London EC1V 4PB
England
(01) 251 2525/6
Telex: 25950 IPI-LON G
Cable: PRESSINT

The IPI was founded in 1951. It has almost 1900 members in 63 countries. Full membership is open to those responsible for the editorial policies of newspapers, magazines and broadcasting stations; associate membership is open to those otherwise concerned with journalism and the media. Its purposes are to further and safeguard the freedom of the press; to achieve understanding between journalists; to promote the free exchange of news; and to improve the practices of journalism. Wherever possible, the IPI takes action when journalists are harassed or imprisoned and when newspapers are threatened by government restrictions. It holds international conferences and seminars; carries out research projects, often in conjunction with other organizations; and holds an annual assembly. Publications: *IPI Report* (see listing on page 345); *Annual Report* on world press freedom; occasional books and pamphlets.

International Press Telecommunications Council (IPTC)
Studio House
Hen and Chickens Court
184 Fleet Street
London EC4A 2DU
England
01-405-2608
Cable: IPTELCOM LONDON PS4
Oliver G. Robinson, Director
   The IPTC was founded in 1965 as the International Press Telecommunications Committee. It has 12 national and international organizations as members. Its purpose is to safeguard and promote the telecommunications interests of the world's press. Publications: *Newsletter*, three times a year, free.

International Publishers Association
Avenue de Miremont 3
1206 Geneva
Switzerland
P.A. Sjögren, President
J.A. Koutchoumow, Director
   Founded in 1896 as the International Publishers Congress, the Association includes professional book publishers' associations in 35 countries. Its purposes are to promote the freedom of publishers to publish and distribute literary works, and to keep the flow of books between countries free of tariffs and other obstacles. Its next congress will be in May-June, 1980, in Stockholm. Publications: reports and congress proceedings.

International Radio and Television Organization (OIRT)
15 U Mrazovky
151-13 Prague 5
Czechoslovakia
   The OIRT was founded in 1946 as the successor to the Union Internationale de Radiodiffusion. It consists of broadcasting services in 25 countries in Europe, Asia and Latin America. Its purposes are to arrange for an exchange of information on technical developments, programs and projects for improvements among its members; and to uphold the interests of broadcasting and television by means of international cooperation. The Inter-

vision Program has ensured direct exchange of television programs since 1960. Publications: *Radio and Television*, bimonthly, $6 per year; *OIRT Information*, monthly, $1.50 per year.

International Telecommunication Union (ITU)
Place des Nations
1211 Geneva 20
Switzerland
(022) 34 60 21
Telex: 23 000 uit ch.

Originally established in 1865 as Union Telegraphique Internationale, the ITU adopted its present title in 1932. Any country can be admitted as a member if it meets the conditions of the International Telecommunication Convention. The ITU Council is composed of 36 members elected by the Plenipotentiary Conference. The ITU includes the International Frequency Registration Board, the International Telegraph and Telephone Consultative Committee, the International Radio Consultative Committee, and a General Secretariat. Its purposes are to gain international cooperation in improvement and rational use of telecommunication services; to promote development of technical facilities and improve efficiency of services; to lend technical assistance and prepare programs for developing countries; to publish the International Frequency Lists, a summary of monitoring information, tables of telegraphic rates, radio communications channels, call signs, and the technical recommendations of the two International Consultative Committees. Publication: *Telecommunication Journal*, monthly.

University of Leicester, Centre for Mass Communication Research
104 Regent Road
Leicester LE1 7LT
England
Professor James D. Halloran, Director

Founded in 1966, the Centre conducts various studies on the mass media and on mass communications both in England and throughout the world. The Centre is multidisciplinary, but the main emphasis is sociological. One of its main purposes is to carry out and present research that can contribute to more enlightened media policies.

Projects have included The Future of Broadcasting; Community and Communication; Media and Pressure Groups; Media and Race; Television and Delinquency; Communication and Health Education; School Culture and Popular Culture; Adolescent Use of the Media; Reporting Conflict; Television Language; Production Processes in Television News and Drama; Mass Media and Violence; International News Study; International News Agencies; The Use of Mass Media in National Development; Pre-School Children and Television; Mass Media, Attitudes and the Welfare State; Ownership and Control of the Mass Media in Britain; and Social Action Programming on Television. There is no formally taught programme, but postgraduate students are awarded PhD and MPhil degrees on the basis of their research. A course leading to MA (Education) is jointly provided with the University School of Education. The staff includes the Director, a Research Fellow, four Research Associates and seven Research Assistants. There are also normally 2-3 Visiting Fellows in any given year. The Centre is also one of the UNESCO-supported regional centres for Mass Communication Research Documentation and is the Headquarters of the International Association for Mass Communication Research.

Nordic Documentation Center for Mass Communications Research (NORDICOM)

The Center consists of four coordinated national units carrying on parallel work. They are:
NORDICOM—Denmark
Statsbiblioteket
Universitetsparken
DK-8000 Arhus C
Denmark
NORDICOM—Finland
University of Tampere
P.O. Box 607
SF-33101 Tampere 10
Finland
NORDICOM—Norway
University of Bergen
Christies gate 15-19
N-5014 Bergen-U
Norway
NORDICOM—Sweden

University of Gothenburg
Box 5048
S-402 21 Gothenburg
Sweden

The Center reaches researchers, educators, and decision makers in government who are concerned with mass communications. It does not initiate research but collects and presents relevant material to contribute to the improvement and advancement of research and public debate. Publications: Bibliographies, which can be ordered from NORDICOM Denmark.

Organization for Economic Co-Operation and Development (OECD)
Subgroup on Information, Computers, and Communications
2 rue Andre Pascal
75775 Paris Cedex 16
France
Hans-Peter Gassman, Director

The Subgroup deals with all aspects of national and international policies which govern information activities in the natural and social sciences and in technology. Its studies cover present and future needs for information; the processing, communication and use of information; national reviews of information policy; the training of information specialists; and the management and economics of information systems, services and networks. Publications: A catalogue of OECD publications, including those of the Subgroup, is available from OECD Publications Center, Suite 1207, 1750 Pennsylvania Ave., N.W., Washington, DC 20006.

Press Research Center (CECOM)
Osrodek Badan Prasoznawczych
Rynek Glowny 23, 31-008 Krakow
Poland
Telex: 032-491

The Centre was founded in 1956 as the scientific and research department of the Worker's Press Publishing Co-operative. It is a national center for research in the field of mass communications/communicator activities, encompassing content analysis, audience, exposure, reception and public opinion. CECOM, an international-regional center for mass communications research documentation for the Central European Countries, was established in 1974 within the framework of the Press Research Centre. CECOM is a part of the UNESCO network of regional documentation centers. Publications: *Mass Communication Research: Current Documentation*, twice a year, $10 per issue; a quarterly and books in Polish.

University of Salzburg, Department of Mass Communication
Sigmund Haffner Gasse 18/3
A-5020 Salzburg
Austria
06222/44511248
Professor Michael Schmolke, Chairman

The Department prepares students for careers in the various fields of mass communications, in media education, and in public relations. It also carries out research projects such as recent ones on the coverage in the Austrian media of the activities of the International Year of the Woman, on the mass media in Austria, and on mass media research in Austria.

Swedish Broadcasting Corporation, Audience and Programme Research Department
S-105 10 Stockholm
Sweden
08/63 10 00.
Telex: 10000 BROADCAST STH
Cable: BROADCAST

The goals of the Audience and Programme Research Department are to gain and disseminate knowledge concerning how radio and television can and do function, on the basis of knowledge of the process of mass communication (the relations between the mass media and individuals, groups and society at large); to provide a basis for decisions regarding radio and television on the levels of policy-making, planning and production; and to provide a basis for discussions of radio, television and other mass media both within and outside the broadcasting organization. On the production level its main task is, through studies of programs, to contribute to the maintenance and further development of a standard of quality that satisfies professional as well as audience demands. On the planning level, through studies, it helps to ensure that segments of the audience with varying needs, backgrounds and habits are able to listen to and view programs that concern them. On the policy-making level, by analyses of programming and audiences, it indicates how the established goals and norms for broadcasting are fulfilled. Publications: Many publications of the Swedish Broadcasting Corporation are in English. Among them are: *Audience and Programme Research*, five times a year, free, presenting summaries of projects both planned and completed; a series of reports emphasizing children's studies, information studies, and audience studies; *Presentation of Projects*, biennial.

The Thomson Foundation
16th Floor
International Press Centre
76 Shoe Lane
London EC4 3JB
England
353-6718/9
Tom Neil, Director

    The Foundation was established in 1962 to help develop mass communications in emerging countries by giving grants and scholarships to individuals in developing countries and in institutions. Courses for senior editorial people from Third World countries are held at the Editorial Study Centre, Havelock Street, Cardiff. Courses for television engineers from developing countries are held at the Thomson Foundation Television College, Kirkhill House, Newton Mearns, Glasgow. The Foundation also sends staff members and other experts overseas to assist in training and investigation.

United Kingdom Post Office Telecommunications
Telecommunications System Strategy Department
Long Range Intelligence Division (THQ/TSS6)
88 Hills Road
Cambridge CB2 IPE
England
I. J. Barton, Head, Information and Services Group

    As one of three Long Range Studies Divisions, the Intelligence Division is concerned with the identification of long-term changes which can have important effects on the development of telecommunications in the United Kingdom, and with the assessment of these effects and their wider economic, social, and environmental implications. Current work is mainly concerned, either directly or indirectly, with the estimation of long-term demand functions for telecommunications services (voice, visual, data, and mobile) which may become available over the next 30 years. Publications include *Long Range Research Reports* and *Long Range Intelligence Bulletins,* covering topics such as "The Effectiveness of Person-to-Person Telecommunications Systems: Research at the Communications Studies Group, University College, London," and "Residential Telecommunications Applications: A General Review." A complete list of publications is available from the above address.

United Nations Educational Scientific and Cultural Organization (UNESCO)
Communication Sector
7 Place de Fontenoy
75700 Paris
France
Alberto Obligado Hazar, Assistant Director General
   for Communications

UNESCO's work in communications ranges from newspapers to computers. It has four major tasks in this field: 1) the free flow of information and book development, through preparation and application of several international instruments, including the Agreement for Facilitating the International Circulation of Auditory and Visual Materials of an Educational, Scientific and Cultural Character; and the Agreement on Importation of Educational, Scientific and Cultural Materials; 2) to assist countries in equipping themselves with the media they need by holding seminars, providing experts, and allocating equipment and fellowships; 3) to promote the use of the media for educational purposes through the UNESCO Space Communication Program, which was conceived with a view to promote increased cultural exchange between nations and a freer flow of information across frontiers; and 4) to disseminate the ideals of the United Nations through publications such as *UNESCO Features,* the *UNESCO Chronicle,* and press releases, and through producing radio and television programs in cooperation with national networks in member states. Publications: UNESCO has published some 70-odd items in the field of communications, including catalogues of films, studies such as "The Effects of Television on Children and Adolescents" and "World Communications," a survey of communications in some 200 countries. Publications are available through UNIPUB, P.O. Box 433, New York, NY 10016.

World Association for Christian Communication (WACC)
122 King's Road
London SW3 4TR
England
(01) 589-1484
Cable: WACC London SW3
Hans W. Florin, General Secretary

WACC is a working fellowship of corporate and individual members from 60 countries who are concerned with the use of modern means of communication for the proclamation of the Gospel in relevance to life. Members include church-related and secular communications organizations. It is concerned with strategy, evaluation and support of projects in print and electronic media development; communication education; research; exchange of information; and cooperation with other international and regional organizations in studies, conferences and events. Activities are centered in six regional associations: Africa, Asia-Pacific, Europe, Latin America-Caribbean, Middle East, and North America. Publications: *ACTION Newsletter* (see listing on page 295); *WACC Journal* (see listing on page 304).

3. LATIN AMERICA

Caribbean Broadcasting Union (CBU)
c/o CARICOM Secretariat
Bank of Guyana Building
Avenue of the Republic
Georgetown
Guyana

The CBU has 27 member organizations consisting of radio and television stations in the 13 Commonwealth Caribbean countries: Belize, the Bahamas, Jamaica, Antigua, St. Kitts/Nevis/Anguilla, Monserrat, Dominica, St. Lucia, St. Vincent, Grenada, Barbados, Trinidad and Tobago, and Guyana. Stations in Surinam, Aruba, Curacao and Bermuda are also full members. The CBU provides assistance to member organizations in the field of management, administration and in the form of training and technical advice. It reviews International Copyright arrangements, negotiates with various sports organizations in the region, advises on copyright and rights of access arrangements, and makes arrangements for the transmission of material to its member systems. It keeps its members in touch with the debate taking place in developing countries on the role of mass communications in development and on such issues as freedom of the press and social responsibility of the media. It also produces radio programs of regional interest on events such as national elections, regional conferences, and major disasters. Publication: *CBU Newsletter*, quarterly, for the staffs of member organizations.

Center for the Study of Advanced Means and Procedures in Education (CEMPAE)
Pedro H. Alegria, General Coodinator
Avenida Insurgentes Sur No. 1480
Mexico 12, D.F.
534-81-55
Rio Tamesi No. 300
Colonia Mexico, Monterrey, N.L.
Mexico
58-99-46

The general purpose of the Center is to promote and design innovative techniques in mass education. It also conducts research in the fields of education and communications and acts in an advisory capacity to similar institutions and organizations. Specific projects include the Open Learning System, a program utilizing tutors and printed and audio-visual programmed learning aids whose purpose is to spread educational opportunities, from the elementary to the post-degree levels, to the rural and working classes of Mexico; the National Program for Adult Education, which develops self-learning texts and trained tutors to provide basic elementary school education to rural and suburban working adults; television channel XHFN-TV in Monterrey, an educational channel which broadcasts educational and cultural programs for the non-culturally privileged audience; radio broadcasts of educational programs created by CEMPAE; and Expression and Communication, a program of instructional materials which help urban and rural elementary teachers develop artistic, physical and technological abilities in their students. CEMPAE has also been involved in numerous research projects that relate education techniques and mass media technology.

Inter-American Association of Broadcasters (IAAB)
Rua Mayrink Veiga 6
13 Andar, ZO
Rio de Janeiro
6B, Brazil

The Association was founded in 1946. Its members include private radio and television companies and radio and television broadcasting associations in both South and North America. Its purpose is to further representation of broadcasting interests in official or private national and international organizations, and to sponsor continental or regional conferences of a technical or educational nature. It bestows a Medal of Merit to individuals or groups which make outstanding contributions to free and private broadcasting. Publications: *Bulletin*, six times a year; monographs.

Inter American Press Association (IAPA)
See listing on page 232.

Interamerican Center for Advanced Studies of Communications in Latin America (CIESPAL)
Avenida Amazonas
1521, Quito
Ecuador
Marco Ordonez, Director

CIESPAL conducts a variety of research and sponsors a two-month training course for professionals in mass communications. It also conducts a book publishing program.

1. AFRICA AND THE MIDDLE EAST

Arab States Broadcasting Union (ASBU)
General Secretariat:
22 (a) Taha Hussein Street
Zamalek, Cairo
Egypt
Cable: ASBUNION
Salah Abdel Kader, Secretary General
Technical Centre:
P.O. Box 2231
Khartoum
Sudan
Ahmed Mahmoud Youssef, Director
Training Centre:
Damascus
Syria
Kheidr El Sha'ar, Director

Full Members of the Union are broadcasting organizations in Algeria, Bahrein, Egypt, Iraq, Jordan, Kuwait, Libya (A.R.), Mauritania, Morocco, Oman, Palestine, Qatar, Saudi Arabia, Somalia, Sudan, Syria, Tunisia, United Arab Emirates, Yemen (A.R.), Yemen (P.D.R.). Broadcasting organizations in four non-Arab countries are Associate Members: France, Pakistan, Spain and Yugoslavia.

Iran Communications and Development Institute
P.O. Box 33-183
Tajrish, Tehran 19
Iran
Telex: 2797-1846
Cable: TELMEL

The Institute was established in 1976. Its research and educational activities are focused on those areas of national development where the communications media can play an important role. Its purposes are to sponsor theoretical research in the fields of communications and development sciences in order to forge the interdisciplinary tools necessary for empirical research; to foster basic research in all facets of Iranian national culture in order to identify and revitalize those cultural elements which enhance integrated national development; to promote applied research in all aspects of Iranian national and regional cultures in order to facilitate the translation of traditional cultural materials into modern media forms; to engage in the development of multi-media educational programs in order to raise the quality of instruction as well as to expand educational opportunities; to promote an understanding of the role of communications support in national development through education and research in order to facilitate national integration and to avoid social problems which arise out of imbalances between different regions and sectors of the population; to assist in the planning of development-support communications systems in such fields as literacy campaigns, agricultural extension services, public health, family planning, telemedicine, teleconferencing, market information, consumer protection, and information utility; and to contribute towards research in the international aspects of communications and development in order to enhance international regional understanding and cooperation between Iran and other countries. Its activities include research projects, conferences, courses and seminars for middle and top management, preparation of a program of higher education, and strengthening of professional ties with individuals and institutions engaged in related research activities both in Iran and abroad. Publications: *Communications and Development Review*, a newsletter; *Communications Policy for National Development: A Comparative Perspective; The Future of Communications Technologies; Mass Communications Policy in Rapidly Developing Societies: Report of the Mashad Symposium; Survey of Social Attitudes in Iran; Social Attitudes and Modernization in Yazd;* and *Continuity and Change in National Development: Reflections on Japan and Iran.*

**Union of National Radio and
   Television Organizations of Africa**
101 Rue Carnot
BP 3237, Dakar
Senegal

The Union was established in 1962. Its membership consists of radio and television organizations throughout Africa. Its functions are to promote the development of African radio and television; to promote cooperation and exchange information among members; and to foster African culture.

5. ASIA AND AUSTRALIA

Asian Broadcasting Union (ABU)
203 Castlereagh Street
Sydney, New South Wales
Australia 61-7405
Charles Moses, Secretary General

The ABU was founded in 1964 to help develop broadcasting media in the Asian/Pacific region and to foster the use of these media in the cause of international understanding. Its members are national broadcasting organizations throughout Asia and the Pacific. Publications: *ABU Newsletter*, monthly; *ABU Technical Review*, bimonthly.

Asian Mass Communication Research and Information Center (AMIC)
39 Newton Road, Singapore 11
Republic of Singapore 515106/7
Telex: FESSINO RS 21731 AMIC
Cable: AMICINFO

Founded in 1971 and jointly sponsored by the Friedrich Ebert Foundation of West Germany and by the Singapore Government, AMIC is one of several regional documentation centers on mass communications cooperating with UNESCO. The Centre's objectives are to serve as a clearinghouse of information regarding mass communication in Asia; to bridge the gap between professional communicator, scholar and administrator; and to promote mass communication teaching, training and research. It collects and diffuses print and audio-visual materials on Asian mass communications, maintains a specialized library, and conducts seminars and refresher courses. AMIC initiated the *Asian Mass Communication Bibliography Series* in 1973, a bibliographical project which involved partners from eleven Asian countries: Hong Kong, India, Indonesia, Korea, Malaysia, Nepal, Pakistan, Philippines, Sri Lanka and Taiwan, with AMIC undertaking the compilation for Singapore. Membership in AMIC is open to individuals and institutions actively involved and interested in the study and practice of mass communications, irrespective of their geographical location. Publications: *Media Asia*, including *AMIC Documentation List*, quarterly, US $6.50 per year, free to members; *Asian Mass Communication Bulletin*, quarterly newsletter, free to members; *AMIC Index of Periodicals*, semiannual, free; *Asian Mass Communication Institutions: a Directory;* and a list of theses in three volumes: 1971, 1972, and 1973/74.

Indian Institute of Mass Communication
D-13, South Extension Part II
New Delhi-110049
India
Cable: MASMEDIA
Professor M.V. Desai, Director

The Institute was founded in 1965 as a national center for advanced study in mass communications. It engages in training, research and development in print media, visuals and films, advertising and campaign planning, radio and television, speech communication, and traditional media. The Institute conducts seminars and training courses, one of which is a post-graduate diploma course in journalism for information personnel and scholars from English-speaking countries in Asia and Africa. It also provides professional advice on manpower and infrastructure problems to media organizations and to professionals in the media. Publication: *Communicator,* quarterly journal, $5 per year.

International Association of Women in Radio and Television
Elisabeth Kirkby, President
35 Marina, 300a Burns Bay Road
Lane Cove, NSW 20066
Australia
Elisabeth Schnell, Secretary-Treasurer
SRG/Studio Zurich
8042 Zurich
Postfach, Switzerland

Members of the Association work in 35 countries throughout the world, including the United States. The Association's purpose is to promote an exchange of professional experience and technical knowledge; to further members' consciousness of the privilege of free speech and the responsibility entailed therein; to improve methods of serving listeners; and to widen the content of women's programs.

Press Foundation of Asia
1632 Indiana Street
P.O. Box 1843
Malate, Manila
Philippines
Cable: PRESSASIA
Amitabha Chowdhury, Executive Trustee

Founded in 1967, the Foundation conducts studies and training programs designed to uplift the standards of the journalism profession in Asia. It is supported by over 200 Asian editors and newspapers. It has helped to set up and has supported several national press institutes in the region. As part of its efforts to speed the flow of information in Asia or concerning Asia, primarily for the use of the mass media, the Foundation established an information bank of contemporary source materials in 1972. It services the Asian press through a specialized news features agency, Depthnews. Publications: *Data Asia*, weekly bulletin of statistics, development events and economic information, $250 per year; *DataFil*, containing systematized data and abstracts on the Philippines, biweekly, $150 per year overseas; *Media Magazine*, monthly, by invitation; *Asian Press and Media Directory*.

9

A GUIDE TO SPECIAL LIBRARIES
AND RESOURCES ON COMMUNICATIONS

This section contains listings of major collections of books, periodicals, and non-print resources of particular interest to the communications researcher. It also includes a bibliography of guides to special libraries and archives.

The libraries and archives listed in this section are affiliated with universities, government agencies, and private business firms. Unless otherwise noted, they are open to the public, though most require that materials be used on the premises.

American Newspaper Publishers Association Library
Post Office Box 17407
Dulles International Airport
Washington, DC 20041
(703) 620-9500 ext. 250
Mrs. Jo Kirks, Librarian

Features works on newspaper publishing, newspaper history, mass communications, journalism techniques, and legal aspects of publishing newspapers. Founded in 1952.

Holdings: 4,000 books, 500 bound periodical volumes, subscriptions to 200 journals. Hours: 9 AM to 4:45 PM. Open to the public for on-site research only.

American Newspaper Publishers Association, Research Institute Library
Easton, PA 18042
(215) 253-6155
Erwin Jaffe, Director

Contains 800 books on printing, paper, ink, and the graphic arts.

American Telephone and Telegraph Company Legal Library
195 Broadway
New York, NY 10007
(212) 393-3651
Marian E. Mager, Librarian

Special collections of ICC, FCC, and state commission reports. Hours: 9 AM to 5 PM.

Annenberg School of Communications Library
University of Pennsylvania
3620 Walnut Street C5
Philadelphia, PA 19174
(215) 243-7027/8
Sandra B. Grilikhes, Librarian

Founded in 1962. Covers theory and research in communication, mass media, interpersonal communication, attitude and opinion research, language behavior, communications economics, ethnographic methods, literature and communications, and other social issues of communication.

Holdings: Special collections—Annenberg faculty publications collection, film catalog collection, collection of annual reports of communication companies; 14,500 bound periodicals and books; 320 current periodicals; 40 pamphlet drawers, which include pamphlets, clippings, reprints, and technical reports.

Open to the public for reference. Microfilm and photocopying facilities are available to the public. Interlibrary loans handled by the Main Library, University of Pennsylvania.

Hours (when classes are in session): Monday through Thursday, 9 AM to 9 PM; Friday, 9 AM to 6 PM; Saturday, 12:00 to 4:30 PM; Sunday, 1 PM to 9 PM. When classes are not in session: weekdays from 9 AM to 5 PM, closed on weekends.

Anthology Film Archives (AFA)
80 Wooster Street
New York, NY   10012
(212) 226-0010
Jonas Mekas, Executive Director

Formerly *Film-Makers' Cinematheque*. Maintains four divisions: film collection, library, preservation, and video library. Research facilities are open to scholars and to the general public. Facilities include visual and written research library, publication of texts on film, nightly public screenings of films in the collection, and preservation of video works. AFA is concerned with the preservation of new American cinema and European avant-garde cinema and encourages presentation of new work. The library contains 4,500 volumes.

Archives of Labor and Urban Affairs
Walter P. Reuther Library
Wayne State University
Detroit, MI   48202
(313) 577-4024
Augelita Espino-McGhee, Librarian

The Newspaper Guild preserves historical records and inactive files in the Archives of Labor and Urban Affairs. In addition to the papers of the international Guild, the Archives contains papers of a number of Guild locals and the personal papers of some Guild members.

Hours: Monday through Friday, 8:30 AM to 5 PM; Saturdays, 9 AM to 5 PM. Materials in the Archives are available to persons with a serious scholarly interest.

Broadcast Pioneers Library
1771 N Street, N.W.
Washington, DC   20036
(202) 223-0088
Catherine Heinz, Director

Established in 1971, the library includes primary sources in tapes, oral history interviews, recordings, research studies, official records, letters, newspaper clippings, books, magazines on the history of radio and television broadcasting.

Hours: Monday through Friday, 9 AM to 5 PM. Open to the public.

Milton Caniff Library
Ohio State University
Library Building, Room 100
242 West 18th Avenue
Columbus, OH   43210
(614) 422-8747

Library of mass communication. Holdings: 11,000 books, 425 periodical volumes, 150 M.A. theses, subscriptions to more than 200 professional and other journals, 500 bound periodical volumes, and 36 newspapers.

Hours: Autumn, Winter and Spring Quarters: 8 AM to 10 PM Monday through Thursday; 8 AM to 5 PM Friday; 10 AM to 2 PM Saturday; 5 PM to 10 PM Sunday. Summer Quarter: 8 AM to 5 PM weekdays; closed Saturday; 1 PM to 7 PM Sunday. Hours vary during the time between quarters. All faculty, staff, students and active alumni may use and borrow from the library. Courtesy privileges extended to some other colleges and universities. Open to the public, but materials cannot be borrowed.

CBS News Special Projects Department Library
524 West 57th Street
New York, NY   10019
(212) 975-2877, 2878, and 2879
Meg M. Dowell, Director

Library of radio and television broadcasting founded in 1940.

Holdings: 25,000 books, 561 vertical files, subscriptions to 280 journals and periodicals, 37 drawers of microfilm.

Hours: Monday through Friday, 10 AM to 6 PM.

Columbia University Journalism Library
Room 304, Journalism Building
116th Street and Broadway
New York, NY   10027
(212) 280-3860
Jonathan D. Beard, Assistant Librarian
    Founded in 1912. Subjects include astronautics (satellites), books and book publishing, telephone communications, computers, corporate communications, the FCC, journalism, motion pictures, radio, television, and cable.
    Holdings: 11,000 books, extensive newspaper clipping collection (over 3 million), subscriptions to 130 American and foreign periodicals and 35 American newspapers.
    Hours: Monday through Friday, 9 AM to 5 PM. Individuals not affiliated with the University may be granted short-term reading privileges upon application to the Library Information Office, Room 234, Butler Library.

Columbia University Oral
   History Research Office
Butler Library
New York, NY   10027
(212) 280-2273
Louis M. Starr, Director
    Founded in 1948, the Office engages in creating, by means of tape-recorded, transcribed interviews with leaders in many fields, primary source materials for the University's Oral History Collection. It also services research requests from scholars, by mail and in person. Recent accessions are given in its annual report, obtainable for the asking. A catalogue, *The Oral History Collection* (1973 edition), is available in paperback ($7.50) or hard cover ($12.50).
    A course on Oral History, conducted by Professor Starr and Elizabeth B. Mason, Associate Director of the Office, is offered in the spring semester, a cross-disciplinary seminar carrying three-point credit toward advanced degrees in anthropology, education, history, journalism, and library service. Post-doctoral candidates may also apply; there are a limited number of scholarships for those who qualify.

Educational Film Library Association (EFLA)
   (See listing on page 125.)

Film Library Information Council (FLIC)
See listing on page 126

Freedom of Information (FOI) Center
Post Office Box 858
Columbia, MO 65201
(314) 882-4856

The Center, located at the University of Missouri School of Journalism, clips major newspapers, professional journals, periodicals, and confidential bulletins to maintain files showing how government, society, and the media affect the content and movement of information. *FOI Digest* is published bi-monthly to summarize information and news about the media and to list recent books and articles in periodicals and law reviews. *FOI Reports*, published monthly, are short studies on subjects of continual interest, such as cable television, censorship and newsman's privilege legislation. *FOI Foundation Series* are studies on freedom of information written by distinguished professors across the country. Published periodically. Subscriptions, costing $12 per year for individuals and $25 per year for organizations, include all Center publications.

Great Plains National Instructional Television Library (GPN)
Post Office Box 80669
Lincoln, NE 68501
(402) 472-2007 or 467-2502
Paul H. Schupbach, Director

Founded in 1962 as a service agency of the University of Nebraska-Lincoln, GPN's mission is to identify, acquire and make available for distribution to schools and ETV stations and agencies (on a rental, lease or sale basis), instruction over a wide subject area spectrum that has been recorded and preserved on video tape, ¾-inch videocassette, and 16mm film. Holdings include nearly 150 separate series and singles, the bulk of which constitute multi-lesson series structured for use in the elementary through college classroom. GPN publishes annual catalogs and monthly updating newsletters, all available on a gratis basis to interested and qualified persons and agencies. Use of GPN-distributed materials does not require a membership fee.

University of Illinois Journalism and Communications Library
122 Gregory Hall
University of Illinois
Urbana, IL 61801
(217) 333-2216
Eleanor Blum, Librarian

Founded in 1933. Covers advertising, book publishing, broadcasting, magazines, newspapers, photography, public relations, communication theory, popular culture, mass communications, publishing, typography, international communications, post office, telephone and telegraph, magazine, film, copyright.

Holdings: over 20,000 books, 825 bound periodical volumes, subscriptions to 200 journals and periodicals and current issues of 20 newspapers (microfilms of about 1,000 newspapers are stored in a separate library).

Hours: Monday through Thursday, 8 AM to 5 PM and 7 PM to 10 PM; Friday, 8 AM to 5 PM; Saturday, 9 AM to 5 PM; Sunday, 1 PM to 10 PM.

International Federation of Film Archives (FIAF)
See listing on page 243

University of Iowa Libraries, Special Collections Department
Iowa City, IA 52242
(319) 353-4854
Robert A. McCown, Manuscripts Librarian

A collection of materials on silent and sound motion pictures, television and journalism, including screenplays, TV scripts, still photos, posters, artists' sketches, clippings, correspondence, editorial comments, production papers, censorship records, financial records and other items. Open for use by scholars. Hours: 9-12 and 1-5, Monday through Friday.

University of Minnesota Journalism Library
121 Murphy Hall
School of Journalism
Minneapolis, MN 55455
(612) 373-3374

Founded in 1941. Subjects include mass communications, newspaper journalism, broadcast journalism, graphic arts, advertising, international communications, and public relations. Special creative writing holdings are in the Thomas Heggen Memorial Library. Holdings: 4,200 books, 1,400 bound periodical volumes, 1,500 pamphlets, subscriptions to 130 journals and periodicals and 25 newspapers.

University of Missouri Journalism Library
117 Walter Williams Hall
Columbia, MO   65201
(314) 882-7502

Subjects are mass communications, including journalism; radio and television broadcasting; public relations; and cinema and photography.

Holdings: 10,000 books, 6,000 bound periodical volumes, subscriptions to 200 journals and periodicals, and 70 domestic and 50 foreign newspapers.

Hours: variable.

Non-members are welcome to use the library facilities but cannot remove materials.

The Museum of Broadcasting
1 East 53rd Street
New York, NY   10022
(212) 752-4690
Information: (212) 752-7684
James Rieser, Technical Director

Supported by the William S. Paley Foundation and by memberships, the Museum of Broadcasting is the first American museum dedicated to the study and preservation of radio and television broadcasting history.

Holdings: The Museum's collection includes significant radio and television programs spanning the period from the 1920s to the present, with emphasis on the earlier years. The Museum also maintains a library of rare radio and television scripts, as well as books and periodicals on broadcasting.

Facilities and Programs: Professionally indexed collections are open to the public. The Broadcast Study Center has custom-designed broadcast consoles for public monitoring of programs in the collection. Morning hours are reserved for use by college and university classes (by arrangement) and for periodical programs on the media for members.

Hours: Tuesday through Saturday, 12:00 noon to 5 PM.

Fees: Members free. Visitors: $1.00 contribution (suggested).

National Archives and Records Service, Audiovisual Archives Division
Washington, DC 20408
(202) 523-3189
James W. Moore, Director

Maintains the noncurrent permanently valuable audiovisual records of the federal government and audiovisual materials acquired from non-federal sources which document federal activities. The Division is composed of three branches:

Still Picture Branch. (202) 523-3236. Joe D. Thomas, Chief.

Holdings: Over 5 million items dating primarily from the 1860s to the present.

Hours: 8:45 AM to 5:15 PM, Monday through Friday.

Motion Picture and Sound Recording Branch. (202) 523-3267. William T. Murphy, Chief.

Holdings: motion pictures, 103,000 reels; sound recordings, 70,000 items; video recordings, 2,000 items. See dating from 1900 to the present.

Hours: 8:45 AM to 5:15 PM, Monday through Friday.

Stock Film Library Branch. 1411 South Fern Street, Arlington, VA 20408. (703) 557-1114. Leon A. Williams, Chief.

Holdings: Over 6,000 reels of non-defense government-produced stock motion picture footage dating from the late 1950s to the present.

Hours: 8:00 AM to 4:30 PM, Monday through Friday.

National Association of Broadcasters Library
1771 N Street, N.W.
Washington, DC 20036
(202) 293-3578
Susan M. Hill, Librarian

The library collection supports the activities of the staff and members of the National Association of Broadcasters, a trade association. Its emphasis is the radio and television broadcasting industry. Founded in 1946.

Holdings: 3,500 books (titles), 5,500 volumes (including bound periodicals), subscriptions to over 200 periodicals, and vertical files.

Hours: Open to the public by appointment, Monday

through Friday, 10 AM to 4 PM.

National Broadcasting Company General Library
Room 1016
30 Rockefeller Plaza
New York, NY 10020
(212) 664-4444, ext. 5307
Founded in 1930.

Holdings: 8,500 books, concentrated on broadcasting and current events; subscriptions to 145 periodicals; over 2,000 reels of microfilm and 35 drawers of clippings. The library is also a subscriber to the *New York Times* Information Bank (a computerized information retrieval system).

Hours: Monday through Friday, 9 AM to 6 PM. Access only for NBC employees.

National Technical Information Service (NTIS)
Department of Commerce
5285 Port Royal Road
Springfield, VA 22161
(202) 724-3509
*Washington Information Center
   and Bookstore*
425 13th Street, N.W.
Washington, DC 20004
(202) 724-3383

Other phone numbers: subscriptions: (703) 557-4630; computer products: (703) 557-4763; new orders for documents and reports: (703) 557-4650; NTISearches: (703) 557-4642; SRIM (Selected Research in Microfiche and Microforms): (703) 557-4640.

Central source for public sale of government-sponsored research, development, and engineering reports and other analyses prepared by federal agencies, their contractors or grantees. Supplies the public with approximately four million documents and microforms annually. An Information Service catalog of special interest documents describes those reports most in demand. Current abstracts are published weekly and semimonthly.

Holdings: Over 900,000 titles, all for sale.

The Peabody Collection
Henry W. Grady School of Journalism
University of Georgia
Athens, GA   30602
(404) 542-3785
Dr. Worth McDougald, Director

The George Foster Peabody Radio and Television Awards were initiated in 1941 when five awards relating to meritorious public service during 1940 were made. All program recordings submitted to the Peabody Awards competitions become the property of the University of Georgia.

Holdings: more than 11,000 program recordings.

Hours: Monday through Friday, 8 AM to 5 PM; closed Saturday and Sunday; holidays in accordance with University of Georgia academic schedule; normally closed Christmas and New Year's week, July 4th, and at certain times between quarters.

RCA Laboratories/David Sarnoff
   Research Center Library
Princeton, NJ   08540
(609) 452-2700, ext. 2608

Founded in 1941. Subjects include radio, electronics and television, as well as physics, chemistry, mathematics, metallurgy, acoustics, computers, space technology. A weekly library bulletin is distributed to all technical personnel.

Holdings: 33,000 books; 7,000 bound periodical volumes; 110 vertical file drawers of company reports; 100 vertical file drawers of pamphlets; numerous vertical files of bibliographies, doctoral dissertations and government reports; subscriptions to over 350 journals.

Hours: 8:30 AM to 5 PM. Open to the general public.

Milo Ryan Phonoarchive
School of Communications, DS-40
University of Washington
Seattle, WA   98195
(206) 543-2660
Donald G. Godfrey, Curator

Established in 1956, the Phonoarchive includes 5,000 KIRO-CBS broadcasts, primarily of World War II. The collection has been meticulously catalogued. *History in Sound* by Milo Ryan and *History in Sound Part II* (a microfiche publication) edited by Donald G. Godfrey are available through the University of Washington Press. The collection has a news/information orientation. Computer assistance is available for research, as the collection has been computerized to yield chronological and subject search information.

Stanford University Communication Department Library
Stanford, CA 94305
(415) 497-1789
Douglas Ferguson, Director

Covers broadcasting, film, journalism, research on processes and effects of mass media, media and international development, and new technologies. Primarily recent material.

Holdings: 3,000 recent volumes (older books are in the main library on the Stanford campus), subscriptions to 40 journalism reviews, 25 broadcasting and film periodicals, and 12 newspapers.

Hours: 9 to 5 weekdays during Fall, Winter and Spring quarters; irregular during the Summer. Open to the general public.

Television Information Office Library
745 Fifth Avenue
New York, NY 10022
(212) 759-6800
James Poteat, Librarian

Founded in 1959. An extensive library and information center covering the social, cultural, and programming aspects of television. The library collection supports the functions of the Television Information Office in providing a continuing information service for educators, students, government agencies, the press, the clergy, librarians, broadcasters, and the general public.

Holdings: 3,500 books, 475 bound periodicals, 123 vertical file drawers, subscriptions to 190 periodicals and 10 newspapers.

Hours: Monday through Friday, 9:30 AM to 5 PM, by appointment.

U. S. Federal Communications Commission Library
1919 M Street, N.W.
Room 639
Washington, DC 20036
(202) 632-7100

Library of communications, electronics, radio, telegraph, telephone, television, public utilities, economics, management and law. Founded in 1934.

Holdings: 37,000 books and bound periodical volumes, 30 vertical files on legislative materials, subscriptions to over 300 periodicals, 350 bound court records, materials from congressional hearings on FCC business from the 60th Congress to the present one.

Hours: Monday through Friday, 8 AM to 4:30 PM. The library is open to the public and will provide assistance in research. Items must be used in the library, but provisions can be made for photocopying.

Vanderbilt Television News Archive
Joint University Libraries
Nashville, TN 37203
(615) 322-2927
James P. Pilkington, Administrator

The Archive was begun in 1968. It maintains a videotape collection of the evening newscasts of the three major television networks—ABC, CBS, and NBC. The collection consists of more than 5,000 hours of news programs, with at least 7½ hours added each week. The collection also includes some additional material, such as Presidential speeches, political conventions, and Watergate hearings. Beginning in January 1972, the Archive has published a monthly index to television news, entitled *Television News Index and Abstracts*. Tapes in the Archive are available for study either on the premises or through rental of the tapes for outside use. Material may be rented—unaltered and as aired—either in complete programs or as compiled subject matter tapes. No material is sold, and none can be duplicated.

G. Robert Vincent Voice Library
c/o Michigan State University Library
East Lansing, MI 48824
(517) 355-5122; nights and weekends: (517) 353-1753
Dr. Maurice A. Crane, Director

Mrs. Pamela Engelbrecht, Librarian
A collection of 20,000 voices from 1888 to the present. Catalogue published by G. K. Hall and Company, Boston, 1975. Hours: weekdays from 8 to 5.

Wisconsin Center for Film and Theatre Research
University of Wisconsin
Madison, WI 53706
(608) 262-9706

Founded in 1960, the Center is a national repository of primary source materials relating to the performing and communication arts in the United States and to their role in social and cultural history. Holdings include more than 150 collections in the performing arts donated by writers, composers, producers, directors, designers, critics, actors, and studios. The Center also houses documents, such as original film scripts, manuscripts of plays, correspondence, pressbooks, posters, and other material. A film library containing over 2,000 feature films, plus cartoons and short subjects, and a television kinescope and film library are also part of the Center. A guide to the collections and a listing of the films are available. Open to the general public.

Wisconsin State Historical Society
Mass Communications History Center
816 State Street
Madison, WI 53706
(608) 262-9561
Janice L. O'Connell, Director

The Mass Communications History Center (MCHC) is the nation's most extensive archive of primary source materials on the development of mass communications in the United States and on the role of the mass media in American history. Established in 1955 with the donation of the papers of H. V. Kaltenborn, the MCHC and the Wisconsin Center for Film and Theatre Research (a separate but cooperative unit) have received donations of materials from nearly 700 organizations and individuals, including eminent journalists, actors, producers, radio and television personalities, playwrights, and broadcasting, advertising, and public relations executives. Except for certain restricted collections, the holdings of the MCHC are available for general research.

A Guide to Special Libraries and Resources on Communications

Ash, Lee, et al. *Subject Collections: A Guide to Special Book Collections and Subject Emphases as Reported by University, College, Public and Special Libraries and Museums in the United States and Canada* (New York: Bowker, 1974—4th ed.): the title pretty much explains this annotated listing of some 35-40,000 references computerized and arranged from survey questionnaires sent to the libraries. A very important and useful source.

Benton, Mildred, comp. *Federal Library Resources: A User's Guide to Research Collections* (New York: Science Associates/International, 1973): alphabetical listing of more than 160 libraries, mainly in the Washington, D.C. area, with annotations on location, personnel, hours, telephones, services provided, and resources. Subject index included. See also the Library of Congress entry below.

Catalog of the Communications Library (Boston: G. K. Hall, 1975, three volumes): the 50,000 library cards of the University of Illinois Communications Library are reproduced here for reference elsewhere. An increasing number of specialized library catalogs are getting the same treatment from specialty publishers.

Library of Congress, National Referral Center. *A Directory of Information Resources in the United States: Federal Government* (Washington: Government Printing Office, 1974): one of several volumes in a series, this volume includes the name, location, areas of interest, publication and information sources of hundreds of libraries. There is also a subject index. The Library of Congress also updates from time to time *Library and Reference Facilities in the Area of the District of Columbia* which includes both government, commercial, and private libraries.

Parch, Grace D., ed. *Directory of Newspaper Libraries in the U. S. and Canada* (New York: Special Libraries Association, 1976): information on 295 papers with a page for each providing location, telephone contacts, hours, resources available, special collections, services provided to media and unaffiliated users.

Performing Arts Resources (New York: Drama Book Specialists/Theater Library Association, 1975-date, annual): under various editors, these volumes provide guides to unique collections of theatrical (including film and broadcasting) collections in the U. S. and Canada. Volume III was to include an index for the first three years (1974-1976).

Rawley-Saldich, Anne. "Access to Television's Past," *Columbia Journalism Review* (November/December 1976), pp. 46-48. Useful current review of conflicting plans and projects to save network news program content.

Schneider, John H., *et al. Survey of Commercially Available Computer-Readable Bibliographic Data Bases* (Washington: American Society for Information Science, 1973): a total of 81 such bases from 55 organizations (40 in the U. S.) are detailed with a full page form of information on each.

Schwartz, Ruth. "Preserving TV Programs: Here Today—Gone Tomorrow," *Journal of Broadcasting* 17:287-300 (Summer 1973): a status report, as of 1972, of some 35 film and videotape collections, including a comparative chart and text describing both the difficulties and importance of such preservation efforts.

Weber, Olga S., *et al. North American Film and Video Directory: A Guide to Media Collections and Services* (New York: Bowker, 1976): arranged by state, this provides details on more than 2,000 libraries and archives with film and videotape collections. It is admittedly quite incomplete (especially for television), and its subject index is not very good, but the locational and collection content information is unavailable in any other single source.

Young, Margaret Labash, *et al. Directory of Special Libraries and Information Centers* (Detroit: Gale Research, 1974—3rd ed.): this three-volume work contains (in Volume I) detailed listings with information on where to find and how to use the various collections, (in Volume II) a geographic and personnel index, and (in Volume III) a binder for periodic updates of the main volume that obviates the need to publish complete new editions.

Young, William C. *American Theatrical Arts: A Guide to Manuscripts and Special Collections in the United States and Canada* (Chicago: American Library Association, 1971): a guide by state of special collections, many of which include film or broadcast materials. Detailed and useful name and subject index.

Readers interested in finding nearby locations of specific books and periodicals should consult the *National*

Union Catalog, which is available in several multi-volume editions in most major university (and some public) libraries.

10

COMMUNICATIONS PERIODICALS

This section, perhaps more than any other in the *Handbook*, reflects the great diversity of interests in and approaches to the field of communications. The publications listed here range from trade journals to scholarly publications, from small, specialized newsletters to large annual directories. Moreover, the number of communications periodicals continues to grow, both as a result of the general increase of interest in communications and of the emergence of new communications technologies.

The section is broken down into the following categories:

1)	Annuals, Directories and Indexes	283
2)	Research	289
3)	Related General Periodicals	295
4)	Advertising and Public Relations	305
5)	Broadcasting	309
6)	Cable and Pay Television	316
7)	Educational/Instructional Media	320
8)	Film and Photography	324
9)	Journalism	335
10)	Journalism Criticism Reviews	342
11)	Print Media	344
12)	Technology and Telecommunications Policy	347

This breakdown demonstrates the difficulty of organizing the multi-disciplinary field of communications into logical categories. *Public Telecommunications Review*, for example, is intended primarily for professionals working in public radio and television and is therefore listed under "Broadcasting." However, because of the range of subjects covered by *PTR* it has also been cross-referenced under "Educational/Instructional Media" and "Telecommunications Technology and Policy."

Publications that are available only to members of an organization are not included in this section. Such periodicals are included with the organizational listing in Section IV, Communications Organizations.

Information on subscription rates was correct as of Spring, 1977. Because frequent rate increases have become more and more common, the reader is advised to check on current prices before entering a subscription to any of the periodicals listed.

1. ANNUALS, DIRECTORIES AND INDEXES

Annual Cost Study for Weekly Newspapers
National Newspaper Association
491 National Press Building
Washington, DC 20045
(202) 783-1651

Analyzes revenues and costs of about 300 newspapers. Participating newspapers are categorized by circulation. $5 to participating newspapers; $25 for nonparticipants.

Annual Review of Marketing
American Marketing Association
222 South Riverside Plaza
Chicago, IL 60606
(312) 648-0536

Provides an integrated review and yearly updating of the various subfields within marketing. Articles specify practical implications of current marketing thought. Each is an original review and synthesis of the published literature in each of the major fields of marketing. Available early 1978. $20 to individuals, $30 to institutions.

Broadcasting Yearbook
Broadcasting Publications, Inc.
1735 DeSales Street, N.W.
Washington, DC 20036
(202) 638-1022

A complete and comprehensive annual listing of facts about all aspects of broadcasting, including full listing for every radio and TV station in the U. S. and Canada, plus FCC rules, ADI market atlases, associations, attorneys, brokers, equipment manufacturers, program services, networks, and representatives. Contains over 160 separate directories. $25 prepaid; $30 billable.

Cable Sourcebook
Broadcasting Publications, Inc.
1735 DeSales Street, N.W.
Washington, DC 20036
(202) 638-1022
Sol Taishoff, editor

Contains up-to-date information on cable owners,

systems, groups, equipment, brokers, consultants, FCC rules, program suppliers, Yellow Pages Buyers Guide, broadcasters in cable, CATV associations and government agencies in the U. S. and Canada. Fully indexed, cross-referenced, with history and outline of cable regulations and developments. Annual. $10.

CATV and Station Coverage Atlas
Television Digest, Inc.
1836 Jefferson Place, N.W.
Washington, DC 20036
(202) 872-9200
　　An annual publication which contains all the FCC rules on cable television rule-making for CATV systems. It also lists equipment manufacturers, translators, and microwaves servicing CATV systems and includes two sets of state maps showing CATV systems, grade B contours of all stations, and 35-mile and 55-mile CATV zone maps. $44.50.

**CATV Systems Directory,
　Map Service and Handbook**
Communications Publishing Corp.
1900 West Yale
Englewood, CO 80110
(303) 761-3770
　　Lists industry statistics, programming and advertising markets, regulations, federal agencies and congressional committees, CATV associations, MSO's and all cable systems in the U. S. and Canada. Annual. $14.95.

Editor & Publisher International Yearbook
850 Third Avenue
New York, NY 10022
(212) 752-7050
　　Annual listing of facts about all aspects of newspapers, executive personnel, circulation, etc. $20 per issue.

Education Media Yearbook
R. R. Bowker Company
1180 Avenue of the Americas
New York, NY 10036
(212) 764-5100
James W. Brown, editor

Contains statistics on employment, funding, associations and programs in the media industry; feature articles on media developments in education, industry, computer science and libraries. $19.95.

Encyclomedias
Media Decisions
342 Madison Avenue
New York, NY   10017
(212) 953-1888
   Annual compendiums to help media planners, media buyers, ad managers, marketing directors, agency account executives and others understand, evaluate and plan media buys. *1977 Newspaper Encyclomedia*: $18. *1977 Consumer Magazine Encyclomedia*: $20. In the planning stage: *Magazine Encyclomedia, Radio Encyclomedia, TV Encyclomedia, Business Publication Encyclomedia* and *Out-of-Home and Yellow Pages Encyclomedia*.

Free Speech Yearbook
Speech Communication Association
5205 Leesburg Pike
Falls Church, VA   22041
(703) 379-1888
Dr. Gregg Phifer, Florida State University, editor
   Sponsored by the SCA Commission on Freedom of Speech. $3 to members, $3.50 to non-members.

Hope Reports AV-USA
Hope Reports, Inc.
919 South Winton Road
Rochester, NY   14618
(716) 244-6630
   Analyzes sales of 130 products in seven basic markets. Annual. $135.

Hudson's Washington News
Media Contacts Directory
2626 Pennsylvania Avenue, N.W.
Washington, DC   20037
(202) 333-5444
Mary Elizabeth Hudson and
   Howard Penn Hudson, editors
   Comprehensive guide to the entire Washington D.C., press corps, broken down by categories. Lists Washing-

ton bureau chiefs, national and international news services, magazine correspondents, syndicated columnists, Canadian and foreign news bureaus and magazines, freelance writers, and photographic services. Revisions issued in April, July and October. $40 per year.

Index of Research Publications
Research Publications and
   Documentation Service
Communications Research Centre
Shirley Bay
P.O. Box 11490
Station "H"
Ottawa, Ontario K2H 8S2
(613) 596-9404
Ted Atkins, manager
   A compilation of research publications indexed by subject and principal author. Annual. Free.

International Film Guide
The Tantivy Press
136–148 Tooley Street
London SE1 2TT
England
Peter Cowie, editor
   Covers the international film, TV film and documentary market. Annual. $5.95. U.S. distributor: A.S. Barnes and Co., P.O. Box 421, Cranbury, NJ 08512. (609) 655-0190.

Journalism Abstracts
Department of Journalism
Ball State University
Muncie, IN 47306
(317) 289-1241
Mark Popovich, editor
   An annual compilation of M.A. theses and doctoral dissertations from schools and departments of journalism and communication in the U. S. $7 per year. Subscriptions should be sent to 430 Murphy Hall, University of Minnesota, 206 Church Street S.E., Minneapolis, MN 55455. (612) 376-7100.

Media Report to Women Index/Directory
Women's Institute for Freedom of the Press
3306 Ross Place, N.W.
Washington, DC   20008
(202) 363-0812
Martha Leslie Allen, editor
   An annual cumulative index to *Media Report to Women* and a directory of women's media groups and individual media women. $8.

NAEB Directory of Public Telecommunications
National Association of Educational Broadcasters
1346 Connecticut Ave, N.W.
Washington, DC 20036
(202) 785-1100
   Contains information about the NAEB and related organizations, individual members, professional councils, institutional associates, public radio and television stations, state agencies, networks and authorities, ITFS systems, and colleges and universities. Annual. $10. Free to members.

National Directory of Weekly Newspapers
National Newspaper Association
491 National Press Building
Washington, DC   20045
(202) 783-1651
   Lists all nondaily newspapers in the United States alphabetically by state. Contains the following information for each listing: name of newspaper, city and address, area designation (agricultural, industrial, mining, oil, resort, suburban, county seat), line rate, publication day, circulation, number of columns, inches per column, column width, production information, advertising policies, publisher's name, telephone, county of publication. Annual (published in April). $20.

Newspaper Fund Journalism Scholarship Guide
The Newspaper Fund, Inc.
P. O. Box 300
Princeton, NJ   08540
(609) 452-2000
   Listing of scholarships, fellowships, assistantships and loans available to journalism students. Annual.

Single copy free; two or more: 50¢ each.

Standard Rate and Data Service
5201 Old Orchard Road
Skokie, IL 60076
(312) 966-8500

Serves as a major source of rate information news for advertisers and agencies; also contains valuable information for PR people. Published in 12 editions: Newspapers, Business Publications, Consumer and Farm Magazines, Network TV, Spot Radio, Spot Television, Direct Mail, Transit Advertising, Weekly Newspapers and Shopping Guides, Canadian Media, Newspaper Circulation Analysis, and Print Media Production Data. Frequency of publication and subscription price varies with each edition.

Television Factbook
Television Digest, Inc.
1836 Jefferson Place, N.W.
Washington, DC 20036
(202) 872-9200

Annual reference work of over 2,000 pages providing details of all TV stations in the world, all CATV systems in the U.S. and Canada, directories of government agencies, trade associations, engineers, attorneys, consultants, brokers—about 150 such categories. Published each winter. $94.50.

Television News Index and Abstracts
Vanderbilt Television News Archive
Joint University Libraries
Nashville, TN 37203
(212) 322-2927

Monthly summary of the evening news broadcasts of the three major television networks, ABC, CBS, and NBC, indexed by names, subjects, etc. Tapes of the newscasts are in the Archives collection. Free.

Topicator
Thompson Bureau
5395 South Miller Street
Littleton, CO 80123
(303) 973-2337

A monthly classified guide to the advertising/ broadcasting trade press. Cumulated quarterly and annually. Includes articles from *Advertising Age, AV Communication Review, Broadcasting, Educational Broadcasting Review, Journal of Broadcasting, Marketing/Communications, Media/Scope, Television Age, Television Digest, Television Quarterly, TV Guide, Variety*. $85 per year.

The Video Handbook
United Business Publications, Inc.
750 Third Avenue
New York, NY   10017
(212) 697-8300
   Authoritative guide to video technology and techniques, intended for reference and for use as a training manual. Annual. $11.25.

Working Press of the Nation
National Research Bureau
424 North Third Street
Burlington, IA   52601
(319) 752-5415
   A comprehensive reference work listing detailed information on newspapers (vol. 1), national magazines (vol. 2), radio and television (vol. 3), feature writers and syndicates (vol. 4), and house magazines (vol. 5). Annual. $154 for all five volumes; $120 for volumes 1, 2 and 3; or $45 each volume. Shipping charges extra.

2. RESEARCH

Canadian Communications Research
  Information Centre Newsletter
255 Albert Street
Post Office Box 1047
Ottawa, Ontario K1P 5V8
(613) 237-3400, ext. 411 or 493
Ash K. Prakash, editor
   Informal bulletin focusing on existing national resources in communications. Includes sections on policy and public issues, research projects, new periodicals, information exchange and research resources, education, and calendar of events. Bimonthly, free. (Also published

in a French edition, *Nouvelles*.)

Communication Quarterly
Department of Speech Communication
227 Sparks Building
Pennsylvania State University
University Park, PA 16802
(814) 865-4201
Thomas W. Benson, editor

An interdisciplinary journal with articles and reviews on all aspects of human communication. $10 for institutions; $15, with membership in Eastern Communication Association, for individuals. Subscriptions to R. Bailey, Executive Secretary, ECA, Department of Speech Communication, University of Rhode Island, Kingston, RI 02881.

Communication Research:
An International Quarterly
Department of Journalism
and Program in Mass Communication
University of Michigan
Ann Arbor, MI 48104
(313) 764-1817
F. Gerald Kline, editor

A quarterly journal dealing with communications research in the fields of political science, psychology, economics, sociology, marketing, speech, and journalism. A major concern is unification of common communications-research interests. $20 per year. Subscriptions to the publisher, Sage Publications, Inc., 275 South Beverly Drive, Beverly Hills, CA 90212.

Communications: Research in Canada
255 Albert Street
Ottawa, Ontario K1P 6A9
(613) 237-3400, ext. 411 or 493

Annual publication focusing on the social science of electronic mass communication but also including content on communications technology. 1974-75 edition: $5.00; 1975-76 edition: $3.00. (Also published in French.)

Human Communication Research
Department of Communication
Michigan State University
Gerald R. Miller, editor
Published by:
International Communication Association
Balcones Research Center
10,100 Burnet Road
Austin, TX 78758
(512) 836-0440, ext. 225

An official publication of the Association devoted to advancing knowledge and understanding about human symbolic transaction. Aside from its broad behavioral science focus, the journal avoids particular methodological or substantive biases. Quarterly. $15 per year U. S. and Canada; $17 elsewhere.

Index of Research Publications
See listing on page 286

International and Intercultural Communication Annual
Speech Communication Association
5205 Leesburg Pike
Falls Church, VA 22041
(703) 379-1888
Nemi Jain, Arizona State University, editor

Sponsored by the SCA Commission on International and Intercultural Communication. $3 to members, $3.50 to non-members.

Journal of Advertising
School of Journalism
University of Georgia
Athens, GA 30602
(404) 542-1704
J. Thomas Russell, editor

The official publication of the American Academy of Advertising. A quarterly journal devoted to encouraging the discovery and development of valid theory and relevant facts regarding the psychological and philosophical aspects of communication, and the relationship between these and other components of the advertising process. $12 per year. Subscriptions should be addressed to Donald Glover, School of Journalism, University of Nebraska,

Lincoln, NE 68588.

Journal of Advertising Research
Advertising Research Foundation
3 East 54th Street
New York, NY 10022
(212) 751-5656

    A bimonthly journal containing original papers on advertising and marketing research. $24 per year to professors and students in the U. S., $35 to others. $27 per year to professors and students elsewhere; $38 to others elsewhere. $60 elsewhere by air mail.

Journal of Applied
   Communications Research (JACR)
Department of Communication
P. O. Drawer NJ
Mississippi State University
Mississippi State, MS 39762
(601) 325-4908/9
Mark Hickson, editor

    Broad coverage of communications research, both mass and other. Twice a year. $4 per year for individuals, $6 for institutions and libraries.

Journal of Broadcasting
School of Journalism
University of Georgia
Athens, GA 30602
(404) 542-1704
Joseph Dominick, editor

    The scholarly research journal of the Broadcast Education Association, which covers political broadcasting, regulatory issues, history and policy, criticism, effects, and other research on all aspects of radio, television and related fields. Quarterly. $17.50 per year; $9 for students. Free to members of the Association.

Journal of Communication
3620 Walnut Street
Philadelphia, PA 19104
(215) 243-6685
George Gerbner, editor

    Published by The Annenberg School Press, in cooperation with the International Communication Association.

A quarterly journal with an interdisciplinary approach to the study of communications. Contains scholarly and research articles on all aspects of interpersonal, group and mass communications. $15 per year. Send subscriptions to P. O. Box 13358, Philadelphia, PA 19101.

Journal of Communication Inquiry
Iowa Center for Communication Study
School of Journalism
University of Iowa
Iowa City, IA 52242
(319) 353-5414

Contains articles of a conceptual or philosophic nature about issues in communication and mass communication. Twice a year. $5.00 per year or $3.00 per issue.

Journal of Marketing Research
Graduate School of Business Administration
Tulane University
New Orleans, LA 70118
(504) 865-4611
Harper W. Boyd, editor

Quarterly journal containing articles on methods, concepts, applications and case histories in marketing research. Business address: American Marketing Association, 222 South Riverside Plaza, Chicago, IL 60606. (312) 648-0536. Joint subscription with *Journal of Marketing*: $9 to members; $18 to non-members in the U. S. and Canada, $20 elsewhere.

Journal of Organizational Communication
International Association of
  Business Communicators (IABC)
870 Market Street, No. 469
San Francisco, CA 94102
(415) 433-3400

Quarterly magazine devoted to in-depth studies of communication concepts, trends, case studies and philosophy. $8 per year. Subscriptions limited to libraries, school and public; educational institutions, and educators.

Journal of Popular Culture
100 University Hall
Bowling Green State University
Bowling Green, OH   43402
(419) 372-2610
Ray B. Browne, editor
   Published by the Popular Culture Association, with coverage of advertising, amusements, art, biography, broadcasting and cinema, humor, comics, fiction, and music. Quarterly. $15 per year, $4 per issue.

Journalism Monographs
School of Journalism
University of Kentucky
Lexington, KY   40506
(606) 258-2786
Bruce H. Westley, editor
   Published by the Association for Education in Journalism. Research monographs published serially (four or more a year) on journalism, communications and many aspects of the media. $10 per year U. S. and Canada; $10.50 elsewhere. Subscriptions should be sent to AEJ Publications, 201 Murphy Hall, University of Minnesota, Minneapolis, MN   55455. (612) 373-3172.

Journalism Quarterly
School of Journalism
Ohio University
Athens, OH   45701
(614) 594-6710
Guido H. Stempel III, editor
   A quarterly journal devoted to research in journalism and mass communications, with book reviews and annotated bibliographies. $12 per year. Subscriptions should be sent to School of Journalism, University of Minnesota, Minneapolis, MN   55455. (612) 373-3172.

Public Opinion Quarterly
Graduate School of Journalism
Columbia University
New York, NY   10027
(212) 280-2991
   Organ of the American Association for Public Opinion Research, editorially sponsored by the Advisory Committee on Communication, Columbia University. Quarterly

journal of research in polling, the mass media, and communications processes. Articles relating to public opinion polls, mass media, survey methods, and communications effects. Subscriptions: $12 per year domestic, $12.80 foreign. Subscriptions should be placed with Columbia University Press, 136 South Broadway, Irvington-on-Hudson, NY 10533.

Public Relations Review:
  A Journal of Research and Comment
College of Journalism
University of Maryland
College Park, MD 20742
(301) 454-2228
Ray E. Hiebert, editor

Published by the Foundation for Public Relations Research and Education. A journal devoted to original research and comment on public relations. Each year one issue is the updated *Comprehensive Bibliography* of public relations. Quarterly. $12 per year.

---

3. GENERAL

ACTION Newsletter
World Association for
  Christian Communication (WACC)
122 King's Road
London SW3 4TR
England
(01) 589-1484

News of events, books, publications, studies and general developments in church-related and development communication. Audience: professional communicators, especially those with a Christian concern, and church leaders related to communication. Ten times a year. $5 a year, sent by air mail.

Audio
North American Publishing Co.
134 North 13th Street
Philadelphia, PA 19107
(215) 564-5170
Gene Pitts, editor
   Formerly *Audio Engineering*. Home high fidelity systems coverage with equipment and record reviews. Monthly. $7 per year.

Billboard
9000 Sunset Boulevard
Los Angeles, CA 90069
(213) 273-7040
   Weekly newspaper for the music/record industry. Provides news reports, reviews, statistical studies and marketing data. $50 per year.

Cash Box
119 West 57th Street
New York, NY 10019
(212) 586-2640
   Trade weekly of the popular music industry, covering the top 100 in music, radio, record sales, etc. $50 per year.

Comm/ent: A Journal of Communications and Entertainment Law
198 McAllister Street
San Francisco, CA 94102
(415) 557-3539
   The first issue of **Comm/ent** was published in Winter, 1976 by Hastings College of Law of the University of California as "the only law journal to deal exclusively with the most recent changes in communications and entertainment law both at home and abroad." It covers topics such as tax incentive financing of motion pictures under the new tax reform act; the expanded coverage of the Equal Time Rule; the constitutional status of "obscene violence"; international regulation of broadcasting; and the effect of current amendments to the Copyright Act. A special section on recent developments in the law will provide a synopsis of current decisions by the FCC, a digest of important state statutes, and a selection of commentaries on upcoming trends in the law. Quarterly. $12 per year.

Communication
Gordon and Breach Science Publishers Ltd.
42, William IV Street
London WC2
England
(01) 836-5125
U. S. office:
One Park Avenue
New York, NY 10016
(212) 689-0360

An international quarterly journal devoted to new conceptual, theoretical and philosophical approaches to the role and consequences of communication in human affairs. Issued twice yearly. Subscriptions: $19.50 per year for individuals, $39 for organizations. Rates are the same for all other countries except Great Britain, where subscriptions are 7.50 pounds for individuals and 19.50 pounds for organizations. Subscriptions should be placed with the London office.

Communication Arts
P. O. Box 10300
Palo Alto, CA 94303
(415) 326-6040

A magazine for professionals in the field of visual communications. Contains outstanding work of individuals in the graphic design and advertising fields. The Art Annual features the best work in illustration and photography juried from over 3,000 entries. The CA Annual is a juried competition for all areas of design and advertising selected from more than 14,000 entries. Six times a year. $24. U.S., $26 Canada, $30 elsewhere.

Communication Notes
Council of Communication Societies
P. O. Box 1074
Silver Spring, MD 20910
(301) 953-7110

A monthly newsletter designed for the communication professional containing news articles about legislative proceedings, judicial decisions and executive actions relating to communication, as well as articles about people and events in communication professional associations. Contains a continuing calendar of forthcoming professional society meetings and society, university, and commercial seminars. Digests selected articles from communication journals, notes the advent of new journals and lists new publications. Monthly. Prepaid: $12 per year in the U. S.; $16 in Canada and Mexico; $24 elsewhere. Billing fee if not prepaid: $3.00.

Communications
Communications Publishing Corporation
1900 West Yale
Englewood, CO   80110
(303) 761-3770

Contains news about the business communications industry. Subjects covered include business management and marketing; evaluation of new equipment; equipment maintenance and service shop operation; public safety and emergency medical systems; business and industrial use of communications equipment; regulation; and other special reports and features. Articles on management and technical subjects comprise the majority of content. Monthly. $14 per year.

Communicontents
Communication Research & Services
Arizona State University
Tempe, AZ   85281
(602) 965-4797

Abstracts of current books related to communication, plus reviews, employment opportunity listings, scholarly articles, etc. Includes works on information systems, interpersonal and organizational communication, plus intercultural, political, instructional, mass, and health communication. Issued quarterly with self-indexing format and year-end index. Subscription rates: 1976 (monthly) and 1977 (quarterly) are $4.00 per year in the U.S., $5.50 per year outside the U.S. 1978 rate not yet announced. Information on back files (1970-1974) and sample issue available.

Daily Variety
1400 Cahuenga Boulevard North
Los Angeles, CA   90028
(213) 469-1141
Thomas M. Pryor, editor

Show business newspaper concentrating on Hollywood film, broadcasting and other aspects of the entertainment business. Daily except Saturdays, Sundays and holidays. $25 for six months, $40 for one year.

Development Communication Report
Clearinghouse on Development Communication
1414 22nd Street, N.W.
Washington, DC 20037
(202) 293-5964

Formerly *ICIT Report*. Presents interviews and articles on the ways in which communication has been and can be used in agriculture, health, nutrition, family planning, and other development areas. Audience consists of people and organizations involved in the use of communications for development in Third World countries. Quarterly. Free.

FOI Digest, FOI Reports and FOI Foundation Series
See listing for **Freedom of Information Center** on page 269.

Footnotes to the Future
Futuremics, Inc.
2850 Connecticut Avenue, N.W.
Washington, DC 20008
(202) 667-5620
Sandra Lauffer, editor

A newsletter featuring new developments in communication, bioethics, education, population, environment and global resources. Monthly. $15.00 per year; students: $7.50.

The Hollywood Reporter
6715 Sunset Boulevard
Hollywood, CA 90028
(213) 464-7411
Tichi Wilkerson, editor-in-chief

Coverage of the motion picture, television and theater scene in Hollywood. Daily. $40 per year.

Hope Reports Perspective
Hope Reports, Inc.
919 South Winton Road
Rochester, NY 14618
(716) 244-6630

A newsletter covering products, systems, markets,

concepts and people. Emphasis on trends and current developments, marketing studies, the use of AV, and the administration of media. Bimonthly. $30 per year.

IABC News
International Association of
  Business Communicators (IABC)
870 Market Street, No. 469
San Francisco, CA 94102
(415) 433-3400

A tabloid containing news on trends, techniques, people, and regulations affecting organizational communication and news items for members. Monthly. $10 per year. Subscriptions limited to school and public libraries, educational institutions, and educators.

Ideas in Sound
Hoke Communications, Inc.
224 7th Street
Garden City, NY 11530
(516) 746-6700

The information bank of Hoke Communications, containing recorded interviews, speeches, seminars from which Hoke editors obtain their editorial material and from which newsletter and magazine subscribers can retrieve specific programs attuned to their specific interests on cassette. Annual. Free upon request.

Impact
Impact Publications
Baker & Bowden
333 North Michigan Avenue
Chicago, IL 60601
(312) 263-2313
Robert L. Baker, editor

Monthly newsletter on communications trends and techniques for editors, public relations executives, and communicators. $15 per year.

In Search/En Quête
Information Services
Department of Communications
300 Slater Street
Ottawa, Ontario K1A 0C8
(613) 995-8185

David Wright, editor

A magazine of information and opinion offering a selection of articles touching on different fields of communication. Its purpose is to provide fresh viewpoints, to add to the reader's general knowledge and to generate an increased awareness of telecommunications. Quarterly. Free.

InterMedia
International Institute of Communications (IIC)
Tavistock Square East
London WC1H 9LG
England
(01) 388-0671
John Howkins, editor

Covers communications issues, policies, systems, events and trends throughout the world. Six times a year, $17 per year. Free to members of IIC.

International Communications Bulletin (ICB)
College of Journalism
University of Maryland
College Park, MD 20742
(301) 454-2228
L. John Martin, editor

Established by the International Communications Division of the Association for Education in Journalism, the *Bulletin* is a newsletter for students, teachers, scholars, researchers and professionals in international communication. Provides a round-up of new and forthcoming developments in communications and includes a section on research notes. Quarterly. $4 per year U. S., Canada and by surface mail overseas; $5 per year air mail overseas.

Mass Comm Review
Department of Journalism
Temple University
Philadelphia, PA 19122
(215) 787-8344 or 787-7383
Edward J. Trayes, editor

Mass Comm Review, an international journal for academics and professionals, is the official publication of the Mass Communications and Society Division of the Association for Education in Journalism. Published in February, April and July. $6 per year.

Mass Media Booknotes
Department of Radio-TV-Film
Temple University
Philadelphia, PA   19122
(215) 855-7778
Christopher H. Sterling, editor

Description and review of about 40 new publications per month on all aspects of mass communication: books, newspapers, magazines, photography and motion pictures, broadcasting, cable and other media. Included are foreign and international communication, popular music and culture, general reference and bibliographies, comics, media production, etc. Full details, price, and ordering information is provided for each item. Special issues devoted to film books (December) and government documents (August). Monthly. $5 per year in the U. S., $6 elsewhere.

Mass Media Newsletter
Mass Media Ministries, Inc.
2116 North Charles Street
Baltimore, MD   21218
(301) 727-3270
Clifford J. York, editor

A nation-wide ecumenical communications resource for churches, schools and community organizations. Special emphasis is placed on individual and institutional development through media education. Includes reviews of current commercial films, selected advance television program information, and multimedia learning resources: short films, filmstrips, cassette tapes, recordings, books, games, resource organizations, special articles, media themes, etc. Twice a month, except monthly in August and December. $10 per year.

The Matrix
Women in Communication, Inc.
P. O. Box 9561
Austin, TX   78766
(512) 452-0119

A journal of the professional society for women in journalism and communications, with professional articles on issues concerning women in the field of communications. Quarterly. $4 per year in the U. S., Canada and Mexico; $5 elsewhere.

Media Industry Newsletter (MIN)
150 East 52nd Street
New York, NY   10017
(212) 751-2670
Ralf Brent, editor
   A newsletter featuring inside news about television, radio, newspapers, magazines, book publishing, cable, new products, marketing, and advertising. Carries a composite stock average of media stocks weekly; summaries of advertising pages; and revenues of magazines, TV networks, radio networks and individual stations. The financial aspects of the media are stressed. Stringer correspondents are maintained in major markets and overseas. Weekly. $58 per year; $15 for a three-month trial.

Media Law Reporter
   See listing on page 190

Media Report to Women
Women's Institute for Freedom of the Press
3306 Ross Place, N.W.
Washington, DC   20008
(202) 363-0812
Donna Allen, editor.
   "What women are doing and thinking about the communications media." Monthly. $15 per year for organizations; $10 per year for individuals. Current *Index/Directory*: $8.

New Books in the Communications Library
College of Communications
122 Gregory Hall
University of Illinois
Urbana, IL   61801
(217) 333-2216
Eleanor Blum, editor
   Quarterly annotated list of new books in the Communications Library, arranged by subject. Free on request.

Print
R. C. Publications, Inc.
355 Lexington Avenue
New York, NY 10036
(212) 682-0830
Martin Fox, editor
   Covers the graphic arts. Monthly. $18 per year.

Technical Communication
428 East Preston Street
Baltimore, MD 21202
(301) 528-4249
   The Journal of the Society for Technical Communication. Covers editing and writing, publishing, education, art andproduction, and management. Also contains regular material on the status of technical manual specifications and standards, book reviews, business review, and announcements of meetings. Quarterly. $17 per year.

Variety
154 West 46th Street
New York, NY 10036
(212) JU 2-2700
   Weekly newspaper of the entertainment industry covering radio, television, theatre, and movies as well as cable television and videocassette developments. Also follows the auditorium/arena scene and nightclubs. $30 per year; foreign $33 per year (sea mail).

WACC Journal
World Association for
   Christian Communications
122 King's Road
London SW3 4TR
England
(01) 589-1484
   Information and analysis of communication theory and practice of relevance to the proclamation of the Gospel. For professional communicators, especially those with Christian concern, and church leaders related to communication. Quarterly. $10 per year.

4. ADVERTISING AND PUBLIC RELATIONS

ABC News Bulletin
Audit Bureau of Circulations (ABC)
123 North Wacker Drive
Chicago, IL 60606
(312) 236-7994
   Periodical on the activities and practices of the Audit Bureau of Circulation and related matters. ABC, an association of 4,000 advertisers, advertising agencies, and publishers in the United States and Canada, audits and reports on 75 percent of all print-media circulation in North America. Quarterly. Free.

Advertising Age
Crain Communications, Inc.
740 Rush Street
Chicago, IL 60611
(312) 649-5200
   National weekly newspaper of advertising and marketing, covering new advertising campaigns, agency appointments, personnel changes and governmental actions affecting advertising and marketing. $20 per year.

Annual Review of Marketing
   See listing on page 283

Broadcasting
   See listing on page 311

Direct Marketing
Hoke Communications, Inc.
224 7th Street
Garden City, NY 11530
(516) 746-6700
   Devoted to direct mail and direct communications, regardless of media or medium. Contains business information on the best ways to keep in touch with identified customers and prospects. Monthly. $15 per year.

Encyclomedias
   See listing on page 285

Friday Report
Hoke Communications, Inc.
224 7th Street
Garden City, NY 11530
(516) 746-6700

A weekly newsletter of direct marketing, "an insider's report of what's happening among major direct response advertisers and their agencies, among the sophisticated, computerized market data centers, which organize the direct marketing function." $48 per year.

The Gallagher Report
Gallagher Report, Inc.
230 Park Avenue
New York, NY 10017
(212) 661-5000

Weekly newsletter about advertising, marketing, sales, and media with forecasts, news, trends, ideas, and latest developments in the advertising, marketing, media, and retail management fields. $60 per year.

Journal of Advertising
See listing on page 291

Journal of Advertising Research
See listing on page 292

Journal of Marketing
American Marketing Association
222 South Riverside Plaza
Chicago, IL 60606
(312) 648-0536

Quarterly journal covering new management techniques, ideas, trends, views and solutions to existing problems in marketing. (See listing for **Journal of Marketing Research** on page   for subscription information.)

Journal of Marketing Research
See listing on page 293

Madison Avenue
545 Madison Avenue
New York, NY 10022
(212) 753-8055
Jenny Greenberg, editor

Covers advertising and marketing. Monthly. $10 per year.

Marketing Communications
United Business Publications, Inc.
750 Third Avenue
New York, NY   10017
(212) 697-8300

Highlights the fundamentals of marketing and advertising mix and reports on advertising successes and research. Six times a year. $5 per year.

Marketing Information Guide
Hoke Communications, Inc.
244 7th Street
Garden City, NY   11530
(516) 746-6700

A compilation of information on books, magazine articles, papers and cassettes of interest to marketing executives. Listings describe the content of the publication or article and tell where to order it. Bimonthly. $12 per year.

Marketing News
American Marketing Association
222 South Riverside Plaza
Chicago, IL   60606
(312) 648-0536

A newspaper reporting on general marketing activities, with emphasis on those sponsored by the Association. Biweekly. Free to members; $10 per year to nonmembers.

Media Decisions
342 Madison Avenue
New York, NY   10017
(212) 953-1888

Deals with concepts and trends in the media and contains non-technical articles about media functions and roles in advertising and marketing. Monthly. $20 per year.

PR Reporter
PR Publishing Company
P. O. Box 600
Dudley House
Exeter, NH   03833

(603) 778-0514

Broad coverage on trends, implications and "think pieces." Written by practitioners who are currently active in the field. Weekly (50 weeks of the year). $35 for six months; $60 per year.

Public Relations Journal
Public Relations Society of America
845 Third Avenue
New York, NY 10022
(212) 826-1750

A magazine for public relations practitioners that provides ideas, techniques, and new approaches to communications problems. Monthly. Free to members of the Society; $12 per year to others.

Public Relations News
127 East 80th Street
New York, NY 10021
(212) TR 9-7090

Covers a broad range of topics and includes case studies of public relations problems. Oldest of the weekly newsletters. $89.50 per year.

Public Relations Quarterly
Hudson Associates
44 West Market Street
Rhinebeck, NY 12572
(914) 876-2081

Stresses trends in public relations and problems in society affecting the field. $12 per year.

Public Relations Review:
  A Journal of Research and Comment
    See listing on page 295

Sales and Marketing Management
633 Third Avenue
New York, NY 10017
(212) 986-4800

Formerly *Sales Management*. Focuses on the tactics of marketing, management of sales forces, market evaluation, and research planning. Semimonthly. $22 per year.

Standard Rate and Data Service
See listing on page 288

Television/Radio Age
See listing on page 315

Topicator
See listing on page 288

5. BROADCASTING

Access
National Citizens
 Committee on Broadcasting
1028 Connecticut Avenue, N.W.
Suite 402
Washington, DC   20036
(202) 466-8407
   Concentrates on media reform, current news and analysis, and investigative reporting concerning media. Monthly. $12 per year.

ACT News
Action for Children's Television (ACT)
46 Austin Street
Newtonville, MA   02160
(617) 527-7870
   Quarterly newsletter that covers legal and broadcast actions and developments in children's programming and advertising, ranging from federal regulatory proceedings to topics related to program content, including the arts, consumerism, role modeling and stereotyping, as well as reviews and descriptions of current research, books, and films. Free with membership in ACT; $15 per year to non-members.

AFTRA Magazine
American Federation of Television
 and Radio Artists (AFTRA)
1350 Avenue of the Americas
New York, NY   10019
(212) 265-0610
   Quarterly magazine sent to 30,000 AFTRA members with articles on future developments in communications and the status of legislation relative to performers in its

jurisdiction. $5 per year.

Better Broadcasts News
American Council for Better Broadcasts
120 East Wilson
Madison, WI 53703
(608) 257-7712 (mornings)

Newsletter published five times a year reporting news of radio and television, with emphasis on efforts by various groups to encourage better broadcasts. Evaluates programs, publishes articles on trends, and lists current reading on broadcasting and future special programs. Free to members; $2 per year for non-members.

Better Radio and Television
National Association for
   Better Broadcasting
P. O. Box 43640
Los Angeles, CA 90043
(213) 474-3283

A journal containing information on public involvement in broadcasting. The winter issue contains "Television for the Family," reviews of commercial programs for the current season. Quarterly. $4 per year.

BM/E (Broadcast Management/Engineering)
Broadband Information Services, Inc.
295 Madison Avenue
New York, NY 10017
(212) 685-5320

A magazine containing articles of interest to those responsible for operating radio/television/cable facilities. Includes a regular feature interpreting FCC rules and regulations. Monthly. $15 per year.

Broadcast Investor
Paul Kagan Associates, Inc.
100 Merrick Road
Rockville Centre, NY 11570
(516) 764-5516

Twice-monthly newsletter on investments in radio and television. $195 per year.

Broadcasting
Broadcasting Publications, Inc.
1735 DeSales Street, N.W.
Washington, DC   20036
(202) 638-1022

A magazine covering business news about national and regional radio and television advertisers and their advertising agencies; radio and television networks and stations; cable television systems; producers and distributors of programs for radio, television and cable television; manufacturers and distributors of equipment for radio, television and cable television; audience-measurement and market-research services; suppliers of music to radio, television and cable television; financing and financial services; sales representatives; telecommunications (relating to radio, television and cable television distribution); home video-recording and video-playback systems and services; governmental bodies dealing with radio, television, cable television and telecommunications. Weekly. $30 per year.

Broadcasting and the Law
Perry Publications
Box 8357
Knoxville, TN   37916
(615) 483-8474

Twice-monthly newsletter and supplements explaining findings and holdings of the Federal Communications Commission, the Courts, Congress and other agencies that affect broadcast operations. Intended for general use by station personnel. Special college rates upon request. $48 per year. Back issues available to 1972 at a cost of $25 per year.

Broadcasting Yearbook
See listing on page 283

Combroad
Commonwealth Broadcasting Association
CBA Secretariat
Broadcasting House
London W1A 1AA
England
(01) 580-4468, exts. 5022/23

Contains articles and news of broadcasting in countries of the British Commonwealth of nations. Quarterly. Free.

Comm/ent: A Journal of Communications and Entertainment Law
See listing on page 296.

CPB Report
Corporation for Public Broadcasting (CPB)
1111 16th Street, N.W.
Washington, DC 20036
(202) 293-6160
　　Newsletter of the Corporation for Public Broadcasting containing news, features and general information of interest to the public broadcasting community. Biweekly. Free.

CTVD
　　See listing on page 326

EBU Review, Geneva edition
European Broadcasting Union (EBU)
1, Rue de Varembé
Case Postale 193
CH-1211 Geneva
Switzerland
　　Journal featuring programs, administration and law containing articles, illustrations, news and information, book reviews, statistics on radio and television throughout the world, with special emphasis on EBU active members: Algeria, Austria, Belgium, Cyprus, Denmark, Finland, France, Germany (Federal Republic), Greece, Iceland, Ireland, Israel, Italy, Jordan, Lebanon, Libya, Luxembourg, Malta, Monaco, Morocco, Netherlands, Norway, Portugal, Spain, Sweden, Switzerland, Tunisia, Turkey, United Kingdom, Vatican State, Yugoslavia. Bimonthly, alternating with Brussels edition, which covers technical matters.

Educational and Industrial Television
　　See listing on page 321

Educational Broadcasting International
　　See listing on page 322

ETV Newsletter
See listing on page 322

Federal Communications Bar Journal
Federal Communications Bar Association
1730 M Street, N.W.
Suite 700
Washington, DC 20036
(202) 331-0606

Contains articles on legal issues relating to the communications industry. Three times a year. $3 per issue; $7.50 per volume. Business office: Suite 615, 1620 Eye Street, N.W., Washington, DC 20036.

Film and Broadcasting Review
See listing on page 326

Journal of Broadcasting
See listing on page 292

Look-Listen Opinion Poll
American Council for Better Broadcasts
120 East Wilson
Madison, WI 53703
(608) 257-7712 (mornings)

Annual poll of adults' and high school students' opinions on programs. The report is sent to networks, national advertisers, the FCC, and interested congressional committees.

NAEB Directory of Public Telecommunications
See listing on page 287

NAEB Letter
See listing on page 323

Pike and Fischer Radio Regulation
See listing on page 190

Public Telecommunications Review
National Association of
  Educational Broadcasters (NAEB)
1346 Connecticut Avenue, N.W.
Washington, DC 20036
(202) 785-1100

Contains research, reporting, opinion and book reviews about public broadcasting, instructional communications, and related fields. Bimonthly. $18 per year in the U. S., Canada and Mexico; $27 elsewhere. Free to members.

Radio and Television Weekly
254 West 31st Street
New York, NY 10001
(212) 594-4120
Cy Kneller, editor
Covers radio, television and the high-fidelity industries. $10 per year.

RTNDA Communicator
See listing on page 340

SMPTE Journal
See listing on page 333

Television Digest
1836 Jefferson Place, N.W.
Washington, DC 20036
(202) 872-9200
Newsletter for executives in broadcasting, consumer electronics, and allied fields. Covers developments in the television and consumer electronics industries, FCC reports, financial reports, cable television activity, and AM-FM radio. Three weekly *Addenda* (TV, AM-FM and CATV) provide complete details of specific activities of the FCC and the industry, such as applications for new stations and cable systems, sales and engineering data. In addition, *Television Digest* periodically issues special supplements, including full texts of FCC decisions, congressional bills, speeches by government and industry officials, in-depth interviews with government and industry officials, etc. Weekly. $198 per year. Also publishes *Television Factbook* (see listing on page 288) and *CATV and Station Coverage Atlas* (see listing on page 284). *Newsletter* with three *Addenda* and *Television Factbook*: $334 per year.

Television Factbook
See listing on page 288

Television International
P. O. Box 2430
Hollywood, CA 90028
(213) 876-2219
Al Preiss, editor
   A magazine for television program exeuctives. Coverage of European and American television technology and programming, including editorials, book reviews, interviews. Distributed in 138 countries. Bimonthly. $15 per year.

Television News Index and Abstracts
   See listing on page 288

Television Quarterly
National Academy of Television
   Arts and Sciences
291 South La Cienega Boulevard
Beverly Hills, CA 90211
(213) 659-0990
   Quarterly magazine of reviews and opinions, primarily by professionals in the U. S. television industry. $7.50 per year.

Television/Radio Age
666 Fifth Avenue
New York, NY 10019
(212) 757-8400
   Trade periodical stressing advertising, with occasional special issues on news, the FCC and foreign television. Biweekly. $12 per year.

Televisions
Washington Community Video Center, Inc.
P. O. Box 21068
Washington, DC 20009
(202) 331-1566
Nick Demartino, editor-publisher
   National coverage of video production, technology, broadcast TV, and cable TV, with sections on history, education and resources. Quarterly. $10 for 10 issues (individuals); $15 for 10 issues (organizations).

Topicator
   See listing on page 288

TV Guide
Radnor, PA   19088
(215) 688-7400
   Weekly magazine with news about all aspects of television and listings of the week's television programs. There are 88 separate regional editions. $13.56 per year.

Variety
   See listing on page 304

The Video Handbook
   See listing on page 289

The Video Publisher
   See listing on page 353

6.   CABLE AND PAY TELEVISION

BM/E (Broadcast Management/Engineering)
   See listing on page 310

Broadcasting
   See listing on page 311

Cable Communications
30 Bloor Street West
Toronto, Ontario M4W 1A2
(416) 924-1214
William Pryde, editor
   A magazine covering the cable television and telecommunications industries. Monthly. $20 per year Canada and the U. S.

Cable Sourcebook
   See listing on page 283

Cablecast
Paul Kagan Associates, Inc.
100 Merrick Road
Rockville Centre, NY   11570
(516) 764-5516
   Newsletter on cable TV finance. Twice a month. $235 per year.

CableLibraries
C. S. Tepfer Publishing Co., Inc.
P. O. Box 565
Ridgefield, CT   06877
(203) 438-3774
 A newsletter for public and other librarians who are involved with producing programs for cable TV or in circulating AV materials to their users. Includes discussions of federal and state regulations, case histories of successful projects, new programming information, etc. Monthly. $15 per year.

Cablelines
Cable Communications Resource Center
2000 K Street, N.W.
Washington, DC   20036
(202) 857-4827
 Monthly newsletter containing articles of interest to minorities in the cable and broadcasting industries.

Cablevision
Titsch Publishing, Inc.
1139 Delaware Plaza
Denver, CO   80204
(800) 525-6370
Paul Maxwell, editor
 A trade journal for the industry. Biweekly. $19.50 per year.

CATV and Station Coverage Atlas
See listing on page 284

CATV Buyer's Guide of Equipment, Services and Manufacturers
Communications Publishing Corp.
1900 West Yale
Englewood, CO   80110
(303) 761-3770
 A product-by-product listing of equipment used by the cable television industry. Annual. $8.95.

CATV Systems Directory, Map Service and Handbook
See listing on page 284

Federal Communications Bar Journal
See listing on page 313

NFLCP Newsletter
P.O. Box 119
Cambridge, MA   02142
A publication of the National Federation of Local Cable Programmers containing news of the Federation and of cable programming in general. Bimonthly. $7.50 per year for individuals; $15 for organizations. Free to members. Subscriptions to: Mickey Brandt, Treasurer, Cable Channel 7, 76 South Spring Road, Vineland, NJ 08360.

Notes from the Center
Cable Television Information Center
2100 M Street, N.W.
Washington, DC   20037
(202) 872-8888
A quarterly newsletter with information on the cable television industry. Free.

Pay Television
P.O. Box 2430
Hollywood, CA   90028
(213) 876-2219
Al Preiss, editor
Covers management and programming aspects of pay television. Bimonthly. $25 per year.

The Pay TV Newsletter
Paul Kagan Associates, Inc.
100 Merrick Road
Rockville Centre, NY   11570
(516) 764-5516
A newsletter on economic, industrial and regulatory developments in pay television. Twice a month. $215 per year.

Perspective on Cable Television
National Cable Television Association
918 16th Street, N.W.
Washington, DC   20006
(202) 457-6700
A bimonthly issue-oriented newsletter concerned

with major developments in the cable television industry. Free to non-members.

Television Digest-CATV Activity Addenda
See listing on page 314

Televisions
See listing on page 315

TVC
Communications Publishing Corporation
1900 West Yale
Englewood, CO   80110
(303) 761-3770

Formerly *TV Communications*. Covers current industry news of products and people in the industry, with feature articles and special reports focusing on system design, engineering, construction, management, finance, subscribers' promotion and pay-cable. Monthly. $17 per year.

Videocassette and CATV Newsletter
Martin Roberts and Associates, Inc.
P. O. Box 5254
Beverly Hills, CA   90210
(213) 273-0381

Contains news of the latest developments in the fields of videocassettes, CATV, and telecommunications. Includes material from foreign correspondents giving the latest information and statistics on the electronic audio-visual field from major manufacturing countries in Asia and Europe. Subscribers also receive three or four in-depth Special Reports each year. Monthly. $42 per year.

Vue
Communications Publishing Corporation
1900 West Yale
Englewood, CO   80110
(303) 761-3770

Formerly *CATV Weekly*. A newsmagazine containing regular news and feature coverage of current industry developments and issues, plus regular sections summarizing VUE system franchise activity, system construction, financial reports, Washington developments, the progress of industry executives, and a weekly "pay cable" report. Weekly. $22 per year.

7. EDUCATIONAL/INSTRUCTIONAL MEDIA

Audio-visual Communications
United Business Publications, Inc.
750 Third Avenue
New York, NY 10017
(212) 697-8300
　　Serves audio-visual specialists. Provides practical case histories and a guide to AV techniques, equipment and services. Includes special reference guides: "Who's Who in AV Presentation," "State of the Art Review," and "AV Equipment and Production Directory." Monthly. $11 per year.

Audiovisual Instruction
Association for Educational
　Communications and Technology (AECT)
1126 16th Street, N.W.
Washington, DC 20036
(202) 833-4180
　　Features articles about innovative educational programs that are using media and technology to improve instruction; about the use, selection and evaluation of instructional materials; and about managing media programs and services. Published ten times during the academic year, with a combined June/July issue. $18 per year in the U. S.; $20 elsewhere.

AV Communication Review
Association for Educational
　Communications and Technology (AECT)
1126 16th Street, N.W.
Washington, DC 20036
(202) 833-4180
　　Devoted to communication, technology, and the teaching/learning process. Includes in-depth articles by leading scholars and practitioners in the field of instructional technology. A book review section covering a wide range of educational liberature and a research abstract section are also featured in each issue. For research workers, theoreticians, graduate students and media practitioners. Quarterly. $19.50 per year in the U.S.; $21.50 elsewhere.

AV Guide
Trade Periodicals, Inc.
434 South Wabash
Chicago, IL   60605
(312) 922-4950
Joe Ziemba, editor

Founded in 1922, *AV Guide* is a newsletter directed at purchasers and users of audiovisual materials. It contains "mini-reviews" of new books, films, filmstrips and equipment as well as news of activities and concepts in the field. Monthly. $6 per year.

Business Screen
Harcourt Brace Jovanovich
757 Third Avenue
New York, NY   10017
(212) 754-4385
Robert Seymour, editor

Special case reports, general views, and articles on business and industrial audio-visual/film production and utilization activities. Bimonthly. $6 per year.

Education Media Yearbook
See listing on page 284

Educational and Industrial Television
C. S. Tepfer Publishing Co., Inc.
P. O. Box 565
Ridgefield, CT   06877
(203) 438-3774

A magazine containing technical and practical information related to making and using television in non-commercial application. Includes information on new products, news, off-the-shelf programs, and literature. Occasional columns include specific production/utilization information, *e.g.*, lighting and graphics. Periodic directories of TV equipment and program sources. Monthly. $12 per year in the U. S.; $14 in Canada and Mexico; $16 elsewhere.

Educational Broadcasting
Brentwood Publishing Corp.
825 South Barrington Avenue
Los Angeles, CA   90049
(213) 826-8388

Detailed review of new technological and software developments in educational media. Ten times a year. $20 per year in the U. S.; $40 elsewhere.

Educational Broadcasting International
The British Council
Tavistock House South
Tavistock Square
London WC1H 9LL
England
(01) 387-0166, ext. 44
Florence Marriott, editor
   Contains articles and features on all aspects of communication policy, planning, and techniques in education, concentrating on radio and television. Reports on developments in educational thought in both developing and industrial countries and acts as a forum for opinion, innovation and case study. Quarterly. In the U.S.: $17.50 for individuals, $25.50 for libraries. Order from International Scholarly Book Services, Inc., P. O. Box 555, Forest Grove, OR 97116.

EDUCOM
Bulletin of the Interuniversity
   Communications Council
P. O. Box 364
Princeton, NJ 08540
(609) 921-7575
   A journal for general readers in colleges and universities focusing on the application of computing, communications and information technology to higher education and reporting on EDUCOM activities. Quarterly. $10 per year.

ETV Newsletter
C. S. Tepfer Publishing Co., Inc.
P. O. Box 565
Ridgefield, CT 06877
(203) 438-3774
   Contains business analyses, up-to-the-minute news, and a special section on new programming of interest to executives and leaders in educational TV, public broadcasting, noncommercial TV, and to manufacturers of TV equipment. Biweekly. $60 per year.

Film Library Quarterly
See listing on page 328

Film News
See listing on page 328

Hope Reports AV-USA
See listing on page 285

Hope Reports Quarterly
Hope Reports, Inc.
919 South Winton Road
Rochester, NY 14618
(716) 244-6630
    Covers sales of 40 key AV products and services, regional sales patterns, and economic indicators. $190 per year.

Media & Methods
401 North Broad Street
Philadelphia, PA 19108
(215) 574-9600
    Formerly *Educators Guide to Media and Methods*. A magazine for professionals in education media, with articles about teaching with multi-media aids. Monthly. $9 per year.

Media Mix
221 West Madison Street
Chicago, IL 60606
(312) 236-7782
    A newsletter covering new films, filmstrips, records, tapes, books, publications, games, idea kits, and other new media and learning experiences. Published monthly from October to June, except for December. $9 per year.

NAEB Directory of Public Telecommunications
See listing on page 287

NAEB Letter
National Association of
  Educational Broadcasters (NAEB)
1346 Connecticut Avenue, N.W.
Washington, DC 20036

(202) 785-1100

A newsletter of member and Association activities in all phases of educational media. Monthly. $15 per year in the U. S., Canada and Mexico; $25 elsewhere.

Public Telecommunications Review
See listing on page 313

Videoplay Report
C. S. Tepfer Publishing Co., Inc.
P. O. Box 565
Ridgefield, CT 06877
(203) 438-3774

Newsletter concerned with trends and developments in program production and use, containing information for producers and distributors of noncommercial video programming. Biweekly. $50 per year.

8. FILM AND PHOTOGRAPHY

American Cinematographer
1728 North Orange Drive
Hollywood, CA 90028
(213) 876-5080

A magazine for directors of photography and others who work with motion picture film. Monthly. $9 per year.

American Cinemeditor
American Cinema Editors, Inc.
422 South Western Avenue
Los Angeles, CA 90020
(213) 386-1946

Covers new developments, equipment and techniques in professional film editing. Quarterly. Free.

American Film
The American Film Institute
The John F. Kennedy Center
  for the Performing Arts
Washington, DC 20566
(202) 833-9300
Hollis Alpert, editor

Articles for a general audience on films and film makers past and present. Ten issues a year. $15, which includes membership in the Institute.

Aperture
Aperture, Inc.
Elm Street
Millerton, NY   12546
(914) 789-4491
Michael E. Hoffman, editor
   A hardcover magazine of fine photography. Quarterly. $17.50 per year.

Camera
C.J. Bucher, Ltd.
CH 6002 Lucerne
Switzerland
Allan Porter, editor
   Publishes portfolios of the work of contemporary photographers and includes brief reports on new equipment, book reviews, and announcements of exhibitions and competitions. Monthly. $10 per year.

Canyon Cinemanews
Industrial Center Building
Room 220
Sausalito, CA   94965
(415) 332-1514
Diane Kitchen, editor
   Articles of interest to student and independent film makers, descriptions of new acquisitions by Canyon Cinema Cooperative, film reviews, interviews with and letters by film makers, occasional book reviews. Bimonthly. $3 per year.

Cineaste
333 Sixth Avenue
New York, NY   10014
(212) 989-3330
Gary Crowdus, editor
   Begun by New York University film students in 1967. Specializes in analysis of radical and political films. Quarterly. $4 per year in the U. S.; $6 elsewhere.

Cinema Canada
Box 398
Outremont Station
Montreal, Quebec H2V 4N3
(514) 272-5354

Jean-Pierre and Connie Tadros, editors
A magazine devoted to both the trade aspect of and to criticism of the Canadian cinema. 10 times a year. $10 per year.

Cinema Journal
Department of Radio-TV-Film
Northwestern University
Evanston, IL 60201
Jack C. Ellis, editor
A journal of scholarly film history, theory and criticism. Reviews books but not films. Semiannual. $7 per year. Subscription to: Publications Order Department, University of Iowa, 17 West College Street, Iowa City, IA 52242.

CTVD
Hampton Books
Route 1, Box 76
Newberry, SC 29108
(803) 276-6870
A review of the serious foreign-language cinema and television press, plus original articles. Published irregularly.

Film and Broadcasting Review
Office for Film and Broadcasting
United States Catholic Conference
1011 First Avenue
Suite 1300
New York, NY 10022
(212) 644-1880
Formerly *Catholic Film Newsletter*. A newsletter reviewing current nationally released 35mm films and notable television programs, with special sections entitled Community Dimensions and Educational Resources. Critical reviews are addressed to the moral and artistic dimensions of films and television programs. Biweekly. $10 per year in the U. S.; $12 per year elsewhere; $20 per year for foreign air mail.

Film & History
The Historians Film Committee
c/o The History Faculty
New Jersey Institute of Technology
323 High Street
Newark, NJ 07102
(201) 645-5224
Martin A. Jackson and
  John E. O'Connor, editors
   A journal for historians and social scientists interested in film for research and teaching, containing articles, reviews and news. The Historians Film Committee is affiliated with the American Historical Association. Quarterly. $5 per year to individuals; $10 to institutions. Add $2 for mailing outside the U. S.

Film Comment
1865 Broadway
New York, NY 10023
(212) 765-5100
   In-depth articles on film history and criticism, national cinemas, and independent productions. Contains reviews and interviews, film production information, filmographies. Bimonthly. $9 per year in the U. S.; $11.50 elsewhere.

Film Culture
GPO Box 1499
New York, NY 10001
Jonas Mekas, editor
   A magazine covering film history, esthetics, criticism, biography, and other film subjects. Specializes in coverage of avant-garde (independent) film. Quarterly. $8 per year in the U. S.; $10 elsewhere.

Film Heritage
Box 652
University of Dayton
Dayton, OH 45469
(513) 229-3241
F. Anthony Macklin, editor
   A journal for those interested in film analysis and history. Contains interviews and reconsiderations of underrated films. Quarterly. $3 per year.

Film Information
Communication Commission
National Council of Churches
475 Riverside Drive
New York, NY 10027
(212) 870-2567
Beatrice Rothenbeucher, editor

Contains evaluations of current theatrical films written by leading Protestant critics, theologians, educators and communications specialists. Subscription includes study guides of films of special interest to the church audience and occasional inserts-reviews of recommended 16mm films. Monthly. $7 per year in the U. S.; $10 elsewhere. Subscriptions to: Film Information, Box 500, Manhattanville Station, New York, NY 10027. (212) 870-2577.

Film Library Quarterly
Box 348
Radio City Station
New York, NY 10019
(212) 790-6549
William Sloan, editor

A journal featuring reviews and articles by key people in the motion picture and audio-visual fields. Quarterly. $10 per year.

Film News
Rohama Lee
d/b/a Film News Company
250 West 57th Street
New York, NY 10019
(212) 581-3596

Stresses previews and reviews of nontheatrical (*i.e.*, 16mm) films and other audio-visual aids, including filmstrips, equipment, and books about film and TV. Published five times a year. $6 per year in the U. S.; $7 in Canada; $7.50 elsewhere.

Film Quarterly
University of California Press
Berkeley, CA 94720
(415) 642-6333

Quarterly journal on films in the U. S. and abroad, with analysis and criticism of specific productions. $6 per year; institutional rates slightly higher.

Filmfacts
P. O. Box 69610
West Station
Los Angeles, CA 90069
Ernest Parmentier, editor

A publication of the Division of Cinema of the University of Southern California. Provides comprehensive information on all foreign and domestic feature films released theatrically in the United States. Published twice a month. $40 per year in the U. S.; $45 elsewhere.

Films in Review
National Board of Review
  of Motion Pictures, Inc.
210 East 68th Street
New York, NY 10021
(213) 988-4916

Published since 1950. Contains filmographies and impressionistic studies of actors and directors of interest to film enthusiasts. Reviews films and offers an annual list of "best" pictures. Monthly, except bimonthly in June/July and August/September. $7.50 per year.

Focus on Film
144 Gloucester Place
London NW1
England
Peter Cowie, publisher

Analyses of films, trends and careers of actors and directors. Emphasis on current releases. Quarterly. $6 per year.

Independent Film Journal
1251 Avenue of the Americas
New York, NY 10020
(212) 246-6460

Trade paper devoted to motion picture theaters and other branches of the film industry. Biweekly. $12 per year.

Industrial Photography
750 Third Avenue
New York, NY 10017

(212) 697-8300
   A magazine for in-house photographers and communications departments, covering production and applications of still photography, audio-visuals, motion pictures, trends in visual communications and relevant new equipment. Monthly. Free to industrial photographers; $13 per year to all others.

International Film Guide
   See listing on page 286

International Photo
   Technik Magazine
Verlag Grossbild Technik
D-8 Munchen 70
Rupert-Mayer-Strasse 45
West Germany
Nicholas Karpf, editor
   Concerned with medium and large format professional photography. Published in both English and German. U. S. distributor: HP Marketing Corporation, 98 Commerce Road, Cedar Grove, NJ   07009. (201) 857-0171. Quarterly. $14 per year.

The Journal of Popular Film
Bowling Green University
   Popular Press
University Hall 101
Bowling Green, OH   43403
(419) 372-2848
   Contains serious articles concerning films and their relationship with their audiences. Includes book reviews. Quarterly. $5 per year.

Journal of the Producers
   Guild of America
8201 Beverly Boulevard
Los Angeles, CA   90048
(213) 651-0084
Lou Greenspan, editor
   A periodical for the industry, covering topics such as problems of distribution, economics, censorship, international production. Quarterly. Free.

Journal of the University Film Association
Department of Radio-Television-Film
Temple University
Philadelphia, PA 19122
(215) 787-8423
Timothy J. Lyons, editor
   Presents historical and theoretical studies concerned with problems of film education. Quarterly. $6 per year.

Jump Cut
3138 West Schubert
Chicago, IL 60647
(312) 252-6616
John Hess and
   Chuck Kleinhans, editors
   Social and esthetic critiques of films and trends, past and present, from a radical/socialist/feminist point of view. Bimonthly. $4 per year in the U. S.; $5 elsewhere. Subscriptions to: P. O. Box 865, Berkeley, CA 94701.

Literature/Film Quarterly
Salisbury State College
Salisbury, MD 21801
(301) 546-3261
Thomas L. Erskine, Gerald R. Barrett
   and James M. Welsh, editors
   Studies of literary sources for films and their interpretation on the screen. Occasional theoretical articles and interviews. $5 per year.

Monthly Film Bulletin
British Film Institute
81 Dean Street
London W1V 6AA
England
(01) 437-4355
Richard Combs, editor
   Lists all credits and provides a plot synopsis and review of each film within a given one-month time period for which a certificate has been issued or which has been passed and certified for public exhibition by the British Board of Film Censors or by a licensing authority in Great Britain. Also carries a feature devoted to assorted topics such as the making of a film or a bibliography relating to a

particular director. $11 per year.

Motion Picture Product Digest
159 West 53rd Street
New York, NY   10019
(212) 247-3100
   Biweekly newsletter for the entertainment industry. $25 per year.

Photo Marketing
Photo Marketing Association
603 Lansing Avenue
Jackson, MI   49202
(517) 783-2809
John W. Dancer, editor
   A magazine for firms and individuals engaged in the amateur photography industry. Monthly. $3 per year.

The Rangefinder
Rangefinder Publishing Company, Inc.
P. O. Box 66925
3511 Centinela Avenue
Los Angeles, CA   90066
(213) 390-3688
Janet Marshall Victor, editor
   Encompasses all phases of professional photography—technical problems, business practices, equipment test reports, processing techniques, future trends. Monthly. $10 per year.

Screen
63 Old Compton Street
London W1V 5PN
England
Ben Brewster, editor
   An intellectual forum for the theory and history of film. Quarterly. $11.50 per year (combined subscription with *Screen Education*).

The Screen Actor
Screen Actors Guild (SAG)
7750 Sunset Boulevard
Hollywood, CA   90046
(213) 876-3030
Judith Rheiner, editor

A magazine intended primarily for SAG members, with news of the Guild and the film and television industries. Quarterly. $4 per year in the U. S.; $7 elsewhere.

Sight & Sound
British Film Institute
81 Dean Street
London W1V 6AA
England
U. S. address:
155 West 15th Street
New York, NY 10001
Penelope Houston, editor
   Reviews of films and news of actors and producers and history of the field. Quarterly. $6 per year.

The Silent Picture
First Media Press
6 East 39th Street
New York, NY 10016
Anthony Slide, editor
   Devoted exclusively to the art and history of the silent cinema. Articles on silent films, players and technicians and related news of interest. $4 per year.

SMPTE Journal
Society of Motion Picture
   and Television Engineers
862 Scarsdale Avenue
Scarsdale, NY 10583
(914) 472-6606
   A journal for managers, scientists and engineers in television, motion pictures and related fields. Covers technical aspects of TV and motion picture production. Includes American standards and recommended practices related to test films of the SMPTE. Monthly. $30 to members; $10 to student members; $35 to non-members.

Soviet Film
14 Kalasny Pereulok
103009, Moscow
U.S.S.R.
Vladimir Shalunovsky, editor
   News of recent productions. Monthly. $5.50 per year.

Studio Photography
PTN Publishing Company, Inc.
250 Fulton Avenue
Hempstead, NY 11550
(516) 489-1300
Barry Tannenbaum, editor

Business magazine of professional photography for portrait, commercial and wedding photographers. Monthly. $7 per year.

Take One
Box 1778
Station B
Montreal 110, Quebec
(514) 843-7733

Discusses film in its interrelationships with the rest of today's society. Film reviews, interviews, articles, book reviews and regular columnists cover the best of today's American, European, major and independent films. Bimonthly. $6 per year in the U. S. and Canada; $9 elsewhere by surface mail; $18 elsewhere by air mail.

Technical Photography
PTN Publishing Company, Inc.
250 Fulton Avenue
Hempstead, NY 11550
(516) 489-1300
David A. Silverman, editor

A journal for industrial, military, and government still, cine and AV professionals. Monthly. $5 per year.

UFA Digest
Department of Drama and Communication
University of New Orleans
Lake Front
New Orleans, LA 70122
H. Wayne Schuth, editor

The official publication of the University Film Association. *Film Research in Progress* is published as part of *UFA Digest*, from two to four times a year. Bimonthly. $2 per year. Subscriptions to: Donald Zimmerman, Department of Communications, Washington State University, Pullman, WA 99163.

Variety.
See listing on page 304

The Velvet Light Trap
Old Hope Schoolhouse
Cottage Grove, WI 53527
John Davis, editor
    Contains serious historical criticism, research and analysis, with emphasis on the American cinema. Each issue is devoted to a single topic or theme. In-depth book reviews. Quarterly. $5 to individuals; $10 to institutions.

9. JOURNALISM

**American Society of
  Newspaper Editors Bulletin**
Box 551
1350 Sullivan Trail
Easton, PA 18042
(215) 252-5502
    A magazine of journalism shop talk covering public affairs, primarily as they refer to editing the nation's daily newspapers. Includes articles analyzing shortcomings of the press and suggestions for improvements in coverage. Nine times a year. $6 per year.

AP World
50 Rockefeller Plaza
New York, NY 10020
(212) 262-4000
Sibby Christensen, editor
    Published by the Associated Press for its member news organizations and for its staff worldwide. Quarterly.

Atlas World Press Review
230 Park Avenue
New York, NY 10017
(212) 889-2900
Alfred Balk, editor
    Reprints and excerpts from foreign periodicals translated into English, offering serious treatment of current issues as seen from different countries. Has a regular department on Press/Broadcasting. Annually selects International Editor of the Year. Monthly. $14 per year in the U. S. and Canada; $17 elsewhere. Subscriptions to:

Atlas, Box 2550, Boulder, CO 80302.

The Catholic Journalist
Catholic Press Association
119 North Park Avenue
Rockville Centre, NY 11570
(516) 766-3400

A newspaper of the Catholic Press Association of the U. S. and Canada. Serves member newspapers, magazines, book publishers and their staffs with news and articles on the Catholic press and allied subjects. Bimonthly. $5 per year.

College Press Review
Department of Journalism
Bradley University
Peoria, IL 61625
(303) 676-7611
John W. Windhauser, editor

Provides opinion and research on the collegiate communications media and related areas. Quarterly. $15 per year; free to members of the National Council of College Publications Advisers.

Communication: Journalism Education Today (C:JET)
Co-editors:
Marjorie Wilson
4933 17th Place
Lubbock, TX 79416
(806) 795-2442
and
Betty Stanley
4726 27th Street
Lubbock, TX 79410
(806) 799-5753

The professional journal of the Journalism Education Association. Prints scholarly articles for and by advisers on such topics as freedom of the press issues for high school students and advisers. Quarterly. Free to members; $16 per year to non-members. Business office: c/o Sister Rita Jeanne, 912 Market Street, La Crosse, WI 54601.

Community College Journalist
Citrus College
Azusa, CA 91702
(213) 335-0521
Jan Rawson, editor

The official publication of the Community College Journalism Association, an affiliate of the Association for Education in Journalism (AEJ). Concerned with issues in journalism education, teaching techniques, and educational policy, especially in relation to the two-year community college instructor and student. Improving articulation with four-year schools is a major emphasis. Quarterly. $7 per year; free to members of the Association. Subscriptions to: W.B. Daugherty, San Antonio College, 1300 San Pedro Avenue, San Antonio, TX 78284.

Direct Line
International Federation of Journalists (IFJ)
I.P.C.
Boulevard Charlemagne 1
1040 Brussels
Belgium
(02) 736.80.15

Contains brief news items of development in the field of press freedom, trade union activities, IFJ interventions, etc. English, French and German editions. Monthly. Free.

Editor and Publisher
See listing on page 345

Guild Reporter
The Newspaper Guild
1125 15th Street, N.W.
Washington, DC 20005
(202) 296-2990

A newspaper containing news of the Guild and the newspaper industry. Semimonthly. $7.50 per year.

Hudson's Washington News Media Contacts Directory
See listing on page 285

I.F.J. Information
International Federation of Journalists
I.P.C.
Boulevard Charlemagne 1
1040 Belgium
(02) 736.80.15

Contains information about members and activities of the IFJ and a section on professional inquiries. English, French and German texts in the same issue. Annual. Free.

Journalism Abstracts
See listing on page 286

The Journalism Educator
Department of Journalism
University of Wyoming
Laramie, WY   82071
(307) 766-1121
William Roepke, editor

Official publication of the Association for Education in Journalism. Promotes excellence in teaching to prepare men and women for news media careers. Quarterly. $6 per year.

Journalism Monographs
See listing on page 294

Journalism Quarterly
See listing on page 294

The Liebling Ledger
The Liebling Group
2416 I Street, N.W.
Washington, DC   20007
Pauline Jennings, editor,
   (202) 965-0936

Begun in September 1973 as an outgrowth of the second A. J. Liebling Counter-Convention, this occasional publication is distributed through Newspaper Guild facilities and is concerned with pooling the information and resources of working journalists and freelancers in order to increase their power and influence on the media. Free.

Mass Comm Review
See listing on page 374

The Masthead
National Conference of Editorial Writers
1725 N Street, N.W.
Washington, DC   20036
(202) 785-1081
   A quarterly magazine devoted to the problems of producing responsible and effective editorial pages. $10 per year.

News Leads
The Urban Policy Research Institute
321 South Beverly Drive
Suite W
Beverly Hills, CA   90212
(213) 553-4161
   A journal of investigative reporting, focusing on California and containing story and source compilations for use by professional journalists and students. Bimonthly. $15 per year to organizations; $10 to individuals; $5 to students.

Newspaper Fund Journalism Scholarship Guide
See listing on page 287

Newspaper Fund Newsletter
The Newspaper Fund, Inc.
P.O. Box 300
Princeton, NJ   08540
(609) 452-2000
   A newsletter for teachers of high school journalism and for publications advisers. Monthly. Free.

Nieman Reports
Society of Nieman Fellows
48 Trowbridge Street
Cambridge, MA   02138
(617) 495-2238
James C. Thomson, Jr., editor
   A quarterly periodical "about newspapering by newspapermen, including reports and articles and stories about the newspaper business, newspaper people and

newspaper stories." $5 per year.

The Quill
The Society of Professional Journalists
Sigma Delta Chi
35 East Wacker Drive
Chicago, IL 60601
(312) 236-6577

Monthly magazine for newspaper reporters and editors, photographers, radio and television newsmen and newswomen, freelance writers, students and teachers of journalism. $10 per year.

Quill and Scroll
Quill and Scroll Society
School of Journalism
University of Iowa
Iowa City, IA 52242
(319) 353-4475

A magazine devoted to high school journalism and publications. Bimonthly during the school year. $3 per year in the U. S.; $4 in Canada; $4.50 elsewhere.

RTNDA Communicator
Radio Television News Directors Association
1735 DeSales Street, N.W.
Washington, DC 20036
(202) 737-8657

Monthly newsletter for radio-television news directors devoted particularly to government regulation and freedom of information but also containing news about the Association and the field of news broadcasting. Free to members; libraries $15 per year.

Scholastic Editor
720 Washington Avenue, S.E.
Suite 205
University of Minnesota
Minneapolis, MN 55414
(612) 373-3180

Monthly publication during school year for high school and college journalists and publication staffs, covering all areas related to college and high school publications. $6.50 one year; $12 two years; $16 three years.

UPI Reporter
United Press International
220 East 42nd Street
New York, NY 10017
(212) 682-0400, ext. 396
H. L. Stevenson, editor

A newsletter primarily for subscribers to the UPI news service, journalism schools and others in the industry. Reports on news coverage throughout the world and comments on journalistic trends and events. Weekly. Free to clients and journalism schools; $25 per year to organizations and individuals in non-media-related professions.

Working Press of the Nation
See listing on page 289

Specialized Newsletters for Journalists

In addition to the periodicals listed above, there are many specialized newsletters published for journalists in a wide variety of fields. Some examples:

ACP Newslog. Associated Church Press, 326 West State Street, Media, PA 19063.

ANPA Public Affairs Newsletter and *ANPA General Bulletin.* American Newspaper Publishers Association, P. O. Box 17407, Dulles International Airport, Washington, DC 20041.

AMWA Newsletter and *Medical Communications.* American Medical Writers Association, 5272 River Road, Suite 290, Bethesda, MD 20016.

AP Log. The Associated Press, 50 Rockefeller Plaza, New York, NY 10020.

APME News and *APME Photo-letter.* Associated Press Managing Editors Association, 50 Rockefeller Plaza, New York, NY 10020.

Aviation/Space Writers Association *Newsletter.* 101 Greenwood Avenue, Jenkintown, PA 19046.

The Byline. American Agricultural Editors Association, 702 Louis Street, Mount Prospect, IL 60056.

Christian Author. Christian Writers Institute, Gunderson Drive and Schmale Road, Wheaton, IL 60187.

Committee of Small Magazine Editors and Publishers (COSMEP) *Newsletter.* Box 703, San Francisco, CA 94101.

Construction Writers Association *Newsletter*. 601 13th Street, N.W., Room 202, Washington, DC 20036.
Education Reporter. Education Writers Association, Box 1289, Bloomington, IN 47401.
Garden Writers Bulletin. c/o Margaret Herbst, 101 Park Avenue, New York, NY 10017.
IABC Journal and *IABC News*. International Association of Business Communicators, 870 Market Street, Suite 469, San Francisco, CA 94102.
IAPA News. Inter American Press Association, 2911 N.W. 39th Street, Miami, FL 33142.
Intercom Newsletter. Society of Technical Writers and Publishers, 1010 Vermont Avenue, N.W., Washington, DC 20005.
National Association of Science Writers, Inc., *Newsletter*. Box H, Seacliff, NY 11579.
Newsprint Facts. Newsprint Information Committee, 633 Third Avenue, New York, NY 10017.
Members Service Bulletin. Inland Daily Press Association, 100 West Monroe Street, Chicago, IL 60603.
Outdoor Writers Association of America *Newsletter*. 4141 West Bradley Road, Milwaukee, WI 53209.
RNA Newsletter. Religion Newswriters Association, 422 South Fifth Street, Minneapolis, MN 55415.
RPRC Counselor. Religious Public Relations Council, c/o David A. Wilson, 17512 Ridgeview Drive, Minnetonka, MN 55343.

10. JOURNALISM CRITICISM REVIEWS

Columbia Journalism Review
700 Journalism Building
Columbia University
New York, NY 10027
(212) 280-3872
James Boylan, editor
   A magazine which appraises the performance of all types of journalism and provides a forum for discussion of problems. Bimonthly. $12 per year. Subscriptions to: 601 Journalism Building. (212) 280-2716.

feed/back
Journalism Department
San Francisco State University
1600 Holloway Avenue
San Francisco, CA 94132
(415) 469-2086 or 469-1689

Reviews the press and broadcast journalism of Northern California with an eye to examining, evaluating and commenting on press performance. Quarterly. $6 per year.

Montana Journalism Review
School of Journalism
University of Montana
Missoula, MT 59801
(406) 243-4001

Journal of reports, research findings, and opinions about the news media, with emphasis on Montana newspapers and radio-TV stations. Includes critical articles on the press. Founded in 1958 as the first journalism review in the United States. Annual. Free.

St. Louis Journalism Review
928a North McKnight Road
St. Louis, MO 63132
(314) 991-1698

A critique of news media in the metropolitan St. Louis area. Bimonthly. $5 per year.

Washington Journalism Review
3122 M Street, N.W.
Washington, DC 20007
(202) 338-2495
Edwin Diamond, senior editor

A nonprofit organization conducting a review of Washington media—newspapers, television, radio, national news bureaus, international press bureaus, FCC, Congress, the Supreme Court. Monthly. $16 per year.

11. PRINT MEDIA

Alternative Media
Alternative Press Syndicate, Inc. (APS)
Box 777
Cooper Station
New York, NY 10003
(212) 674-6550
   A magazine for and about the alternative press. Bimonthly. $6 per year.

**Annual Cost Study
   for Weekly Newspapers**
   See listing on page 283

**Biennial Survey of Newspaper
   Printing Equipment**
National Newspaper Association
491 National Press Building
Washington, DC 20045
(202) 783-1651
   Published as a result of a survey of newspapers which gathers composition and printing information, primarily in production areas of composition, camera, printing, and mailroom, in order to learn what types of equipment are being used, what has been spent on such equipment, and projected expenditures for the upcoming year. $10 per copy.

Bulletin
The Columbia Scholastic
   Press Advisors' Association (CSPAA)
Box 11
Central Mail Room
Columbia University
New York, NY 10027
(212) 280-4480
   Welcomes articles based on research but humanized in terms of specific situations, clarifying examples, and the human problems concerned. Also welcomes articles expressing a specific point of view, or "how-to-do-it" solutions to recurring problems in school publications. Quarterly (summer, spring, fall and winter). $5 per year.

Communication Arts
   See listing on page 297

Content
22 Laurier Avenue
Toronto, Ontario M4X 1S3
(416) 920-6699 and 920-7733
Barrie Zwicker, editor
"Canada's national news media magazine." 11 times a year. $6.50 per year in Canada; $7.50 in the U. S.; $8.50 elsewhere.

Editor and Publisher
850 Third Avenue
New York, NY   10022
(212) 752-7050
A magazine covering news of events and trends in newspaper business/management, labor, photography, journalism, syndicates, advertising, public relations and printing. Weekly. $12.50 per year.

Editor and Publisher International Yearbook
See listing on page 345

Folio
125 Elm Street
P. O. Box 697
New Canaan, CT   06840
(203) 972-0761
Howard Ravis, editor
"The magazine for magazine management." Monthly. $15 per year.

Hudson's Washington News Media Contacts Directory
See listing on page 285

IPI Report
International Press Institute
Lindenplatz 6
8048 Zurich
Switzerland
London Secretariat:
City University
280 St. John Street
London EC1V 4PB
England

Reports of events and developments concerning the press and the media; reports on press freedom cases throughout the world; and news of IPI activities. Monthly. 40 Swiss francs, or $20 per year.

**National Directory of
  Weekly Newspapers**
See listing on page 287

Press Censorship Newsletter
The Reporters Committee
  for Freedom of the Press
1750 Pennsylvania Avenue, N.W.
Room 1112
Washington, DC 20006
(202) 347-6888
   A compendium of all important legislative, executive and judicial actions affecting the press at federal, state and local levels. $15 per year.

Print
See listing on page 304

Printing and Publishing
U. S. Department of Commerce
Domestic and International
  Business Administration
Washington, DC 20230
(202) 377-4115
William S. Lofquist, editor
   A review of trends in the printing and publishing industry. Emphasizes use of government statistics and provides analyses that are often not available elsewhere. Quarterly. $3 per year. Subscriptions to: Superintendent of Documents, Government Printing Office, Washington, DC 20402.

Publishers' Auxiliary
National Newspaper Association
491 National Press Building
Washington, DC 20045
(202) 783-1651
   Newspaper focusing on news of and affecting community newspapers. Regular features on Washington developments, law and the press, production and equipment,

advertising, marketing, distribution, circulation and promotion. Also covers writing, editing and photography techniques, layout and design, newspaper plant design, and newspaper buying and selling. Semimonthly. $10 per year.

Publishers Weekly
R. R. Bowker Company
1180 Avenue of the Americas
New York, NY   10036
(212) 764-5100
 A magazine covering news and trends mainly in the book industry, with information about books and promotions, personnel changes, bookselling and marketing, production and design, copyright legislation, and advance reviews of forthcoming books. Weekly. $30 per year in the U. S.; $33 in Canada, Postal Union of the Americas and Spain; $35 per year elsewhere. Subscriptions to: P. O. Box 67, Whitinsville, MA   01588.

School Press Review
Columbia Scholastic Press Association
Box 11
Central Mail Room
Columbia University
New York, NY   10027
(212) 280-4480
 Contains articles and information helpful to student journalists, news of school press conventions, seminars, summer workshops, and special meetings, as well as current book reviews, reprints of current student writings and photography, and how-to material on new techniques, innovations, and production methods in publishing and editing student media of all types. Monthly (October through May). $6 per year.

12. TECHNOLOGY AND TELECOMMUNICATIONS POLICY

**Annual Review of Information
  Science and Technology**
American Society for Information Science
1155 16th Street, N.W.
Washington, DC   20036
(202) 659-3644

Editor:
Prof. Martha E. Williams
University of Illinois
(217) 333-8462
   Contains approximately 10 chapters on various topics of concern to information scientists and library professionals. Annual. ASIS members: $28; ASIS affiliates: $31.50; non-members: $35.

Bell Journal of Economics
American Telephone and Telegraph Company
195 Broadway
New York, NY 10007
(212) 393-9800
Dr. P. W. MacAvoy, editor
   Formerly *Bell Journal of Economics and Management Science*. Semiannual. Free.

Bell Laboratories Record
Bell Telephone Laboratories, Inc.
600 Mountain Avenue
Murray Hill, NJ 07974
(201) 782-3000
William J. Bucci, editor
   Contains semi-technical articles on accomplishments within the Bell System, including information on breakthroughs in research. 11 times a year. $10 per year, plus $1 for postage. Subscriptions to: Bell Telephone Laboratories, Whippany Road, Whippany, NJ 07981.

Bell System Technical Journal
Bell Telephone Laboratories, Inc.
600 Mountain Avenue
Murray Hill, NJ 07974
G.E. Schindler, Jr., editor
   Covers personnel and developments of a technical nature in the entire Bell system. 10 times a year. $15 per year. Subscriptions to: Bell Telephone Laboratories, Whippany Road, Whippany, NJ 07981.

BM/E (Broadcast Management/Engineering)
   See listing on page 310

Bulletin of the American Society for Information Science
1155 16th Street, N.W.,
Washington, DC 20036
(202) 659-3644
Lois F. Lunin, editor, (310) 523-0191
Contains articles on topics of interest to information professionals as well as news about the Society. It is aimed primarily at ASIS members, although there are approximately 400 other subscribers. Bimonthly. Free to ASIS members and affiliates; $27.50 to non-members.

Business Radio/Action
National Association of Business
 and Educational Radio
1330 New Hampshire Avenue, N.W.
Washington, DC 20036
(202) 659-8334
Intended for users of land mobile radio communications in business and nonprofit organizations, as well as independent dealers and radio service facility operators. Special attention is given to regulatory matters and new technological developments. Monthly. $5 per year.

IEEE Spectrum
Institute of Electrical
 and Electronics Engineers
345 East 47th Street
New York, NY 10017
(212) 644-7566
Donald Christiansen, editor
Technical journal in communications and related electronics field. Monthly.

Information Science Abstracts
Computer Science Department
Yale University
New Haven, CT 06520
(203) 776-2844
Ben-Ami Lipetz, editor
The principal English-language abstracting and indexing service for information science, library science, and documentation, and for such related fields as special librarianship, education, administration, editing, publishing, and communication. Provides heavy cross-

referencing between abstracts of related publications as an aid to searching. Sponsored by the American Society for Information Science, the Division of Chemical Information of the American Chemical Society, and the Special Libraries Association, *Abstracts* is published by Documentation Abstracts, Inc., a nonprofit corporation. Work is under way to develop a computer-searchable data base of *Information Science Abstracts* to supplement the published version. Both current and full retrospective coverage are planned. Published in six bimonthly abstracts issues and an annual volume index issue. $95 per year, plus $4 for subscriptions outside the U. S. Send subscriptions to: Documentation Abstracts, Inc., P. O. Box 8510, Philadelphia, PA 19101.

Jola Technical Communications
American Library Association
Information Science Automation Division
50 East Huron Street
Chicago, IL   60611
(312) 944-6780

A section published quarterly in the *Journal of Library Automation*, which is devoted to reporting the latest information in the areas of library automation, information retrieval, and information technology. Related areas of multi-media and A-V are included.

Journal of the American Society for Information Science
1155 16th Street, N.W.
Washington, DC   20036
(202) 659-3644
Arthur W. Elias, editor, (215) 568-4016

Contains scholarly articles on information science and technology. Audience consists of ASIS members, plus 1,500 other subscribers, including libraries, technical centers, and individuals, throughout the world. Bimonthly. Free to ASIS members; $22.50 per year to ASIS affiliates; $45 per year to non-members.

Multicast
Paul Kagan Associates, Inc.
100 Merrick Road
Rockville Centre, NY   11570
(516) 764-5516

A newsletter on Multipoint Distribution Service (MDS), FCC-authorized closed circuit, omnidirectional microwave common carrier transmission. Twice a month. $195 per year.

Pike and Fischer Radio Regulation
See listing on page 190

Public Telecommunications Review
See listing on page 374

Public Utilities Fortnightly
Public Utilities Reports, Inc.
1828 L Street, N.W.
Washington, DC 20036
(202) 293-5910

Biweekly magazine with current news and opinion about problems facing the utilities industry under the established system of regulation. $45 per year for 26 issues.

RCA Review
RCA Laboratories
Princeton, NJ 08540
(609) 452-2700
R. F. Ciafone, editor

Technically oriented journal on RCA developments and projects. Quarterly. $6 per year worldwide.

Telecommunication Journal
International Telecommunication Union
Place des Nations
CH 1211, Geneva 20
Switzerland
(022) 34 60 21

A publication of the ITU, the specialized agency of the United Nations for telecommunications, which was founded in 1865 and which has 153 member countries. Covers new ideas and achievements throughout the world, new products, information on satellites, information for radio amateurs, new accessions to the ITU film library, new books, official announcements of the Union, and news of conferences and meetings external to the ITU. Editions in French and Spanish as well as English. Monthly. 75 Swiss francs per year; special rates for delivery by air mail.

Telecommunications
610 Washington Street
Dedham, MA 02026
(617) 326-8220
James Hughes, editor

Covers data communications, teleprocessing and transmission. Monthly, except semimonthly in September with the publication of the *Telecommunications Handbook and Buyers Guide*. Free upon written request to qualified persons working directly in the communications industry. Other subscriptions $25 per year.

Telecommunications Policy
IPC Science and Technology Press Ltd.
IPC House
32 High Street
Guildford, Surrey GU1 3EW
England
Editor:
Lawrence Day
620 Belmont, Room 1105
Montreal, Quebec H3C 3G4

Covers all aspects of the assessment, control, and management of developments in telecommunications and information systems. Quarterly. $78 per year. Subscriptions to: IPC Business Press (Sales and Distribution), Oakfield House, Perrymount Road, Haywards Heath, Sussex, England RH16 3DH.

Telecommunications Reports
Telecommunications Publishing Company
1204 National Press Building
Washington, DC 20045
(202) 347-2654

Weekly news coverage of legislative, regulatory, tax, and business developments affecting the telecommunications industry, including satellite communications. Thorough coverage of FCC rulings, hearings, reports. $125 per year; $100 per year for overseas, nonprofit, and noncommunications entities. All postage extra.

Telephony
Telephony Publishing Corp.
53 West Jackson Boulevard
Chicago, IL 60604
(312) 922-2435

Weekly news magazine covering regulatory, legislative, judicial and organizational developments in matters affecting telecommunications throughout the world, with emphasis on the United States and Canada. $9.50 per year.

Telephone Engineer & Management
402 West Liberty Drive
Wheaton, IL 60187
(312) 653-4040

A semimonthly magazine containing information on legislation and regulation of the telephone industry, including FCC actions. Edited for administrative executives in all departments of the telephone industry. $8.50 per year.

Televisions
See listing on page 315

The Video Publisher
Knowledge Industry Publications
2 Corporate Park Drive
White Plains, NY 10604
(914) 694-8686
Seth Goldstein, managing editor

A newsletter covering developments in television programming, distribution and syndication, plus developments in programming in all aspects of cable TV, including pay TV, and in videocassettes and video discs. Twice a month. $75 per year.

Video Trade News
C. S. Tepfer Publishing Co., Inc.
P. O. Box 565
Ridgefield, CT 06877
(203) 438-3774

A trade publication featuring news of the video business community and new video technology. Monthly. $6 per year in the U. S.; $8 elsewhere.

Videocassette and CATV Newsletter
See listing on page 319

Videography
United Business Publications, Inc.
750 Third Avenue
New York, NY 10017
(212) 697-8300

Covers the entire field of video. Includes special sections on hardware and software as well as news columns. Monthly. $10 per year.

VideoNews
Phillips Publishing Company
8401 Connecticut Avenue
Chevy Chase, MD 20015
(301) 652-5522
Jerry Norton, editor

Formerly *Broadband Communications Report* and *Vidnews*. A newsletter reporting on developments in the video field, with emphasis on consumer information and video technology, plus aspects of cable and other emerging technologies. Biweekly. $87 per year in the U. S. and Canada; $98 elsewhere.

11

A SELECTION OF
BOOKS ON COMMUNICATIONS

On the following pages will be found a selective listing of the more recent and useful books on the various communications industries. The emphasis is on currently-available titles having reference value. Excluded are bibliographies, which are found in Section XII, books of a practical how-to nature (production and direction texts), and volumes in languages other than English.

Books are divided into the following sections:
1) General Titles   357
2) History and Development   358
3) Communications Technology   359
4) Structure and Economics   360
5) Journalism   362
6) General Media Content   363
7) Audience and Effects   364
8) Regulatory Policy   365
9) U.S. Communications Abroad   367
10) Foreign and International Communications   369

To keep this section from becoming too long, titles are listed only once. Though most books deal with more than one industry, listings are alphabetized according to their principal emphasis without further subdivision. With only a few exceptions, listings are not annotated.

While the stress here is on mass communications (books, magazines, newspapers, broadcasting and film), "fringe media" (comics, recordings) are briefly covered, and several titles refer to common carrier communication (telephone, specialized carriers, etc.). Any such choice is an arbitrary one, but the attempt here has been to provide a reasonable choice of current reference-value works which, taken together, provide the essential information on American communications industries.

1. GENERAL TITLES

Blake, Reed H., and Edwin O. Haroldsen. *A Taxonomy of Concepts in Communication*. New York: Hastings House, 1975. 158 pp.
Lamberton, Donald M., ed. "The Information Revolution," *The Annals* Vol. 412. Philadelphia: American Academy of Political and Social Science, 1974. 162 pp.
Machlup, Fritz. *The Production and Distribution of Knowledge in the United States*. Princeton, N.J.: Princeton University Press, 1962. 416 pp.
McLuhan, Marshall. *Understanding Media: The Extensions of Man*. New York: McGraw-Hill, 1964. 364 pp.
McQuail, Denis. *Towards a Sociology of Mass Communications*. London: Collier-Macmillan, 1969. 122 pp.
Monaco, James. *How to Read a Film: The Art, Technology, Language, History, and Theory of Film and Media*. New York: Oxford University Press, 1977. 502 pp.
National Information Policy: Report to the President of the United States. Washington: Government Printing Office (for the National Commission on Libraries and Information Science, as submitted by the Staff of the Domestic Council Committee on the Right of Privacy), 1976. 233 pp.
Pool, Ithiel de Sola, and Wilbur Schramm, eds. *Handbook of Communication*. Chicago: Rand McNally College Publishing Co., 1973. 1011 pp.
Schramm, Wilbur. *Men, Messages, and Media: A Look at Human Communication*. New York: Harper & Row, 1973. 341 pp.
Schramm, Wilbur, and William L. Rivers. *Responsibility in Mass Communication*. New York: Harper & Row, 1969. 314 pp.
Sterling, Christopher H., and Timothy R. Haight, eds. *The Mass Media: Aspen Guide to Communication Industry Trends*. New York: Praeger Special Studies (hardcover), and Palo Alto: Aspen Institute (paperback), 1977. A statistical abstract of all media, arranged in sections on growth, ownership, economics, content, employment, audience, and U.S. media abroad, covered historically from 1900 to the present.
Wright, Charles R. *Mass Communication: A Sociological Perspective*. New York: Random House, 1975. 179 pp.

2. HISTORY AND DEVELOPMENT
(See also: 3, 6 and 8)

Barnouw, Erik. *A History of Broadcasting in the United States*. New York: Oxford University Press, 1966-70 (three volumes: A Tower in Babel; The Golden Web; The Image Empire). The same author and publisher issued a one-volume television-emphasis condensation as *Tube of Plenty* (1975).
Bohn, Thomas W., and Richard L. Stromgren. *Light and Shadows: A History of Motion Pictures*. Port Washington, N.Y.: Alfred Publishing Co., 1975. 537 pp. There are many one-volume histories of film available—this is one of the more inclusive and recent.
Brooks, John. *Telephone: The First Hundred Years*. New York: Harper & Row, 1976. 369 pp.
Clarke, Arthur C. *Voice Across the Sea*. New York: Harper & Row, 1974 (2nd ed.). 226 pp.
Emery, Edwin. *The Press and America: An Interpretive History of the Mass Media*. Englewood Cliffs, N.J.: Prentice-Hall, 1972 (3rd ed.). 788 pp. Title misleading: deals only with newspapers and magazines but gives the standard history of those.
Gelatt, Roland. *The Fabulous Phonograph: 1877-1977*. New York: Macmillan, 1977 (3rd ed.). 349 pp.
Harlow, Alvin F. *Old Wires and New Waves: The History of the Telegraph, Telephone and Wireless*. New York: Appleton-Century, 1936 (reprinted by Arno Press in 1971). 548 pp.
Johnson, Elmer D. *Communication: An Introduction to the History of Writing, Printing, Books and Libraries*. Metuchen, N.J.: Scarecrow Press, 1973 (4th ed.). 322 pp. Heavy emphasis on libraries, but with good bibliography for all topics listed.
Jowett, Garth. *Film: The Democratic Art*. Boston: Little-Brown, 1976. 518 pp. A social history of American film.
Lichty, Lawrence W., and Malachi C. Topping, eds. *American Broadcasting: A Sourcebook on the History of Radio and Television*. New York: Hastings House, 1975. 723 pp.
Manvell, Roger, ed. *The International Encyclopedia of Film*. New York: Crown, 1972. 574 pp.
Newhall, Beaumont. *The History of Photography From 1839 to the Present Day*. New York: Museum of

Modern Art, 1964. (4th ed.). 216 pp. There are several one-volume histories—this is a long-lasting classic.
Nye, Russel B. *The Unembarrassed Muse: The Popular Arts in America*. New York: Dial Press, 1970. 497 pp. Mainly print, theater and music.
Reitberger, Reinhold, and Wolfgang Fuchs. *Comics: Anatomy of a Mass Medium*. Boston: Little, Brown, 1972. 264 pp.
Rosewater, Victor. *History of Cooperative News-Gathering in the United States*. New York: Appleton, 1930 (reprinted by Johnson Reprint in 1971). 430 pp. Definitive history of news agencies to 1930.
Saettler, Paul. *A History of Instructional Technology*. New York: McGraw-Hill, 1968. 399 pp.
Sterling, Christopher H., and John M. Kittross. *Stay Tuned: A Concise History of American Broadcasting*. Belmont, Calif.: Wadsworth, 1978. 550 pp.
Tebbel, John. *The Media in America*. New York: Crowell, 1975. 422 pp. Integrated history of books, newspapers and magazines. The author is writing *A History of Book Publishing in the United States* (Bowker, 1972-date, four volumes), the definitive history.
Wood, James Playsted. *The Story of Advertising*. New York: Ronald Press, 1958. 512 pp.
———. *Magazines in the United States*. New York: Ronald Press, 1971 (3rd ed.). 476 pp.

3. COMMUNICATIONS TECHNOLOGY (See also: 2)

Bagdikian, Ben H. *The Information Machines: Their Impact on Men and the Media*. New York: Harper & Row, 1971. 359 pp.
Bretz, Rudy. *A Taxonomy of Communication Media*. Englewood Cliffs, N.J.: Educational Technology Publications, 1971. 128 pp.
"Fiftieth Anniversary Edition," *Proceedings of the Institute of Radio Engineers* 50:5:529–1448 (May 1962). Includes 113 papers on communications and electronics, both of historical and then-current nature.
Gaskell, Philip. *A New Introduction to Bibliography*. New York: Oxford University Press, 1972. 438 pp. Development of the techniques of book printing, design, paper, composition, and production from 1500 to date in Europe and the U.S.
Gerbner, George, Larry P. Gross, and William H. Melody,

eds. *Communications Technology and Social Policy: Understanding the New "Cultural Revolution"* (New York: John Wiley, 1973. 573 pp.

Happé, Bernard. *Basic Motion Picture Technology*. New York: Hastings House, 1970. 371 pp.

Jenkins, Reese V. *Images and Enterprise: Technology and the American Photographic Industry, 1839–1925*. Baltimore: Johns Hopkins University Press, 1975. 371 pp.

Limbacher, James L. *Four aspects of the Film: Color, Sound, 3-D, and Widescreen*. New York: Brussel & Brussel, 1968. 387 pp.

Maclaurin, W. Rupert, with R. Joyce Harman. *Invention and Innovation in the Radio Industry*. New York: Macmillan, 1949 (reprinted by Arno Press in 1971). 304 pp. Broadcast radio and television to about 1941.

Marsh, Ken Morton Schiff. *Independent Video: A Complete Guide to the Physics, Operation and Application of the New Television for the Student, the Artist and for Community TV*. San Francisco: Straight Arrow Books (Simon and Schuster), 1974. 212 pp. Excellent clear diagrams on how television system works.

Martin, James. *Future Developments in Telecommunications*. Englewood Cliffs, N.J.: Prentice-Hall, 1971. 413 pp.

Polcyn, Kenneth. *An Educator's Guide to Communication Satellite Technology*. Washington: Academy for Educational Development, 1973. 99 pp.

"Sixtieth Anniversary Issue," *SMPTE Journal* 85: 449–551 (July 1976). 15 articles on the development of television and film technology and applications.

Spottiswoode, Raymond, general editor. *The Focal Encyclopedia of Film and Television Techniques*. New York: Hastings House, 1969. 1100 pp.

Straus, Victor. *The Printing Industry: An Introduction to its Many Branches, Processes and Products*. New York: Bowker, 1967. 815 pp.

4. STRUCTURE AND ECONOMICS

Baer, Walter S., et al. *Concentration of Mass Media Ownership: Assessing the State of Current Knowledge*. Santa Monica, Calif.: Rand Corp., 1974. 202 pp.

Barton, Roger, ed. *Handbook of Advertising Management*. New York: McGraw-Hill, 1970. 1050 pp.

Bluem, A. William and Jason E. Squire. *The Movie Business: American Film Industry Practice.* New York: Hastings House, 1972. 368 pp.

Borchardt, Kurt. *Structure and Performance of the U.S. Communications Industry: Government Regulation and Company Planning.* Cambridge, Mass.: Harvard University Press, 1970. 180 pp.

Bunce, Richard. *Television in the Corporate Interest.* New York: Praeger Special Studies, 1976. 150 pp. Ownership trends.

Cater, Douglass, and Michael J. Nyhan, *The Future of Public Broadcasting.* New York: Praeger Special Studies, 1976. 372 pp.

Denisoff, R. Serge. *Solid Gold: The Popular Record Industry.* New Brunswick, N.J.: Transaction Books, 1975. 504 pp.

Dessauer, John P. *Book Publishing: What it Is, What it Does.* New York: Bowker, 1975. 231 pp.

Ford, James L. C. *Magazines for Millions: The Story of Specialized Publications.* Carbondale: Southern Illinois University Press, 1969. 320 pp.

Head, Sydney W. *Broadcasting in America: A Survey of Television and Radio.* Boston: Houghton Mifflin, 1976. (3rd ed.). 629 pp.

Noll, Roger G., Merton J. Peck and John J. McGowan. *Economic Aspects of Television Regulation.* Washington: Brookings Institution, 1973. 342.

Owen, Bruce M. *Economics and Freedom of Expression: Media Structure and the First Amendment.* Cambridge, Mass.: Ballinger Publishing Co., 1975. 202 pp.

———, Jack H. Beebe and Willard G. Manning, Jr. *Television Economics.* Lexington, Mass.: Lexington Books (D.C. Heath), 1974. 218 pp.

Porat, Marc. *The Information Economy.* Washington: Government Printing Office, 1977. Nine volumes of Office Telecommunications "Special Publications" series on information sector of U.S. economy, with historical and current text and data series.

Publishers Weekly, editors of. *The Business of Publishing: A PW Anthology.* New York: Bowker, 1976. 303 pp.

Wood, Donald N., and Donald G. Wylie. *Educational Telecommunications.* Belmont, Calif.: Wadsworth Publishing Co., 1977. 370 pp.

Wright, John S., et al. *Advertising.* New York: McGraw-Hill, 1977 (4th ed.). 769 pp. Or one of the other current one-volume introductory texts.

5. JOURNALISM

Adler, Ruth. *A Day in The Life of the New York Times.* Philadelphia: Lippincott, 1971. 242 pp.

Barrett, Marvin, ed. *The Alfred I. duPont-Columbia university Survey of Broadcast Journalism.* New York: Grosset & Dunlap (to 1972); Crowell (since 1972), biennial. Main title varies somewhat each year.

Blanchard, Robert O., ed. *Congress and the News Media.* New York: Hastings House, 1974. 506 pp.

Bloom, Melvyn H. *Public Relations and Presidential Campaigns: A Crisis in Democracy.* New York: Crowell, 1973. 349 pp.

Braestrup, Peter. *Big Story: How the American Press and Television Reported and Interpreted the Crisis of Tet 1968 in Vietnam and Washington.* Boulder, Colo.: Westview Press, 1977 1500 pp. (two volumes).

Chaffee, Steven H., ed. *Political Communication: Issues and Strategies for Research.* Beverly Hills, Calif.: Sage Publications, 1975. 319 pp.

Chester, Edward W. *Radio, Television and American Politics.* New York: Sheed & Ward, 1969. 342 pp. Historical review from 1920 through 1968 campaigns.

Epstein, Edward Jay. *News from Nowhere: Television and the News.* New York: Random House, 1973. 321 pp. Anatomy of the network news operations.

Hulteng, John l. *The Messenger's Motives: Ethical Problems of the News Media.* Englewood Cliffs, N.J.: Prentice-Hall, 1976. 262 pp.

Johnstone, John W. C., Edward J. Slawski, and William W. Bowman. *The News People: A Sociological Portrait of American Journalists and Their Work.* Urbana: University of Illinois Press, 1976. 257 pp.

Kraus, Sidney, and Dennis Davis. *The Effects of Mass Communication on Political Behavior.* University Park, Pa.: Pennsylvania State University Press, 1976. 308 pp.

Krieghbaum, Hillier. *Pressures on the Press.* New York: Crowell, 1972. 248 pp.

MacDougall, Curtis D. *The Press and its Problems.* Dubuque, Iowa: Wm. C. Brown, 1964. 532 pp.

Martin, L. John, ed. "Role of the Mass Media in American Politics," *The Annals*, Vol. 427. Philadelphia: American Academy of Political and Social Science, 1976. 133 pp.

Porter, William E. *Assault on the Media: The Nixon Years.* Ann Arbor: University of Michigan Press, 1976. 320 pp. Documented review arranged chronologically, 1969–1974.

Rivers, William L. *The Adversaries: Politics and the Press.* Boston: Beacon Press, 1971. 273 pp.

Swanberg, W. A. *Luce and His Empire.* New York: Scribner's, 1972. 529 pp. Slashing attack on, and the story of, Time Inc. and its publications.

Talese, Gay. *The Kingdom and the Power.* New York: World, 1969. 650 pp. Behind the scenes for the past 15 years at *The New York Times.*

Wolf, Frank. *Television Programming for News and Public Affairs: A Quantitative Analysis of Networks and Stations.* New York: Praeger Special Studies, 1972. 203 pp.

6. GENERAL MEDIA CONTENT (See also: 2)

Andrew, J. Dudley. *The Major Film Theories: An Introduction.* New York: Oxford University Press, 1976. 278 pp.

Cantor, Muriel G. *The Hollywood TV Producer: His Work and His Audience.* New York: Basic Books, 1972. 264 pp.

Daniels, Les. *Living in Fear: A History of Horror in the Mass Media.* New York: Scribners, 1975. 248 pp.

David, Nina. *TV Season.* Phoenix. Ariz.: Oryx Press, 1976-date, annual. ca 200 pp. Annual listing of network and syndicated programs with credits and content details.

Dunning, John. *Tune in Yesterday: The Ultimate Encyclopedia of Old-Time Radio, 1925–1976.* Englewood Cliffs, N.J.: Prentice-Hall, 1976. 703 pp. Alphabetical listing and discussion of network radio programs, their characters and themes.

Hackett, Alice Payne, and James Henry Burke. *80 Years of Best Sellers.* New York: Bowker, 1977 (4th ed.). 265 pp. Listing and brief discussion of book trends from 1895 to date. For more analysis and content information, see Frank Luther Mott's *Golden Multitudes: The Story of Best Sellers in the United States.* New York: Macmillan, 1947 [reprinted by Bowker, 1973]. 357 pp.

Hohenberg, John. *The Pulitzer Prizes: A History of the Awards in Books, Drama, Music, and Journalism, Based on the Private Files over Six Decades.* New York: Columbia University Press, 1974. 434 pp.

Horn, Maurice, ed. *The World Encyclopedia of Comics.* New York: Chelsea House Publishers, 1976. 785 pp. The definitive resource on all aspects of the subject.

Madsen, Roy. *The Impact of Film: How Ideas are Communicated Through Cinema and Television.* New York: Macmillan, 1973. 571 pp. Film genre and form and what they contribute to content.

Mendelsohn, Harold. *Mass Entertainment.* New Haven, Conn.: College and University Press, 1966. 203 pp. Theoretical defense of entertainment function.

Newcomb, Horace. *TV: The Most Popular Art.* New York: Doubleday Anchor Books, 1974. 272 pp.

Palmer, Tony. *All You Need is Love: The Story of Popular Music.* New York: Viking Press/Grossman, 1976. 322 pp. The literature on this subject is huge and there are many histories, reference books, and volumes of opinion—this is one of the best recent overall discussions integrating all types.

Real, Michael R. *Mass-Mediated Culture.* Englewood Cliffs, N.J.: Prentice-Hall, 1977. 289 pp.

Stedman, Raymond William. *The Serials: Suspense and Drama by Installment.* Norman: University of Oklahoma Press, 1977 (2nd ed.). 550 pp. As presented in films, radio, and television.

Terrace, Vincent. *The Complete Encyclopedia of Television Programs, 1947–1976.* Cranbury, N. J. A.: S. Barnes, 1976 (two volumes). 914 pp. Alphabetical listing of network and syndicated programs with credits and some trend information

7. AUDIENCE AND EFFECTS

Bower, Robert T. *Television and the Public.* New York: Holt, Rinehart & Winston, 1973. 205 pp. National survey of audience likes, dislikes, and viewing habits, compared to similar study of a decade earlier.

Chu, Godwin C., and Wilbur Schramm. *Learning from Television: What the Research Says.* Washington: National Association of Educational Broadcasters, 1967, with updated version issued in 1974. 127 pp.

Davison, W. Phillips, and Frederick T. C. Yu, eds. *Mass*

Communication Research: Major Issues and Future Directions. New York: Praeger Special Studies, 1974. 248 pp.

Greenberg, Bradley, and Brenda Dervin, *Use of the Mass Media by the Urban Poor.* New York: Praeger Special Studies, 1970. 190 pp.

Goodhardt, G. J., A. S. C. Ehrenberg, and M. A. Collins. *The Television Audience: Patterns of Viewing.* Lexington, Mass.: Lexington Books, 1975. 157 pp. British study with comparison to American findings.

Jarvie, I. C. *Movies and Society.* New York: Basic Books, 1970. 394 pp.

Klapper, Joseph T. *The Effects of Mass Communication.* New York: Free Press, 1960. 302 pp. Long a standard study, this is now dated, although its lengthy discussion on persuasion is still useful.

Liebert, Robert M., John M. Neale, and Emily S. Davidson. *The Early Window: Effects of Television on Children and Youth.* New York: Pergamon Press, 1973. 193 pp.

Noble, Grant. *Children in Front of the Small Screen.* Beverly Hills, Calif.: Sage Publications, 1975. 256 pp.

Pool, Ithiel de Sola, ed. *The Social Impact of the Telephone.* Cambridge, Mass.: MIT Press, 1977. 20 essays focusing on current impact on different aspects of society.

Schramm, Wilbur, and Donald F. Roberts, eds. *The Process and Effects of Mass Communication.* Urbana: University of Illinois Press, 1971 (2nd ed.). 997 pp.

Short, John, Ederyn Williams, and Bruce Christie. *The Social Psychology of Telecommunications.* New York: Wiley, 1976. 195 pp. Impact of the telephone and other kinds of interpersonal electronic communication.

Stein, Aletha Huston, and Lynette Kohn Friedrich. *Impact of Television on Children and Youth.* Chicago: University of Chicago Press, 1975. 72 pp.

The Television Audience. Northbrook, Ill.: A. C. Nielsen Co., 1959-date, annual. Detailed review with tables, charts, and text on programs and audience patterns of the previous season.

8. REGULATORY POLICY

Ashley, Paul P., in collaboration with Camden M. Hall. *Say It Safely: Legal Limits in Publishing, Radio, and Television.* Seattle: University of Washington Press,

1976 (5th ed.). 238 pp. Handy short introduction to basic points of law.

Carmen, Ira H. *Movies, Censorship and the Law.* Ann Arbor: University of Michigan Press, 1966. 339 pp.

Committee on Interstate and Foreign Commerce, Subcommittee on Communications (House of Representatives). *Options Papers.* Washington: GPO, 1977 (95th Cong., 1st Sess.). 664 pp. Nine staff papers on possible telecommunications regulation options under sonsideration in rewrite process for 1934 Act.

Copyright Revision Act of 1976: Law, Explanation Committee Reports. Chicago: Commerce Clearinghouse Inc., 1976. 279 pp. One of the best one-volume compilations on the new act.

DeVol, Kenneth S., ed. *Mass Media and the Supreme Court: The Legacy of the Warren Years.* New York: Hastings House, 1976 (2nd ed.). 400 pp. Cases and comment.

Francois, William E. *Mass Media Law and Regulation.* Columbus, Ohio: Ohio State University Press, 1975. 470 pp. Best in-depth introduction.

Franklin, Marc A. *Cases and Materials on Mass Medial Law.* Mineola, N.Y.: Foundation Press, 1976. 878 pp.

Friendly, Fred W. *The Good Guys, the Bad Guys, and the First Amendment: Free Speech vs. Fairness in Broadcasting.* New York: Random House, 1976. 269 pp.

Georgetown Law Journal, editors. *Media and the First Amendment in a Free Society.* Amherst, Mass.: University of Massachusetts Press, 1973. 250 pp.

Grundfest, Joseph A. *Citizen Participation in Broadcast Licensing Before the FCC.* Santa Monica, Calif.: Rand Corp., 1976. 195 pp.

Guimary, Donald L. *Citizens' Groups and Broadcasting.* New York: Praeger Special Studies, 1975. 171 pp.

Herring, James M., and Gerald C. Gross. *Telecommunications: Economics and Regulation.* New York: McGraw-Hill, 1936 (reprinted by Arno Press in 1974). 544 pp. Includes broadcasting and common carrier development and issues.

Jones, William K., ed. *Cases and Materials on Electronic Mass Media.* Mineola, N.Y.: Foundation Press, 1976. 474 pp.

Kahn, Frank J., ed. *Documents of American Broadcasting* Englewood Cliffs, N.J.: Prentice-Hall, 1978 (3rd ed.).

700 pp. Now arranged chronologically rather than by topic as before.

Levin, Harvey J. *The Invisible Resource: Use and Regulation of the Radio Spectrum.* Baltimore: Johns Hopkins Press, 1971. 432 pp. Definitive work on the subject.

National Association of Broadcasters. *Legal Guide to FCC Broadcast Rules, Regulations and Policies.* Washington: NAB, 1977. Loose-leaf service to be regularly updated—at present, the best single source of concise and current information.

Office of Telecommunications Policy, Executive Office of the President. *The Radio Frequency Spectrum: United States Use and Management.* Washington: Government Printing Office, 1975 (3rd ed.). 200 pp. Frequently revised.

President's Task Force on Communications Policy. *Final Report.* Washington: Government Printing Office, 1969. 528 pp. Most recent of the broad-view special commissions.

Randall, Richard S. *Censorship of the Movies: The Social and Political Control of a Mass Medium.* Madison: University of Wisconsin Press, 1968. 280 pp.

Schmidt, Benno C., Jr. *Freedom of the Press vs. Public Access.* New York: Praeger Special Studies, 1976. 296 pp. Best work to date on "access" questions.

Shapiro, Andrew O. *Media Access: Your Rights to Express Your Views on Radio and Television.* Boston: Little, Brown, 1976. 297 pp.

Simons, Howard, and Joseph A. Califano, Jr. *The Media and the Law.* New York: Praeger Special Studies, 1976. 220 pp. Series of case studies of journalistic need vs. government regulation and how journalists and officials would face each.

9. U.S. COMMUNICATIONS ABROAD

Elder, Robert E. *The Information Machine: The United States Information Agency and United States Foreign Policy.* Syracuse, N.Y.: Syracuse University Press, 1968. 356 pp.

Gordon, George N., and Irving A. Falk. *The War of Ideas: America's International Identity Crisis.* New York: Hastings House, 1973. 362 pp.

Guback, Thomas H. *The International Film Industry: Western Europe and America Since 1945.*

Bloomington: Indiana University Press, 1969. 244 pp.
Henderson John W. *The United States Information Agency.* New York: Praeger, 1969. 324 pp.
MacMahon, Arthur W. *Memorandum on the Postwar International Information Program of the United States.* Washington: Department of State, 1945 (reprinted by Arno Press in 1972). 135 pp. Existing status and post-war projections for all media—useful for historical background.
Nordenstreng, Kaarle, and Tapio Varis. "Television Traffic: A One-Way Street? A Survey and Analysis of the International Flow of Television Programme Material." *Reports and Papers on Mass Communication, No. 70.* Paris: Unesco (New York: Unipub), 1973. 62 pp.
Presidential Study Commission on International Radio Broadcasting. *Report: The Right to Know.* Washington: Government Printing Office, 1973. 91 pp.
Read, William H. *America's Mass Media Merchants.* Baltimore: Johns Hopkins University Press, 1977. 208 pp. Focuses on the wire services, news magazines, *Readers Digest,* motion pictures, and television films.
Schiller, Herbert I. *Mass Communications and American Empire.* Boston: Beacon Press, 1969. 170 pp. Strong attack on economic imperialism.
———. *Communication and Cultural Domination.* White Plains, N.Y.: International Arts and Sciences Press, 1976. 127 pp. Continuation of above.
Sorenson, Thomas C. *The Word War: The Story of American Propaganda.* New York: Harper & Row, 1968. 337 pp. Heavy focus on the Murrow years of the early 1960s at USIA.
Thomson, Charles A. H. *Overseas Information Service of the United States Government.* Washington: Brookings Institution, 1948 (reprinted by Arno Press in 1972). 397 pp. Historical background for today: details on operation of OWI in World War II, and immediate post-war U.S. information reaction to Cold War.
Tunstall, Jeremy. *The Media are American: Anglo-American Media in the World.* New York: Columbia University Press, 1977. 352 pp.
United States Treaties and other International Agreements Pertaining to Telecommunications. Washington: Office of Telecommunication (Government Printing Office), 1974. 175 pp.Wells, Alan. *Picture Tube Imperialism? The Impact of U.S. Television*

on Latin America. Maryknoll, N.Y.: Orbis Books, 1972. 197 pp.

10. FOREIGN AND INTERNATIONAL COMMUNICATIONS

Cherry, Colin. *World Communications: Threat or Promise? A Socio-Technical Approach.* New York: Wiley, 1971. 229 pp. Press, media, and common carrier/mail communications are dealt with.
Fischer, Heinz-Dietrich, and John C. Merrill, eds. *International and Intercultural Communication.* New York: Hastings House, 1976 (2nd ed.). 524 pp.
Gerbner, George, ed. *Mass Media Policies inChanging Cultures.* New York: Wiley/Interscience, 1977. 291 pp. 23 original articles on media in various regions and countries.
Hale, Julian. *Radio Power: Propaganda and International Broadcasting.* Philadelphia: Temple University Press, 1975. 195 pp.
Head, Sydney W., ed. *Broadcasting in Africa: A Continental Survey of Radio and Television.* Philadelphia: Temple University Press, 1974. 453 pp.
Hollander, Gayle Durham. *Soviet Political Indoctrination: Developments in Mass Media and Propaganda Since Stalin.* New York: Praeger Special Studies, 1972. 245 pp.
Hopkins, Mark W. *Mass Media in the Soviet Union.* New York: Pegasus, 1970. 384 pp.
Leive, David M. *International Telecommunications and International Law: The Regulation of the Radio Spectrum.* Dobbs Ferry, N.Y.: Oceana Publications, 1970. 386 pp.
Liu, Alan P. L. *Communications and National Integration in Communist China.* Berkeley: University of California Press, 1971. 225 pp.
Martin, L. John, ed. "Propaganda in International Affairs," *The Annals* Vol. 398. Philadelphia: American Academy of Political and Social Science, 1971. 139 pp.
Merrill, John C., Carter R. Bryan, and Marvin Alisky. *The Foreign Press: A Survey of the World's Journalism.* Baton Rouge: Louisiana State University Press, 1970. 366 pp.
Namurois, Albert. *Structures and Organization of Broadcasting in the Framework of Radiocommunications.*

Geneva: European Broadcasting Union, 1972. 210 pp. Well-organized comparative analysis of broadcast systems.

Roetter, Charles. *The Art of Psychological Warfare, 1914-1945.* New York: Stein & Day, 1975. 199 pp. A short historical review of propaganda's background.

Schramm, Wilbur, and Daniel Lerner, eds. *Communication and Change: The Last Ten Years—and the Next.* Honolulu: University of Hawaii Press (East-West Center), 1976. 371 pp. Papers to update the same editors' *Communication and Change in the Developing Countries,* 1967.

Singer, Benjamin D., ed. *Communications in Canadian Society.* Toronto: Copp Clark Publishing, 1975 (2nd ed.). 484 pp. Perhaps the best single-volume overview of Canadian media.

Smith, Anthony. *The Shadow in the Cave: The Broadcaster, His Audience, and the State.* Urbana: University of Illinois Press, 1974. 351 pp. Comparative review of U.S., several European countries, and Japan.

Smith, Delbert D. *Communication via Satellite: A Vision in Retrospect.* Leyden, The Netherlands: A. W. Sijthoff, 1976. 335 pp. Interrelationship between technology, politics, and economics—the background of Comsat and Intelsat.

Taubert, Sigfred, ed. *The Book Trade of the World.* New York: Bowker, 1974-78 (three volumes). I deals with Europe and international trends generally; II covers the Americas, Australia and New Zealand; and III covers Africa and Asia.

Unesco, *Communication Policies.* Paris: Unesco (New York: Unipub), 1975-77 (series). Short monographs, one per country, with several on Europe and Latin America published thus far.

World Communications: A 200 Country Survey of Press, Radio, Television, Film. Paris: Unesco (New York: Unipub), 1975 (5th ed.). 533 pp. The standard one-volume reference for the media covered.

12

A SELECTION ON COMMUNICATIONS BIBLIOGRAPHIES

As a key to the contents of the hundreds of periodicals listed in Section X, and to indicate the extent of book-length publications in mass communications, the following pages offer a brief annotated guide to the more important bibliographies dealing with media subjects. The approximately 125 titles listed here, divided by topic, stress the more recent publication trends in media research; many older bibliographies now mainly of historical interest have been left out in the interest of space. Asterisks indicate especially valuable items. Many of the periodicals listed in Section X contain book review sections or published bibliographies from time to time—*Topicator, Mass Media Booknotes, Journalism Quarterly, Journal of Broadcasting,* and *New Books in the Journalism and Communications Library.* Two caveats: only English-language material is included here (there are also many useful foreign language bibliographies); and all titles are listed but once, so the reader may wish to scan several related categories.

1)	General Media	373
2)	Media Economics	375
3)	Law and Regulatory Policy	376
4)	Educational and Instructional Media	377
5)	Media Audience Research	379
6)	Foreign and International Media	381
7)	Media in Developing Nations	384
8)	Journalism and Print Media	385
9)	Broadcasting	388
10)	Cable and New Technologies	389
11)	Motion Pictures	391
12)	Guides to Media Archives/Libraries	395

1. GENERAL MEDIA

Agee, Warren K., Phillip H. Ault, and Edwin Emery. *Introduction to Mass Communications*. New York: Harper & Row, 1976 (5th ed.). 469 pp. A good annotated bibliography divided by topic appears on pp. 418-453 and includes books, periodicals, reports and organizations.

*Blum, Eleanor. *Basic Books in the Mass Media*. Urbana, Ill.: University of Illinois Press, 1972. 252 pp. The best single key to finding data on any aspect of media, this typescript volume is divided into sections by media and is well-indexed and annotated for its more than 600 entries.

* "Communications and the Arts," Volume 31 of *Comprehensive Dissertation Index*. Ann Arbor: Xerox University Microfilms, 1973. This is a 37 volume indexed set which provides subject, author, and title indexes to *Dissertation Abstracts*. Entries on mass communication appear in this volume, pp. 195-267, with library and information science on pp. 127-194, covering dissertations completed in the years 1861—1972. The publisher is now issuing annually a five-volume update to this basic index, and entries for each year on mass communications and library-information science appear in Volume 3. Each book contains how-to-use information. Together, these index volumes and the abstracts in the main publication provide definitive access to nearly all doctoral dissertations in all fields presented to American universities. See also on this list: *Journalism Abstracts* (section 8), and Kittross (section 9).

Danielson, Wayne, and G. C. Wilhoit, Jr. *A Computerized Bibliography of Mass Communication Research, 1944-1964*. New York: Magazine Publishers Association, 1967. 399 pp. A key-word-in-context index to over 2,300 periodical and book citations on all aspects of media (with an understandable emphasis on magazines) for the two-decade period indicated. Key-word index takes half of book, while bibliography with full citations (and keyed to index by a serial number) takes second half.

Friedman, Leslie, comp. *Sex Role Stereotyping in the Mass Media: An Annotated Bibliography*. New York: Garland Publishing Co., 1977. 300 pp. Including print and non-print material this guide has sections on children's media, popular culture, the mass media in general, men in media, minority group portrayals, impact of the stereotyping on career choices. Cross-referenced with an author index.

Matlon, Ronald and Irene. *Index to Journals In Communication Studies Through 1974.* Falls Church, Va.: Speech Communication Association, 1976. 365 pp. Chronological tables of contents as well as detailed combined indexes to 10 speech journals, plus *Journal of Communication, Journalism Quarterly,* and *Journal of Broadcasting,* from their inception through 1974 issues.

Pool, Ithiel de Sola, et al., eds. *Handbook of Communication.* Chicago: Rand McNally, 1973. 1011 pp. A review of the entire field of communication (including mass media) in 31 sections, each of which is essentially an analysis of research and other literature to about 1970. Each article has a supplementary bibliography, and items listed are discussed in the articles, making the whole book something of an annotated bibliography to a vast field.

Public Opinion Quarterly, editors of. *Cumulative Index to the Public Opinion Quarterly, Volumes 1-31 (1937-1967).* New York: Columbia University Press, 1968. 110 pp. Some 200 topics headings plus indexes by author, geography, and book reviews. Indispensable guide to the major periodical in the field.

Sterling, Christopher H. *The Media Sourcebook: Comparative Reviews and Listings of Textbooks in Mass Communications.* Washington: National Association of Educational Broadcasters, 1974. 53 pp. Reprint of six articles from NAEB journals providing comparative evaluations of some 350 volumes suitable for text use in mass communications generally, and broadcasting specifically, all published in the 1960-73 period. The series is updated in the February 1975 and subsequent February issues of *Public Telecommunications Review.* See also Sterling's "Mass Communication Texts and Readers: An Overview for 1974/75," *Mass Comm Review* 2:1:24-40 (December 1974). Some 90 currently in-print volumes are discussed, compared, and classified in both chart and text. Discussion restricted to general books on mass communications suitable for broad-based introductory courses. The latter is to be published in updated form in early 1978.

2. MEDIA ECONOMICS

Baer, Walter S., Henry Geller, Joseph A. Grundfest, and Karen B. Possner. *Concentration of Mass Media Ownership: Assessing the State of Current Knowledge.* Report R-1584-NSF, Santa Monica, Calif.: Rand Corporation, 1974. 202 pp. The best analysis of writing and research on media ownership, with lengthy discussion of findings and a detailed listing of all writings (pp. 173-202).

Bockman, Marilyn M. *Selected Bibliography of Books on Advertising.* New York: American Association of Advertising Agencies, 1975. 6 pp. Unannotated but topically-divided listing.

*Daniels, Lorna M. *Business Information Sources.* Berkeley: University of California Press, 1976. 439 pp. Well organized and annotated 20 sections with details on hundreds of books, trade annuals, periodicals, statistical and indexing services, government reports and both domestic and foreign analyses of all aspects of business and industry. Lacks specific section on communications but provides much related data throughout.

Owen, Bruce M., et al. *A Selected Bibliography in the Economics of the Mass Media* (Memorandum 99) and *Mass Communication and Economics: A Bibliography* (Memorandum 156). Stanford, Calif.: Stanford University, Center for Research in Economic Growth, August 1970 and October 1973. 83 and 68 pp. Alphabetical listings with subject-matter designation numbers of several hundred periodical articles, books, and reports on all aspects of advertising and media economics. Not annotated. (See also Wechsler, below.)

Ramond, Charles. *Advertising Research: The State of the Art:* New York: Association of National Advertisers, Inc., 1976. 148 pp. Narrative, topically-organized discussion of findings of studies listed on pp. 117-136. It is limited to "studies which showed how advertising works and which led (or could have led) to improved performance ... methodological studies are therefore included when they show how to improve the practice of advertising research itself." Still, one of the few guides to an expanding field of the literature of communication.

Wechsler, Andrew R. *Economics and Freedom of Expression: A Bibliography*. Stanford, Calif.: Stanford University Center for Research in Economic Growth, January 1974. 51 pp. Focuses on post-1960 material (only most important earlier data included) in an unannotated alphabetical listing. Part I lists books, reports and articles; II covers court decisions and laws. (See also Owen, above.)

3. **LAW AND REGULATORY POLICY**
   (See also Section VI, "A Guide to Government Policymaking Bodies in Communications")

*"A Bibliography of Articles on Broadcasting in Law Periodicals: 1920-1968." *Journal of Broadcasting* 14:83-156 (Winter 1969-1970). A combination of three articles, two providing annotated bibliographies, the third an unannotated listing with a detailed subject index. Up to 1968, this is unsurpassed. For an update covering the 1968-74 period, see *Client* 2:3 (Spring 1975).

Gandy, Oscar H., Jr., et al. *Media and Government: An Annotated Bibliography*. Stanford, Calif.: Stanford University Institute for Communication Research, 1975. 93 pp. Divided into sections on nature of the news media, government information systems, impact of government on the media, and impact of media on government.

Lamoreux, Stephen. *The Right of Privacy—A Bibliography of 71 Years: 1890-1961*. Pullman, Wash.: Washington State University, Department of Journalism, 1961. 53 pp. Some 280 items (mainly periodical citations) are annotated and divided into about 20 topical categories.

"Media and the First Amendment in a Free Society." *Georgetown Law Journal* 60:863-1099 (March 1972). Reprinted by University of Massachusetts Press, 1973. A special issue that is a good introduction to major controversies and the literature on them; footnotes (often annotated) take up half the issue.

*President's Task Force on Communications Policy. *Bibliography [on Communications Policy]*. Springfield,

Va.: National Technical Information Service, U. S. Department of Commerce, 1969. 172 pp. Unannotated listing of documents, reports, and articles on the problems in and control of telecommunications.

Seipp, David J. *Privacy and Disclosure: Regulation of Information Systems, A Bibliographic Survey*. Cambridge, Mass.: Harvard Program on Information Technologies and Public Policy, 1975. 100 pp. Topically-divided analysis (Part I) and listings (Part II) of material on privacy and its relation to politics and technology. Excellent broad coverage of increasingly complex area.

Sperry, Robert. "A Selected Bibliography of Works on the Federal Communications Commission." *Journal of Broadcasting* 12:83-93; updated in 14:377-389 (Summer 1970) and again in 19:55-113 (Winter 1975). Unannotated but fairly complete listings of articles, law review discussions, government documents, and FCC releases dealing with the Commission and its activities. Second supplement covers 1967-1969, while third covers 1970-1973 inclusive.

Weinhaus, Carol, ed. *Bibliographic Tools, Volume II: Legislative Guide*. Cambridge, Mass.: Harvard University Program on Information Technologies and Public Policy, 1976 (4th ed.). 108 pp. A programmed guide to materials on federal legislation, presidential documents, federal agencies and departments, and two reprints from *Journal of Broadcasting* and *Client* on the specifics of broadcast regulation. One of more complete and easily used guides to the maze of government publication in this field. (Volume I of *Bibliographic Tools* includes a short annotated guide to books and reports of a general nature on information technology.)

4. EDUCATIONAL AND INSTRUCTIONAL MEDIA

*Brown, James W., ed.*Educational Media Yearbook*. New York: Bowker, 1973-date (annual). Lengthy section each year of annotated listings of periodicals, books, and reports dealing with all aspects of educational media. Perhaps the best single reference bibliography in this area, with good index.

*Chu, Godwin C., and Wilbur Schramm. *Learning From Television: What the Research Says*. Washington,

D.C.: National Association of Educational Broadcasters, 1968. 116 pp. Review discussion of topics in instructional television keyed to bibliography pp. 103-115, making whole book a literature review, and best to date. [1974 reprint includes 11-page update introduction.]

Dale, Edgar, et al. *Motion Pictures in Education: A Summary of the Literature.* New York: H. W. Wilson, 1938 (reprinted by Arno Press, 1970). 472 pp. Well-annotated discussion of literature up to the mid-1930s, much of which is still applicable today. Divided into six topical divisions, with extensive literature overview discussions.

Lingel, Robert. *Educational Broadcasting: A Bibliography.* Chicago: University of Chicago Press, 1932. 162 pp. Subject-divided and semi-annotated, with useful 23 pages on radio law. Author and subject indexes. Covers books, periodicals, government documents.

Lumsdaine, A. A., and M. A. May. "Mass Communication and Educational Media." *Annual Review of Psychology*, Vol. 16. Palo Alto, Calif.: Annual Reviews, 1965. Pp. 475-534. Review discussion keyed to lengthy bibliography, with some overlap to Chu and Schramm, above.

Ohliger, John, and David Gueulette. *Media and Adult Learning: A Bibliography with Abstracts, Annotations and Quotations.* New York: Garland Publishing, 1975. 486 pp. Some 1,600 citations divided into 59 categories—but lacking an overall index.

Ramey, James W. *Television in Medical Training and Research: A Survey and Annotated Bibliography.* Washington, D.C.: U. S. Government Printing Office, 1965. 155 pp. Covers 1947-65 period with overall essay followed by extended annotations of key articles, papers, books, speeches and reports, divided by topic.

Reid, J. Christopher, and Donald W. MacLennan. *Research in Instructional Television and Film.* Washington, D.C.: U. S. Government Printing Office, Office of Education, 1967. 216 pp. Indexed and annotated discussion of some 330 studies done after 1950. This study is an update to C. F. Hoban and E. B. Van Ormer, *Instructional Film Research, 1918-1950* (Port Washington, N.Y.: U. S. Naval Training Devices Center, 1959; reprinted by Arno Press, 1971), which had some 200 annotated items.

Taggart, Dorothy T. *A Guide to Sources in Educational Media and Technology*. Metuchen, N.J.: Scarecrow Press, 1975. 156 pp. A guide to building library collections in this area, the book has 18 chapter topic sections covering over 400 annotated items. Indexed but badly dated in some places.

5. MEDIA AUDIENCE RESEARCH

Adler, Richard P., et al. *Research on the Effects of Television Advertising on Children: Review and Recommendations*. Washington, D.C.: National Science Foundation, 1977. 404 pp. Review discussion of the primary and secondary behavioral research literature on television advertising and children, organized around current policy issues. Includes detailed technical reviews of 21 "key studies" and a 40-page comprehensive bibliography.

Atkin, Charles K., John P. Murray, and Oguz B. Nayman, eds. *Television and Social Behavior: An Annotated Bibliography of Research Focusing on Television's Impact on Children*. Rockville, Md.: National Institutes of Mental Health, U. S. Public Health Service, 1971. 150 pp. Three hundred annotated studies, supplemented with another 250 listed but not discussed citations. Author index.

*Comstock, George, and Marilyn Fisher. *Television and Human Behavior: A Guide to the Pertinent Scientific Literature*. Report R-1746-CF, Santa Monica, Calif.: Rand Corporation, 1975. 344 pp. First in a series of three studies, this offers 2,300 references with brief annotations, including research still in process in 1974-75. In addition, offers 11 specialized bibliographies.

*Comstock, George, et al. *Television and Human Behavior: The Key Studies*. Report R-1747-CF, Santa Monica, Calif.: Rand Corporation, 1975. 251 pp. More detailed coverage of some 450 journal articles, books, and other studies thought particularly important, and culled from the volume just above. Comparative evaluations.

*Comstock, George, and Georg Lindsey. *Television and Human Behavior: The Research Horizon: Future and Present*. Report R-1748-CF, Santa Monica, Calif.: Rand Corporation, 1975. 120 pp. Third in the series, this details ongoing current projects and in-press manuscripts. This three volume series is the finest and most detailed survey of its kind—a natural starting point for future work.

Davison, W. Phillips, and Frederick T. C. Yu, eds. *Mass Communication Research: Major Issues and Future Directions.* New York: Praeger Special Studies, 1974. 248 pp. Review of current knowledge in selected topic areas, keyed to bibliography pp. 202-236. Compare with Kline and Tichenor, below.

"Effects of Mass Media," *Annual Review of Psychology.* See below, "Mass Communication," *Annual Review of Psychology.*

Gordon, Thomas F., and Mary Ellen Verna. *Mass Media and Socialization: A Selected Bibliography.* PhiladeLphia: Temple University, School of Communications and Theater, 1973. 47 pp. Unannotated but topically organized listing of articles, reports, and books.

Hansen, Donald A., and J. Herschel Parsons, eds. *Mass Communication: A Research Bibliography.* Santa Barbara, Calif.: Glendessary Press, 1968. 144 pp. Some 3,000 items included in a topically organized but unannotated bibliography, which stresses audience effects and includes other topics as well.

Kline, F. Gerald, and Phillip J. Tichenor, eds. *Current Perspectives in Mass Communication Research.* Beverly Hills, Calif.: Sage, 1972. 320 pp. Nine major and original articles reviewing literature of mass communications, with bibliographies attached to each. Compare with Davison and Yu, above.

* "Mass Communication," from 1977 "Effects of Mass Media," *Annual Review of Psychology.* Palo Alto, Calif.: Annual Reviews, 1959-date, annual. This is a special section providing a narrative discussion and listing of related literature for a specific period of time. The specific sections, by recognized scholars, and excellent overviews, are as follows:

Vol. 13 (1962), pp. 251-284, by Wilbur Schramm. Covers late 1950s.

Vol. 19 (1968), pp. 351-386, by Percy Tannenbaum and Bradley Greenberg. Deals with 1961-66 period, and provides 217 research citations.

Vol. 22 (1971), pp. 309-336, by Walter Weiss. About

180 items from 1967-1970 period.
Vol. 28 (1977), pp. "Effects of Mass Media," pp.141-173, by Robert M. Liebert and Neala S. Schwartzberg. 276 items from 1970 to April, 1976.
McQuail, Denis. *Towards a Sociology of Mass Communications*. New York: Macmillan, 1969. 122 pp. Review of research knowledge supplemented by annotated bibliography on pp. 97-121.
Schramm, Wilbur. *The Effects of Television on Children and Adolescents: An Annotated Bibliography with an Introductory Overview of Research Results*. Paris: UNESCO Reports and Papers on Mass Communication No. 43, 1964. 54 pp. The title sums it up—covers articles on behavioral research (survey, experiment or clinical study) only.

6. FOREIGN AND INTERNATIONAL MEDIA
(See also: 7)

Bibliography: Some Canadian Writings on the Mass Media. Ottawa, Ont.: Canadian Radio-Television Commission, 1974. 99 pp. Alphabetical nonannotated listing of 1,075 items with a subject index.
British Broadcasting Corporation. *British Broadcasting: A Selected Bibliography, 1922-1972*. London: BBC Publications, 1972. 49 pp. More than 700 references, divided into 13 major categories—all carefully indexed and annotated. Includes much material on their colonial broadcasting in Africa and Asia and external broadcasting elsewhere. Offers some material on commercial broadcasting in Britain. Still useful is the 1958 edition for more detail on earlier materials.
Browne, Donald R. "Broadcasting in Industrially-Developed Nations: An Annotated Bibliography." *Journal of Broadcasting* 19:341-354 (Summer 1975). Restricted to book-length studies, this is divided by country.
Fackelman, Macy P., and Kimberly A. Krekel. *International Telecommunications Bibliography*. Washington, D.C.: U. S. Government Printing Office, (Office of Telecommunications, Department of Commerce), 1976. ca. 200 pp. Annotated material on and from the U. S. and other countries on technology of media, international organization, financial and technical

cooperation, international telecommunication law, etc., with author and subject index.

Harwood, Kenneth A. "A World Bibliography of Selected Periodicals on Broadcasting, Revised." *Journal of Broadcasting* 16:131-146 (Spring 1972). Some 350 periodicals listed, with addresses, to supplement and update the original report, 5:251-278 (Summer 1961).

International Telecommunication Union, Central Library. *List of Periodicals*. Geneva: International Telecommunication Union, 1976 (annual). 76 pp. Listing alphabetically, by key-word-in-title, and geographically of titles held by the ITU library; a good supplement to Harwood, above.

Kato, Hidetoshi. *Japanese Research on Mass Communication: Selected Abstracts*. Honolulu, Hi.: University Press of Hawaii, 1974. 128 pp. Nearly 100 studies are detailed.

Lasswell, Harold D., Ralph D. Casey, and Bruce Lannes Smith. *Propaganda and Promotional Activities: An Annotated Bibliography*. Minneapolis, Minn.: University of Minnesota Press, 1935 (reprinted by University of Chicago Press, 1969). 450 pp. Several thousand citations divided topically and most briefly annotated, covering material up to about 1934. See two volumes by Smith, below, which are updates.

Lichty, Lawrence W., comp. *World and International Broadcasting: A Bibliography*. Washington, D.C.: Association for Professional Broadcasting Education, 1971. ca. 800 pp. Topically and geographically organized listing (unannotated) of citations through the 1960s; probably the biggest on broadcasting alone ever attempted. For a similarly-organized update, see Benno Signitzer, "Comparative Systems of Broadcasting: A Bibliography, 1970-1973," in Charles Sherman and Donald Browne, eds., *Issues in International Broadcasting: Broadcast Monographs No. 2*, Washington, D.C.: Broadcast Education Association, 1976, pp. 135-171.

List of Documents and Publications in the Field of Mass Communication. Paris: Unesco, 1976-date, irregular. This serial document is an annotated and carefully indexed English accessions list for the main Unesco Secretariat in Paris. Part 1 of each issue is a listing in masterfile number order (different in each issue), while Part 2 provides the indexes by subject, title, series, personal name, and meeting and corporate body (cumulative, thus replacing earlier issues). As this cumulates, it should become one of the premier record and searching aids for all aspects of mass communication as published in countries around the world.

Marxism and the Mass Media: Towards a Basic Bibliography. Bagnolet, France: International General, International Mass Media Research Center, 1972-date, irregular. A cumulative bibliography which consists of a haphazardly arranged series of annotations (heavy on the political comment as might be expected), with good subject, author, and country indexes which make the material accessible. The five parts published thus far have nearly 700 entries.

Mowlana, Hamid. *International Communication: A Selected Bibliography.* Dubuque, Iowa: Kendall/Hunt, 1971. 130 pp. Some 1450 citations (not annotated) divided by topic, with author and subject indexes.

Nafziger, Ralph O. *International News and the Press: Communications, Organization of News-Gathering, International Affairs, and the Foreign Press—An Annotated Bibliography.* New York: H. W. Wilson, 1940 (reprinted by Arno Press, 1972). Detailed subject-divided listing up to World War II, which is heavily annotated and indexed by author.

Richstad, Jim, and Jackie Bowen, eds. *International Communication Policy and Flow: A Selected Annotated Bibliography.* Honolulu: East-West Communication Institute, 1976. 103 pp. Over 220 entries in this selective bibliography with lengthy annotations are supplemented with an author and subject descriptor index. The abstracts are quite complete.

*Smith, Bruce Lannes, Harold D. Lasswell, and Ralph D. Casey, comps. *Propaganda, Communication, and Public Opinion.* Princeton, N.J.: Princeton University Press, 1946. 435 pp. An update of Lasswell, Casey, and Smith, above, this volume covers the 1934-1944 period with more than 2,500 citations, nearly all annotated and divided by topic, with more of an international flavor than the 1935 volume. See also Smith and Smith, below.

*Smith, Bruce Lannes, and Chitra M. Smith. *International Communication and Political Opinion: A

Guide to the Literature. Princeton, N.J.: Princeton University Press, 1956. 325 pp. The last of three volumes (see Lasswell and the Smith volumes cited above), this book annotated some 2,600 studies in the 1943-55 period, dealing totally with international communications. Together the three books are definitive to 1955.

7. MEDIA IN DEVELOPING NATIONS (See also: 6)

Asian Mass Communication Bibliography Series. Singapore: Asian Mass Communication Research and Information Centre, 1975-date. A series of annotated paperback country-defined books. Each is subject-divided and has an author index. Annotations are extensive—often of paragraph length. Titles issued thus far:
  1. Malaysia (91 pp.)
  2. India (216 pp.)
  3. Hong Kong and Macao (30 pp.)
  4. Philippines (335 pp.)

*Hachten, William A. *Mass Communication in Africa: An Annotated Bibliography.* Madison, Wis.: University of Wisconsin, Center for International Communication Studies, 1971. 121 pp. Annotated listing of over 500 (mainly print media) items. See also Head and Beck, below.

Head, Sydney W., and Lois Beck. *The Bibliography of African Broadcasting: An Annotated Guide.* Philadelphia: Temple University, School of Communications and Theater, 1973. 60 pp. More than 450 items. See also Hachten, above.

*Lent, John. *Asian Mass Communications: A Comprehensive Bibliography.* Philadelphia: Temple University, School of Communications and Theater, 1975. 720 pp. Some 15,000 items (partially annotated) listed by region, then country, and finally by topics within countries. Includes discussion of research centers in each country. Definitive.

*Lent, John, ed. "Selected Information Sources," *Journal of Broadcasting* (as listed below). Each installment offers semi-annotated listings by region and country stressing most recent books, reports, articles and newspapers. Titles published thus far include: (each by different author, Lent doing first two)

"Asian Mass Communications" 19:321-340 (Summer 1975)

"Caribbean Mass Communications" 20:111-125 (Winter 1976)

"African Mass Communications" 20:381-415 (Summer 1976)

Publications expected for segments on the Pacific, the Middle East, Eastern Europe, and Latin America.

Rahim, Syed A., ed. *Communication Policy and Planning for Development: A Selected Annotated Bibliography.* Honolulu, Hi.: East-West Communication Institute, 1976. 285 pp. Nearly 400 entries with subject, author, and country indexes. Annotations are extensive and coverage is broad, including many policy-planning items not specifically relating to the development process.

A Sourcebook on Radio's Role in Development. Washington: Clearinghouse on Development Communication, n.d. but 1976. 85 pp. Some 600 annotated entries (including double listings under more than one category) discussed by type of document, by issue covered (policy and planning, innovation, audience, cost, and support), and strategies (open broadcast, instruction, farm forum, radio school, and animation). Includes address list of document sources. Very useful, complete, and up-to-date.

*Van Bol, Jean-Marie, and Abdelfattah Fakhfakh. *The Use of Mass Media in the Developing Countries.* Brussels: International Center for African Social and Economic Documentation, 1971. 750 pp. A magnificently organized and annotated volume, this covers 2,500 citations in many different languages dealing with media in development; the best bibliography on the subject to date.

8. JOURNALISM AND PRINT MEDIA

*Bishop, Robert L. *Public Relations: A Comprehensive Bibliography—Articles and Books on Public Relations, Communication Theory, Public Opinion, and Propaganda, 1964-1972.* Ann Arbor, Mich.: University of Michigan Press (Publications Distribution Service), 1974. 212 pp. 4,500 entries are annotated in this subject-divided and indexed update to Cutlip (see below).

Bishop, Robert L. "Public Relations: A Comprehensive Bibliography—Articles and Books on Public Relations, Communication Theory, Public Opinion, and Propaganda, 1973-74," *Public Relations Review* 1:4 (Supplement) 1-200 (Winter 1975-76). The first of an annual series of updates, this is in the same form and arrangement, complete with short annotations, as the work above. One issue each year will be devoted to the previous year's publication (e.g. 1977 issue contains material for 1975—76).

Canon, Carl L., comp. *Journalism: A Bibliography.* New York: New York Public Library, 1924 (reprinted by Gale Research Co., 1967). 360 pp. Comprehensive annotated discussion of sources on American and British journalism in the 19th and early 20th centuries. Extensively subject-divided and a standard source up to about 1920.

Cutlip, Scott M. *A Public Relations Bibliography.* Madison, Wisc.: University of Wisconsin Press, 1965 (2nd ed.). 305 pp. A typescript volume that is topically organized and annotates nearly 6,000 citations with varying relations to mass media. See Bishop, above.

Freedom of Information Center. *Index: FOI Reports* (FOI Report 341) and *Annotated Bibliography* (FOI Report 344). Columbia, Mo.: University of Missouri School of Journalism (FOI Center), 1975. 12 and 17 pp. Details on the monthly *FOI Report* series from 1958 to 1975.

Hausman, Linda Weiner. "Criticism of the Press in U. S. Periodicals, 1900-1939: An Annotated Bibliography." *Journalism Monographs*, No. 4 (August 1967). 49 pp. More than 500 well-annotated entries divided into eight sections, including a bit on radio and the wire services. Restricted to periodical citations.

Journalism Abstracts: M.A., M.S., Ph.D. Theses in Journalism and Mass Communication. Minneapolis: University of Minnesota (Association for Education in Journalism), 1963-date, annual. Collection of abstracts first of Ph.D. level, and then Master's level studies, with subject and author listings. Somewhat duplicates *Dissertation Abstracts*, but more selective (incomplete), though easier to use. See also: Kittross, under broadcasting.

Journalism Quarterly, editors of. *Cumulative Index, Vol-*

umes 1-40, 1924-1963 and *Cumulative Index, Volumes 41-50, 1964-1973*. Minneapolis, minn.: Association for Education in Journalism, 1964 and 1974. 120 and 79 pp. Subject and author guides to the major scholarly quarterly's first half century.

*Kaid, Lynda Lee, Keith R. Sanders, and Robert O. Hirsch. *Political Campaign Communication: A Bibliography and Guide to the Literature*. Metuchen, N.J.: Scarecrow Press, 1974. 211 pp. Unannotated listing of hundreds of periodical citations, annotated discussion of 50 most important books in this field, and a general guide to the increasing political communication literature. Only work of its kind.

Kempkes, Wolfgang. *International Bibliography of Comics Literature*. New York: Bowker, 1974. 190 pp. Unannotated listing of nearly 5,000 books and articles, divided topically and presented in German and English.

*McCoy, Ralph E. *Freedom of the Press: An Annotated Bibliography*. Carbondale, Ill.: Southern Illinois University Press, 1968. ca. 500 pp. Alphabetical listing of over 8,000 books, pamphlets, articles, etc. Basic work covers up to 1965 and there is an addendum with 1965-1968 material. Indexed. Perhaps the most handsome and ambitious of the media bibliographies with often lengthy annotations.

*McQuail, Denis. *Review of Sociological Writing on the Press*. London: HMSO, 1976. 86 pp. The second working paper of the British Royal Commission on the Press, this is a narrative bibliographical discussion, divided into more than 12 subject categories, and stressing American and British research efforts. There is a full bibliography, and author index.

*Price, Warren C. *The Literature of Journalism: An Annotated Bibliography*. Minneapolis, Minn.: University of Minnesota Press, 1959. ca. 500 pp. A topically organized volume with over 3,100 books discussed and indexed. Some coverage of broadcasting and other related media. Updated by Price and Pickett, below.

Price, Warren C., and Calder M. Pickett. *An Annotated Journalism Bibliography: 1958-1968*. Minneapolis, Minn.: University of Minnesota Press, 1970. 285 pp. Over 2,100 books arranged alphabetically (with a subject index) to update volume above.

Schacht, J. H. *A Bibliography for the Study of Magazines*.

Urbana, Ill.: University of Illinois, College of Communications, 1972 (3rd ed.). 51 pp. A topically organized and briefly annotated listing of books and articles on magazine publishing.

Wolseley, Roland E. *The Journalist's Bookshelf: An Annotated Bibliography of United States Journalism.* Philadelphia, Pa.: Chilton, 1961 (7th ed.). 225 pp. Some 1,300 titles arranged into over 20 categories, with about half devoted to studies of specific papers and journalists.

9. BROADCASTING

"A Bibliography of Selected Bibliographies in Radio, Television, and Tele-Film: 1958-1968." *Educational Broadcasting Review* 3:2:62-69 (April 1969). Unannotated listing divided into seven topics.

Cooper, Isabella M. *Bibliography on Educational Broadcasting.* Chicago: University of Chicago Press, 1942 (reprinted by Arno Press, 1971). 576 pp. Coverage is far broader than title indicates, being the best annotated discussion of broadcasting literature up to 1940. Some 1,800 items are annotated, topically divided, and indexed by title and author.

Hamill, Patricia Beall. *Radio and Television: A Selected Bibliography.* Washington, D.C.: U. S. Government Printing Office, 1960. 46 pp. The last in a once-often-revised booklet of subject-divided and annotated entries, this deals mainly with book-length material. Handy now as a guide to the literature of the 1950s.

*Head, Sydney W. *Broadcasting in America.* Boston: Houghton Mifflin, 1976 (3rd ed.). 640 pp. The best single volume on U. S. radio-TV now contains more than 100 pages of narrative subject-divided bibliography and listings of book and periodical citations on pp. 511-612. For the moment, the best up-to-date discussion of literature on broadcasting.

Journal of Broadcasting (see p. 292). Constantly publishes bibliographies on all aspects of broadcasting—several are listed here. See "Topic and Author Index to Volume I through Volume XV," in the Fall 1971 issue (15:453-503), and subsequent annual indices.

Kittross, John M., comp. *Theses and Dissertations in Broadcasting: 1920-1972.* Philadelphia: Broadcast

Education Association, 1977. About 250 pp. The most complete listing of its kind, this is a computer printed and indexed listing of some 4,400 titles with a modified-key-word and 40 topic-heading indexes. Based on various published listings to 1966, and a national survey for the 1966-72 period.

Paulu, Burton. *Radio-Television Bibliography: Books and Magazine Articles on the Nontechnical Aspects of Broadcasting: 1949-1952.* Urbana, Ill.: National Association of Educational Broadcasters, 1952. 129 pp. Topically-divided but not annotated coverage of four-year period.

Poteet, G. Howard. *Published Radio, Television, and Film Scripts: A Bibliography.* Troy, N.Y.: Whiston Publishing Co., 1975. 245 pp. First 125 pp. is radio script listing (1,251 of them), 40 pp. cover TV (400 scripts), and the rest is film. List is in program or film title order and is not annotated. (See section 11 for film.)

Rose, Oscar. *Radio Broadcasting and Television: An Annotated Bibliography.* New York: H. W. Wilson, 1947. 120 pp. Useful subject-divided discussion of book-length studies on U. S. broadcasting up to about 1945. Author and title indexes.

Television Information Office. *Bibliographies.* New York: Television Information Office, 1962-1964. Topics covered in these booklets, which include annotated entries but apparently are not kept up-to-date, include "Television and Education," "Television Careers," and "Television in Government and Politics." As these are part of a public relations effort, the views covered are basically favorable to TV. Inquire at TIO concerning revisions and new titles.

Topicator. See listing on page 288. Wright, Charles R. "Television and Radio Program Ratings and Measurements: A Selected and Annotated Bibliography." *Evaluation of Statistical Methods Used in Obtaining Broadcast Ratings9* U. S. Congress, House Report 193, 87th Congress, 1st Session (1961), pp. 140-163 (shorter version in *Journal of Broadcasting* 5:165-186, Spring 1961). Topically arranged and very detailed.

10. CABLE AND NEW TECHNOLOGIES

Bibliocable. Washington, D.C.: Cable Television Information Center, Urban Institute, 1972 and 1974 update.

24 and 20 pp. Detailed annotations and how-to-get-it information on some 150 books, articles, reports, and documents on all aspects of cable communications. Periodically updated.

BCTV: Bibliography on Cable Television. San Francisco: Communications Library, 1975-date, quarterly. Accumulating cable bibliography covering books, selected news and magazine articles, dissertations, organizational publications and material from Canada. Back issues available.

Communication Satellites and Social Services: Focus on Users and Evaluations, An Annotated Bibliography. Los Angeles: University of Southern California, Learning Systems Center, 1975. To be revised late in 1977, this first version contained 225 selections focusing on educational, medical, agricultural and other public and social service delivery by satellite programs.

Control of the Direct Broadcast Satellite: Values in Conflict. Palo Alto, Calif.: Aspen Institute Program on Communications and Society, 1974. 156 pp. "Selected Bibliography" is topically arranged on pp. 145-154.

D'Amato, Charles R. "A Selected Bibliography: Recent Materials Relating to Development, Potential and Problems of Communications Satellites." *Communications Satellites: Are The Users Ready?* Medford, Mass.: Tufts University, Edward R. Murrow Center of Public Diplomacy, 1966. 109 pp. Bibliography on pp. 82-109 is subject-divided and semi-annotated. Useful guide to early literature.

Gillespie, Gilbert. *Public Access Cable Television in the United States and Canada with an Annotated Bibliography.* New York: Praeger Special Studies, 1975. 157 pp. See pp. 103-157.

Grogan, Denis. *Science and Technology: An Introduction to the Literature.* Hamden, Conn.: Linnet Books, 1976 (3rd ed.). 343 pp. Useful narrative discussion divided into 22 chapters by type of publication (books, bibliographies, microforms, etc.) and covering entire field, with many communications-related titles.

Kildow, Judith Tegger. "Bibliography." *Intelsat: Policy-Maker's Dilemma.* New York: Praeger Special Studies, 1973. 118 pp. See pp. 91-108 for an unannotated alphabetical listing.

*LeDuc, Don R. "A Selective Bibliography on the Evolution of CATV: 1950-1970." *Journal of Broadcasting* 15:195-234 (Spring 1971). A topically and chronologically arranged but unannotated listing of citations, mainly periodical articles. Probably definitive up to 1970.

Shervis, Katherine, comp. *The Educational and Social Use of Communications Satellites: A Bibliography* (1970); *Legal and Political Aspects of Satellite Telecommunication: An Annotated Bibliography* (1970); and *Satellite Teleconferencing: An Annotated Bibliography* (1972). Madison, Wisc.: University of Wisconsin Edsat Center, 1970-72. 42, 126, and 130 pp. Computer-generated listings with both author and permuted (key word) indexes.

Shiers, George, and May Shiers. *Bibliography of the History of Electronics*. Metuchen, N.J.: Scarecrow Press, 1972. 336 pp. Annotations on some 1,800 items dealing with telegraph, telephone, and broadcasting subjects, among others. Topically divided with author and subject indexes. Definitive.

11. MOTION PICTURES

*Aceto, Vincent J., Jane Graves, and Fred Silva, eds. *Film Literature Index: Annual Cumulation*. New York: Bowker, 1975-date. ca 500 pp., annual. Volumes have appeared for 1973, 1974, and 1975 material, based on the quarterly journal of the same title, and covering some 250 periodicals, some selectively (especially the many non-film general titles). Listing is in a single alphabetical form, including author-title-subject references. Also see Jones, below.

*Batty, Linda. *Retrospective Index to Film Periodicals: 1930-1971*. New York: Bowker, 1975. 425 pp. Coverage of 19 English-language journals content in three parts: reviews of films, film subjects, and film book review citations. Semi-annotated. Designed to supplement *International Index* (see below).

*Boni, Albert, ed. *Photographic Literature* and *Photographic Literature 1960-1970*. Hastings-on-Hudson, N.Y.: Morgan and Morgan, 1962 and 1972. 333 and 535 pp. The definitive bibliography on all aspects of photography, with most items annotated within a topical arrangement with indexes. Includes motion pictures and some television.

Bouman, Jan C. "Bibliography on Filmology as Related to the Social Sciences," *Reports and Papers on Mass Communication No. 9.* Paris: Unesco, February 1954. 42 pp. Author-arranged listing in English and French (regardless of original language of item cited) of several hundred pre-1953 studies on film.

Bowles, Stephen E. *Index to Critical Film Reviews in British and American Film Periodicals.* New York: Burt Franklin, 1974 (two volumes). 782 pp. Some 20,000 citations to reviews of 6,000 films are listed along with 3,000 reviews of 1,200 film books. Covers the 1930-1972 period as seen on the pages of 29 film periodicals. Most complete listing of its kind.

Cinemabilia Catalogue of Film Literature. New York: Cinemabilia Book Store, 1972. 264 pp. Though essentially a sales catalog, and unannotated, this, with Larry Edmunds' catalog listed below, is a fine guide to the vast number of film publications—easily several thousand being listed here.

Dyment, Alan G., ed. *Literature of the Film: A Bibliographic Guide to the Film as Art and Entertainment, 1936-1970.* Detroit, Mich.: Gale Research Co., 1975. 398 pp. Some 1,300 annotated entries (all books) in ten subject areas.

Enser, A. G. S. *Filmed Books and Plays, 1928-1974.* New York: Academic Press, 1974. 549 pp. Some 10,000 entries with elaborate cross-listing by authors and variant titles of books and plays from which films have been made.

Fielding, Raymond. "Bibliographic Survey of Theses and Dissertations on the Subject of Film at U. S. Universities, 1916-1974." *Journal of the University Film Association* 26:3 (1974), 24:3 (1972), 21:4 (1969) and 20:2 (1968). A nonannotated listing by school (and by author within each school), with each segment of the series being additive rather than cumulative.

The Film Index: A Bibliography, The Film as Art. New York: H. W. Wilson and Museum of Modern Art, 1941 (reprinted by Arno Press, 1966). 723 pp. Carefully organized and annotated discussions of thousands of books and articles on the film up to 1940. See MacCann, below.

*Gerlach, John C., and Lana Gerlach. *The Critical Index: A Bibliography of Articles on Film in English, 1946-1973, Arranged by Names and Topics.* New York: Columbia University, Teachers College Press, 1974. 726 pp. A very carefully arranged, annotated and indexed bibliography printed by computer. A fine guide to the periodical literature of the postwar years on film.

Heinzkill, Richard. *Film Criticism: An Index to Critics' Anthologies.* Metuchen, N.J.: Scarecrow Press, 1975. 151 pp. Covers 40 books of anthologies (each done by or representing a single critic), and indexes names, films and subjects covered.

The Influence of the Cinema on Children and Adolescents: An Annotated Bibliography. Paris: UNESCO Reports and Papers on Mass Communication No. 31, 1961. Detailed annotations covering entries from about 1930 to the late 1950s.

*Jarvie, I. C. *Movies and Society.* New York: Basic Books, 1970. 394 pp. Contains excellent annotated bibliography of important film books on pp. 229-336.

Journal of the University Film Association (see p. 331). Regularly prints bibliographies on all aspects of film, including Richard Vincent's "An Introduction to Film Bibliographies," 28:3:39-43 (Summer 1976), and the same author's "A Bibliography of Film Reference Resources," 29:3:43-56 (Summer 1977), Fielding's list of dissertations (see above), and such specialized material as Daniel Appelman's "A Bibliography of Latin American Cinema," 28:2:41-47 (Spring 1976).

Jones, Karen, ed. *International Index to Film Periodicals.* New York: St. Martin's Press, 1975-date. 550 pp. Annual (material for calendar year 1974 is first to be covered) subject-divided guide to 80 world film periodicals, assembled by 26 national film archives, and carefully indexed. Also see Aceto, above.

Kowolski, Rosemary Ribich. *Women and Film: A Bibliography.* Metuchen, N.J.: Scarecrow Press, 1976. 278 pp. Some 2,300 annotated entries, divided into major sections on women as performers; as film-makers; images of women; and women columnists and critics. 25%page index. The introduction clearly indicates limitations and selectivity in the bibliography.

Larry Edmunds Bookshop, Inc., Cinema Catalog. Hollywood, Calif.: Larry Edmunds Bookshop, 1972. 524 pp. Like Cinemabilia catalog above, this provides a wealth of semi-annotated information on film books and other materials.

*MacCann, Richard Dyer, and Edward S. Perry. *The New*

Film Index: A Bibliography of Magazine Articles in English, 1930-1970. New York: Dutton, 1975. 522 pp. Some 12,000 annotated periodical article entries under 278 categories to update *The Film Index* (above). Unlike the earlier work, this does not list books or films, nor does it include film reviews, all of which can be found in other bibliographies in this listing. An excellent 50-page index concludes this most important postwar film reference bibliography.

MacCann, Richard Dyer. "Reference Works for Film Study." *Cinema Journal* 14:2:72-79 (Winter 1974-75). Deals only with the feature film, but covers books, periodicals and other citations divided by topic. Reprinted in Perry, *Performing Arts Resources, Volume Two* (see section 12 of this bibliography).

McCarty, Clifford. *Published Screenplays: A Checklist.* Kent, Ohio: Kent State University Press, 1972. 126 pp. Includes all kinds of films, as long as screenplay is in English, and was commercially published. Includes brief annotations on source for each. (See Poteet, Section 9.)

Nachbar, John G. *Western Films: An Annotated Critical Bibliography.* New York: Garland Publishing Co., 1975. 98 pp. Analysis of 500 items (books, articles, reviews, etc.) in English on all aspects of western films. Ten subject categories plus bibliography and indexes.

Powers, Anne. *Blacks in American Movies: A Selected Bibliography.* Metuchen, N.J.: Scarecrow Press, 1974. 167 pp. Topically organized, semi-annotated listings with alphabetical, chronological, author, and subject indexes. Contains introductory essay as well.

*Rehrauer, George. *Cinema Booklist* and *Supplement One.* metuchen, N.J.: Scarecrow Press, 1972 and 1974. 473 and 405 pp. The most complete annotated discussion of film books (no periodical articles here), arranged alphabetically by title with subject and author indexes. Annotations sometimes quite lengthy. *Supplement Two* due in 1977.

Schuster, Mel, comp. *Motion Picture Directors: A Bibliography of Magazine and Periodical Articles, 1900-1972.* Metuchen, N.J.: Scarecrow Press, 1973. 418 pp. Unannotated and divided by name of the director and chronologically within each person.

Schuster, Mel, comp. *Motion Picture Performers: A Bibli-*

ography of Magazine and Periodical Articles, 1900-1969 and *Supplement One*. Metuchen, N.J.: Scarecrow Press, 1971 and 1976. 702 and 793 pp. Total of 5,500 performers covered with unannotated listings chronologically under each. Supplement takes coverage to 1974 and broadens coverage as well.

12. **GUIDE TO MEDIA ARCHIVES/LIBRARIES**
    (See also Section IX, "A Guide to Special Libraries and Resources on Communications")

Hounshell, David A., comp. *Manuscripts in U. S. Depositories Relating to the History of Electrical Science and Technology*. Washington, D.C.: Smithsonian Institution, Division of Electricity and Nuclear Energy, 1973. 116 pp. Arranged by *National Union Catalog* symbols and indexed, this includes much communications-related material.

Perry, Ted, ed. *Performing Arts Resources*. New York: Drama Books Specialists/Theater Library Association, 1974-date (annual). Each volume contains 15-20 articles detailing contents of various theater and media archives. First volume contains information on several film and television collections, containing both actual video material and documents. Second volume includes details on one broadcast and two film archive articles. This looks to be a valuable guide to a growing number of such non-book collections.

Rose, Ernest D. *World Film and Television Study Resources: A Reference Guide to Major Training Centres and Archives*. Bonn-Bad Godesberg, Germany: Friedrich-Ebert-Stiftung, 1974. 421 pp. The first such international guide since a 1950 UNESCO effort, this reviews both schools and archives of film and TV material in all areas of the world with addresses and other details.

Veinstein, André. *Performing Arts Libraries and Museums of the World*. Paris: UNESCO, 1967.

Weber, Olga S. *North American Film and Video Directory: A Guide to Media Collections and Services*. New York: R. R. Bowker, 1976. 284 pp. U. S. and Canadian collections, some 2,000 of them, are listed by state and city with details on collection size and content, loan policies, annual budget, key personnel, etc. While best for film sources (it's very incomplete for video materials), this is clearly the basis for an inclusive oft-updated guide.

Whalon, Marion K. *Performing Arts Research: A Guide to Information Sources*. Detroit, Mich.: Gale Research Co., 1976. 280 pp. Annotated guide to directories, handbooks, dictionaries, sources for reviews, bibliographies, indexes, abstracts, and audiovisual material on theater and films. Some of the material is tangential, but most refers in some way to media content. Well-indexed.

Young, William C. *American Theatrical Arts: A Guide to Manuscripts and Special Collections in the United States and Canada*. Chicago: American Library Association, 1971. 166 pp. Details on 138 collections of scripts and other manuscript materials (much including or relating to media), with a 60-page subject index. Good details on specific items in each collection.

13

A SELECTION OF FILMS
ON COMMUNICATIONS

Previous editions of the *Handbook* have concentrated solely on print resources on communications. This edition now includes information on nonprint resources, specifically films and videocassettes, which are suitable for supplementary classroom use.

A wide variety of films on the various aspects of communications for short-term use. Rental fees vary widely, ranging from as little as $5 for a short film to as much as $60 or more, depending on the length, age, quality and popularity of a particular film. Some films can be borrowed free of charge.

A wide variety of films on the various aspects of communications have been produced, and many of them can be easily obtained for short-term use. Rental fees vary widely, ranging from as little as $5 for a short film to as much as $60 or more, depending on the length, age, quality and popularity of a particular film. Some films can be borrowed free of charge.

The listings in this section are divided into the following categories:

1)	Free Loan	399
2)	Advertising	400
3)	Broadcast History	401
4)	Film History	402
5)	Film Study	404
6)	Issues and Controversies	406
7)	Politics	409
8)	Popular Music	409
9)	Printing and Graphic Arts	410
10)	Television Documentaries and Study	411
11)	Theory, Technology and Future Developments	413
12)	Writing	414

A list of libraries from which rental films and videocassettes can be obtained is included at the end of this section.

1. FREE LOAN

Advertising and Competition
An overview of advertising's relation to and interrelationship with marketing and general economic conditions. Panelists include Willie May Rogers of *Good Housekeeping*, Prof. Charles Ramond of Columbia University and Isadore Barmash of the *New York Times*. Available from ANA Information Center, Association of National Advertisers, 155 East 44th Street, New York, NY 10017. 1968, 28 min., color.

The Golden Standard
A promotional film produced by the Audit Bureau of Circulation which discusses the purpose and influence of the ABC. Film deals with advertising, media selection, and the positive determination of circulation facts. Available from Modern Talking Picture Service, Inc., 2323 New Hyde Park Road, New Hyde Park, NY 11040. (Offices in other cities—check phone book). 18 min., color.

The Journalists
Harry Reasoner narrates this film about careers in journalism. Film features a series of interviews with noted journalists. Produced by Sigma Delta Chi and available for free loan from Modern Talking Picture Service, Inc. 26 min., color.

Nielsen Station Index
Emphasis in this film is on local ratings, the steps taken to give local television stations an accurate measure of viewer preference, and program selection. Free loan from the producer: Public Relations, A.C. Nielsen Company, Nielsen Plaza, Northbrook, IL 60062. 17 min., color.

Nielsen Television Index
Illustrates the steps necessary to secure the national television viewer ratings. (Book well ahead, since this film is in heavy demand.) Public Relations, A.C. Nielsen Company, Nielsen Plaza, Northbrook, Il 60062. 14 min., color.

The Score
Documentary which explores the process of writing music for TV and motion pictures. Several composers discuss their work and Jerry Goldsmith conducts his own film score with a 60-piece orchestra. Considerable emphasis is given to the music itself. Free loan from the pro-

ducer: Broadcast Music, Inc. (Attention: Russell Sanjek), 40 West 57th Street, New York, NY 10019. Two versions available. 30 min. or 59 min., 1974.

Stalking the Wild Cranberry
A delightful view of the making of the Euell Gibbons Grape-nuts TV commercial. Traces the creation of the commercial from conception through storyboard and actual filming. Produced for Benton and Bowles Advertising Agency but available from: Ms. Bonnie Adams, Modern-Mass Media Inc., 315 Springfield Avenue, Summit, NJ 07901. 1973, 17 min., color.

World on the Line . . . Via Global Communications
Emphasis is on the expanding technology of global communications. Illustrates establishment and operation of the Washington-Moscow hot line, computer telex, facsimile transmission, satellite station operations, and teleprinting. A promotional film produced by RCA and available from Modern Talking Picture Service, Inc. 11 min., color.

2. ADVERTISING

But First This Message
Analysis of commercial TV content for children, including excerpts from TV shows and commercials. Includes comments from professionals working with children and reactions from children. Provides basis for discussion about TV for children. Available only from the producer: Action for Children's Television, 46 Austin Street, Newton, MA 02160. 1974, 15 min., color.

Buy Line
Examines contemporary advertising (mostly TV). Opens with rapid montage of typical TV commercials, then examines each ad. Deals with psychological seduction, disclaimers, false and misleading statements, fantasy appeals. Interviews a group of typical consumers and shares their opinions about advertising's place in our economy. 1972, 13 min., color.

CLIO Awards: Special Educational Reel
Selection of 30 TV commercials that have won awards for creative excellence in recent years. Humorous and extremely well done; excellent for stimulating discussions on advertising and marketing. Updated each

year. Available from the producer: CLIO Awards, 30 East 60th Street, New York, NY 10022. Also available from the same source are reels of award-winning commercials for each year since 1960, special product category reels, technique reels (eight categories), and EFFIE winners (marketing effectiveness). 30 min., color.

Forty Years to Now
Nostalgic documentary on four decades of advertising from the pages of *Fortune*. Time capsule of selections from 60,000 individual ad layouts. Ads range through personality endorsements, patriotic sloganeering, the plastic age, electronics, and space. Film ends on a critical note asking if American business's printed word can make the needed jump into the 1970s when greater emphasis must be placed on commitment and responsibility. 1969, 24 min., color.

Marketing As a Career
Advertising executive Fairfax M. Cone (Foote, Cone & Belding) is interviewed by Prof. William T. Kelley. Cone describes the kinds of people likely to succeed in advertising. 1966, 30 min.

Sixty Second Spot: The Making of a Television Commercial
Traces the steps necessary to create and produce a commercial message. Examines the interaction between advertising agency and independent producer. 1974, 25 min., color.

Super Up
Commentary on advertising pressures in our culture. Signs, billboards, cars, TV, and a thousand familiar images are juxtaposed to form a fascinating mosaic. Somewhat experimental and avant-garde. 1968. 12 min.. color

TV Advertising (videocassette)
An exploration of television advertising practices with people who make TV commercials and those who are critical of the present system. 1973, 59 min.

3. BROADCAST HISTORY

Great Radio Comedians
A three-part film, though each of the parts may be rented independently. Part one deals with the transition from vaudeville to radio and features a segment from a

Burns and Allen comedy sketch. Part two deals with the late 1930s and early 1940s and includes a sketch by Jack Benny and other radio stars. Part three is probably the best in the series and includes a discussion of the lost art of radio comedy, as well as a re-enactment of Fred Allen's "Allen's Alley" sketch. 1974, 35 min., 26 min., 27 min., color.

Making of a Live Television Show
Behind the scenes of the 23rd Annual Emmy Awards Show. Producer Bob Finkel and Director Bill Foster introduce viewers to the "what, who, and how" of live television production. Film uses triple split screen to show events on stage and in the control room. Good introduction to TV production. 1972, 26 min., color.

Television Land
An entertaining potpourri of TV clips from 1948 to 1970. Some memorable fluffs illustrate the hazards of live television. 1971, 12 min., color.

4. FILM HISTORY

Film Firsts: Parts One and Two
Part one surveys early examples. Revives first stereotypes of cowboys, villains, comedians, glamour girls, and gives examples of technical improvements such as animation, camera movement, and underwater photography. Part two places emphasis on the stars of early films and the roles they created. Each part available separately. 1963, 27 min. (each).

First Flickers
Excerpts from the Library of Congress paper print collection of films produced between 1894 and 1912. Early stars include Mary Pickford and Mack Sennett, as well as sequences from the first film ever copyrighted and two versions of *The Great Train Robbery*. Produced by NBC. 1969, 27 min., color.

Golden Age of Comedy
A fantastic collection of comedy bits selected by the producer from over 2,000 films. Contains slapstick, pie throwing, car wrecking, pants falling, and manhole disappearances. Includes Laurel and Hardy, Will Rogers, Jean Harlow, Carole Lombard, Ben Turpin, and Harry Langdon. Winner of two Academy Awards. 1958, 85 min.

Great Train Robbery
Edwin S. Porter's primitive but classic "western." One of the few early story films. Considered by many as the forerunner of later Hollywood westerns. Silent. A "fun-film" ideal for those wishing a taste of this early period. 1904, 8 min.

Kiss and Other 1895 Films
A good selection of four one-scene, one-angle vignettes from the 1895–1901 period. The oldest of the collection, *The Kiss*, is a 15-second spectacular (for its day) made in Edison's experimental studio. Silent. 6 min.

Life of an American Fireman
First effort to discover narrative potentials for the motion picture. Pioneer director Edwin S. Porter edited this film to present two parallel lines of action progressing simultaneously until they intersect. Cast includes about 300 firemen, plus a mother and child whom the firemen save from a burning building. Silent. 1902, 10 min.

Man of Aran
Robert Flaherty's classic documentary showing the life of a family on one of the Aran Islands, west of Ireland. Emphasis is on realism and man's survival in a rugged environment. Excellent for those who wish to probe more deeply into film history and the early documentary. 1934, 77 min.

Movies Learn to Talk
Rather basic. Development of sound films from early experiments to *The Jazz Singer* in 1927 and the polished and sophisticated sound-film of today. Includes glimpses of 34 personalities and excerpts from 12 silent and sound movies. 1960, 26 min.

Nanook of the North
Classic pioneering documentary by Robert Flaherty. Focuses on the life of an Eskimo family. Originally silent, but most rental prints have a sound track which was created to supplement the film. 1922, 55 min.

Origins of the Motion Picture
Historical record from DaVinci to Edison, showing the work of Plateau, Daguerre, Muybridge, Morey, Edison, Armat, and Dickson. 1955, 21 min.

5. FILM STUDY

The American Film

Uses excerpts from five classic films—*High Noon* (Zinneman), *North by Northwest* (Hitchcock), *Friendly Persuasion* (Wyler), *On the Waterfront* (Kazan), and *Shane* (Stevens) to examine the American cinema as an art form. Comments by Charlton Heston on the objectives, themes, techniques, and work of the individual directors. 1967, 37 min., color.

Angry Screen

Uses scenes from *Birth of a Nation* and *Triumph of the Will* as well as scenes from selected American films to demonstrate how the motion picture can alter emotions, influence attitudes, and arouse concern over various social conditions. From the "Hollywood and the Stars" series originally produced for television by David Wolper. 1964, 26 min.

Art of the Motion Picture

Contains a beginning film vocabulary and gives examples of five basic elements in film making: composition, lighting, editing, filming of movement, and use of sound. Illustrates how the filmmaker uses these elements to express his ideas. 1971, 20 min., color.

Basic Film Terms: A Visual Dictionary

Made specifically for courses in film technique and film appreciation. Demonstrates various shots, lenses and camera movements. Gives visual definitions of editing and sound recording methods and terms. 1970, 15 min., color.

Cinema: The Living Camera (Toward the Year 2000 Series)

Film critics Pauline Kael and Judith Crist, along with anti-establishment filmmaker Melvin Van Peebles, outline the future revolution in filmmaking. Illustrates new editing techniques and uses sequences from *Sweet Sweetback's Badasss Song* to illustrate how minority groups will use film as a weapon. 1972, 24 min., color.

Directed by John Ford

Footage from twenty-seven of Ford's films is combined with interviews with Ford himself and with three of Ford's favorite actors—Henry Fonda, James Stewart, and John Wayne. This film was produced by the American Film Institute, directed by Peter Bogdanovich, and narrated by Orson Welles. 1973, 102 min., color.

Film: Art of the Impossible
Emphasizes the ease with which an audience is deceived into accepting impossible action by simple editing techniques. Some excellent examples of editing from a number of films including *Downhill Racer, Potemkin, Lawrence of Arabia, King Kong,* and *Birth of a Nation.* Also includes analysis of a television spot made for Lyndon Johnson's presidential campaign. Film clips illustrate tools of the director's trade, including script, casting choices, sets and costumes, direction of actors, and music. 1972, 30 min., color.

Film Graphics: Abstract Aspects of Editing
Emphasizes basic principles of film editing. Film progresses from classical painting to still photography to motion picture photography, to demonstrate that the same structural principles are inherent in all three. Animation, slow motion, and freeze-frame photography are used in a critical analysis of the famous "Odessa Steps" sequence from Eisenstein's *Potemkin.* Film clips from Bunuel and Vertov are also utilized. 1973, 14 min., color.

Grierson
Presents the life and contributions of pioneer documentary filmmaker John Grierson. Discusses Grierson's social concerns, his work with Robert Flaherty, and his role in the organization of the National Film Board of Canada. 1973, 58 min., color.

Hollywood: The Dream Factory
Examines what the Hollywood film industry was like before the major studios suffered financial breakdown and the star system fell apart. Clips from many M-G-M movies made during the 1930s, 1940s and 1950s. Produced by M-G-M for television and narrated by Dick Cavett. 1972, 50 min., color.

Interpretations and Values (Film Editing)
Outstanding example of film editing techniques. Uses a dramatic sequence from TV's *Gunsmoke* that includes hand-to-hand fighting between the series hero and adversary. First shows all 25 shots selected for workprint and assembled in script order, then shows three edited versions, including the one used on TV. 1964, 30 min.

Life and Times of John Huston, Esq.
   Biography of the director in cinema-verité style. In Huston's Irish castle the film director discusses his life, reviews his successes and failures, and outlines his philosophy. One portion of the film shows Huston directing *Reflections in a Golden Eye.* 1966, 60 min.

Making a Sound Film
   Primarily for 16mm production classes but may be used to illustrate basic techniques. Demonstrates synchronous shooting and editing, use of "voice over," music, and sound effects. 1973, 14 min., color.

Olympia Diving Sequence
   Extraordinary sequence from the lengthy documentary *Olympia* by Nazi filmmaker Leni Riefenstahl. Remarkable cinematography and editing often described as the purest expression of filmic art. (The entire documentary is also available but is better suited for a class in film history.) 1938, 4 min.

Underground Film (videocassette)
   The underground film movement, from filmmaker to distributor to exhibitor to audience. 1971, 29 min.

Understanding Movies—1973
   Viewers follow a dramatic "chase" scene through the streets of a large city and then examine that scene to illustrate various aspects of filmmaking, use of sound, camera angles, and lighting effects to illustrate how film can communicate suspense, realism, and personal response to the characters on the screen. Not to be confused with a 1951 film of the same title intended for teachers of English. 1973, 13 min., color.

Western Hero
   Historical survey of the western movie and various types of western heroes. Interesting historical footage, including scenes from early westerns and more recent classics such as *The Iron Horse, Stagecoach,* and *High Noon.* Originally part of the CBS "20th Century Series," with narration by Walter Cronkite. 1963, 26 min.

6. **ISSUES AND CONTROVERSIES**

Black History: Lost, Stolen or Strayed
   Bill Cosby narrates this CBS documentary, which examines the role of the media, particularly motion pic-

tures, in the building and perpetuation of the black stereotype. Film includes footage from *Birth of a Nation,* several Shirley Temple movies, an Amos 'n' Andy TV kinescope, and other examples. It is best to use only that portion of the film which deals with media, although the entire film may be viewed if more convenient. 1968, 54 min.

Free Press, Fair Trial
Discusses the conflict between the constitutional guarantees of a free press and the right to a fair trial. Examines the claims of former Vice President Spiro Agnew and others that extensive press coverage can affect the outcome of trials. 1975, 30 min.

Free Press vs. Fair Trial By Jury—The Sheppard Case
Extensive coverage of a classic case history. Documentary footage plus re-enactments of the crime give the viewer a realistic feeling of the tensions and pressures of the time. Sheppard's lawyer unsuccessfully protests circus atmosphere of the court. Columnists Dorothy Kilgallen and Paul Holmes express opinions on TV that can be heard by the jury. Appeal lawyer F. Lee Bailey is followed in his successful attempt to bring the case to the Supreme Court, which overturns the original verdict. Readings from the decision emphasize the need to protect both the press and the defendant in future trials. 1970, 27 min., color.

Freedom of the Press (videocassette)
An examination of the First Amendment guarantee of freedom of the press and its meaning for the news media and the public. 1973, 58 min.

Journalism: Mirror, Mirror on the Wall
Comparative analysis of news reporting of a single event—a peace demonstration—by the Public Television Laboratory, NBC's David Brinkley, the *Washington Post,* United Press International, and the *New York Times.* Joseph Lyford, journalism professor at the University of California, comments on the deficiencies in the various stories, while editors and reporters defend their coverage. 1967, 52 min.

Mightier Than the Sword: Zenger and Freedom of the Press
Dramatization of the Zenger libel case of 1734. Footage edited from a Hollywood feature-length film. 1962, 23

min.

People's Right to Know: Police Versus Reporters
Documents a news photographer's experiences during the 1968 Democratic National Convention in Chicago. The photographer recounts how police harassed and beat him and others, against a background of photographers and news film. 1969, 12 min.

The Question of Television Violence
Film report of the hearings conducted by former Sen. John Pastore and his Senate Communications Subcommittee. Condensation of four days of testimony by network spokesmen, social scientists, and representatives of various pressure groups. Produced by the National Film Board of Canada. 1971, 56 min., color.

The Rating Game
Explores the rating system used to determine television programming successes and failures. Describes the sampling methods used by the A.C. Nielsen Company and discusses the investigations by a congressional committee on the ratings controversy. Produced by CBS. 1965, 60 min.

TV, The Anonymous Teacher
Interview of experts concerned about the effects of television upon children. Discusses the concept of "incidental learning" and suggests that television has a strong influence on children. 1976, 15 min., color.

What's Happening to Television
A critical view of program material. Network executives, news commentators, critics, writers, the president of A.C. Nielsen, and the chairman of the FCC present their ideas as to what is good about TV programming, what is bad, and where and how changes can be made. Portions of TV programs being discussed are shown. An NET production. 1966, 60 min.

Whole World Is Watching
Explores the question of bias in television newscasting. Interviews with David Brinkley, Walter Cronkite, Sen. John Pastore, and media critic John Fischer. Brinkley contends that objectivity is impossible and that he strives for fairness. Topics include TV coverage of the 1968 Democratic National Convention, restraints upon television, and possible influences by advertisers on what

news is broadcast. 1968, 55 min.

7. POLITICS

Campaign: American Style
CBS documentary which explores political campaigns and particularly advertising techniques, the hiring of political advisors, public opinion sampling, and the use of computers to analyze and predict voter behavior. Discusses the concepts of "image" and "exposure" and presents an in-depth analysis of a campaign which exemplifies the new "American Style." 1968, 39 min., color.

Electric Flag
Intercuts scenes of the making of the feature film *The Candidate* with historical footage from actual election campaigns. Illustrates that the making of a film and the making of a political candidate are similar in that media are used in both cases to manipulate images and thus "create" reality. Discusses how TV creates and sells a candidate's image. 1972, 12 min., color.

Television: A Political Machine
Uses the 1968 Indiana presidential campaign to examine the role of TV in electoral politics. Considers the candidate as a TV personality; examines announcements that resemble news reports. 1968, 14 min.

Television and Politics
This CBS documentary examines political commercials which use "Madison Avenue" techniques to package and sell politicians. A portion of the film gives a brief history of political TV commercials from 1948 (Harry Truman) to the present. Mike Wallace questions politicians and political consultants on their use of TV to influence the American voter. Some discussion of the need for reform in the use of paid political announcements. 1972, 26 min., color.

8. POPULAR MUSIC

Anatomy of a Hit
Jazz critic Ralph Gleason examines the popular music business. During the film he traces the preparation of recorded music, describes the operation of a "Top 40" radio station, and talks with the composer of a hit record.

1964, 90 min.

American Music: From Folk to Jazz and Pop
Traces the roots of popular music and jazz in American history. Many old-time performers are shown, as well as several popular folk singers and rock-and-roll groups. 1967, 54 min.

9. PRINTING AND GRAPHIC ARTS

Daguerre—The Birth of Photography
Traces the early history of photography. Discusses the work of Daguerre, Niepce, and other photographic pioneers. 1971, 29 min.

Language of the Camera Eye
Ansel Adams and Beaumont Newhall analyze the still photographs of Edward Weston, Cartier-Bresson, Edward Steichen, Alfred Stieglitz and others. Originally produced by KQED-TV. 1959, 29 min.

Naked Eye
Development of the camera and of photography. Traces the work of pioneer photographers Matthew Brady, William Jackson, and Louis Daguerre and of modern photographers Margaret Bourke-White, Alfred Eisenstadt, and Edward Weston. Academy Award nominee, narrated by Raymond Massey. 1957, 70 min.

Newspaper Layout
Basic treatment of the subject. Illustrates four principles of good make-up: balance, use of white space, accenting hot spots, and elimination of ornaments. Selected pages from daily newspapers are compared to emphasize these principles. Discusses headlines and typography. 1972, 14 min., color.

Story of Printing
Traces the history of printing, beginning with Oriental block printing, through Gutenberg, the introduction of printing into England by Caxton, and the first printing of newspapers in the 18th century. Explains how the Industrial Revolution modernized presses and depicts continuous reel machinery. 1950, 47 min.

The Tiger's Tail: Thomas Nast Vs. Boss Tweed
Adapted from *The Cavalcade of America* TV program. Emphasizes the significance of the editorial cartoon in

American journalism. Somewhat elementary. 1965, 20 min.

Today's Newspaper
Film tour of a newspaper plant. Stresses the need for newspapers and professional journalists to change with the times. 1972, 22 min., color.

Typesetting
Basic but well-visualized introduction to the process of linecasting (linotype). Useful for those seeking a film in graphic arts. 1969, 35 min.

10. TELEVISION DOCUMENTARIES AND STUDY

Anderson Platoon
Revealing study of the day-to-day effects of the Vietnam War on a U.S. Army platoon during a six-week period in 1966. Film captures the spirit of comradeship, humor, homesickness, stoicism, and determination that holds the platoon together. Originally made for French TV but available with English narration. Highest international awards, including the Academy Award. 1969, 65 min.

Banks and the Poor
Controversial NET documentary which infuriated banking interests, antagonized critics of public broadcasting, and incurred congressional wrath. Exposes bank practices which maintain slums; reveals conflicts of interest among certain congressmen and bank directors. Film can serve to illustrate the documentary format and/or the need to insulate the financing of public broadcasting from political pressures. 1970, 59 min.

Harvest of Shame
The classic TV documentary and Edward R. Murrow's last important work. An excellent example of the "hard" documentary calculated to generate viewer concern and action. This sympathetic treatment of migrant farm workers triggered an avalanche of telegrams and mail when it was first aired. The film is an excellent example of Murrow's style and one of the most important documentaries ever made for television. 1960, 54 min.

Hawaii Now: Hawaii Five-O (videocassette)
A documentary film shot on location in Honolulu showing how the CBS television series Hawaii Five-O is put together. Shows the actors, production staff and the

crew as the go through a day's work. 1971, 30.

Hunger in America
Controversial and bold CBS documentary which prompted citizen outcry and congressional inquiry. Blends personal interviews and narrated on-the-scene sequences. One of the few "hard" documentaries of recent vintage. 1968, 54 min., color.

Making of a Documentary
Pre-planning, research, shooting, and editing of a TV documentary. Cameramen shot 40 hours of film for a special, *Catholic Dilemma*, which was then edited to a final one-hour version costing $120,000. Techniques of lighting, cross-cutting, jump cuts, reverse shots, and sound are explained, with editorial options discussed. Originally released by CBS News. 1973, 22 min., color.

Murrow Versus McCarthy
The classic confrontation from the CBS "See It Now" series. Edward R. Murrow questions the methods employed by Sen. Joseph McCarthy. Includes film of the Senate subcommittee investigations as well as Murrow's analysis of McCarthy's investigative tactics and McCarthy's replies. Murrow was one of the first public figures to attack McCarthy, and historians cite this program as instrumental in the move to defuse McCarthy and end "McCarthyism." 1954, 45 min.

Pensions: The Broken Promise
NBC documentary which sparked a "Fairness Doctrine" complaint and litigation, as well as the Pension Reform Act of 1974. A critical and provocative examination of company pension plans and Social Security. One of the few "hard" documentaries from the current period. 1972, 39 min., color.

Selling of the Pentagon
Peabody Award-winning exposé of the Pentagon's public relations activities. This CBS documentary, narrated by Roger Mudd, touched off a storm of criticism by supporters of the Defense establishment who were angered by the network attack, and particularly by the use of film editing to present sequences out of context. The latter complaint prompted some change in CBS News editing policies. 1971, 52 min.

11. THEORY, TECHNOLOGY, AND FUTURE DEVELOPMENTS

Cable: The Immediate Future

Produced by the Cable Television Information Center, a nonprofit advisory group. Designed to alert viewers to the importance and potential of cable television. Low-cost rental ($7.50). Available from the Distribution Branch, National Audio-Visual Center, General Services Administration, Washington, DC 20409. 1972, 10 min.

Communication Primer

Excellent overview of the Shannon-Weaver model, the concept of "noise," and the utilization of redundancy in language. Good basic film for those unfamiliar with basic theories of communication. 1962, 23 min., color.

Communications: Wired World (Toward the Year 2000 Series)

Guided demonstration of the potential of communications in the year 2000, when super-computers will make it possible for every person to communicate with any other person. Interview with Marshall McLuhan and other communications experts. Touchtone phones and computers, conference television, and two-way cable. 1971, 24 min., color.

The Liveliest Wire (videocassette)

A survey of the history of cable television, explaining some of its current uses and giving projections for the future. 1973, 59 min.

Media: Massaging the Mind (Toward the Year 2000 Series)

Newspaper, TV, magazines, and radio are discussed by Gloria Steinem, Joe McGinnis, former editor of *Look* Magazine William Arthur, and media expert Ernest Dichter. Newspapers are folding because unions will not recognize advanced methods. The *Village Voice* makes no attempt to "balance" opinions, because the right wing cannot express itself as well as the left. Commercial TV cannot serve special interests (ballet), and politicians get training to project a TV image. Also laser satellites and future programming. 1972, 24 min., color.

Space for Man (videocassette)

A look at how space technology has benefited man in the past and what it can do in the future: how a communications satellite brings medical aid to a remote village via two-way television; how satellites will carry cultural and educational programs to India; how space-derived telemetry systems provide vital information on accident victims; the use of Landsat, the earth resources satellite, in forestry, agriculture and weather forecasting; Peter Glazer's proposed 25-mile wide solar cell platform; space colonization; and future directions for the space program that will benefit mankind. 1975, 120 min.

This Is Marshall McLuhan: The Medium Is the Message
   Outstanding film and one of the best ways to introduce students to McLuhan and his ideas. Good coverage of television vs. movies, "hot" and "cool" media, the future of education, and the meaning behind McLuhan's title *The Medium Is the Message*. Originally seen on NBC-TV. 1968, 55 min., color.

Tomorrow's TV: Get What You Want or Like What You Get
   Examines competitive struggle of cable TV operators against motion picture industry and commercial broadcasters. Discusses the financial base for each medium and Federal Communication Commission policies which deal with the regulation of broadcasting. 1969, 62 min.

Turning Points: The Cable Revolution (videocassette)
   Explores the system's capabilities for use in classrooms and for home shopping, and takes up the question of private versus government regulation. Covers the development of a two-way capability for CATV, the use of CATV in job-training programs, and the use of CATV as a source of programming for minority groups. 1973, 29 min.

12. WRITING

Artists in America: Jerry McNeely (videocassette)
   A portrait of a professor of television drama who is also a Hollywood network television writer. How he works and creates in both worlds. 1970, 29 min.

Story of a Writer
   Science-fiction author Ray Bradbury is the subject in a film that reveals the working habits of a creative writer. Rather basic, but one of the few films available in this area. 1963, 25 min.

Writers on Writing
   Viewers learn how four writers work: Harry Golden, Ray Bradbury, Frederick Shroyer, and Richard Armour.

Film uses question and answer technique as writers reveal their sources of ideas, their methods, what they think of critics, etc. 1965, 28 min., color.

Rental Films

Rental films are available from a number of sources, among them major universities that maintain film libraries. Seven of the largest such libraries are:

Audio-Visual Center
6 Willard Building
Penn State University
University Park, PA 16802

Media Center
Florida State University
Tallahassee, FL 32306

Audio-Visual Center
University of Iowa
Iowa City, IA 52242

Extension Media Center
University of California
2223 Fulton Street
Berkeley, CA 94720

Film Library
Syracuse University
1455 E. Covin Street
Syracuse, NY 13210

Audio-Visual Center
Indiana University
Bloomington, IN 47401

Central Arizona Film Co-op
Arizona State University
Tempe, AZ 85281

Catalogs from these and other film rental libraries are generally available upon request.

Videocassettes

Rental and purchase information on the 3/4" videocassettes listed is available from:

The Public Television Library
475 L'Enfant Plaza S.W.
Washington, DC 20024

Announcing a companion volume to the ASPEN HANDBOOK ON THE MEDIA:

THE MASS MEDIA: ASPEN GUIDE TO COMMUNICATION INDUSTRY TRENDS

Edited by Christopher Sterling and Timothy Haight

THIS NEW ASPEN GUIDE is the first comprehensive statistical overview of the American communication industry, both domestic and international, from 1900 to the present. The editors have gathered and analyzed historical and descriptive statistical information on the American mass media from academic, industry, trade, and government sources. This information is presented and discussed in a topical, cross-related format, with a focus on the inter-relationships and trends among the various industries. The industries covered in this volume are books, newspapers, magazines, motion pictures, recordings (disc and tape), radio (AM and FM), television, and cable.

The purpose of this sourcebook is to make the public sector more aware of both trends and issues in communication industries and to encourage further cross-disciplinary work. Therefore, the editors' analysis strives to identify (1) the information that is currently available, (2) the information that is still needed, and (3) the information that might be usable as "communications indicators." The volume also includes a detailed listing of bibliographical references, as well as further reading suggestions for background and extended data searches.

THE MASS MEDIA: ASPEN GUIDE TO COMMUNICATION INDUSTRY TRENDS is organized according to the following topics:

- *GROWTH OF THE MEDIA*
- *MEDIA OWNERSHIP AND CONTROL*
- *MEDIA ECONOMICS*
- *EMPLOYMENT AND TRAINING*
- *MEDIA CONTENT TRENDS*
- *AUDIENCE SIZE AND CHARACTER*
- *INTERNATIONAL INTERESTS OF THE AMERICAN MEDIA*

THE EDITORS:

Christopher H. Sterling is a professor in the Department of Radio-Television-Film, Temple University. He is also editor of *Mass Media Booknotes*.

Timothy R. Haight is associated with the Institute for Communications Research, Stanford University.

Winter, 1977. 600 pages. Paper edition ISBN: 0-275-85760-3. $11.95. Cloth edition (through Praeger Pub.) ISBN: 0-275-24020-7. $20.00. LC 76-24370.

THE MASS MEDIA is a joint publishing venture of the Aspen Institute Program on Communications and Society and Praeger Publishers, Inc. The paper edition ($11.95) is available for sale through the Aspen Institute Publication Office. The cloth edition ($20.00) can be ordered from Praeger Publishers, 200 Park Avenue, New York, NY 10017.

An order form for the paper edition can be found on the last page of this book.

INDEX

A

A. A. A. A. Educational Foundation, The, 91
AAF/ADS, 107
ABC News Bulletin, 305
ABC Television Network, Research Services Department, 67
Abt Associates, 67
Academy for Educational Development, 67
Access, 309
Accuracy in Media (AIM), 157
ACT News, 309
Action for Children's Television (ACT), 157, 400
ACTION Newsletter, 295
Adenauer Foundation, The Konrad (KAF), 236
Advertising Age, 305
Advertising Council, 107
Advertising Research Foundation (ARF), 107
AFTRA Magazine, 309
Agency for Instructional Television (AIT), 118
Alpha Epsilon Rho, 111
Alternative Media, 344
Alternative Press Syndicate, Inc. (APS), 143
American Academy of Advertising (AAA), 108
American Advertising Federation, 108
American Association for Public Opinion Research (AAPOR), 148
American Association of Advertising Agencies (AAAA), 91, 108
American Cinematographer, 324
American Cinemeditor, 324
American Council for Better Broadcasts (ACBB), 158
American Council on Education for Journalism, 129
American Federation of Information Processing Societies (AFIPS), 136
American Federation of Television and Radio Artists (AFTRA), 111
American Film, 324
American Film Institute (AFI), 99, 123, 404
American Humanist Association, The, 102
American Library Association (ALA)
    Information Science and Automation Division (ISAD), 136
American Marketing Association (AMA), 109
American Newspaper Publishers Association (ANPA), 21, 143
    Library, 265
    Research Institute Library, 265
American Press Institute (API), 130
American Science Film Association (ASFA), 119
American Society for Information Science (ASIS), 137
American Society of Journalists and Authors, 130
American Society of Magazine Editors (ASME), 130
American Society of Newspaper Editors, 131
    Bulletin, 335

American Telephone and Telegraph Company Legal Library, 265
American University, The, 3, 96
American Women in Radio and Television, Inc. (AWRT), 111
Annenberg School of Communications, The, University of Pennsylvania, 40
    Library, 265
Annenberg School of Communications, University of Southern California, 42
Annual Cost Study for Weekly Newspapers, 283
Annual Review of Information Science and Technology, 347
Annual Review of Marketing, 283
ANPA News Research Center, 48
ANPA Research Institute, The, 69
Anthology Film Archives (AFA), 266
Antitrust Division, Department of Justice, 175
AP World, 335
Aperture, 325
Arab States Broadcasting Union (ASBU), 257
Arbitron Company, The, 70
Archives of Labor and Urban Affairs, 266
Arizona State University
    College of Law, 211
    Department of Mass Communications, 4
Asian Broadcasting Union (ABU), 259
Asian Mass Communication Research and Information Center (AMIC), 259
Aspen Institute for Humanistic Studies, 98
    Program on Communications and Society, 71, 95, 101, 102
Associated Press Managing Editors Association, 131
Association for Educational Communications and Technology (AECT), 119
Association for Education in Journalism (AEJ), 131
Association of American Publishers (AAP), 143
Association of Canadian Advertisers, 109
Association of Maximum Service Telecasters, Inc. (MST), 112
Association of Media Producers (AMP), 120
Association of Public Radio Stations (APRS), 116
Atlas World Press Review, 335
Audio, 296
Audio-visual Communications, 320
Audiovisual Instruction, 320
AV Communication Review, 320
AV Guide, 321

B

Batelle Memorial Institute, 72
Bell Journal of Economics, 348
Bell Laboratories Record, 348
Bell System Technical Journal, 348

Bell Telephone Laboratories, 72
Benton Foundation, The William, 92
"Best of Families, The," 114
Bestvision, 141
Better Broadcasts News, 310
Better Radio and Television, 310
Biennial Survey of Newspaper Printing Equipment, 344
Bilingual Children's Television, Inc. (BC/TV), 112
Billboard, 296
BM/E (Broadcast Management/Engineering), 310
Boston University
    School of Law, 211
    School of Public Communication, 5
Brigham Young University, 5
British Broadcasting Corporation (BBC), 237
Broadcast Education Association, 113
Broadcast Investor, 310
Broadcast Pioneers Library, 267
Broadcasting, 311
Broadcasting and the Law, 311
Broadcasting Yearbook, 283
Brookings Institution, The, 73
Brooklyn College, City University of New York, 6
Bulletin, 344
Bulletin of the American Society for Information Science, 349
Bureau of Social Science Research, The (BSSR), 74
Business Radio/Action, 349
Business Screen, 321
Butler Library, 268

C

Cable Arts Foundation, 137
Cable Communications, 316
Cable Sourcebook, 283
Cable Television Information Center, 139
Cablecast, 316
Cablecommunications Resource Center, 139
CableLibraries, 317
Cablelines, 317
Cablevision, 317
California, University of, Berkeley, 7, 95, 96
    Mass Communications Project, 7
    School of Law, 211
California State University, Chico, 8
California, University of, Los Angeles
    School of Law, 167, 212

422   Index

California, University of, San Francisco, 7
Camera, 325
Canada Council, 200
Canada Post, 197
Canadian Association of Broadcasters, 113
Canadian Broadcasting Corporation, 201
Canadian Cable Television Association, 139
Canadian Communications Research Information Centre (CCRIC), 74
    Newsletter, 289
Canadian Daily Newspaper Publishers Association (CDNPA), 144
Canadian Film Development Corporation, 201
Canadian provincial ministries, 206
Canadian Radio-television and Telecommunications Commission, 197, 201
Canadian Transport Commission, 202
Caniff Library, Milton, 267
Canyon Cinemanews, 325
Caribbean Broadcasting Union (CBU), 254
Carleton University, 8
Carnegie Corporation of New York, 93
Cash Box, 296
Catholic Journalist, 336
Catholic Media Council, 237
Catholic Press Association of the U. S. and Canada, 144
Catholic University of America, The
    Columbus School of Law, 212
CATV and Station Coverage Atlas, 284
CATV Buyer's Guide of Equipment, Services and Manufacturers, 317
CATV Systems Directory, Map Service and Handbook, 284
CBS Broadcast Group, Research Department, 75
CBS News Special Projects Department Library, 267
Center for Research in Children's Television, 18
Center for the Study of Advanced Means and Procedures in Education
    (CEMPAE), 255
Center for Understanding Media, 148
Central Missouri State University, 9
Centre for Public Opinion and Broadcasting Research (OBOPSP), 238
Children's Broadcast Institute, The, 158
Children's Television Workshop (CTW), 18, 114
Cincinnati, University of
    College of Law, 212
    Department of Communication, 9
    Division of Broadcasting, 10
Cineaste, 325
Cinema Canada, 325
Cinema Journal, 326,
Cineamerica, 141
Citizens Communications Center, 159
Citizens for Better TV, Inc. (CBTV), 159
Citizens' Research Foundation (CRF), 76

Clearinghouse on Development Communication, 231
College Press Review, 336
College Press Service, Inc. (CPS), 145
Colorado State University
    Department of Speech and Theater Arts, 10
    Department of Technical Journalism, 11
Columbia Journalism Review, 279, 342
Columbia University
    Center for Advanced Study of Communication and Public Affairs, The, 12
    Graduate School of Journalism, 11
    Journalism Library, 268
    Oral History Research Office, 268
    School of Law, 213
Columbus School of Law, 212
Combroad, 311
Comic Magazine Association of America (CMAA), 145
Comm/ent: A Journal of Communications and Entertainment Law, 296
Committee for Economic Development (CED), 76
Committee for Open Media (COM), 160
Committee on Children's Television (CCT), 160
Commonwealth Broadcasting Association (CBA), 238
Commonwealth Press Union (CPU), 238
Communication, 297
Communication Arts, 297
Communication: Journalism Education Today (C:JET), 336
Communication Notes, 297
Communication Quarterly, 290
Communication Research: An International Quarterly, 290
Communications, 298
Communications Canada, 197
Communications: Research in Canada, 290
Communications Satellite Corporation (COMSAT), 177
Communicontents, 298
Community College Journalist, 337
Consortium of University Film Centers (CUFC), 124
Consumer and Corporate Affairs, 198
Content, 345
Copyright Office, Library of Congress, 177
Cornell University
    Program on Science, Technology and Society, 13
    School of Law, 214
Corporation for Public Broadcasting (CPB), 177
Council for Public Interest Law, 161
Council of Communication Societies, 149
Council on Children, Media and Merchandising (CCMM), 161
Council on International Nontheatrical Events (CINE), 125
CPB Report, 312
CTVD, 326

CTW (Children's Television Workshop), 18, 114
Current Index to Journals in Education (CIJE), 47

D

Daily Variety, 298
Denver, University of
    Communication Arts Center, 13
    Denver Research Institute, 14
Detroit, University of
    School of Law, 215
Development Communication Report, 299
Direct Line, 337
Direct Marketing, 305
DISTRIPRESS: Association for the Promotion of the International Circulation of the Press, 239
Ditchley Foundation, The, 239
Duke University, 96
    Institute of Policy Sciences and Public Affairs, 15

E

Early Learning Center, The, 96
East-West Communication Institute, 231
EBU Review, Geneva edition, 312
Editor and Publisher, 345
Editor and Publisher International Yearbook, 284
Education Media Yearbook, 284
Education, Office of, Department of Health, Education and Welfare, 175
Educational and Industrial Television, 321
Educational Broadcasting, 321
Educational Broadcasting Corporation, 101
Educational Broadcasting International, 322
Educational Communication Association (ECA), 121
Educational Film Library Association (EFLA), 125
Educational Press Association of America (ED Press), 121
EDUCOM, 121
EDUCOM, 322
"Electric Company, The," 114
Encyclomedias, 285
ERIC Clearinghouse on Information Resources, 46
ETV Newsletter, 322
European Broadcasting Union (EBU), 240

F

Federal Communications Bar Journal, 313
Federal Communications Commission (FCC), 181, 193
Federal Court of Canada, 204
Federal Trade Commission (FTC), 184, 193
Federation of Motion Picture Councils (FMPC), 162
feed/back, 343
Film Advisory Board (FAB), 162
Film and Broadcasting Review, 326
Film & History, 327
Film Comment, 327
Film Culture, 327
Film Heritage, 327
Film Information, 328
Film Library Information Council (FLIC), 126
Film Library Quarterly, 328
Film News, 328
Film Quarterly, 328
Film rental libraries, 415
Filmfacts, 329
Films in Review, 329
Florida, University of
    College of Journalism and Communications, 15
    Communication Research Center, 16
Focus on Film, 329
Folio, 345
Footnotes to the Future, 299
Ford Foundation, The, 4, 93
Fordham University
    School of Law, 215
Foundation for Public Relations Research and Education, 110
Free Speech Yearbook, 285
Freedom of Information Clearinghouse, 162
Freedom of Information (FOI) Center, 269
Friday Report, 306
Fund for Investigative Journalism, The, 94

G

Gallagher Report, The, 306
Gannett Urban Journalism Center, Frank E., 36
General Accounting Office. 177
George Washington University, 92, 93
    National Law Center, The, 216
Georgetown University Law Center, 216

426   Index

Georgia, University of
    Grady School of Journalism and Mass Communications, Henry W., 16, 274
Goldmark Communications Corporation, 76
Grady School of Journalism, Henry W., 16, 274
Great Plains National Instructional Television Library (GPN), 269
Guild Reporter, 337

H

Hartford, University of
    New England Instructional Television Research Center (NETREC), 17
Harvard University, 95, 96, 102
    Center for Research in Children's Television, 18
    Law School, 217
    Program on Information Resources Policy, 18
Hawaii, University of, Honolulu, 231
Hawaii, University of, Manoa, 18
Hollywood Home Theatre, 142
Hollywood Reporter, The, 299
Home Box Office, 142
Hope Reports AV-USA, 285
Hope Reports Perspective, 299
Hope Reports Quarterly, 323
Horizon House International (HHI), 77
House of Commons, Parliament of Canada, 203
House of Representatives Committees and Subcommittees, 178
Howard University
    School of Law, 218
Hudson's Washington News Media Contacts Directory, 285
Human Communication Research, 291

I

IABC News, 300
Ideas in Sound, 300
IEEE Spectrum, 349
I.F.J. Information, 338
Illinois, University of, 21
    College of Communications, 19
    Institute of Communications Research, 19
    Journalism and Communications Library, 270
    Visual Aids Service, 124

Impact, 300
In Search/En Quete, 300
Independent Film Journal, 329
Index of Research Publications, 286
Indian Institute of Mass Communication, 260
Indiana University, Indianapolis
    Department of Telecommunications, 22
    Poynter Center on American Institutions, The, 22
    School of Journalism, 20
    School of Law, 218
Industrial Photography, 329
Information Futures, 77
Information Science Abstracts, 349
Institute for Democratic Communication, 5
Institute for the Future, 78
Institute of Scientific and Technical Communicators, Ltd. (ISTC), 240
Inter American Press Association (IAPA), 232
Inter-American Association of Broadcasters (IAAB), 256
Interamerican Center for Advanced Studies of Communications in Latin America (CIESPAL), 256
Interdepartment Radio Advisory Committee, 175
InterMedia, 301
International Advertising Association (IAA), 232
International and Intercultural Communication Annual, 291
International Association for Mass Communication Research, 241
International Association of Business Communicators (IABC), 233
International Association of Independent Producers (IAIP), 233
International Association of Women in Radio and Television, 260
International Broadcast Institute Ltd. (IBI), 102, 245
International Catholic Association for Radio and Television (UNDA), 241
International Catholic Union of the Press (ICUP), 242
International Communication Association (ICA), 150
International Communication Policy, Office of, Department of State, 176
International Communications Bulletin (ICB), 301
International Council for Technical Communication (INTECOM), 242
International Development Research Centre, 233
International Federation of Film Archives (FIAF), 243
International Federation of Journalists (IFJ), 243
International Federation of Newspaper Publishers (FIEJ), 243
International Federation of the Periodical Press, 244
International Film and Television Council (IFTC), 244
International Film Guide, 286
International Institute of Communications Ltd. (IIC), 102, 245
International Labor Press Association (ILPA), 234
International Organization of Journalists (IOJ), 245
International Photo Technik Magazine, 330
International Press Institute (IPI), 246
International Press Telecommunications Council (IPTC), 247
International Publishers Association, 247

International Radio and Television Organization (OIRT), 247
International Radio and Television Society (IRTS), 234
International Society of Weekly Newspaper Editors (ISWNE), 234
International Telecommunication Union (ITU), 248
International Telecommunications Satellite Organization (INTELSAT), 177, 235
Iowa Freedom of Information Council, 150
Iowa, University of
    College of Law, 219
    Department of Speech and Dramatic Art, 25
    Libraries, Special Collections Department, 270
    School of Journalism, 23, 133
IPI Report, 345
Iran Communications and Development Institute, 257

J

Joint Committee on Congressional Operations, 178
Joint Council on Educational Telecommunications (JCET), 114
Jola Technical Communications, 350
Journal of Advertising, 17, 291
Journal of Advertising Research, 292
Journal of Applied Communications Research (JACR), 292
Journal of Broadcasting, 17, 174, 188, 279, 292, 388
Journal of Communication, 292
Journal of Communication Inquiry, 293
Journal of Marketing, 306
Journal of Marketing Research, 293
Journal of Organizational Communication, 293
Journal of Popular Culture, 294
Journal of Popular Film, The, 330
Journal of the American Society for Information Science, 350
Journal of the Producers Guild of America, 330
Journal of the University Film Association, 331
Journalism Abstracts, 286
Journalism Education Association (JEA), 132
Journalism Educator, The, 338
Journalism Monographs, 294
Journalism Quarterly, 294
Jump Cut, 331

K

Kalba Bowen Associates, Inc., 79

Kansas, University of
    Department of Radio-Television-Film, 128
    School of Law, 219
    White School of Journalism, William Allen, 26
Kentucky, University of, 26

L

Leicester, University of, Centre for Mass Communication Research, 248
Liebling Ledger, The, 338
Lilly Endowment, Inc., 94
Lincoln Center for the Performing Arts, 97, 103
Literature/Film Quarterly, 331
Little, Inc., Arthur D., 80
London Graduate School of Business, 97
Look-Listen Opinion Poll, 313
Loyola Law School, 219

M

Madison Avenue, 306
Magazine Publishers Association (MPA), 146
Management and Budget, Executive Office of the President, 176
Marketing Communications, 307
Marketing Information Guide, 307
Marketing News, 307
Marketing Science Institute (MSI), 80
Markle Foundation, The, 3, 95
Marshall-Wythe School of Law, 227
Maryland, University of
    College of Journalism, 27
    School of Law. 220
Mass Comm Review, 301, 374
Mass Communications History Center (MCHC), 277
Mass Media Booknotes, 302
Mass Media Newsletter, 302
Massachusetts Institute of Technology (MIT), 95, 103
    Center for International Studies, 27
Masthead, The, 339
Matrix, The, 302
Media Access Project (MAP), 95, 163
Media & Methods, 323
Media Credit Association, 150

Media Decisions, 307
Media Industry Newsletter (MIN), 303
Media Law Reporter, 190
Media Mix, 323
Media Report to Women, 303
Media Report to Women Index/Directory, 287
Medill School of Journalism, 36
METREK Division, The MITRE Corporation, 81
Michigan State University
    College of Communication Arts and Sciences, 28
    Institute of Public Utilities, 29
    Vincent Voice Library, G. Robert, 276
Michigan, University of, 28, 96, 97
    Graduate School of Business Administration, 29
    Interdepartmental Program in Mass Communication, 28
    Law School, 220
Mid-America, University of (UMA), 30
Ministry of State for Science and Technology, 199
Minnesota, University of, 95
    Department of Speech-Communication, 31
    Journalism Library, 270
    School of Journalism and Mass Communications, 30
Missouri, University of
    Freedom of Information Center, 269
    Journalism Library, 271
    Law School, 221
    School of Journalism, 32, 129
Modern Media Institute, Inc., 151
Montana Journalism Review, 343
Monthly Film Bulletin, 331
Montreal, University of, 33
Motion Picture Association of America, Inc., 126
Motion Picture Product Digest, 332
Multicast, 350
Museum of Broadcasting, The, 271

N

NAEB Directory of Public Telecommunications, 287
NAEB Letter, 323
National Academy of Television Arts and Sciences (NATAS), 115
National Archives and Records Service, Audiovisual Archives Division, 272
National Association for Better Broadcasting (NABB), 163
National Association of Broadcasters (NAB), 97, 115
    Library, 272
National Association of Educational Broadcasters (NAEB), 115

National Audio-Visual Association (NAVA), 122
National Black Media Coalition (NBMC), 164
National Board of Review of Motion Pictures (NBRMP), 126
National Broadcasting Company
    General Library, 273
    Social Research Department, 81
National Cable Television Association (NCTA), 140
National Cartoonists Society, 151
National Center on Educational Media and Materials for the Handicapped (NCEMMH), 123
National Citizens Committee on Broadcasting (NCCB), 96, 164
National Conference of Editorial Writers, 132
National Council of the Churches of Christ—Communication Commission, 164
National Council on the Aging, 96
National Directory of Weekly Newspapers, 287
National Endowment for the Arts, 98
National Endowment for the Humanities, 98
National Federation of Local Cable Programmers (NFLCP), 140
National Federation of Press Women (NFPW), 133
National Film Board of Canada, 202, 405, 408
National Free Lance Photographers Association (NFLPA), 127
National Gay Task Force (NGTF), 165
National Institute of Education, 30
National Institute of Mental Health (NIMH), 99
National Law Center, The, 216
National League of Cities (NLC), 151
National News Council (NNC), 95, 133
National Newspaper Association (NNA), 146
National Opinion Research Center, 97
National Organization for Women (NOW), Task Force on Broadcast Media and the FCC, 165
National Press Photographers Association (NPPA), 127
National Public Radio (NPR), 116
National Religious Broadcasters (NRB), 116
National Research Council (NRC), 82
National Science Foundation (NSF), 99, 186
National Sisters Communications Services, The, 166
National Technical Information Service (NTIS), 273
Nebraska, University of, Lincoln
    College of Law, 221
Network Project, The, 166
New Books in the Communications Library, 303
New England Instructional Television Research Center (NETREC), 17
Newhouse School of Public Communications, S. I., 47
News Leads, 339
Newspaper Fund, The, 100
Newspaper Fund Journalism Scholarship Guide, 287
Newspaper Fund Newsletter, 339

Newspaper Guild, The, AFL-CIO, CLC, 147
Newsprint Information Committee, 147
New York University
    School of Law, 221
    School of the Arts, 33, 95
NFLCP Newsletter, 318
Nielsen Company, A. C., 83, 399, 408
Nieman Reports, 339
Nordic Documentation Center for Mass Communications Research
    (NORDICOM), 249
North Carolina, University of, Chapel Hill, 95
    Department of Radio, Television and Motion Pictures, 34
    School of Journalism, 34
Northern Illinois University, 35, 234
Northwestern University
    Medill School of Journalism, 36
    School of Law, 222
    Transportation Center, College of Arts and Sciences, 36
Notes from the Center, 318
"Nova," 93

O

Ohio State University, 123
    Caniff Library, Milton, 267
    College of Law, 222
    School of Journalism, 38
Ohio University, 37
University of Oklahoma Law Center, 223
Optical Systems, 142
Oregon, University of
    Division of Broadcast Services and Televised Instruction, 39
    Communication Research Center, 39
    School of Journalism, 39
    Department of Speech, 40
Organization for Economic Co-Operation and Development (OECD), 250

P

Pay Television, 318
Pay TV Newsletter, The, 318
Pay TV Services, 142
Peabody Collection, The, 274
Pennsylvania, University of, 95
    Annenberg School of Communications, The, 40

Index   433

Perspective on Cable Television, 318
Photo Marketing, 332
Pike and Fischer Radio Regulation, 190
Population Education, Inc., 96
Poynter Center on American Institutions, The, 22
Practising Law Institute (PLI), 223
Press Censorship Newsletter, 346
Press Foundation of Asia, 261
Press Research Center (CECOM), 250
Princeton University, 97
Print, 304
Printing and Publishing, 346
Prism TV, 142
PR Reporter, 307
Public Advertising Council, 167
Public Broadcasting Service (PBS), 117
Public Communication, Inc., 167
Public Interest Satellite Association (PISA), 167
Public Media Center, Inc. (PMC), 168
Public Opinion Quarterly, 12, 294, 374
Public Relations Journal, 308
Public Relations News, 308
Public Relations Quarterly, 308
Public Relations Review: A Journal of Research and Comment, 295
Public Relations Society of America, Inc. (PRSA), 110
Public Service Satellite Consortium (PSSC), 140
Public Telecommunications Review, 313, 374
Public Utilities Fortnightly, 351
Publishers' Auxiliary, 346
Publishers Information Bureau, 148
Publishers Weekly, 347

Q

Quill and Scroll, 340
Quill and Scroll Society, 133
Quill, The, 340

R

Radio and Television Weekly, 314
Radio-Television News Directors Association (RTNDA), 117
Rand Corporation, 83, 96

Rangefinder, The, 332
RCA Laboratories/David Sarnoff Research Center Library, 274
RCA Review, 351
Recording Industry Association of America (RIAA), 152
Reporters Committee for Freedom of the Press, The, 169
Reuther Library, Walter P., 266
Rice University, 41
Rockefeller Brothers Fund (RBF), 101
Rockefeller Foundation, The, 102
Roper Organization, Inc., The, 84
RTNDA Communicator, 340
Rutgers University, Camden
    School of Law, 224
Rutgers University, Newark
    School of Law, 224
Ryan Phonoarchive, The Milo, 274

S

St. Louis Journalism Review, 343
Sales and Marketing Management, 308
Salzburg, University of, Department of Mass Communication, 251
San Francisco, University of
    School of Law, 225
Sarnoff Research Center Library, David, 274
Scholastic Editor, 340
School Press Review, 347
Screen, 332
Screen Actor, The, 332
Secretary of State, Canada, 199
Senate Committees and Subcommittees, 180
Senate, Parliament of Canada, 204
"Sesame Street," 96, 114
Showtime, 142
Sight & Sound, 333
Silent Picture, The, 333
Simon Fraser University, 41
Sloan Foundation, The Alfred D., 102
SMPTE Journal, 333
Social Science Research Council (SSRC), 85
Society for Cinema Studies (SCS), 128
Society for Collegiate Journalists (SCJ), 134
Society for Technical Communication (STC), 152
Society of Motion Picture and Television Engineers (SMPTE), 128
Society of Professional Journalists, Sigma Delta Chi, 134
Southern California, University of
    Annenberg School of Communications, 42

Southern Illinois University, 44
Soviet Film, 333
Speech Communication Association (SCA), 153, 285
SRI International, 86
Standard Rate and Data Service, 288
Stanford Research Institute (SRI), 86
Stanford University
    Communication Department Library, 275
    Department of Communication, 45
    Department of Economics, 46
    Institute for Communication Research, 45
    Law School, 225
Statistics Canada, 199
Studio Photography, 334
Support Center, The, 169
Supreme Court of Canada, 205
Supreme Court of the United States, 186
Swedish Broadcasting Corporation, Audience and Programme Research Department, 251
Syracuse University, 21, 96
    ANPA News Research Center, 48
    Canadian Communications Program, 48
    Communications Research Center, 48
    Department of Television and Radio, 49
    ERIC Clearinghouse on Information Resources, 46
    Newhouse School of Public Communications, 47
Systems Applications, Inc. (SAI), 86

T

Take One, 334
Technical Communication, 304
Technical Photography, 334
Technology Assessment, Office of, 177
Telecommunication Journal, 351
Telecommunications, 352
Telecommunications, Office of, Department of Commerce, 176
Telecommunications Policy, 352
Telecommunications Policy, Office of, 176
Telecommunications Reports, 352
Teleglobe Canada, 202
Telemation Program Services, 142
Telephone Engineer & Management, 353
Telephony, 353
Telesat Canada, 203
Television Digest, 314
Television Factbook, 288

Television Information Office (TIO), 118
    Library, 275
Television International, 315
Television News Index and Abstracts, 288
Television Quarterly, 315
Television/Radio Age, 315
Televisions, 315
Temple University, 128
    Institute for Survey Research, 49
    School of Communications and Theatre, 49
    School of Law, 226
Tennessee, University of, 50
Texas, University of, Austin
    School of Communication, 51
    School of Law, 226
Thomson Foundation, The, 252
Topicator, 288
Transport Canada, 200
TV Guide, 316
TVC, 319
Twentieth Century Fund, The, 103

U

UFA Digest, 334
Union of National Radio and Television Organizations of Africa, 258
United Church of Christ, Office of Communication, 102, 170
United Kingdom Post Office Telecommunications, 252
United Nations Correspondents Association (UNCA), 236
United Nations Educational, Scientific and Cultural Organization
    (UNESCO), 74, 253
United States Information Agency, 176
University Film Association (UFA), 128
UPI Reporter, 341
Urban Policy Research Institute, 170
U. S. Court of Appeals for the District of Columbia Circuit, 187
U. S. Federal Communications Commission Library, 276
Utah, University of, 52

V

Vanderbilt Television News Archive, 276
Variety, 304

Velvet Light Trap, The, 335
Video Handbook, The, 289
Video Publisher, The, 353
Video Trade News, 353
Videocassette and CATV Newsletter, 319
Videography, 354
VideoNews, 354
Videoplay Report, 324
"Villa Alegre," 112
Vincent Voice Library, G. Robert, 276
Vue, 319

W

WACC Journal, 304
Washburn University
    School of Law, 227
Washington Journalism Center, 135
Washington Journalism Review, 343
Washington State University, 55
Washington, University of
    Center for Quantitative Studies in Social Science, 54
    Ryan Phonarchive, The Milo, 274
    School of Communications, 53
Washington University, St. Louis, 53
Wayne State University
    Reuther Library, Walter P., 266
Western Ontario, University of, 55
White School of Journalism, William Allen, 26
William and Mary, College of
    Marshall-Wythe School of Law, 227
Windsor, University of, 57
Wisconsin Center for Film and Theatre Research, 277
Wisconsin State Historical Society Mass Communications History
    Center, 277
Wisconsin, University of, Madison, 99
    Department of Agricultural Journalism, 57
    Department of Communication Arts, 58
    School of Journalism and Mass Communication, 58
    Wisconsin Center for Film and Theatre Research, 277
Wisconsin, University of, Milwaukee, 59
Women in Communications, Inc. (WICI), 154
Women's Institute for Freedom of the Press, The, 135
Working Press of the Nation, 289
World Association for Christian Communication (WACC), 254

Y

Yale University, 102
    Law School, 227
Yankelovich, Skelly and White, Inc., 87

ABOUT THE EDITORS

William L. Rivers is Paul C. Edwards Professor of Communication at Stanford University, where he has taught since 1962. He has served as a consultant to the Twentieth Century Fund, the RAND Corporation, the Education Program of the Ford Foundation, and U.S.A.I.D., and he was project director of a Markle Foundation-funded study on government-media relations. Dr. Rivers is the author, co-author and editor of 17 books, including the first two editions of the *Aspen Handbook on the Media* and the recently published *Mass Media Issues: Articles and Commentaries*. Earlier titles included *The Adversaries: Politics and the Press* and *The Opinionmakers*.

Wallace Thompson is a writer and editor who has had five of his own books published in the United States and Great Britain and has edited seven others. He is a member of the National Committee on U. S.-China Relations, a director of Shelter Institute, and served as an advisor to The Asia Society. He was formerly president of a publishing house, Word Wheel Books, Inc., and for many years was executive director of The American Society for Eastern Arts. He has served both in the United States and overseas with The Asia Foundation and U.S.I.A.

Michael J. Nyhan is co-editor (with William Rivers) of the *Aspen Notebook on Government and the Media* and (with Douglass Cater) of *The Future of Public Broadcasting*. He has served as assistant director of the Aspen Institute Program on Communications and Society. Previously he served overseas with the U.S.A.I.D. and with the Peace Corps.

RELATED TITLES
Published by
Praeger Special Studies

Published in cooperation with the Aspen Institute Program on Communications and Society:

* FREEDOM OF THE PRESS VS. PUBLIC ACCESS
Benno C. Schmidt, Jr.

* THE FUTURE OF PUBLIC BROADCASTING
edited by Douglass Cater
and Michael J. Nyhan

* THE MASS MEDIA: Aspen Guide to Communication
Industry Trends
Christopher H. Sterling
Timothy Haight

TELEVISION AS A CULTURAL FORCE
edited by Richard Adler
and Douglass Cater

TELEVISION AS A SOCIAL FORCE
edited by Douglass Cater
and Richard Adler

Also published by Praeger Special Studies:

CHILDREN'S TELEVISION: An Analysis of Programming
and Advertising
F. Earle Barcus

COMMUNICATIONS TECHNOLOGY AND DEMOCRATIC
PARTICIPATION
Kenneth C. Laudon

* THE MEDIA AND THE LAW
edited by Howard Simons
and Joseph A. Califano, Jr.

PUBLIC BROADCASTING: The Role of the Federal
Government 1912-1976
George H. Gibson

TELEVISION IN THE CORPORATE INTEREST
Richard Bunce

* Also available in paperback as a PSS Student Edition.

ASPEN INSTITUTE PUBLICATIONS
P.O. Box 1652
Palo Alto, CA 94302

We are anxious to have your feedback on this edition of the **Aspen Handbook on the Media** and thus would appreciate it if you could fill out this form and send it to us postpaid.

1) Your evaluation of the usefulness of the **Handbook**:

2) Are there any obvious omissions of institutions, programs, or publications within the categories in the **Handbook**?

3) Are there any additional categories which might be included in future editions?

4) Are there any factual or other inaccuracies in the text?

NAME _____
ORGANIZATION _____
ADDRESS _____
_____ ZIP _____
DATE _____

☐ *Please send me a catalog of Aspen publications.*

FIRST CLASS
Permit 926
Palo Alto, CA 94301

Business Reply Mail

No Postage Stamp Necessary if Mailed in the U.S.A.

Postage will be paid by

The Editors
Aspen Handbook on the Media
Aspen Institute Publications
P.O. Box 1652
Palo Alto, CA 94302

First Class

ORDER FORM

Please send me a copy of the paper edition of:

THE MASS MEDIA: ASPEN GUIDE TO COMMUNICATION INDUSTRY TRENDS

edited by Christopher H. Sterling and Timothy R. Haight.

☐ I am enclosing a check or money order for $11.95, payable to **Aspen Institute Publications.** (California residents please add $ .78 sales tax.)

☐ Please bill me. I understand that a charge for shipping and handling will be added.

☐ Please send me information on other Aspen publications on communications.

NAME _____
TITLE _____
ORGANIZATION _____
ADDRESS _____
_____ **ZIP** _____

*(The cloth edition must be ordered from Praeger Publishers,
200 Park Avenue, New York, NY 10017.)*

ASPEN INSTITUTE PUBLICATIONS
P.O. Box 1652
Palo Alto, California 94302

FIRST CLASS
Permit 926
Palo Alto, CA 94301

Business Reply Mail

No Postage Stamp Necessary if Mailed in the U.S.A.

Postage will be paid by

ASPEN INSTITUTE PUBLICATIONS
P.O. Box 1652
Palo Alto, CA 94302

First Class